The Pope Encyclopedia

The Pope Encyclopedia

AN A TO Z OF THE HOLY SEE

Matthew Bunson

CROWN TRADE PAPERBACKS • NEW YORK

Published by Crown Trade Paperbacks, 201 East 50th Street, New York, New York 10022. Member of the Crown Publishing Group.

Random House, Inc. New York, Toronto, London, Sydney, Auckland

CROWN TRADE PAPERBACKS and colophon are trademarks of Crown Publishers, Inc.

Manufactured in the United States of America

Designed by June Bennett-Tantillo

Vatican map by Sandee Cohen

Library of Congress Cataloging-in-Publication Data
Bunson, Matthew.
    The pope encyclopedia: an A to Z of the Holy Sea / Matthew Bunson.—
    1st pbk. ed.
        p.   cm.
    1. Papacy—Dictionaries.   2. Popes—Biography—Dictionaries.
I. Title.
BX955.2.B86   1995
262'.13'03—dc20   95-23290
                                                                          CIP

ISBN 0-517-88256-6

10 9 8 7 6 5 4 3 2 1

First Edition

Acknowledgments

❁

There are a great many individuals to whom a special debt of gratitude is owed for their very kind assistance in the preparation of this book. Among them are: His Excellency, the Most Reverend John P. Foley, President of the Pontifical Commission for Social Communications; Signor Arturo Mari of *L'Osservatore Romano;* Don Niccoló Suffi of the Libreria Editrice Vaticana; Don Bowden of Wide World Photos; Sarah Davis of Catholic News Service; the staff of the Sahara West Library; Dakila Divina; Elke Villa of Crown Publicity; and most of all, Jane Cavolina of Crown Publishers for her confidence, enthusiasm, and friendship—without her this book would not have been possible.

Introduction

❀

On a bright, humid morning in January 1995, a crowd of some 5 million worshipers gathered in the streets of Manila, in the Philippines, to hear a mass presided over by a frail-looking seventy-four-year-old man dressed in white. The largest single assembly ever for such a celebration, the throng had come out of curiosity, out of personal faith, and, most of all, out of deep reverence for the figure who stood so far away at the altar that most could not see him and many were unable even to hear him. His very presence was sufficient for the devout, however, for that distant figure, that barely heard voice, was the Pope. To those who had come together that day—as with the nearly 1 billion other members of the Catholic Church around the globe— he stood as the Vicar of Christ on Earth, the Supreme Pontiff, the Bishop of Rome, the successor of St. Peter, and one of the most influential political and religious leaders in the world.

The Pope Encyclopedia is intended to serve as the first-ever comprehensive A-to-Z guide to the entire papacy, the most visible of all spiritual shepherds and the world's oldest surviving temporal ruler as absolute sovereign of the State of Vatican City. This A to Z of the Holy See offers coverage of the popes—from the reign of St. Peter to the current pontiff (as of this writing), John Paul II, said in the custom of former times to be "reigning gloriously"—and the entire mystique-shrouded papal government from which the mission and administration of the Church is directed. The reader will find entries on the Roman Curia, the College of Cardinals, the Swiss Guard, and such lesser-known offices as the Vatican Bank, the Fabric of St. Peter's, and the Camerlengo. There are also entries on artists, churches and basilicas, palaces, and the Vatican museums, all of which are glorious expressions of the rich history of papal patronage of the arts.

Above all, this book is about the 263 highly varied individuals who have served as Bishop of Rome in direct succession to St. Peter. It is hoped that this volume will offer a respectful but honest account of each pope's reign, with much attention paid not merely to dates and facts of their time in office, but insights into their natures, characters, habits, and often very human foibles. The reader will encounter the ascetic Pius VII, who languished as a prisoner of Napoleon; the Smiling Pope, John Paul I, who while Patriarch of Venice wandered the city in sandals and ate seaweed pizza with students; the humanist Paul II who ate himself to death on melons; the Polish philosopher and playwright John Paul II who helped topple the Soviet empire; and the great St. Peter who was crucified upside down on the Vatican Hill by the Romans after declaring himself unworthy to die in the same manner as Christ. At times the behaviors and weaknesses of the popes were shocking and make for quite lamentable reading. However, the words of Pope St. Leo I the Great have remained remarkably true: The dignity of Peter is not tarnished by the unworthiness of his successor; for each Alexander VI, Leo X, and John XII there is a Gregory I, Gregory VII, Pius V, and Pius X.

Each pontiff has left his mark on the Church and on human history, and regardless of the lengths of their times in office, the popes have reigned collectively for 2,000 years through calamity, ruin, hope, opportunity, and challenge. The Holy See has endured, despite the predictions—and often the genuine wishes of its enemies—that the papacy had entered its final years. Many opponents have sat in eager anticipation of outliving the popes, from the Roman and Holy Roman emperors, to Napoleon and Hitler. They are gone, but the popes are still with us, their relevance to the modern world given poignant testimony by the 5 million on that humid day in Manila.

Note: The reader will find next to the entries of many popes a small shield; these are the papal coats of arms used by each pontiff since 1198. Please see *Coat of Arms* for other details.

Thou art Peter and on this rock I will build my Church. And the gates of Hell will not stand against it. I will give you the Keys of the Kingdom of Heaven: whatever you bind on earth will be bound in heaven; whatever you loose on earth will be loosed in heaven.

—MATTHEW 16:18–19

The papacy is not a static institution, frozen once for all in its present form. And popes are not just mass-produced series of figures in white who appear on distant balconies and mouth interchangeable platitudes. It matters very much who is pope. Each pope makes his own distinctive contribution.

—Peter Hebblethwaite,
The Year of the Three Popes

❀ ACADEMY OF SCIENCES, PONTIFICAL An internationally respected organization comprised of scientists, including Nobel Laureates, who provide the pope with their advice on scientific affairs; the academy also promotes research, prepares papers and addresses, and seeks to advance the study and appreciation of science within the Church. The academy dates to August 17, 1603, when Pope Clement VIII established what was called the *Linceorum Academia* (Academy of the Lynxes, from the custom of the lynx representing intellectual attainment). One of its early members was Galileo Galilei, who was to have trouble with the Church over his theories on the solar system. Pope Pius IX in 1847 renamed it the *Pontificia Academia dei Nuovi Lincei*. It was seized in 1870 by the Italian government, forcing Pope Leo XIII to reconstitute the academy on his own initiative in 1887. A major series of changes was undertaken by Pope Pius XI (1922–1939). In 1922 he commanded that the scientists should meet in the Vatican Gardens, in the beautiful retreat called the Casina of Pius IV. He then renamed it in 1936 the Pontifical Academy of Sciences with a membership of seventy. Today, the academy has members from nearly thirty countries. Appointments are for life and are based entirely on merit and achievement in respective fields of science and mathematics; the scientists do not have to be Catholic.

❀ ACCLAMATIO A highly unusual but nevertheless entirely valid form of electing a new pope. *Acclamatio,* Latin for acclamation, is the unanimous proclaiming of an individual to be pope by the cardinals taking part in a conclave. Along with scrutiny (or regular voting) and compromise, it is one of the three recognized types of election. Such a surprise step must not be undertaken through prior consultation among the cardinals and is certainly never the product of negotiations. Entirely spontaneous and done without voting, *acclamatio* is called "quasi-inspirational," implying that the election is guided by the inspiration of the Holy Spirit. The two most recent elections by *acclamatio* (that are known) were Emilio Altieri as Clement X (1670–1676) and Benedetto Odescalchi as Innocent XI

(1676–1689). The latter was supposedly praying in the papal chapel during the conclave when he was suddenly surrounded by his fellow cardinals and proclaimed their pontiff. In a touching scene, the cardinals overcame his protests by kneeling, one by one, and kissing his hand. An interesting depiction of election by acclamation was presented by Morris West in the novel *Shoes of the Fisherman.* (See also *Conclave* and *Elections, Papal.*)

❀ **ACTA APOSTOLICAE SEDIS**   A journal whose title means "Acts of the Apostolic See" that is the official record of the acts and decrees of the Holy See. Known also by the abbreviation AAS, the journal publishes all papal decrees and enactments—texts of encyclicals, constitutions, and papal and curial audiences. It also offers the declarations of the various dicasteries of the Roman Curia and any new facets of canon law. All new decrees of canon law are said to be in effect three months from the date of their publication. The journal was formally launched by a decree promulgated by Pope St. Pius X on September 29, 1908; its first issue was published on January 1, 1909. Printed by the Libreria Editrice Vaticana, it is available by subscription, but it is not recommended for the average Catholic layperson, given the complexity of the decrees and the use of Latin. (See also *Acta Sanctae Sedis.*)

❀ **ACTA SANCTAE SEDIS**   A publication whose title means "Acts of the Holy See" that was the predecessor of the journal *Acta Apostolicae Sedis.* It was begun in 1895 and was intended to provide the means for the Holy See to publish important public documents that might be issued by the popes and their government. Originally an unofficial publication, it was made official on May 23, 1904, an important designation that gave it much prestige. It was superseded in 1909 by the *Acta Apostolicae Sedis.*

❀ **ACTIVITIES OF THE HOLY SEE**   Properly, *L'Attivita della Santa Sede,* the Vatican yearbook, an annual record of the activities of the pope and the goings-on of the Vatican administration. The volume provides complete documentation for the undertakings of the pontiff, including all of his audiences, pronouncements, messages, travels, and meetings with heads of state, various diplomats, and notable individuals. It also provides glimpses into the daily life of the pope. The yearbook offers as well an accounting of the work and administrative status of the Roman Curia, including all of its congregations, commissions, tribunals, and offices. Less formal than the *Annuario Pontificio,* the *Activities of the Holy See* is a useful compendium on the papacy, giving the reader—at least one with some knowledge of Italian—a complete understanding of how active the year is for the pope. (See also *Annuario Pontificio*.)

❀ **ADEODATUS**   See *Deusdedit, St.*

❀ **ADEODATUS II, ST.**   Pope from 672 to 676. Also known as Deusdedit II, he was monk of the Benedictine Order and a Roman by birth, entering at a young age the community of St. Erasmus on the Caelian Hill in the Eternal City. Little is known about his reign, but he was probably quite old when elected on April 11, 672. He repaired many of the churches in Rome that had fallen into disrepair. He is called Adeodatus because Pope Deusdedit is sometimes termed Adeodatus I. He died on June 17, 676. Successor: Donus.

❀ **ADMINISTRATION OF THE PATRIMONY OF THE HOLY SEE (APSA)**   The department of the Roman Curia that has authority over the extensive states of the Apostolic See; the office is one of three main financial departments of the Curia, with the Vatican Bank and the Prefecture for Economic Affairs of the Holy See. The origins of the administration date to the Middle Ages when the position of treasurer became increasingly important with the acquisitions of property by the papacy in Avignon during the fourteenth century. Its present shape was initiated in 1967 under the reforms of Pope Paul VI. It has two principal areas of oversight: the general administrative needs of the Roman Curia and control of the liquid assets of the Holy See, including its real estate and investment strategy. There are two divisions: Ordinary and Extraordinary. The president is a cardinal.

❀ **ADRIAN I**   Pope from 772 to 795. Also known as Hadrian I, he was a very able pontiff, perhaps best known for forging a close relationship with the Franks and for having the longest reign (twenty-three years) until the time of Pope Pius VI (1774–1799). Adrian was born in Rome to a noble family, but in childhood he was left an orphan and was raised by his much respected uncle Theodotus. After serving under Popes Paul I and Stephen III (IV), he was elected to succeed Stephen on February 1, 772. Adrian was immediately confronted with the ongoing troubles caused by the Lombards in Italy. Having continued Stephen's policy of maintaining cordial dealings with the Franks, Adrian stunned the Lombards by making a formal request to the young Frankish king Charlemagne to invade Italy and rid them both of a longstanding enemy. Charlemagne accepted, drove across the Alps, relieved Rome, and deposed the last Lombard ruler, Desiderius, in 774, claiming the iron crown of the Lombards for himself. While Adrian was forced to give tacit acceptance to Charlemagne's involvement in papal affairs, he had won for the Church liberation from an inveterate foe and an alliance with an empire that was clearly on the rise. Relations remained friendly throughout his reign. (See also *Donation of Pepin.*) He also rebuilt the churches of Rome and the city walls, dying on December 25, 795. Successor: St. Leo III.

❀ **ADRIAN II**   Pope from 867 to 872. Adrian was born in Rome in 792 to a noble Roman family that had already produced Popes Stephen IV (V) and Sergius II. He had been married prior to his ordination, and was made a cardinal in 842 by Gregory IV. Given several important positions in the papal government, he was so revered by the Romans that twice, in 855 and 858, he won election to the throne of St. Peter, declining each time. Finally, on December 14, 867, the papal crown was offered a third time. Despite his age, he accepted, succeeding Nicholas I, in large measure because he desired to end the petty squabbling and bloodshed that had followed his predecessor's death. His election did not bring peace, however, for Rome was brutally sacked by the rapacious Duke Lambert of Spoleto. In a personal tragedy, Adrian's daughter was raped and then murdered savagely by a brother of the one-time antipope Anastasius. Suspecting Anastasius of complicity, Adrian condemned and excommunicated him, but within a year he had granted forgiveness and restored him to his post as papal archivist. Adrian suffered from a vacillating nature, making little use of the extensive powers then available to the pontiff thanks to the efforts of Nicholas. His reign witnessed the loss of the Balkans to the Eastern Church, a result of the decision of King Boris I of Bulgaria to accept missionaries from Constantinople, but he also sponsored the missionary activities of Sts. Cyril and Methodius among the Slavs, sanctioning the use of the Slavonic language in the liturgy, an important innovation. He died toward the end of 872. Successor: John VIII.

❀ **ADRIAN III, ST.**   Pope from 884 to 885. A Roman by birth, he is a little known pontiff, chosen on May 17, 884, to succeed Marinus I after an interregnum of a mere two days. His brief pontificate was characterized by a conciliatory policy toward the Eastern Church, with which the Western Church had not been on cordial terms. He also gave badly needed aid to the Romans during a famine. Adrian was probably involved in the often bitter feuding that pervaded the city in his era, once supposedly having a noble woman whipped and led naked through the streets as part of a vendetta related to the assassination of Pope John VIII in 884. He also ordered an official of the Lateran Palace, George of the Aventine, to be blinded for being an enemy of the deceased John. Adrian died in September 885 while on his way to Worms to confer with Emperor Charles III the Fat and to attend the imperial diet. His death was possibly not by natural causes. Buried in an abbey at Nonantula, he was soon given veneration by the locals. Formal recognition of his sainthood was made by Pope Leo XIII in 1891. Successor: Stephen V (VI).

❀ **ADRIAN IV**   Pope from 1154 to 1159, the only Englishman to be elected to the throne of St. Peter. Nicholas Breakspear was born near St. Albans around 1100, the son of a lowly royal clerk. After studying in France, he entered the Augustinian monastery of St. Rufus at Avignon, becoming abbot there in 1137. Pope Eugene III made him a cardinal around 1144 because of his recognized abilities but also because of the unhappiness of the monks in the abbey; Nicholas, it seems, was a severe disciplinarian and his relations with his monks had become quite strained. Around 1150, Eugene appointed him his legate, or representative, to Scandinavia, with the arduous task of reorganizing the Church. The cardinal proved brilliant in this mission, so much so that on December 4, 1154, he was elected unanimously to succeed Anastasius IV (d. 1154). Adrian wasted little time in using his authority as pope, defending and advancing the rights of the papacy against the troublesome commune of Rome and King William I of Sicily (r. 1154–1166) who was threatening papal territory. Adding to the troubles faced by the pontiff was Arnold of Brescia, the radical religious reformer who had once called Pope Eugene "a man of blood." Placing Rome under interdict after the mortal wounding of one of his cardinals in broad daylight on the Via Sacra, Adrian fled to Viterbo and secured the cooperation of Emperor Frederick I Barbarossa (then visiting Rome). Arnold was arrested, placed on trial, condemned, hanged, and burned at the stake in 1155. This did little to end Adrian's struggle with the Roman commune, a conflict that was still unresolved at his death, although Adrian was able to return to Rome in 1156. His relations with Frederick were not particularly ebullient, either, as the two had a major disagreement over Adrian's firm stand that the imperial crown was a *beneficium* or gift of the pope. This disagreement would continue over the years and would plague the dealings of the popes and emperors. Adrian also issued the bull *Laudabiliter,* granting to King Henry II of England recognition of his overlordship of Ireland. Its authenticity has long been studied by scholars. Adrian was reportedly affable and, as noted by his friend John of Salisbury, was willing to listen to criticism. Successor: Alexander III.

ADRIAN V Pope from July 4 to August 18, 1276, one of the most briefly reigning pontiffs. He was born around 1205 in Genoa and was originally known as Ottobono Fieschi. Pope Innocent IV, his uncle, made him a cardinal in 1251, and Pope Clement III sent him to England in 1256. While there, Fieschi distinguished himself by making peace between King Henry III and his barons. Taking part in the conclave to choose a successor to Innocent V (d. June 22, 1276), Fieschi, who was highly respected by his fellow cardinals, was elected after such long and contentious deliberations that the overseer of the conclave, Charles of Anjou, cut the cardinals' rations and refused to give them relief from the stifling Roman heat. Several elderly cardinals, in fact, nearly died from the unbearable temperatures. Fieschi took the name Adrian and promptly left Rome for the more agreeable atmosphere of Viterbo. Once there, he dropped dead without ever being ordained, crowned, or consecrated. Dante placed him in purgatory in the *Divine Comedy* for possible avarice. Successor: John XXI.

ADRIAN VI Pope from 1522 to 1523, Adrian was long distinguished as being the last non-Italian pope until the election of Karol Wojtyla as Pope John Paul II in 1978. He was also one of only two modern pontiffs (with Marcellus II) to retain his baptismal name after election. Adrian Florensz Pedal was born in Utrecht in 1456 to poor parents. He studied with the mystical group known as the Brethren of the Common Life, receiving from them a strong tendency toward asceticism. Entering the University of Louvain, he later became a professor of theology in 1492 and in 1507 was named tutor to the future Emperor Charles V by Emperor Maximilian. From 1516–1517, he served as regent in Spain (then part of the Holy Roman Empire) with the formidable Spanish cardinal Ximenes (on Charles's behalf) wielding virtually total control over the country. He also worked as Inquisitor of Aragon, Navarre, Castile, and Leon, and in 1517 was appointed a cardinal. Known to be a proponent of badly needed reform for the Church and renowned for his religious zeal, he was elected to succeed the profligate Leo X on January 9, 1522, by a unanimous vote.

Adrian's reign would prove both brief and tragic. Sincerely devoted to reform, he soon found many cardinals resisting any planned changes in the Curia, or Church administration. He was further disheartened by his inability to rally the Christian states in alliance against the Ottoman Turks who, under Sultan Suleiman the Magnificent, were sweeping across the Mediterranean. Adrian was also faced with a problem closer to home. The ever irascible Romans took an instant dislike to him. Upon learning of his election, they expressed displeasure that a "northern barbarian" was going to be their pontiff. Their unhappiness only increased when word spread of Adrian's work as an Inquisitor, and their worst fears seemed to be confirmed when the new pope refused to continue Leo's patronage of painters. The program, although popular with the Romans, had helped to empty the coffers of the papal treasury and had placed Adrian in a severe financial predicament. Opposed by many cardinals, unable to garner support against the Turks, and hated by the faithful of his own diocese, Adrian fell ill in August, dying on September 14, disillusioned and disappointed. Had he lived, it is possible that he might have brought real change to the Church. As it was, reform was still years away. His passing was greeted with celebrations in Rome; the papal doctor was even sent flowers and good wishes for having failed in keeping him alive. Successor: Clement VII.

✿ **AGAPITUS I, ST.** Pope from 535 to 536, also called Agapetus I, he reigned for only ten months. The son of a Roman priest named Gordianus, he suffered the murder of his father at the hands of supporters of the antipope Lawrence, in 502. Entering the Church, Agapitus became an archdeacon, serving in this post at the time of his election on May 13, 535, in succession to John II. The main achievement of his reign was to secure the deposition of the Patriarch of Constantinople, Anthemius, on charges of being a heretic for adhering to Monophysitism. Agapitus was in Constantinople in 536, having been sent there by King Theodahad of the Ostrogoths (r. 534–536) with the mission of trying to talk the Byzantine Emperor Justinian I (r. 527–565) out of invading Italy to reestablish Byzantine control, an event with ominous overtones for the Goths. Unable to resist the request, Agapitus accepted, selling off some sacred vessels to pay for the journey. It proved a waste of time because Justinian was determined to launch the venture, although the emperor gave the pontiff a mighty welcome at Constantinople. He died there on April 22, 536, but was brought back to Rome and interred in St. Peter's. Successor: St. Silverius.

✿ **AGAPITUS II** Pope from 946 to 955. Also known as Agapetus II, he was one of the popes elected during the period in which the papacy was dominated by Alberic II, the nobleman who ruled over Rome from 932 to 954. Agapitus was a Roman by birth, but little is known of his life prior to election as successor to Marinus II on May 10, 946. He owed his elevation to Alberic and remained in that prince's shadow for his entire pontificate, although he exercised somewhat greater independence in the political realm than his predecessors. He thus was able to support Emperor Otto I in his plans for the evangelization of the North and to work for the restoration of discipline among the clergy. While honored as a spiritual and virtuous pontiff by the people of Christendom, Agapitus could not overcome the supremacy of Alberic and so accepted the situation trying to rule effectively within those limitations. His final year, however, was blackened by his unavoidable acceptance of Alberic's last command before his death in 954 that his own illegitimate son, Octavian, should succeed Agapitus. This highly noncanonical event took place soon after Agapitus died in December 955. Octavian, as John XII, would be one of history's most scandalous popes. Successor: John XII.

⚘ **AGATHO, ST.** Pope from 678 to 681. He was perhaps originally from Sicily and was known to be a Benedictine monk, extremely well versed in both Greek and Latin. According to some reports of his reign, at the time of his election he was supposedly one hundred years old. If so, he was quite spry for his age, with a brief but active pontificate. His most important act was to send papal legates to the Sixth Ecumenical (or General) Council held in Constantinople in 680—the so-called Trullan Council—at which the heresy of Monothelitism was condemned. Agatho had prefaced the council with a synod in Rome in 680 that produced an anti-Monothelite formula, which found acceptance in Constantinople. Two of his legates to the Greek assembly were future popes, John V and Constantine. Unfortunately, the pope was dead before the decrees of the council could reach Rome for his approval. Considered very generous despite the financial difficulties faced by the Holy See, Agatho was also said to possess quite an affable nature and an excellent sense of humor. Successor: Leo II.

⚘ **ALBERT** Also Adalbert, an antipope who was a successor to the antipope Theodoric, reigning briefly in 1101. Few details have survived of his early life, but he was apparently the cardinal bishop of Silva Candida having been consecrated by the antipope Clement III around 1184. The supporters of Clement had elected Theodoric, but after his arrest and imprisonment by the adherents of the legitimate pontiff, Paschal II, they turned to Albert. News of his elevation was the cause of rioting and violence in the streets of Rome. Albert panicked and fled to the safety of a patron. This individual handed him over to Paschal. Albert was publicly humiliated, stripped of all signs of office, and condemned to life imprisonment in a monastery near Naples where the charmless Norman knights maintained a watch over him. He died at some unknown later date.

❀ **ALBERTI, LEON BATTISTA** An Italian architect and humanist (1404–1472) who performed a variety of services on behalf of the papacy, most notably the great Renaissance pontiff Nicholas V (1447–1455). Alberti was originally from Genoa, the illegitimate son of an exiled banker from Florence. He was raised in Venice, studied in Bologna and Padua, and was later granted a post as a secretary in the Curia in Rome. When the ban on his family was finally lifted in 1432, Alberti was able to visit Florence; he returned there two years later with Pope Eugene IV (1431–1447). Over the next years, Alberti worked for the popes. Also a sculptor, painter, and scholar, he is best known for his architectural contributions, helping to foster appreciation for classical form and style through his famed book *De re aedificatoria,* on architecture, dedicated to Pope Nicholas in 1452. Alberti was hired by Nicholas to design an ambitious rebuilding of the Leonine City in Rome, including a beautification of the Vatican and St. Peter's. Alberti was to comment on the pope: Rome "has become a city of gold . . . It was the care of the pontiff to adorn the city." Alberti's work was cut short by Nicholas's death, although Alberti had set the tone for the immense work undertaken in Renaissance Rome by such notables as Bramante, Michelangelo, and Raphael. Alberti also wrote treatises on humanism and painting, and poetry. He died in Rome.

❀ **ALBORNOZ, GIL DE** A Spanish cardinal and statesman (d. 1367) who helped restore order to the Papal States while the popes were in residence in Avignon. Known in full as Alvarez Carillo Gil de Albornoz, he was born at Cuenca, New Castile, and was related to both royal houses of Aragon and Leon. After studying law at Toulouse, he entered the Church and was swiftly promoted. By 1338, he was named Archbishop of Toledo. In 1340 he participated in the campaign of King Alfonso XI against the Moors, saving the king's life during the fighting at Rio Salado on October 30, 1340. A proponent of reform and morals, he clashed with Alfonso's successor Pedro the Cruel (who came to the throne in 1350). Denouncing Pedro's violent and dissolute nature, Albornoz was forced to flee Spain. He went to Avignon, where Pope Clement VI made him a cardinal in late 1350. Two years later, the pope sent him to Italy with the seemingly impossible task of restoring the control of the popes over the Papal States, which had sunk into near total chaos since the popes had left Italy for Avignon. To carry out his task, Albornoz received vast powers in a bull issued on June 30, 1353. The next years witnessed severe fighting and political intrigue as the cardinal grappled with recalcitrant Roman nobles, local barons, and brigands. By 1356, peace had been restored and Albornoz was received at Avignon in October 1357 by Pope Innocent VI (1352–1362) and was granted the title *Pater Ecclesiae* ("Father of the Church"). He was soon recalled by the pope because his successor in Italy, Abbot Androin de la Roche, had failed miserably in maneuvering around the cunning Roman nobles and was now in a difficult position. Fighting erupted once more, brought to a close with a treaty signed in 1364 between the cardinal and Bernabo Visconti of Milan.

❀ **ALEXANDER I, ST.**   Pope from 105 to 115, the fifth successor to St. Peter and the sixth pope overall. The dates of his reign are somewhat uncertain, although it is clear that he followed St. Evaristus. His reign is largely unknown in any reliable details. According to tradition long held in the Roman Church, he was a Roman by birth and was responsible for introducing water mixed with salt for the blessing of homes. There is also a legend that he was martyred during the reign of Emperor Trajan (98–117), decapitated on the Via Nomentana in Rome. It is likely that this was the result of confusion over a martyr who was found in a semi-subterranean cemetery in 1855 on the via and who had been beheaded. As the early testimony about Alexander's martyrdom is silent, it is considered doubtful that he died a martyr. Successor: Sixtus I, St.

❀ **ALEXANDER II**   Pope from 1061 to 1073, known originally as Anselm, he was born at Baggio, near Milan. A student of the famed teacher and theologian Lanfranc of Bec, he was ordained around 1055 at Milan and subsequently earned a reputation for speaking against simony and clerical incontinence. So troublesome was he to the Archbishop of Milan, Guido, that the prelate and his clergy sent Anselm off to the court of Emperor Henry III to be rid of him. Anselm, however, quickly impressed the ruler and in 1057 was named Bishop of Lucca. He soon became a fixture in the reforming circles of the Church, working with such notables as Hildebrand (the future Gregory VII) and St. Peter Damiani. In 1061, Nicholas II died and the cardinals assembled to choose his successor. This election was notable for being the first held after the decree of 1059 investing the right of election exclusively to the cardinals. With the support of Hildebrand and his followers, Anselm was chosen, taking the name Alexander. As per the decree of 1059, the cardinals did not ask the blessing of Emperor Henry IV, causing the Germans to name an antipope, Honorius II (Cadalus of Parma, a representative of the old school against reform and the loser in the election). Honorius had the sponsorship of the emperor, but not the claims of legitimacy, and Alexander never surrendered his tight control over the papal administration, pushing ahead with his reform program for the Church. Honorius finally died in 1072, although Henry's support had waned in the previous years. Alexander used various legates and assorted synods to combat simony and other irregularities. He also gave his blessing to the invasion of England by William the Conqueror in 1066 and elevated his old teacher Lanfranc to the see of Canterbury. His death on April 21, 1073, left the reform of the Church incomplete. Successor: St. Gregory VII.

❀ **ALEXANDER III**   Pope from 1159 to 1181, Orlando Bandinelli was born in Siena around 1100, the son of a respected family. He grew up to become one of the foremost legal experts of his age, teaching in Bologna from 1139 to 1142 as a professor of law. He authored a commentary on the famed canonist Gratian (twelfth century), was a canon in Pisa, and was finally called to Rome by Pope Eugene III (1145–1153). Once installed in the Curia in Rome, Bandinelli had a swift series of promotions. Eugene made him a cardinal deacon in 1150, a cardinal priest in 1151, and then chancellor in 1153. Throughout the pontificate of Adrian IV (1154–1159), he was his closest counselor, proving a devoted enemy of Emperor Frederick I Barbarossa whose ambitions toward Italy he sought to curtail. In the election that followed Adrian's death, a minority voted for Cardinal Ottaviano while the majority chose the anti-imperial candidate Bandinelli on September 7, 1159. Hostilities soon erupted. Bandinelli sought refuge in the Vatican fortress and was consecrated on September 20, taking the name Alexander (III) at Ninfa, near Velletri. Ottaviano was also consecrated under the name Victor IV and was henceforth an antipope. The conflict with Frederick would rage throughout Alexander's reign and would encompass several antipopes in succession: Victor IV, Paschal III, and Callistus III. Owing to the violence in Italy, the pope departed the peninsula in 1162 and sought the safety of France. He returned in 1165, but soon left again for the more secure surroundings of Benevento. After years of negotiations and alliance making, he helped craft the Lombard League in Italy, which smashed Frederick at the Battle of Legnano in 1176. Peace was signed the next year, although this proved only a temporary respite.

Alexander upheld Church rights against King Henry II of England, inflicting a very severe punishment on the king for the murder of St. Thomas Becket in Canterbury Cathedral on December 29, 1170, although Alexander was not one of Thomas's greatest supporters. He also presided over the Third Lateran Council (or Eleventh General or Ecumenical Council). Its most famous decree was to require the election of a pope by a two-thirds majority of the cardinals. Forced out of Rome once more in 1179 by the Roman commune, he never returned because of the presence of yet another antipope, Innocent III; he died a wandering pontiff at Civita Castellana on August 30, 1181. Successor: Lucius III.

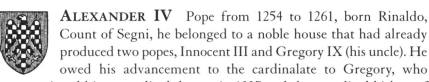 **ALEXANDER IV** Pope from 1254 to 1261, born Rinaldo, Count of Segni, he belonged to a noble house that had already produced two popes, Innocent III and Gregory IX (his uncle). He owed his advancement to the cardinalate to Gregory, who appointed him a cardinal deacon in 1227 and then cardinal bishop of Ostia. His main work as a cardinal was in defending and aiding the mendicant orders, in particular the Franciscans. His election to the papacy was owed possibly in part to his previous dealings with Emperor Frederick II (d. 1250), whose dynasty, the Hohenstaufens, was always on the minds of the cardinals. As it was, the conclave was held in Naples, where Innocent IV had died, and the cardinals were forced to remain there because the mayor, eager for the prestige of hosting the election in his city, had closed and locked the gates. The chronicler Matthew Paris described Alexander IV as assiduous in prayer and strict in abstinence, but easily influenced by the whispering of flatterers and inclined to listen to the evil words of avaricious persons. He chose as the simplest course the continuation of the papacy's hostility toward the Hohenstaufens, excommunicating Frederick's illegitimate son Manfred, who was serving as regent to infant Conradin, the son of Frederick's chosen heir Conrad IV, who had died in 1254. In seeking to encompass Manfred's destruction, Alexander entered into a short-lived alliance with Henry III, King of England, granting the Kingdom of Sicily to Henry's son, Edmund of Lancaster. This fell through and papal troops were defeated in Sicily. Alexander thus had the displeasure of watching Manfred conquer much of central Italy, including most of the Papal States. The pope was forced to reside in Viterbo owing to the hostility of the nobles who elected Manfred a senator in 1261. There were only eight cardinals at the time of his death to choose the next pope because he had not named any new ones. Successor: Urban IV.

ALEXANDER V Antipope from 1409 to 1410, one of the rival claimants to the Chair of St. Peter during the Great Western Schism (1378–1417). Originally Pietro Philarghi, and also called Pietro di Candia, he was born on Crete (or Candia as it was then known). Of Greek descent, he did not know his parents and was a wandering beggar boy until helped by a member of the Franciscans. Around 1357, he entered the order himself on Crete, subsequently studying in Padua, Oxford, and Paris. He taught in Franciscan houses in Russia, Bohemia, and Poland, and lectured in Paris on the *Sentences* of Peter Lombard, which were then the basis of theological study. His lectures are today much prized by scholars. Going to Pavia, where he held a chair in theology from 1386, he came to the attention of Gian Galeazzo Visconti (the future Duke of Milan) who became a patron, helping to secure his rapid promotion. By 1402, Pietro was Archbishop of Milan. Three years later he became a cardinal, playing a role in the negotiations leading to the Council of Pisa in 1409, which sought to end the Great Schism. The council members elected him pope and called upon the other two claimants, Pope Gregory XII and antipope Benedict XIII to resign. This they would not do and so the Church had three popes. Alexander promised to bring reform, but he soon disappointed by giving lavish gifts to his friends with a munificence that was staggering to his supporters. His zeal for reform soon cooled and his reign proved brief. After ten months, he died suddenly at Bologna on May 3, 1410. It was long suspected, perhaps without foundation, that his friend and ally, Cardinal Baldassare Cossa, had poisoned him. Cossa would succeed him as antipope John XXIII.

ALEXANDER VI Pope from 1492 to 1503, arguably the most infamous successor to the throne of St. Peter, described by the Florentine historian Francesco Guicciardini as "more evil and more lucky than perhaps any pope before him." Born at Jativa, near Valencia, Rodrigo de Borja y Borja was a member of the increasingly powerful Borgia family. His uncle, Alfonso de Borja, one-time Bishop of Valencia, was elected pope as Callistus III in April 1455 and soon bestowed many offices upon his nephew. In February 1456, Rodrigo was made a cardinal (without ordination) and the next year became vice-chancellor of the Holy See. While an Italianized Spaniard, Rodrigo proved adroit at political maneuverings, amassing a truly vast personal fortune and influencing the election of Sixtus IV (1471–1484). Meanwhile, he enjoyed a decidedly unreligious life, fathering numerous children and earning a sharp rebuke from Pope

Pius II. His favorite mistress was the Roman aristocrat Vannozza Catanei by whom he would sire four children: Juan, Cesare, Lucrezia, and Jofre. Vannozza led a discreet life, and after his election to the papacy, Rodrigo married her off.

Rodrigo had long harbored ambitions toward the papacy, but he failed to secure his own elevation in succession to Sixtus. He tried again after Innocent VIII died in July 1492, using lavish bribes and promises and a reputation for administrative skill to secure the needed majority of votes by the cardinals on August 11, 1492. His initial acts seemed to point to a promising reign. Civil order was restored in the Eternal City, a general reform of the Curia was proclaimed, and a crusade against the Ottoman Turks was proposed. But Alexander quickly forgot his plans and instead devoted his attentions to his precious causes: the ruthless advancement of the House of Borgia and wholehearted fondness for riches and extravagant dissipation. His son Cesare was made a cardinal at the age of eighteen—one of five Borgias to be made princes of the Church. He had high hopes for his first son, but plans (such as the throne of Naples) were cut short by Juan's murder in 1497. Juan had dined with Cesare and was found brutally stabbed and floating in the Tiber the next morning. When Alexander tearfully commanded his son's body be dragged out of the water, sharp-tongued Romans observed that the pontiff truly was a fisher of men. Rumors placed the crime at the feet of the pope, but real guilt almost certainly belonged to Cesare, who was ever jealous of Juan's power.

The death of his son stunned Alexander, prompting him to make serious efforts at reforming his life. His reform proved fleeting. The bull he intended to issue for the revitalization of the Church was never promulgated. Instead, he sank back into assisting Cesare's bloody subjugation of the nobles of Rome and the Papal States. By the time of his death, the States of the Church were essentially a fiefdom of the House of Borgia. He did involve himself in several other notable affairs, such as the feud with the Florentine dictator Savonarola (who was burned at the stake in 1498) and the division of the New World between Spain and Portugal through a bull issued in 1493–1494. He also celebrated a jubilee, but in typical fashion the sums brought in by selling indulgences were given to Cesare to pay for his campaigns. A patron of the arts, Alexander restored Castel Sant'Angelo, had the Borgia Apartments in the Vatican decorated by Pinturicchio, and even had Michelangelo draw up plans for a new St. Peter's. Alexander died quite suddenly on August 18, 1503, his demise immediately attributed to poison. The story at the time was that he and Cesare (who fell ill but recovered) had accidentally taken an evil brew intended for one of Alexander's cardinals. He perhaps actually died of malaria. His reign, looked upon as one of the darkest in papal history, was subject to wild slander, with chroniclers enthusiastically reporting orgies, poisonings, and even incest. While these were exaggerations, Alexander nevertheless epitomized the worst excesses of the period and the need for genuine reform in the papacy. Successor: Pius III.

 ALEXANDER VII Pope from 1655 to 1667, Fabio Chigi was born at Siena in 1599, was a grandnephew of Pope St. Pius V, and belonged to a genuinely prestigious noble Italian family. He suffered through a miserable childhood because of chronic illness, studying under tutors because he was unable to attend school. Nevertheless, at the age of twenty-seven, Fabio earned doctorates in theology, philosophy, and law from the University of Siena, the long result of a voracious appetite for reading. In 1626, he entered into the service of the Church, receiving appoint-

Pope Alexander VII, the patron of Bernini.

ment as vice-legate of Ferrara by Pope Urban VIII in 1627. Through the patronage of several cardinals, he became Inquisitor of Malta and was consecrated a bishop. From 1639 to 1651, he was papal nuncio in Cologne, taking part in the negotiations that finally ended the bloody Thirty Years' War. Innocent named Fabio secretary of state in 1651, elevating him to the cardinalate in 1652. Innocent died in 1655 and in the ensuing conclave that lasted eighty days, Fabio emerged as the favorite candidate, winning unanimous election on April 7. A deeply spiritual personality who read the writings of Francis de Sales (whom he canonized in 1665), Alexander was a notable patron of the arts and scholars whose company he enjoyed. His reign was marked, however, by general decline in papal power and prestige in the wake of the Thirty Years' War, and the pope was forced to accept humiliating terms in a dispute with France and its crafty Cardinal Mazarin. His relations with Venice were better, winning the right of the Jesuits to return there after their expulsion some years before. In doctrinal matters, he opposed Jansenism, finding common ground with King Louis XIV of France on the subject. He was also pleased with the baptism of Queen Christina of Sweden in 1655 after her abdication of the throne, but he soon found her lavish court in Rome a burden on his treasury and his patience. His coat of arms is visible still in St. Peter's Square, placed there to commemorate the work of Gian Lorenzo Bernini of enclosing the square with colonnades, the same magnificent structure standing today. He died on May 22, 1667; Bernini created his tomb, one of the finest in Rome. Successor: Clement IX. (See also *Cardinal nephew* and *Secretariat of State.*)

ALEXANDER VIII Pope from 1689 to 1691. The son of the chancellor of Venice, Pietro Ottoboni was born in April 1610 in Venice, receiving an excellent education in keeping with the wealth and position of his noble family. After studying at Padua, he traveled to Rome and was given a post by Pope Urban VIII (1623–1644). Pope Innocent X made him a cardinal at the behest of the Venetians in 1652, naming him Bishop of Brescia in 1654. His election came when he was already seventy-nine, so his pontificate would not be a long one. The chief achievement of his reign was a reconciliation

Pope Alexander VIII.

with King Louis XIV of France, who returned Avignon and Venaissin, which he had seized in a dispute with Alexander VII (1655–1667). Alexander did condemn the Gallican Articles of 1682, which had denied the authority of the pope over the French Church, and attacked both Jansenism and Quietism, two movements of unorthodox Catholic belief. In Rome and the Papal States, he reduced the crushing taxes, improved social conditions, and was conspicuous in enriching the

Vatican Library with manuscripts, including those of Queen Christina of Sweden, who had been baptized into the faith in 1655. Alexander also gave aid to Venice in their war with the Ottoman Turks. Unfortunately, his generous nature also prompted him to revive the nepotism that Innocent X had thoroughly discouraged. He died on February 1, 1691. Successor: Innocent XII.

❀ **ANACLETUS, ST.**   Pope from 76 to 88, the second successor to St. Peter, and the third pope overall. Also called Cletus or Anencletus (meaning "blameless"), he is unfortunately rather obscure. It is possible that he was a Greek by origin, and Eusebius of Caesarea observed that he died during the reign of Emperor Domitian. He is honored as a martyr and is credited with establishing the organization of Rome into twenty-five parishes. Successor: St. Clement I.

❀ **ANACLETUS II**   Antipope from 1130 to 1138. The Church holds that Anacletus was an antipope, although some scholars argue for his legitimate claims against Pope Innocent II (1130–1143). Originally named Pietro Pierleone, he was born in Rome, studying in Paris before becoming a monk in the famed monastery of Cluny. Made a cardinal in 1111 or 1112 by Paschal II, he was a reliable legate for the popes and was a possible successor to Pope Honorius II in 1130. The burial of Honorius was hastily arranged, however, by the powerful Chancellor Aimeric, who also took immediate steps to secure the swift, secret, and somewhat irregular election of Gregorio Papareschi as Innocent II. A large group of cardinals, supported by the Roman people and clergy, met later the same day (February 14) and duly elected Pierleone. The dispute caused a breach in the Church. Anacletus was supported by most of the Romans and the house of Frangipani, but Innocent had the backing of Emperor Lothair II, the Byzantine Emperor John II Comnenus, and, most of all, St. Bernard of Clairvaux, who traveled across Europe battering down any thought of Anacletus's legitimacy. The crisis was resolved only in 1138 when Anacletus died (on January 25), although his followers elected a short-reigning successor, Victor IV. Throughout, Anacletus had been holed up in the impregnable fortress of the Leonine City in Rome.

❀ **ANASTASIUS I, ST.**   Pope from 399 to 401. Anastasius was the successor to Siricius and was a Roman by birth. The main event of note in his reign was his condemnation of some writings by the complex theologian Origen. He was admired by the fiery St. Jerome. Successor: St. Innocent I.

❀ **ANASTASIUS II**   Pope from 496 to 498. A Roman and the son of a priest named Peter, Anastasius was elected pope on November 24, 496. His pontificate would be dominated by the ongoing breach with the Eastern Church called the Acacian Schism (482–519) over a number of theological points. Anastasius attempted to bring about a reconciliation, sending two bishops to Constantinople with a letter; while not reversing any of Rome's positions, the pope made it clear to the emperor that he was willing to negotiate a settlement. This caused much controversy in the West and the pope was accused of being led into error by the Byzantine deacon Photinus, who had come to Rome to advance the talks. Anastasius died suddenly on November 19, 498, before any serious progress could be made toward a resolution. The split with the Byzantines would continue until the time of Pope St. Hormisdas (514–523), but the breach with the East was only widening. Dante placed his tomb in hell in the *Inferno* (XI. 6–9), and he was long abused as a traitor to the cause of the West. Successor: St. Symmachus.

❀ **ANASTASIUS III**   Pope from 911 to 913. He was the son of a Roman named Lucian and was born in Rome. Unfortunately, nothing is known with certainty about his early life or career, but he was elected pope around April 911. The papacy at this time was utterly dominated by the House of Theophylact, so it is assumed that Anastasius had virtually no authority on his own. He did manage to give some order to the ecclesiastical divisions of the German Church. He died probably in June 913, although some lists put the month at August or even November. Successor: Lando.

❀ **ANASTASIUS IV**   Pope from 1153 to 1154. Originally called Corrado di Suburra, he was from Rome as his name would indicate (from the Suburra, a quarter in Rome). His career included elevation to the cardinalate by Pope Paschal II around 1111 and his staunch support of Pope Innocent II against the antipope Anacletus II. During the period that Anacletus was in control of Rome (1130–1138), Corrado remained in or near the Eternal City as Innocent's vicar to the city, a task not without some danger. In the conclave that followed the death of Eugene III, Corrado was elected on the very day, July 8, of his predecessor's demise. He was crowned on July 12, in the Lateran of which he was reportedly fond and on which he would spend considerable funds for its beautification. He also worked to restore the Pantheon, the famed Roman edifice that would be looted by the Barberini in the seventeenth century. His relations with the Romans were so tranquil that the pontiff actually resided in the city, something that had been impossible for his predecessor and would be unthinkable for his successor. Already old when elected, Anastasius died on December 3, 1154; he was buried in his beloved Lateran. Successor: Adrian IV.

❀ **ANASTASIUS BIBLIOTHECARUS**   A Greek theologian and one of the greatest scholars of his age (d. *c.* 878) who allowed himself to be elected an antipope in 855 by the enemies of Pope Benedict III. Called "the Librarian" (in the Greek *bibliothecarus*), he was educated by Greek monks and was widely honored for his learning. By nature, however, he lacked discipline and was unable to hold the support of those who had chosen him. He stepped down and was reconciled to the Church. His brilliance kept him from suffering any serious punishment, and several popes actually gave him appointments. Nicholas I made him an abbot, and he was the papal librarian through the reigns of Adrian II (867–872) and John VIII (872–882).

❀ **ANICETUS, ST.**   Pope from 155 to 166, the tenth successor to St. Peter and the eleventh pope overall. According to the *Liber Pontificalis,* he was a Syrian, born in Emesa. Chosen as the successor to St. Pius I, he devoted his principal energies to opposing several heresies that were then plaguing the Christian community. He was visited by St. Polycarp, the much revered bishop of Smyrna, and the two conferred on such matters as the proper date of Easter, which was then the source of some controversy within the Church. He may have died a martyr. Successor: St. Soter.

❀ **ANNUARIO PONTIFICIO**   The "Pontifical Directory," an annual record of the entire Catholic Church published by the Libreria Editrice Vaticana, the Vatican publishing house. It is printed by the Vatican Polyglot Press, and its statistics are compiled by the Central Statistics Office. The *Annuario* presents a massive listing of statistics and biographies of the important leaders and officeholders in the Church. It also provides details on the offices of the Roman Curia and the Diplomatic Corps. The biographies include all members of the College of Cardinals, bishops, and the superiors of the major religious orders, complete with addresses and telephone numbers. There is also a list of all officially recognized popes, with accepted dates of the reigns and other pertinent information.

    The *Annuario* dates back to the compendium *Notizie,* which was first published by the Holy See in 1716. It was given the name *Annuario Pontificio* in 1860. This was changed to the *Catholic Directory* in 1872, but the title *Annuario* was restored in 1912. In 1885, the publication was stated to be official; this was dropped in 1924. It is customary to say that it is "unofficially official," a designation that notes its reliability as the source for information on the Church's entire organization. The *Annuario* is a positively indispensable source for anyone with an interest in the Vatican and the goings-on of the Church. It can be ordered from the Libreria Editrice for around $100, including postage and handling. Readers should be aware, however, that it is published in Italian, with some portions in Latin. Customarily, a special white volume is presented to the pope each year. Pope John Paul I (1978) confessed to using the book just after his election to familiarize himself with the members of the Curia who were to serve him.

�֍ **ANTERUS, ST.** Pope for several weeks from 235 to 236, he was elected to succeed St. Pontianus on November 21, 235, after that pontiff abdicated and allowed a successor to be named when he was sent to the dreaded mines of Sardinia, from which few persons ever came back alive. Anterus was possibly put to death by Roman authorities for collecting the acts of Christian martyrs and placing them for safekeeping in the archives of the young Church in Rome. The source for his martyrdom, the *Liber Pontificalis,* is not corroborated by the *Liberian Catalogue* of the fourth century, which notes that Anterus "fell asleep"; this was the term used for denoting that a pope had died of natural causes. The date of death is placed at January 3, 236. He was buried in the papal crypt in the cemetery of St. Callistus. His tomb was discovered in 1854. Successor: St. Fabian.

✖ **ANTIPOPE** A rival claimant to the papacy who might be elected, appointed, installed, or even proclaim himself to be the legitimate pontiff; such an individual is said by the Church to have assumed the title of pope illegally or in opposition to the legitimate pope. The antipope was a fairly common occurrence during the Middle Ages, and most were often pathetic Churchmen who were propped up by powerful rulers, such as a Holy Roman Emperor, during a feud with the Holy See over various issues. Their authority was frequently very limited and, after the resolution of a conflict, the king who created them might convince them to step down or simply abandon them to the whim or caprices of the real successor to St. Peter. Other antipopes were genuinely notable prelates who came to stand as real threats to the authentic pope. Among them were Benedict XIII (1394–1423) and John XXIII (1410–1415). Some antipopes were also present in the early Church, when competing parties in Rome might offer their own candi-

Antipopes
(217–1449)

Hippolytus—217–235

Novatian—251–258

Felix II—355–365

Ursinus—366–367

Eulalius—418–419

Lawrence—498–506

Dioscorus—530

Theodore—687

Paschal—687

Constantine—767–768

Philip—768

John—844

Anastasius—855

Christopher—903–904

Boniface VII—974, 984–985

John XVI—997–998

Gregory VI—1012

Benedict X—1058–1059

Honorius II—1061–1064

Clement III—1080–1100

Theodoric—1100–1101

Albert—1101

Sylvester IV—1105–1111

Gregory VIII—1118–1121

Celestine II—1124

Anacletus II—1130–1138

Victor IV—1138

Victor IV—1159–1164

Paschal III—1164–1168

Callistus III—1168–1178

Innocent III—1179–1180

Nicholas V—1328–1330

Clement VII—1378–1394

Benedict XIII—1394–1423

Alexander V—1409–1410

John XXIII—1410–1415

Clement VIII—1423–1429

Benedict XIV—1425–1430

Felix V—1439–1449

date for the papacy. In sorting out the lists of antipopes, scholars and experts have been confronted with serious questions over legitimacy, proper dates, accurate historical records, and in some cases the absence of supporting evidence. Church authorities, however, maintain the list of recognized popes and antipopes. In all, there have been some thirty-nine antipopes, from Hippolytus (217–235) to Felix V (1439–1449). (See table; see also under individual antipopes for details.)

❀ **APOSTOLIC CONSTITUTION**   A term denoting an important document issued by the pope that is concerned with some legislative matter and has a bearing on the very lives of Catholics. It may have a universal scope affecting the entire Church, or it may be of limited degree or have limited aims that are nevertheless of much value or importance. Examples of Apostolic Constitutions are *Sacrae Disciplinae Leges* (1983), which officially promulgated the Church's revised Code of Canon Law, and *Pastor Bonus* (1988), which signaled the extensive reform of the Roman Curia by Pope John Paul II. The average Catholic never reads or even hears about most Apostolic Constitutions, but the decrees might deeply affect their religious activities and are one of the principle means used by the popes to shape and guide the faith. All such decrees are published in the *Acta Apostolicae Sedis* and are translated into a host of languages. In Church history, the constitutions are often termed "bulls." (See also *Bull, Apostolic*.)

❀ **APOSTOLIC DELEGATE**   One of the official representatives of the Holy See (with nuncios, pro-nuncios, and others) who are sent around the world. The apostolic delegate (or delegate) is sent to those countries that do not have formal diplomatic relations with the Holy See. His status is not considered diplomatic and is entirely ecclesiastical. This means that he represents the pope to the bishops and Church in a specific country. (See also *Legate, Papal* and *Pontifical Ecclesiastical Academy*.)

❀ **APOSTOLIC PALACE**   Or the Papal Palace, the residence of the popes located within the Vatican City State in Rome. The palace of the popes has undergone a considerable amount of development over the centuries and is today a complicated melange of styles and tastes, the product of different pontiffs in different eras leaving their own architectural and artistic marks on the growing residence. Assorted palaces were constructed over the years, such as the buildings of Leo III and Gregory IV in the ninth century, but a new palace was built by Eugene III (1145–1153), enlarged by Pope Innocent III (1198–1216), with addi-

Residences of the Popes

While the popes today make their official home in the Vatican, throughout most of papal history they resided at the Lateran Palace, which became their home in the early fourth century. During the Middle Ages, they spent many years away from Rome owing to squabbles with the Romans, the dangers posed by ever-scheming noble families of Rome, or the frequent seizure of the city by Holy Roman emperors as part of some struggle with the papacy. The longest period during which the Vicars of Christ lived outside of the Eternal City was from 1309 to 1377, when they were ensconced in Avignon. Other cities that served as a residence, perhaps for a few years, to wandering popes included Anagni, Orvieto, and Viterbo (which had its own papal palace). From the time that Gregory XI (1370–1378) finally went back to Rome, the popes have resided at the Vatican, with a few notable exceptions. Clement VII (1523–1534) first fled Rome following the sack of the city by imperial troops in 1527 and lived for a time in Orvieto. Pius VI (1774–1799) and Pius VII (1800–1823) were both arrested, in 1798 and 1809 respectively, by the French and deported. Pius VI lived in Florence, Briançon, and Valence, dying in exile, and Pius VII was incarcerated in Savona and Fontainebleau, and hid in Genoa briefly in 1815 when Napoleon returned from Elba to launch his 100 days campaign. Pius IX (1846–1878) had to flee a revolution in Rome in 1848, escaping to Gaeta, near Rome, dressed as a simple priest.

In Rome, popes have lived in the Lateran Palace and the Vatican Palace, but they also have resided in Castel Sant' Angelo (when things became rather politically uncomfortable), the Quirinal Palace (which had better air in the summer and which was taken by King Victor Emmanuel II in 1870, prompting Pius IX to declare that buckets of holy water could not wash clean such a desecration), and Castel Gandolfo (allowing the popes to escape Rome's oppressive heat) in the cool Alban Hills, just outside the city. (See also *Avignon; Castel Gandolfo; Castel Sant'Angelo;* and *Lateran Palace.*)

A throne room from the Apostolic Palace, used for various private audiences and meetings of the cardinals with the pope; a photo from the time of Vatican Council II (1962–1965). (AP/WIDE WORLD PHOTOS.)

tions made by Nicholas III (1277–1280), who spent most of his time there. The palace, like Rome, was largely abandoned by the popes during the Avignon Papacy (1309–1377), but, upon the return of the papacy under Gregory XI (1370–1378) to the Eternal City, the Lateran was so decayed that he opted for the marginally better surroundings of the Vatican Palace. Here the popes have lived ever since.

The real founder of the modern Vatican Palace was the energetic humanist Nicholas V (1447–1455). He was followed by other builders: Sixtus IV (1471–1484), founder of the Sistine Chapel; Innocent VIII (1484–1492); Alexander VI (1492–1503); Julius II (1503–1513), patron of Michelangelo, Raphael, and Bramante; Leo X (1513–1521); and Paul III (1534–1549). The last of the great builders of the sixteenth century was Sixtus V (1585–1590) who constructed the palace in which the popes live today, along the plans of the architect Domenico Fontana, from 1589 to the summer of 1590. The whole project was finally finished by Clement VIII (1592–1605). It remained for the succeeding popes to introduce assorted interior improvements, but most contented themselves with aggrandizing St. Peter's Basilica. One shining exception was Alexander VII (1655–1667), who used the genius of Gian Lorenzo Bernini to renovate the Sala Ducale in the palace and, most important, to create the Scala Regia, arguably the foremost Baroque architectural masterpiece in Rome.

The palace would see ambitious building programs under Clement XIV (1769–1674), Pius VI (1774–1799), and Pius VII (1800–1823), each of whom concentrated on the construction of palaces to house the rapidly blossoming Vatican Museums. Today the palace serves as it always has, as the nerve center of the Catholic Church, the home of the Supreme Pontiff and his most important officials. While little is seen by the public (most of it is off limits to tourists), it is itself a repository of the artistic legacy of the West and the devotion of the popes to the attainment of genuine cultural greatness. (See also *Museums, Vatican.*)

❀ **APOSTOLIC SEE**   See *Holy See.*

❀ **APOSTOLIC SUCCESSION**   An important teaching by the Church that describes the unbroken line of succession that stretches from the Apostles to the bishops of today. It is based on the tradition that Christ gave to the keeping of his disciples the sacred ministry he had begun on earth. The Apostles then served as the leaders of the first Christian communities, granting the authority they had received to their successors. This meant that the successors could teach, preach, and administer the sacraments to all the faithful. In turn, these successors passed on the authority to yet another generation, and so on. It is said that every priest and every bishop is able to trace his ordination all the way back to the very days of Christ in an unbroken line.

❀ **ARCHBISHOP**   A title borne by a bishop who has added authority and jurisdiction over an archdiocese. As a bishop in his own right, the archbishop is the head of his own diocese, but this see is considered the primary one of an ecclesiastical province, which is comprised of one or several dioceses. The archbishop may also be given the rank of metropolitan, which means that he possesses a certain authority over the dioceses around him, called suffragan dioceses. There is yet another type of archbishop found within the Church, namely a titular archbishop. This prelate is considered to receive the honorific title of archbishop as a personal honor from the pope. Called *ad personam* (to the person), the archbishop is considered an actual title holder but has no authority over a diocese. Titular archbishops are most often found in the Vatican departments and as diplomats sent by the pope around the world. Many archbishops are destined to become cardinals. The pope is also considered an archbishop. In his many titles, he is styled the Archbishop and Metropolitan of the Roman Province. His jurisdiction extends to all of the suffragan dioceses around Rome, called the suburbicarian dioceses. (See also *Rome, Bishop of* and *Suburbicarian Dioceses.*)

❀ **ARCHIVES, VATICAN**   Properly, the Vatican Secret Archives, the extensive collection of records, documents, and materials preserved in the Vatican. The archive is called secret because of its traditional purpose, to serve as the private official archive of the Pope and the Curia without provision for public interest or scrutiny. While the archive is today partially open to scholars, it remains essentially the private possession of the papacy, and even experts are permitted into it only with specific purposes and with the permission of the pope. It is the most mysterious institution in the papal city, for in its more than thirty miles of shelving are reputed to be the accumulated records of scandals, secrets, and revelations of the most shocking and explosive kind, blithely boxed and filed away with the insouciance born of centuries of silence and discretion. The Vatican Archives were begun in the modern sense by Pope Paul V (1605–1621) in 1612 when he ordered all papal records and documents moved from wherever they might be situated to the Vatican. Unfortunately, few of the records prior to the reign of Innocent III (1198–1216) have been preserved. This was due to the disasters that struck the Holy See and Rome, the losses incurred by the wandering of the popes (as Rome was often not a safe place in which to live), and the fragile nature of many documents, made all the more so by the habit of the officials of the Papal Chancery to use papyrus paper until at least the eleventh century.

Once established, the archive was intimately connected with the Papal Library, a situation changed by Pope Urban VIII in 1630 when he made its head, Felice Cantelori, solely responsible for the archive; he had previously been both head librarian and chief archivist. In 1810, Napoleon ordered the recently seized Vatican to surrender the entire archive, moving it to Paris. Most of the documents were returned in 1815, but many somehow never found their way back to Rome and are still spread across Europe. Today, the archive is a superbly organized collection that encompasses not merely the documented history of the papacy, but much of human history. Among its most fascinating possessions are the appeal of King Henry VIII to Pope Clement VII for a divorce, the abdication document of Queen Christina of Sweden in 1654, the court proceedings against Galileo Galilei, and letters from Napoleon, Michelangelo, Erasmus, Lucrezia Borgia, and even a nephew of Genghis Khan. Also supposedly found in the archive (dismissed by staff members) is the final message of Fatima concerning the end of the world. The

Vatican Archives are under the direction of the Cardinal Archivist of the Holy Roman Church, appointed by the pope; actual operating authority is in the hands of the prefect, assisted by the vice-prefect and a surprisingly small staff. (See also *Library, Vatican.*)

❀ **ASSOCIATION OF VATICAN LAY EMPLOYEES** The quasi-union of Vatican employees that was formed in 1980 in order to provide representation in the Holy See for the needs and demands of the several thousand lay workers within Vatican City. The organization was initially unofficial, but in 1981, at the prodding of some of its more active members, the union asked for and received recognition from Pope John Paul II. In the 1980s, the union represented around 1,600 employees. The department of the papal government charged with dealing with the employees is the Labor Office of the Apostolic See (ULSA— *Ufficio del Lavoro della Sede Apostolica*). It handles all negotiations and especially settles any disputes that may arise. It was launched on January 1, 1989, by a *motu proprio* (a papal decree, effective March 1, 1989) that was in accordance with the extensive changes brought about by the pope in the Curia and government of Vatican City through the apostolic constitution *Pastor Bonus* in 1988. According to the Labor Office (1993 statistics), salaries for the 3,400 employees ranged from $960 to $1,500 a month. A pension plan agreed to in October 1992 stipulated that pensions would range from $18,000 to $23,000 a year. While not large by some standards, the salaries and pensions were generous when compared to the small salary given to the diocesan priests working in the Vatican (priests and religious belonging to religious orders— Dominicans, Jesuits, Franciscans, etc.—are not paid any salary, being entirely dependent upon their own orders).

❀ **AUDIENCES, PAPAL** The various audiences held by the pope each week, unless he is ill or unable for whatever reason to participate. The papal audiences can be one of several types, ranging from the official audience, to the semi-private, to the well-known public audience, which is normally held each week on Wednesday at noon. The public audience can take place either in the Vatican or at Castel Gandolfo when the pope is on vacation. When held at the Vatican, there are normally two possible locations for the audience: the Audience Hall or in St. Peter's Square. The square of St. Peter's is filled to bursting several hours before the start with an exceedingly international crowd. A set of announcers, each speaking a different language, greets the crowd and informs them about the meaning of the papal audience and address.

Assassinated Pontiffs

Over the centuries, many popes have been murdered or assassinated. The first to receive this dubious honor was Pope John VIII, who in 882 was first poisoned and then clubbed to death by scheming court members. Most murders happened in the Middle Ages, especially during a period described by a scholar named Cardinal Baronius in his *Annales ecclesiastici* as the Iron Age of the Papacy, from 867 to 964 when powerful families such as the Crescentii or Theophylact had pontiffs elected, deposed, and killed to advance their political ambitions in Rome or as vengeance for some action taken by the pope that might have offended them or inconvenienced some plan or plot. Of the twenty-six popes during this era, seven died by violence. In modern times, fortunately, no pope has been assassinated so far as any official record has proven. This has not stopped conspiracy theorists or the highly imaginative from speculating on the worst. Theories and claims of murderous cabals blossomed in ghoulish fashion following the deaths of Popes Clement XIV in 1774 and the sudden passing of John Paul I in 1978. Pope Clement was reportedly so racked with guilt over disbanding the Jesuits that he spent his last years terrified of being poisoned. After his death, so prevalent were stories about his possible murder that a full postmortem was conducted. It found nothing, but enemies of the Jesuits spread lies that they had done the dirty deed. In the case of John Paul I, some theorized that he had been killed by the Soviets; other more exotic and even laughable proposals placed possible guilt with the Jesuits again (the pope was supposedly planning to disband the order), the Freemasons and the secret organization in Europe called P-2, officials at the Vatican Bank, or even high-ranking members of the Curia. These were dismissed out of hand by the Vatican, which brought in its own investigator, who found no evidence of a plot or even a cover-up. (See *John Paul I.*) Pope John Paul II was nearly murdered in St.

Peter's Square in 1981 by Mehmet Ali Agca, a Turkish gunman who was perhaps working for the Bulgarians and the KGB. The following is a list of murdered pontiffs and the way in which they are thought to have been removed:

John VIII (872–882): Poisoned and clubbed to death

Adrian III, St. (884–885): Rumored poisoned

Stephen VI (896–897): Strangled

Leo V (903): Murdered

John X (914–928): Suffocated under a pillow

Stephen VII (VIII) (928–931): Possibly murdered

Stephen VIII (IX) (939–942): Mutilated and died from injuries

John XII (955–964): Suffered a stroke while with a mistress or murdered by an outraged husband

Benedict VI (973–974): Strangled by a priest

John XIV (983–984): Starved to death or poisoned

Gregory V (996–999): Rumored poisoned, probably malaria

Sergius IV (1009–1012): Possibly murdered

Clement II (1046–1047): Rumored poisoned

Damasus II (1048): Rumored murdered

Boniface VIII (1294–1303): Died from abuse received while a captive of the French in Anagni

N.B. This list does not include the antipopes, who routinely died by violence or execution, such as Boniface VII (974, 984–985), who was murdered by a mob and left under a statue of Marcus Aurelius to be stabbed by passersby.

The Swiss Guard then march into position, preparing the way for the pope himself. The Supreme Pontiff enters the square from the Arch of the Bells riding in the famed Popemobile. He descends from the transport near the throne, which has been set up with meticulous care before the entrance of St. Peter, his coat of arms hanging elegantly behind him. Customarily, he then personally greets the various dignitaries, guests, and Church figures in the VIP section near the throne. Taking his throne, the pope reads his address, which can range from a pronouncement on theological matters to a complex exposition on contemporary affairs such as world peace, human sexuality, or economics. While lost on the majority of the crowd and recited in Italian, the address is often closely watched by analysts and theologians and may contain papal teachings that have far-reaching consequences. Once finished with his sermon, John Paul II will give individual greetings in a dazzling array of languages. There might be some entertainment by a group of pilgrims singing for the pope, and gifts are often presented from groups who have come to Rome from across the globe. The pope then departs, passing slowly and often coming into contact with the faithful, a procession of perennial concern to the Vatican security department, which remembers well the assassination attempt on the pope in 1981. The second type of audience is the semi-private one, held in the Vatican Palace, in the Audience Chambers. These may include a group of pilgrims, perhaps under the direction of some notable religious figure, a well-known Catholic public leader, or interested participants in a canonization or beatification. The semi-private audience is similar to the older and highly treasured custom of the *baciamano,* the "kissing of the hand" held for select Catholics in the period prior to John Paul II.

Pope John Paul II greets a crowd in a semi-private audience. (Courtesy L'Osservatore Romano, Città del Vaticano.)

Time-honored ceremonies remain for the official or state visits held several times a year in the Vatican, when heads of state or monarchs pay a call upon the pope. All pomp and circumstance equal to the station of the visitor are coordinated by the appropriate Vatican offices, and the Swiss Guard, along with high-ranking Curial officials, cardinals, other prelates, and the most illustrious laypersons attached to the Holy See are present in the Courtyard of St. Damase to greet the esteemed or powerful visitors. The guests are ceremoniously walked through the magnificent corridors of the Apostolic Palace and into one of the more private sancta of the palace, such as the Papal Library. There they might have a private session that can extend to several hours and cover high affairs of state. Afterward, they make a joint public statement, the visitor from time to time awed by the surroundings into minor gaffes, such as the time when then President Jimmy Carter introduced the pope to his own Vatican officials and assembled dignitaries in his own Apostolic Palace. The state audiences may have considerable political meaning and symbolism; a demonstration of this was given in 1994 when the pope met with the newly appointed ambassador to the Holy See from Israel.

❀ **AULA, THE**   The name, meaning "Auditorium," that is used for the Nervi Audience Hall in the Vatican or the Paul VI Audience Hall (the *Salone delle Udienze*). The Aula is the newest major building in the entire city-state and the first large addition to the venerable city in several centuries (if one does not count the extensive underground vaulting installed over the last few years). The vaulted, double parabola hall was designed by the Italian architect Pier Luigi Nervi (d. 1979) and dedicated in 1971. It normally holds around 6,000 for a typical papal audience but can accommodate up to 12,000. Aside from the main hall, there are smaller rooms suitable for private audiences (replete with several papal thrones). Architecturally, the hall utilizes a gentle slope in the seats to provide everyone with a clear view of the central focus of every eye, the man in white seated or standing upon the dais. The ceiling is extremely well lit with soft light, the vault conveying a sense of airiness only partially reinforced by the oval windows on each side of the hall. These were originally created by the Hungarian artist Giovanni Hajnal, who put delicately colored glass between ribbing to match the effect of the ceiling (Nervi reportedly was not at all happy with Hajnal's work). Even more striking is the massive bronze sculpture dominating the back of the dais. It resembles interlacing coral with a sharp and complicated network of branches from which a Risen

Christ seems to be ascending. The bronze was cast by Pericle Fazzini and dedicated in 1977 in honor of Pope Paul's eightieth birthday. The hall is perched somewhat claustrophobically behind the *Palazzo Santo Uffizio* (the Palace of the Holy Office) and across from the Teutonic College to the left of St. Peter's. (See also *Audiences, Papal.*)

❀ **AVIGNON**   A city in southern France, in the Vaucluse *département*, in Provence, best known for serving as the residence of the popes from 1309 until 1377. Avignon was not a particularly important city until the start of the fourteenth century, when it was the property of the ruling family of Naples. In 1309, under the stern influence of King Philip IV the Fair of France, Pope Clement V (1305–1314) decided to live in the city. The popes were boarders in a city that they did not own. When it became clear that the popes were not going to be moving any time soon Pope Clement VI (1342–1352) purchased Avignon from Queen Joanna I of Naples in 1348. It would remain in papal hands until 1791, when it was seized by France. Under the popes, Avignon received a vigorous building program, the most notable of which was the Papal Palace, distinguished by its high and somber Gothic towers. More towers were to flank the fortifications erected by the popes or their representatives for the defense of their property and the various churches, especially the Church of St. Peter. Thanks to the popes, the city underwent an eruption of growth as bankers from Italy came to do business with papal servants, artists arrived to seek employment, and people from surrounding areas came to its walls to trade and sell their wares and vegetables. The popes also started a university to attract scholars to the city. This commerce was artificial, however, and Petrarch was to complain that it was filthy, full of disease, and overrun by prostitutes. Decline set in almost immediately after Gregory XI (1370–1378) decided to move back to Rome. The city was once more the seat of papal claimants during the Great Western Schism (1378–1417). Government remained in the hands of a papal representative. At various times, the French kings would seize the city to express their displeasure with the pope. The final takeover was in 1791 by French revolutionaries who were eager to dismember the papacy. After the long wars caused by Napoleon, Pope Pius VII (1800–1823) did not demand the restoration of the city by the Congress of Vienna, being content to receive back the Papal States in Italy. The Papal Palace today is a favorite tourist site. (See also *Babylonian Captivity.*)

B

Babylonian Captivity The name first used by Petrarch and other writers to describe the period from 1309 to 1377 when the popes resided at Avignon. Also called the Avignon Papacy, the term was coined by Petrarch to compare the presence of the popes in a French city to the exile of the Jewish people in Babylonia. He was prompted in his description by the squalor and immorality of the city, ranking this terrible condition as a kind of imprisonment of the papacy. The first pope to reside in Avignon was Clement V (1305–1314) who was under the thumb of the ruthless French king Philip IV the Fair. Philip made it clear to the pope that he did not want him ruling the Church from Italy and so forced him to wander across Gascony and Provence. Tiring of a migratory existence, Clement settled at Avignon in March 1309. Avignon had advantages much to the liking of Clement: it was owned by the Angevin rulers of Naples and was situated in the papal county of Venaissin in southern France. It was also close to the sea, had a quiet and well-behaved population (unlike Rome), was centrally located in Western Christendom, and offered a certain amount of independence with walls and towers that could be reinforced and strengthened. Clement first lived in a Dominican priory, with the intention of making his habitation of it only temporary. The popes would remain in Avignon for seventy years. Clement's successor, John XXII, slept in the Dominican house for a while, but eventually moved to the nicer surroundings of the bishop's palace. There was still a sense of impermanence to his provisions. He was followed by Benedict XII (1334–1342). This French pope, like his predecessors, made some statements about going back to Italy, but he was discouraged in this by the cardinals and the French crown. So, he decided to make Avignon more of a papal city. The archives of the Holy See were moved from Assisi (where they had been kept) to Avignon, the Curia was built up and made a permanent fixture in the Avignon court, and the command was given to construct a palace for the pope. It soon seemed that the popes might not ever leave. This was especially the case under Clement VI (1342–1352). He devoted much effort to enjoying the papacy, making his court a place of celebrations, banquets, and artists. He also purchased the entire city from Queen Joanna of Naples in 1348 for some 80,000 gold florins. Still not content, he started work on a new palace. The ideal aspect of Avignon began to decline over the next years, as the streets became crowded with merchants, prostitutes, and peasants. The city also was threatened by roving bands of soldiers—called free companies—that were the bane of France during the Hundred Years' War, which was raging in the country. Avignon was occupied by them in 1357, and Innocent VI (1352–1362) had to buy them off. Urban V (1362–1370) tried to return to Rome, but came back in September 1370, severely disappointed with the state of affairs in Italy. His successor, Gregory XI (1370–1378) made the final decision to go back to Rome, at the urging of St. Catherine of Siena. The Babylonian Captivity formally ended on January 17, 1377, when Gregory entered Rome. (See also *Avignon*.)

❀ **BACIAMANO**   One of the old forms of court ceremonial that was held as part of papal audiences, the *baciamano* was a kind of semi-private audience with the Holy Father that was attended by a variety of fortunate laypersons. Meaning "kissing of the hand," it was normally granted to certain individuals who had a letter of recommendation from their bishop and who, in the opinion of the court officials, were suitable material to be presented to the pope. They were ushered together as a group into the Apostolic Palace, perhaps one of the Noble Apartments. There they would line up in single file and the pontiff would move smoothly down the line, shaking hands with the lucky, allowing his ring to be kissed (hence the name of the ceremony), and conversing very briefly. It was custom for the pope to give each person a commemorative medal and to bless any cards, medals, or rosaries that they might present to him. For those attending the *baciamano,* the event was one of the most memorable they might experience. This was especially true with such imperious popes as Pius IX and Pius XII, when the papacy still cultivated a sense of grandeur and omnipotence. The *baciamano* effectively died out in its traditional sense during the reigns of John XXIII and Paul VI, but the basic *baciamano* is still in existence, given its own style by John Paul II and his talented staff. (See also *Audiences, Papal.*)

❀ **BALDACCHINO**   Also baldachinum, a domelike canopy made of wood, stone, or metal that is erected over the main or high altar in many churches. It can be supported on four columns, although some versions are suspended by chains. The word *baldacchino* is from Baldocco, the Italian form for Baghdad, the city from which came the precious cloths used in decorating the canopy. A baldacchino is found in the Lateran and in the Basilica of St. Paul Outside the Walls, but the most famous of all is the one designed for Pope Urban VIII by Bernini. Commissioned in 1624 and completed in 1633, the baldacchino was placed over the main altar of St. Peter's basilica, the altar at which only the pope himself may preside. One of the foremost of all baroque creations, the baldacchino towers over the altar and the tomb of St. Peter beneath. It is topped by a gilded gold cross and adorned with angels and the coat of arms of the Barberini family (of which Pope Urban was the most illustrious member)—three bees. Supporting the top are four columns, 95 feet high,

The baldacchino of Bernini, St. Peter's Basilica. (AP/WIDE WORLD PHOTOS.)

made of swirling bronze. The metal for the columns was taken from the ribs of the cupola, which were then recovered in lead, and from the crossbeams of the Pantheon, the one-time temple built by Emperor Marcus Aurelius, a structure so grand even the barbarians plundering Rome in the fifth century dared not touch it. The looting of the Pantheon prompted the Romans to bemoan *"Quod non fecerunt barbari, fecerunt Barberini"* ("What the barbarians did not do, the Barberini did").

❀ **BANK, VATICAN**   The financial institution of the Holy See that administers the banking needs of the population and officials of the Vatican City State. Known officially as the *Institutio per le Opere di Religione* (Institute for Works of Religion, IOR), the bank is one of the best known of the financial departments in the Vatican, with the

Prefecture for the Economic Affairs of the Holy See, the Administration of the Patrimony of the Apostolic See (APSA), and the Council of Cardinals for the Study of Organizational and Economic Problems of the Holy See. Aside from fulfilling the ordinary and day-to-day banking needs of the diplomats, heads of religious orders, special clients, and others who work in or are associated with the Vatican, the bank makes important contributions to the investment strategy of the Holy See. The bank also has authority over funds that are, as the title of the bank itself declares, works of religion—the numerous programs around the world devoted to the care of souls.

The IOR dates back to the organization founded in 1887 by Pope Leo XIII under the title Administration of Religious Works, set up to administer funds for religious endeavors. In 1942, Pope Pius XII replaced this office with the formally established IOR. Pius, however, changed its overall mission by charging it with the oversight of all monies, as well as property, cash, and bonds, that were transferred or entrusted to the bank for those works of religion; it was also to administer the funds of the many religious orders of the Church. The IOR played a significant role in the safeguarding of the Church's finances during the turbulent years of the Second World War, using its international associations to take precautions against the threat of a Nazi takeover of the Vatican. The Vatican Bank is best known today for the sensational scandals to which its name was attached in the late 1970s and early 1980s. Over the last years, the Vatican has attempted to repair the damage both to the reputation and credibility of the IOR, culminating in the March 1, 1990, reform of the bank at the command of Pope John Paul II, part of his program of changes pertaining to papal finances.

❀ **BARBERINI, HOUSE OF**   One of the great noble families of Rome that produced the memorable pontiff Urban VIII (1623–1644). The Barberini were originally from Tuscany, in the area of Barberino in the Else Valley. They moved to Florence and then to Rome, deriving their vast wealth from the mercantile exploits of Francesco Barberini (1528–1600). In 1623, Maffeo Barberini was elected pope, devoting much of his reign to advancing the wealth and possessions of the house through a notorious degree of nepotism. The pope made cardinals of his nephews Francesco (d. 1679) and Antonio the Younger (d. 1671), and his brother Antonio the Elder (d. 1646). Other family members were given powerful positions. Francesco served as Cardinal Secretary of State, but his principal achievement was to help organize the

Barberini Library. Devoted patrons of the arts and learning, the house outraged many Romans by its ruthless plundering of the city's riches to pay for their building programs and the wanton destruction of ancient buildings and sites to provide materials for their own palace. One of the worst affronts was the stripping of bronze from the Pantheon for Bernini's baldacchino in St. Peter's and to make cannon. Amassing enemies, the Barberini were confronted by an alliance headed by the noble house of Fornese, suffering a crushing defeat at the Battle of Lagoscuro in 1644, the same year that Urban died. His successor, the humorless Innocent X, launched an investigation into abuses of Church funds by the Barberini cardinals. They fled Italy and found sanctuary with Cardinal Mazarin in France, a personage little inclined to hand them over. A reconciliation was achieved in 1653, but the glory days of the house were over. The line died out in 1736 and the family's property passed to the House of Colonna, another line with long ties to the papacy. The Barberini collection of rare manuscripts came into the hands of the Vatican in 1902 under Pope Leo XIII; it was attached to the Vatican Library. (See also *Baldacchino*.)

❀ **BARQUE OF PETER**   The symbolic representation of the throne of St. Peter as a ship or boat. It is derived from Peter's profession as a fisherman prior to being called to be a disciple by Christ. The image is used often when describing the ship of state steered by each pope. The pope also wears the Ring of the Fisherman and the Shoes of the Fisherman, each serving to remind the successor of Peter that he is to be, like Peter, a fisher of men, and that the Holy See was founded by a humble fisherman chosen by God for a remarkable task. In referring to the papacy, Msgr. Ronald Knox remarked that when traveling on the Church's ship of state, one should not get too close to the engine room.

❀ **BASILICA**   A type of Roman architecture that was adopted by the Church as a distinctive design for places of worship used by Church leaders. Rome emerged as the center of the great basilicas. Three were built by Emperor Constantine the Great (d. 337): St. Peter's (the old basilica), St. John Lateran (S. Giovanni in Laterano), and St. Paul's Outside the Walls (S. Paolo fuori le Mura). There are four major basilicas in Rome: St. Peter's, St. Paul's Outside the Walls, St. John Lateran, and Santa Maria Maggiore. Each possesses an altar that may be used only by the pope. St. John Lateran is also the pope's cathedral.

❀ **BEATTISSIMUS PATER**   A Latin term meaning "Most Blessed (or Holy) Father." It is used as a form of reverential address when speaking to the pope.

❀ **BELVEDERE PALACE**   A palace originally built in the Vatican by Pope Innocent VIII (1484–1492) and today used as one of the major parts of the Vatican Museums. The palace was constructed by Innocent to serve as a summer residence at the northern end of the Vatican complex. Its name was taken from the superb view the palace offered of the city. Subsequent popes made additions to the palace: Alexander VI added the Borgia Tower and Julius II connected the palace to the main Apostolic complex through a series of galleries and courtyards, commissioned in 1503 and designed by Donato Bramante. (See also *Museums, Vatican.*)

❀ **BENEDICT I**   Pope from 575 to 579. An obscure pontiff, he was elected to succeed Pope John II. He was consecrated in June 575. His reign came at a time when Italy was in the throes of severe economic, political, and social crisis, plagued by invasions by Germans and famine. Benedict probably worked to improve the situation, but died on July 30, 579, during a siege of Rome by the Lombards. Successor: Pelagius II.

❀ **BENEDICT II, ST.**   Pope from 684 to 685, a Roman by birth, Benedict was elected to succeed St. Leo II in 683, but he was not consecrated until June 26, 684, owing to delays in securing the approval of the Byzantine emperor in Constantinople, which was then mandatory. Benedict was able to win from the Byzantine ruler Constantine the right to receive recognition from the Byzantine official in Italy, the Exarch of Ravenna. This enabled the popes to avoid serious delays from the time of their election to their consecration. He also restored a large number of churches in Rome. He was described as humble and kind, dying on May 8, 685. Successor: John V.

❀ **BENEDICT III**   Pope from 855 to 858, born in Rome, he was the son of a man named Peter, receiving ordination as a deacon by Gregory IV and elevation as a cardinal priest by Leo IV. When Leo died (July 17, 855), the Churchman first chosen was Adrian (II), but he refused and so Benedict was elected. He sent legates to Emperor Louis II to request recognition, but before consecration was permitted, Benedict was under attack by a party of imperial agents who advanced their candidate Anastasius Bibliothecarus. The antipope was brought to Rome, and Benedict, unable to resist the imperial troops, was pushed off the throne and thrown into prison. The Romans themselves rose up and expressed their desire for Benedict. The imperial party acquiesced rather than face violence, and Benedict was finally consecrated on September 29, 855. His main achievement was to repair churches in Rome that had been damaged by the Saracens in their raids. He also struggled to rebuild areas flooded by the Tiber. He died on April 17, 858. Successor: St. Nicholas I.

❀ **BENEDICT IV**   Pope from 900 to 903, Benedict was the son of Mammalus and was a Roman by birth. The details of his election are obscure, owing to the terrible condition of the papacy in the late ninth and early tenth centuries. His reign is known mainly for his excommunication of Baldwin II, Count of Flanders, for the murder of Fulk, Archbishop of Reims, and the coronation of Louis the Blind as Holy Roman Emperor. He died in the middle of 903. Successor: Leo V.

❀ **BENEDICT V**   Pope from 964 to 966, he was born in Rome and earned such a reputation for learning that he was called Grammaticus. His election came at a difficult time for the Church, for in 963 Emperor Otto I forcibly deposed Pope John XII and replaced him with Leo VIII, having him consecrated on December 4. The Romans, however, who would not warm to Leo, seized the first opportunity to depose that pontiff and reinstall John. After his death in May 964 they decided on Benedict; his reign began on May 22, 964. An angry Otto I besieged Rome and, on June 23, Benedict was surrendered into his hands. The pope gave up freely, enduring severe humiliation at the hands of the emperor and the deposed Leo. Leo reportedly broke the staff carried by the pope over his head to demonstrate his shattered power. Surprisingly, in this age of violence, Benedict was not put to death. He was instead carried off to Germany, dying in Hamburg on July 4, 966. Some papal lists consider him an antipope; others view Leo VIII as the usurper. Successor: John XIII.

❀ **BENEDICT VI**   Pope from 973 to 974. Probably a Roman, he was a cardinal at the time of his election to succeed John XIII, probably in the fall of 972. His consecration was not performed, however, until January 19, 973, because of the usual delays in winning approval of the Holy Roman Emperor, in this case, Otto I. His pontificate was short and ended most unpleasantly. The Crescenti family, which sought to dominate Rome, used the period of instability in the empire following Otto's death in 973 to seize Benedict and throw him into Castel

Sant'Angelo. The pope languished there for about two months until the antipope Boniface VII, who had been installed by the Crescenti, had him strangled in July 974. Successor: Benedict VII.

❀ **BENEDICT VII**   Pope from 974 to 983. The legitimate successor to Benedict VI, who had been removed and deposed by the Crescenti family and their creation, antipope Boniface VII. Benedict was a member of the Roman nobility, a relative of Alberic II, the powerful political figure who had ruled Rome from 932 to 954. His election was made possible through the intervention of the imperial representative Count Sicco, who refused to recognize Boniface. Boniface was forced to flee, and Benedict was elected, being acceptable to the Roman nobility. He was not secure on his throne, however, and in 980, Boniface instigated a coup, driving Benedict from the city and forcing him to seek the aid of Emperor Otto II. Benedict returned in 981 with imperial troops. After his return, he worked closely with the emperor, opposing simony and encouraging monasticism. His reign, while plagued by upheaval and dependence upon the emperor, marked a revival in the fortunes of the papacy. He died on July 10, 983. Successor: John XIV.

❀ **BENEDICT VIII**   Pope from 1012 to 1024. Born around 980, this nobleman was originally named Theophylact and belonged to the House of the Tusculani. He owed his election to the papal throne to the sudden rise of his family to preeminence in Rome at the expense of the Crescenti family, which had dominated the Holy See in the tenth century. Some point to the sudden, even suspicious, deaths of Pope Sergius IV (a dependent of the Crescenti) and John II Crescentius, as evidence that Benedict may have been given the papacy at the expense of these two political obstacles. Regardless, he was installed on May 17, 1012, taking the name Benedict and thus certifying Sergius's innovation of changing one's name at the moment of election. He was soon opposed, however, by the Crescenti remnant, crushing his enemies with brute force and driving a rival, Gregory, from Rome. To strengthen himself even further, Benedict placed his brother Romanus (the future John XIX) in charge of civil affairs in the city. Despite this bloody start to his reign, Benedict proved an able pontiff who helped revive the papacy after long being in eclipse in Rome. He resisted the raids of the Saracens, defeating them in battle in 1016–1017. An alliance with the Normans in southern Italy helped the pope to reduce even further the influence of the Byzantines. Concerned for the well-being of the Church, Benedict organized the Synod of Pavia in 1022 where, with

Emperor Henry II, he enacted a number of reforms, focusing espe-
cially against simony and promoting clerical celibacy. Benedict died on
April 9, 1024. He was the first of several popes from the House of
Tusculani. Successor: John XIX.

❀ **BENEDICT IX**   Pope from 1032 to 1044, again in 1045, and once more
in 1047–1048. One of the most corrupt and notorious of all popes,
Benedict IX is distinguished for selling the throne of St. Peter and for
being the only pontiff to reign for three different periods. The nephew
of the two Tusculani popes Benedict VIII and John XIX, he was the son
of Count Alberic II of Tusculum, receiving an arranged election as pope
through the bribes of his father. Consecrated on October 21, 1032, he was
reportedly only ten or twelve at the time—this is probably not accurate;
he was most likely in his twenties. Regardless, the next twelve years were
spent in utterly dissolute fashion. He was scandalous, sensual, and violent, remaining on the throne only by the threat of arms. Finally, in 1044,
the Romans rose up against him through the conspiring of the Crescenti
family. Benedict was driven from the city, and on January 20, 1045, the
Crescenti installed John of Sabina as Sylvester III. Benedict refused to
give up, excommunicating Sylvester and returning to power on March
10. This time, he could last only two months. On May 1, he took the out-
rageous step of selling the throne to his godfather Giovanni Graziano, a
priest who took the name Gregory VI; technically, he accepted a bribe to
step down, but realistically, he had been given the money in return for
the office. By the next year, Benedict had come to regret his act. He thus
reappeared in Rome, marking the presence of three popes, himself,
Gregory VI, and Sylvester III. Summoned to the Synod of Sutri in 1046,
he refused to go, remaining behind the walls of the fortress of Tusculum.
Nevertheless, the synod, under the ruler Henry III of Germany, deposed
all three and appointed Suidger of Bamberg as Clement II. Clement
soon died (perhaps by poison) and Benedict installed himself on
November 8, 1047. He was forced out yet again at the command of
Emperor Henry on July 16, 1048, in favor of Damasus II. Benedict
refused to recognize his deposition, spouting vitriol at Damasus and his
successor Leo IX from his fortress. There is a long tradition that just
before his death, Benedict renounced his terrible life and died a penitent
at Grottaferrata in the Alban Hills. His date of death is uncertain.
Successors: Sylvester III, Gregory VI, Clement II, and Damasus II.

❀ **BENEDICT X**   Antipope from April 1058 to January 1059. Known
originally as John Mincius, he was Bishop of Velletri at the time of his

irregular election as pope following the death of Stephen IX (X) on March 29, 1058. The election was orchestrated by a party of nobles headed by the Tusculani, who wanted to have a reliable pope installed before a full conclave could be held under the influence of Hildebrand (later Gregory VII), the famed reformer who was away in Germany. The nobles hoped to have the reformers give up any opposition, but they responded by fleeing Rome and condemning Benedict. In December 1058, the reforming and legally supported cardinals elected Pope Nicholas II. Benedict managed to hang on until January of the next year, when he fled. Captured in the fall of 1059, he was placed on trial, stripped of all pretense of office, and ordered imprisoned in the monastery of Sant'Agnese on the Via Nomentana. He died there around 1073.

BENEDICT XI Pope from 1303 to 1304, the successor to Boniface VIII (1294–1303). Born in Treviso, Italy, in 1240, Niccolo Boccasini entered the Dominicans at the age of fourteen. In 1296, he became the Master General (or head) of the order. Two years later, Boniface named him a cardinal. He distinguished himself by remaining faithful to the pope during the closing period of the bitter struggle between the pope and King Philip IV the Fair of France. He was, in fact, only one of two cardinals to stay at Boniface's side during the terrible ordeal suffered by him in Anagni in 1303, when servants of King Philip seized and abused the pope for several days. Boccasini was thus much honored by the cardinals who gathered after Boniface died on October 11, 1303, to elect a successor and was their choice, by unanimous vote on October 22, 1303. His pontificate of a mere eight months was marked by an easing of the difficult situation with France. He absolved the king and his subjects of the censures placed upon them by Boniface and forgave the Colonna cardinals for their actions against their pontiff. He did not forgive Guillaume de Nogaret and Sciarra Colonna, however, for their crimes in Anagni, summoning them before a pontifical tribunal. Benedict died suddenly at Perugia on July 7, 1304. His death was possibly by poison. He was beatified by Clement XIV in 1773. Successor: Clement V.

BENEDICT XII Pope from 1334 to 1342, the third of the Avignon popes. Born Jacques Fournier in Saverdun in the province of Toulouse, France, he was possibly the son of a miller. At a young age he entered the Cistercians and became a monk. Emerging as a popular theologian in the order, he was elected abbot of

Fontfroide in 1311 and Bishop of Pamiers in 1317. While there, he mercilessly extirpated the last of the heretic Albigensians. Pope John XXII appointed him a cardinal in 1327. On December 20, 1334, he was elected to succeed John on the first ballot, which came as somewhat a surprise, given his relative obscurity among the cardinals. Consecrated on January 8, 1335, he immediately made clear his intention to lead a simple life as pope. He continued to wear his monk's habit and, proclaiming that the pope must be like Melchizedek (an Old Testament priest and king), without family, refused to take part in traditional nepotism. A reformer by desire and inclination, he brought a number of changes to the clergy, the Curia, and the religious orders; some of his reforms were rescinded by his successors, but others were reiterated by the Council of Trent. At first seriously considering moving the papacy back to Rome, he was talked out of this by his French cardinals. Instead, he worked to improve Avignon by curbing local expenditures on the Curia, sending away the many hangers-on among the clergy seeking preferments in the papal court, and tore down the old episcopal residence, replacing it with the Palace of the Popes. (See *Avignon.*) During his reign, France and England entered into the Hundred Years' War, a conflict he tried unsuccessfully to prevent. He also sent aid to the Romans to rebuild churches and to help the inhabitants, who were suffering in the absence of the papacy. His pontificate is also noted for the sharp decline of papal influence in the States of the Church in Italy. He died on April 24, 1342, at Avignon. He was much abused in the satires of Petrarch, who was angry at his friend's refusal to return to Rome. Successor: Clement VI.

BENEDICT XIII Antipope from 1394 to 1417 (or 1423), one of the rivals for the papal throne during the Great Western Schism (1378–1417). Pedro de Luna was born around 1328 in Aragon. A professor of canon law in Montpellier, he was appointed a cardinal by Pope Gregory IX in 1375. A participant in the conclave that elected Pope Urban VI in 1378, he had long supported the eccentric pontiff, but ultimately abandoned him in favor of antipope Clement VII. He served Clement quite well as a legate, using his charm and diplomacy to win over Castile and Aragon to the claimant's cause. Having stated his resolve to seek an end to the schism, even if it meant his abdication in the process, Pedro was elected to succeed Clement on September 28, 1394. Not surprisingly, he refused to step down as a means of solving the crisis in the Church, preferring to negotiate a settlement. His obstinacy was rooted in a sincere belief that he was the legitimate pope, a resolve that was unshakable in the face of calls to abdicate from the French, Germans, and English. Negotiations failed as well with the legitimate Popes Boniface IX, Innocent VII, and Gregory XII. At the Council of Pisa in 1409, Benedict was declared deposed, along with Pope Gregory. The situation in the Church was only made worse by the council's election of a third pope, Alexander V. Benedict remained firm in his position even after 1417 when the Council of Constance (1414–1417) upheld his deposition. Given backing by Castile and a few other states, he still would not step down, despite the general resolution of the schism by the council. Living at Peñiscola, he continued to style himself pope, creating four cardinals in 1422. He died on May 23, 1423. His body, except for his skull, was broken and crushed by invading French troops in 1811, the remains thrown away. He is still remembered fondly in Peñiscola as Papa Luna.

BENEDICT XIII Pope from 1724 to 1730, Pietro Francesco Orsini was born on February 2, 1649, into the famed Orsini family, which had produced numerous popes over the centuries. (See *Orsini, House of.*) He was drawn to the religious life, entering the Dominicans at the age of sixteen, a move much to the chagrin of his parents, who were appalled that their firstborn should not inherit the estates and title of his uncle, the duke of Bracciano. They appealed to Pope Clement IX not to permit his entry, but the pope responded by granting admission, cutting his time as a novice in half to permit him swifter entrance into the order. Pietro did not disappoint his superiors, becoming a professor at the age of twenty-one. In 1672, his relative, Clement X, made him a cardinal. As a cardinal he remained a simple friar, choosing to become Archbishop of Manfredonia because it was poorer than his other option, the archdiocese of Salerno. In 1724 he entered his fifth conclave after Innocent XII died. This

Pope Benedict XIII.

assembly was soon unable to reach a majority owing to the bickering among various factions of the cardinals. After nine weeks, they decided on Orsini, the choice based on his goodness and his obvious neutrality. In desperation, he refused (an irony, given his family's past), but finally accepted and took the name Benedict XIV, changing it to XIII after it was pointed out that the last Benedict by that number was an antipope. He was a superbly spiritual pontiff, spending long hours in prayer with the rosary. He also heard confessions in St. Peter's and visited the sick and the poor. Dedicated to curbing the extravagant habits of the Roman and Curial clergy, he ordered less flamboyant dress among the clergy, and even commanded that cardinals not wear wigs. The lottery, a favorite pastime in Rome, was banned. Unfortunately, he paid less attention to other matters, entrusting them completely to the unscrupulous hands of Cardinal Niccolo Coscia, who looted the papal treasury and whose mastery of the papal administration ended only with Benedict's death on February 23, 1730. Successor: Clement XII.

BENEDICT XIV Pope from 1740 to 1758, one of the most cheerful, witty, and moderate of popes. Prospero Lorenzo Lambertini was born at Bologna on March 31, 1675. In 1694, he was awarded doctorates in theology and canon law, entering the service of the Church through the Curia. His rise was rapid, culminating with his position as advisor to Benedict XIII (1724–1730) and elevation to the cardinalate in 1728. Entering the conclave in 1740 to find a successor to Clement XII, he was much liked and honored as the foremost scholar of the College of Cardinals but not considered a favorite. The proceedings dragged on for an amazing six months, the longest conclave in modern history, with the cardinals divided over numerous issues and intrigues. At one point, Cardinal Lambertini reportedly said in jest, "If you wish to elect a saint, choose Gotti; a statesman, Aldobrandini; an honest man, elect me." His name, already thrown around as a good compromise candidate, was seized upon by the cardinals, who elected him pope on August 17, 1740. He took the name Benedict in honor of his friend and patron Benedict XIII. He came to the throne in the midst of the Enlightenment and proved an able pontiff. Clearly of a moderate disposition in some areas, he ordered the Index of Forbidden Books to exercise restraint in its examinations of writings, reduced the taxes paid by the inhabitants of the Papal States, and was on excellent terms with many of the leading intellectual figures of the time, including Voltaire. That author dedicated his book *Mahomet* to Benedict, declaring that he was "the pride of Rome and the father of the world." Respect was given to him by Frederick the Great, Horace Walpole (who wrote that the pope was "a man whom neither wit nor power could spoil"), and even the Sultan of the Ottoman Empire, whom Benedict referred to as the "Good Turk." He used his authority where he could, but he perceived even before his election that the Holy See had lost much of its temporal power. He thus made concessions to Spain, Portugal, Naples, and Sardinia, but stood firm on matters of doctrine, condemning freemasonry and even forbidding the reading of Voltaire's works. The decision to curtail certain practices used by the Jesuits in winning converts to the faith in China and India cut down sharply on new Catholics, but he preferred that to teaching a faith that was not authentic. His relations with most states were excellent, including England and various Protestant countries. Benedict's passing on May 3, 1758, was greeted by silence on the part of satirists and acerbic writers of the era. Successor: Clement XIII.

BENEDICT XIV Two very unusual counter-antipopes, meaning that they were elected to be antipopes as rivals to another antipope. A bizarre event, it occurred twice. The first was in 1425 when Bernard Garnier became Benedict XIV against antipope Clement VIII (a rival of Pope Martin V). He held the office until 1430, when Clement abdicated. He was called the Invisible Pope for being so shy in his affairs. The second was Jean Carrier, who died a prisoner in the castle of Foix. Both were supporters of antipope Benedict XIII.

BENEDICT XV Pope from 1914 to 1922, his reign dominated by World War I (1914 to 1918). Giacomo della Chiesa, born in Genoa in 1854, expressed a desire from a young age for the priesthood, but his father insisted that he first secure a degree in civil law from the University of Genoa. Winning a doctorate in law in 1875, he entered the Capranica Seminary in Rome and received ordination on December 21, 1878, in the Lateran Basilica. He subsequently earned doctorates in theology (1879) and canon law (1880), receiving admission into the Academy of Noble Ecclesiastics, the training academy of Vatican diplomats. In 1882, he was appointed secretary to Mariano Rampolla, the future cardinal, secretary of state, and candidate for pope who had just been named nuncio to Spain. As Rampolla climbed the Vatican ladder, della Chiesa was himself swiftly promoted in the Secretariat of State, becoming undersecretary of state in 1901. In 1907, Pope St. Pius X appointed him Archbishop of Bologna; he was made cardinal in 1914, a mere three months before his election to succeed Pius. His election on

September 3, 1914, was unanticipated, but it was probably prompted by the recognition of the cardinals that a steady and competent diplomat would be needed to steer the Church through the troubled waters of the next years. Benedict was immediately confronted by the First World War, which had erupted at the same time as Pius's death in August. With the difficult situation of having Catholic countries at war with each other and seeing the terrible destruction brought by the conflict, Benedict adopted a strict policy of neutrality while laboring desperately to end the fighting and bring relief to the millions of refugees and innocent victims. The possibility of a negotiated peace reached its most promising moment in 1917, when he proposed a seven-point peace plan. Germany was favorably disposed to the idea, but of the Allies, only the United States under Woodrow Wilson answered in any meaningful sense. The hopes of a settlement were dashed permanently by the entry of the United States into the war. (Interestingly, the seven points can be seen in the

Pope Benedict XV, pontiff during World War I.

framework of Wilson's own Fourteen Points.) Owing to his neutral stand, Benedict was punished by the victorious allies by being excluded from the peace talks at Versailles, but he was utterly undeterred in promoting peace and giving assistance to the victims across the globe, sending aid as far away as China. His reign also witnessed the issuing of the new code of canon law in 1917, the publication of twelve encyclicals, and the establishing of a diplomatic representative from Great Britain for the first time in three hundred years. In recognition of his efforts on behalf of peace, he was honored with a statue by the Turks in Constantinople (later Istanbul). Successor: Pius XI.

BERNINI, GIAN LORENZO Italian Baroque sculptor and architect (1598–1680), who made significant contributions to the immense artistic patrimony of the Holy See. Born in Naples, he first studied sculpture under his father, securing the patronage of the Borghese family. At the age of eleven, a bust he carved caught the eye of Pope Paul V, who charged then Cardinal Barberini with the lad's education. He subsequently became the favorite artist and architect to three popes and is generally credited with transforming Rome into a Baroque city. The list of his accomplishments in the Eternal City is a long one, including the "Ecstacy of St. Teresa" (1646) in the church of Santa Maria della Vittoria, the facade of Sant'Andria al Quirinale, and the Palazzo Barberini. Most notable, however, were his creations within the Vatican and St. Peter's Basilica.

Bernini's first great papal patron was Pope Urban VIII (1623–1644), the former Maffeo Cardinal Barberini, who once declared to the artist, "O Cavalier, it is your great fortune to see the election of Cardinal Barberini pope, but much greater is our own that the Cavalier Bernini lives during our pontificate." For Pope Urban, he created the famed baldacchino of St. Peter's (1624–1633), the statue of St. Longinus (1629–1638), and Urban's tomb (1628–1647). He fell out of favor with the Barberini pope when his plan for the construction of towers atop St. Peter's began causing the basilica's roof to sag. While he executed several projects for Pope Innocent X (1644–1655) in Rome, Bernini's next period of activity was for Pope Alexander VII (1655–1667). For him he carved the *Cathedra Petri* (1657–1666), the tomb of Alexander (1671–1678), and, perhaps his greatest architectural achievement, the enclosing colonnade in the Square of St. Peter's (1656–1667). He also was responsible for the second of the two fountains in the square (1667), the equestrian statue of Constantine in St. Peter's, and the renowned Scala Regia (the Royal Stairs), one of the most breathtaking areas of the entire history-rich Vatican complex. (See also *Baldacchino* and *Cathedra Petri*.)

🕸 **BIGLIETTO**   See *Cardinal.*

🕸 **BISHOP**   One of the successors of the Apostles who receives what is termed the "fullness of Christ's priesthood," with the power and authority to administer all of the sacraments, including that of ordaining priests and participation in the consecration of bishops. The name bishop is taken from the Greek *episcopos* (overseer) and implies the position of the bishop as a direct successor of the Apostles. The members of the episcopal order are empowered to take part in directing the Church through the collegial government under the pope and by assembling together in councils and working on an individual basis as heads of dioceses. It is often forgotten that the pope is himself only a bishop in the technical sense. He is not elected Supreme Pontiff but Bishop of Rome; his authority over the Universal Church stems from his place as successor to St. Peter over the primatial see in the Church, through which he becomes Vicar of Christ and Supreme Pontiff. (See also *Apostolic Succession.*)

❁ **BLACK POPE** The nickname traditionally given to the head (or general) of the Jesuits (Society of Jesus) in recognition of his influence and power within the Church. The name is today rather anachronistic.

❁ **BLESSINGS, PAPAL** The granting of a blessing by the Holy Father, usually to a huge throng gathered in St. Peter's Square before the basilica or, more commonly, the Apostolic Apartments. The most routinely seen papal blessing is that given by him each Sunday from the window of his apartment. For this regular event—weather and health permitting—the pope will stand on a small platform to be seen by as many of the faithful as possible. The blessings are given in the audiences held in the Aula (Nervi Audience Hall), in masses held in St. Peter's, the Lateran, or in any of the hundreds of different countries and cities he might visit during a pontificate. One interesting phenomenon of the blessing is the custom of holding up rosaries, holy cards, crosses, statues, and photographs while the pope performs the actual blessing. It is not uncommon to see vendors raising buckets and boxes of religious articles to receive a blessing. These are then sold at a higher price under the assumption that they have greater spiritual value, having been blessed by the Holy Father, even though the individual selling them may have needed binoculars to see the pope given the size of the crowds. (See also *Audiences, Papal.*)

❁ **BONIFACE I, ST.** Pope from 418 to 422. A presbyter in Rome, Boniface was supposedly ordained by Pope St. Damasus I and was also an assistant to Pope St. Innocent I for a time in Constantinople. On December 28, 418, he was elected to succeed Pope Zosimus by the Roman clergy. The same day, however, a small faction of deacons chose as their candidate Eulalius, both consecrated on the same day (December 29). Boniface was thus confronted with considerable upheaval in Rome, finally making appeal to Pope Honorius at Ravenna. The emperor decided in his favor and Eulalius was eventually expelled from Rome after disobeying the emperor's command not to reenter the city. With the issue finally resolved in April 419, Boniface settled into his office and demonstrated genuine administrative skill and competence. The heresy of Pelagianism was condemned and Boniface earned the enthusiastic support of St. Augustine. He also issued a decree forbidding slaves from receiving Holy Orders and those under severe financial difficulties from serving in the local government. He died on September 4, 422. Successor: St. Celestine I.

❀ **BONIFACE II** Pope from 530 to 532, the first German pontiff. Of Gothic descent, he distinguished himself in the reign of Pope Felix IV as an archdeacon and political counselor. Fearing the struggle that might occur over the succession after his death, Felix made formal statement of his intention that Boniface should succeed him; he placed the pallium of papal authority on his shoulders and threatened excommunication to any who might oppose him. Not surprisingly, immediately after Felix died, most of the Roman clergy gathered together and elected Dioscorus pope, thereby preventing what they thought to be the repellant situation of having a German as their pontiff. Both Boniface and Dioscorus were consecrated on the same day, September 22, 530. The schism in the Church did not last long, however, for Dioscorus died on October 14. Boniface took immediate steps to reconcile the Romans, convening a synod and condemning Dioscorus. He then summoned a second synod, proposing a decree by which he assumed the right to name his successor. This was much opposed in the city (although the clergy agreed to honor his desire for Vigilius to succeed him) and opposed by the Byzantines. Boniface soon rescinded it, burning it before the clergy and the Roman senate at a third synod. In a fourth synod, he advanced papal claims to jurisdiction over the territory Illyricum (along the Danube), the source of conflict with the East for many years to come. He also opposed the heresy of Semi-Pelagianism. He died in October 532. Successor: John II.

❀ **BONIFACE III** Pope from February 19 to November 12, 607. A Roman by birth, but of Greek descent, he served as a trusted deacon to Pope Gregory I the Great (590–604) and had been used by him as a legate to Constantinople in 603. While there, he established excellent relations with Emperor Phocas (r. 602–610). Elected pope after the death of Sabinian in February 606, he waited a year for consecration, perhaps because of delays in securing recognition from Phocas (which seems unlikely) or because of an unsettled situation in Rome. His reign had two main achievements: he secured from Phocas the important recognition of the Roman see as head of all the churches and ordered that in future papal elections there should be no campaigning for the office during the lifetime of a pope and only until three days after his burial. Successor: Boniface IV.

✻ **BONIFACE IV, ST.** Pope from 608 to 615. The son of a physician, Boniface was elected to succeed Boniface III after an interregnum of some nine months. He had been an ardent admirer of Pope Gregory I the Great (590–604), serving as a deacon in the Roman Church and being entrusted by Gregory with the distribution of patrimonies. Committed to monasticism, he turned his residence into a monastery and relied upon his spiritual nature to help him endure the disasters striking Italy; there were famines, plagues, and earthquakes. Boniface is notable for securing permission from Emperor Phocas in Constantinople to transform the Pantheon into a Christian church. It was renamed Santa Maria ad Martyres (but was also called Santa Maria Rotunda, from the shape of the Pantheon). The bones of martyrs, removed from the Catacombs and filling twenty-eight carts, were placed beneath the high altar. The pope died in monastic retirement and was buried in the portico of St. Peter's. Successor: Adeodatus I.

✻ **BONIFACE V** Pope from 619 to 625. A native of Naples, he was the successor to Pope Deusdedit after an interregnum of more than a year. Prior to his consecration on October 25, 619, Rome was menaced by a force of Byzantines who, under the local Byzantine commander (the exarch) Eleutherius, rebelled against the empire. The city was spared only by the murder of Eleutherius by his own troops. Boniface is known for having helped to establish the idea of sanctuary and was exceedingly fond of the English Church. Successor: Honorius I.

✻ **BONIFACE VI** Pope for fifteen days in April 896. A Roman, he was elected to succeed Formosus soon after the latter's death on April 4, 896; he was chosen as a result of riots by the populace. His past was somewhat checkered as he had been twice stripped of his clerical office by Pope John VIII. If he was lacking in moral qualifications to be pope, he never had time to demonstrate it, for he died quite suddenly. Given the bleak nature of the papacy and Rome at the time, it is possible he was murdered, although he suffered from gout. In 898, Pope John IX condemned the irregular method of his election. Successor: Stephen VI (VII).

✤ **BONIFACE VII** Antipope in 974 and again from 984 to 985. Known also as Boniface Franco, he was the son of one Ferrucius and was a cardinal in 972 at the time of the death of John XIII. A favorite candidate of the Crescenti family, he was advanced for the papacy, but the imperial party picked Benedict VI and secured the approval of Emperor Otto I. In 974, however, the Crescenti arranged the overthrow of Benedict through an insurrection. The pope was seized, thrown into prison, and Franco was consecrated pope as Boniface VII. When word arrived that the imperial representative Count Sicco was on his way to Rome, Boniface ordered Benedict strangled. Sickened by the crime, the Romans rose up, removed Boniface, and besieged him in Castel Sant'Angelo; they were soon joined by Count Sicco and imperial troops. Boniface managed to escape with some of the papal treasury to southern Italy. He then moved on to Constantinople. In 984 he was back in Rome. With backing from the Byzantines, as well as allies in Rome, Boniface imprisoned Pope John XIV and had him murdered in August. This time he managed to stay on the throne for nearly a year, crushing opposition in the city, including having one cardinal blinded for obstinacy. His death came on July 20, 895; he may have been assassinated or deposed and then murdered by a mob. Regardless, his body was dragged through the streets, stripped naked, and beneath the statue of Marcus Aurelius exposed to abuse by crowds. The favorite pastime was piercing his corpse with spears. After a gruesome night, several clerics carried away the body and gave it a decent burial. Right up to the moment of his death, Boniface considered himself the legitimate pope, and until 1904 several lists considered him so as well. He is one of the bloodiest of all claimants to the papal throne.

BONIFACE VIII Pope from 1294 to 1303. His reign marked the zenith of the papacy's claims of both temporal and spiritual supremacy over all of Christendom; his conception of himself and his role as pope can be summed up in one of his favorite maxims —often shouted at his cardinals—*"Ego sum Caesar, ego imperator!"* ("I am Caesar, I am emperor!"). Born Benedetto Gaetani at Anagni, he was a member of the House of Gaetani (or Caetani) and on his mother's side a nephew of Pope Alexander IV. After studying at Todi, Spoleto, and Bologna, he held a variety of posts in the papal service and was made a cardinal deacon in 1281 by Pope Martin IV (1281–1285) and cardinal priest by Pope Nicholas IV (1288–1292). He was exceedingly successful as papal legate to France (1290–1291), subsequently playing a major role in the disastrous pontificate of St. Celestine V (1294). He gave to the unfortunate pope advice on matters of canon law, including a certain amount of encouragement to abdicate. In the conclave that followed Celestine's resignation, Gaetani was elected on December 24, 1294, receiving formal consecration in Rome on January 23, 1295.

His pontificate would end in abject calamity for the papacy. Boniface was firmly convinced of the dire need to restore the prestige and power of the Holy See, but his own vision of this was no longer realistic, given the weakened position of the popes and the nationalist movements then developing in Europe. He was further debilitated by his own intemperate disposition, his violent anger, and his blindness to the altered social and political climate. All of his shortcomings were to influence his bitter dealings with King Philip IV the Fair of France. In 1296, Boniface decided to use his authority to end the ongoing Hundred Years' War between France and England by declaring a ban on the taxation of clergy to pay for war by issuing the bull *Clericis Laicos* (February 25, 1296). In response, Philip placed a prohibition on exports and ejected merchants, thereby crippling the economy of the Papal States, which were heavily dependent

The imperious Pope Boniface VIII, from a fresco by Giotto. (CATHOLIC NEWS SERVICE.)

upon trade. Boniface retreated in July 1297, permitting taxation in emergencies. Naturally, war was an emergency. Peace would not long endure between the pope and king, however, and in 1301 Boniface reacted aggressively to the trial by King Philip of a papal legate. The pope issued the bull *Ausculta fili* (December 5, 1301). The next year he went even further, promulgating the bull *Unam Sanctam* (November 18, 1302).

Unam Sanctam established the final and grandest of papal claims, declaring that there were two swords in the world, the spiritual and temporal, and both were under the control of the Church; the spiritual is wielded by the Church and the temporal by the civil authority under the direction of the clergy; the temporal sword is subordinate to the spiritual and is ever judged by it. The crowning moment of the decree was its statement: "Now, therefore, we declare, say, determine, and pronounce that for every human creature it is essential for their salvation to be subject to the authority of the Roman Pontiff."

What followed was one of the most terrible events in the history of the papacy. On September 7, 1303, Boniface was seized at Anagni by King Philip's lieutenant, Guillaume de Nogaret, with the aid of the pope's enemies the House of Colonna, whose town of Palestrina Boniface had burned to the ground and two of whose members in the College of Cardinals he had had expelled for conspiring against him. The pope was brutalized for several days and was only rescued by angry townspeople. Taken back to Rome, Boniface never recovered from the treatment he had received, dying on October 12, 1303. On the more positive side, Boniface reorganized the papal archives, catalogued the papal library, founded schools, and issued a legal compilation that would help form the basis of much in subsequent canon law. Successor: Benedict XI.

 BONIFACE IX   Pope from 1389 to 1404, the second legitimate pontiff of the Great Western Schism. Born Pietro Tomacelli, he came from a noble but poor family of Naples around 1350. Little is known about his earlier career, but Pope Urban VI made him a cardinal deacon in 1381 and a cardinal priest in 1385. Not known for his theological depth or education, he nevertheless possessed gifts as a diplomat and was both sturdy and affable. It was probably as a result of his stable and tactful nature that he was elected to succeed the highly erratic and eccentric Urban on November 2, 1389. He wasted little time after his election in excommunicating his rival Clement VII and in 1391 refused to compromise in settling the schism then dividing the Church. He made his main focus the restoring of prestige and respect for the papacy, using his charm to solidify the support of England, Germany, Hungary, and most of Italy. Closer to home, he at first enjoyed excellent dealings with the Romans, but these soon deteriorated as the pope sought to extend his authority to ensure a solid political base, and he was forced to depart the city for Perugia and Assisi. Finally, adopting as a good excuse a conspiracy to assassinate him, Boniface seized absolute control of Rome in 1398. He exterminated any pretense of civic republican government and established himself as a kind of benevolent dictator. The populace generally agreed with his policies, especially his rebuilding of Castel Sant'Angelo, and the fortifying of the bridges of Rome. After Clement's death in 1394, Boniface refused to enter into negotiations with antipope Benedict XIII (Pedro de Luna), feeling confident enough in his position to greet his overtures with disdain. This had the positive effect of maintaining the legitimate papacy at a tenuous time, but it dragged out the schism into the next century. Even as death approached, Boniface refused to treat his rival seriously or on anything approaching equal terms. Boniface fell seriously ill after two casual meetings with Benedict's representatives, dying on October 1, 1404. Despite restoring much of the vitality of the papacy, Boniface earned a fearsome reputation as a shameless nepotist and was utterly unscrupulous when it came to raising money for his cause. Successor: Innocent VII.

❀ **BORGIA APARTMENT**   A series of six chambers situated in the southern end of the Vatican Museums, near the Apostolic Palace and the Sistine Chapel. The Borgia Apartment was built in 1492 at the command of Pope Alexander VI (1492–1503), the last Borgia pope, to serve as his private residence and chambers; here he died in 1503. The apartment would be used by his successors for the next century until superseded by the papal apartments currently in use. It is located directly beneath the Raphael Loggia and Raphael Stanze and is decorated with frescoes by the renowned artist Pinturicchio. For those with an interest in the House of Borgia, the apartment offers a number of notable sights. There is the Borgia symbol, the bull, on the ceiling in the fourth room, and a portrait of Alexander can be seen in the fresco on the Resurrection in the fifth; his reprehensible son Cesare is believed to be included in the fresco, standing near the pope. The infamous daughter Lucrezia Borgia was long thought to be honored in the fourth room, posing as St. Catherine the Blonde, but this is considered unlikely. Aside from the fifteenth-century art, the apartment currently is part of the collection of modern religious art, launched in 1973 under Pope Paul VI.

❀ **BORGIA, HOUSE OF**   See under *Alexander VI, Borgia Apartment,* and *Callistus III.*

❀ **BORGIA TOWER**   See *Towers, Vatican.*

❀ **BORGO, THE**   The quarter situated to the east of Vatican City, from the Vatican to Castel Sant'Angelo, filling out the land between St. Peter's Basilica and the Tiber. Its name is derived from the German word *burg,* or town. One of the most interesting sections surrounding the Vatican City State, the Borgo originated out of hostels called *episcopia* that were used to house the bishops who came to Rome to say mass in St. Peter's on the Vatican Hill. From this beginning came the collection of hostels, hospitals, commercial sites, and pilgrim centers built to meet the needs of the many pilgrims who routinely journeyed to Rome to visit the tomb of Peter and give worship in the old Basilica of St. Peter's. The Borgo also became the residence for the many clerics who served in the Vatican establishment. Foreigners eventually settled there, inaugurating the custom of living near Peter's tomb. This became a tradition among members of the Saxon Kings of Wessex, starting with King Ine of Wessex who began foreign colonies, called "schools," in 725. The kings would retire from their thrones and travel to Rome where, by St. Peter's, they would spend their days in prayer, meditation, and good works.

As the Vatican was frequently attacked during the early Middle Ages by Saracens and other marauders, the Borgo was subjected to pillage, looting, and fire. The most notable attack was in 846 when most of the quarter was burned. In response, Pope Leo IV erected the Leonine Wall around the Vatican and the Borgo, thereby establishing the Leonine City. (See *Leonine City.*) For a long time, the Borgo was actually more important than the rest of Rome across the Tiber, but it was not officially recognized as part of the district system by the papal administration until the fifteenth century. (See *Conciliazione, Via della* for other details.)

�֎ **BRAMANTE, DONATO**   Italian painter and architect (1444–1514), who enjoyed the patronage of the Holy See, in particular Pope Julius II (1503–1513). Born in Monte Asdrualdo, he developed quickly as an artist, his long career effectively divided into two work periods: in Milan and Rome. After laboring for the Sforzas of Milan, Bramante journeyed to Rome in 1499 where he secured the support of Pope Alexander VI (1492–1503) and then the formidable Julius II. For Julius, Bramante executed a number of buildings, courtyards, and galleries that form a central place in the modern Vatican Museums. In 1503, for example, he created the Belvedere Courtyard. He also designed the Cortile della Pigna (Court of the Pine) and the Bramante Stairway, the spiral staircase in a tower toward the eastern end of the Museums laid out in such a fashion to permit his patron Julius—ever in a hurry—to ride up its length on horseback to reach his apartments. His greatest plan, of course, was for St. Peter's Basilica, although he never saw the completed work, which took over a century to complete. As his plans, however, called for the complete demolition of the old basilica, he was criticized by many contemporaries and was satirically called "Ruinate." The pope nevertheless allowed little sympathy for the ancient church, forging ahead with Bramante's vision.

❀ **BRIEF, APOSTOLIC**   A type of papal document, a brief is normally a papal letter given less weight and solemnity than a bull, but still bearing some official purpose and import. It is customarily not signed by the pope himself, but by the cardinal secretary of state or his representative. To make clear its official nature, however, the brief is sealed and authenticated with the so-called Seal of the Fisherman, a wax seal emblazoned with the symbol of the Fisherman.

❀ **BULL, APOSTOLIC**   A type of papal letter, so named from the Latin term *bulla* (seal), that is of greater weight and import than the Apostolic Brief. The *bulla* itself is the wax or lead seal, shaped like a disk that is attached to the document to certify its formal nature as coming from the pope himself. The *bulla* was understood initially to mean only this metal seal (usually a round plate) that was added to the papal documents, a wider application to the entire letter, plus the seal, coming into use sometime in the thirteenth century. For around the next two hundred years, the bull was the name given to all papal letters and pronouncements, regardless of their purpose or nature. Around 1431, however, during the reign of Pope Eugene IV, a clarification of papal documents took place. Thus, the pope could send a brief and then a bull. Bulls today are considered the most solemn of all papal letters, although the name bull is technically not official, given its history and varying nomenclature. (See also *Papal Letters.*) The *bullarium* was the name given to a collection of papal bulls, normally arranged in chronological order.

❧ **CADAVER SYNOD** One of the most gruesome events in papal history, held in January 897 by Pope Stephen VI (VII) during which the corpse of Pope Formosus (891–896) was exhumed and placed on trial. The terrible synod was orchestrated by Lambert of Spoleto (d. 898), who was a bitter political enemy of Formosus, never forgiving him for appealing in 893 to Arnulf, King of the East Franks for aid against the Spoletan family, especially his father Guido (Guy) III of Spoleto (d. 894) and for crowning Arnulf emperor after the pontiff had already reconfirmed his father emperor and had crowned Lambert co-emperor. Lambert had emerged as virtual ruler of Italy with the departure of Arnulf in 896 after the latter's bout of paralysis had cut short his hopes of stamping out the Spoletan party. Lambert harbored plans for revenge against Formosus, but the pontiff died shortly after Arnulf's retreat back to Germany. Following the very brief pontificate of Boniface VI (April 896), Stephen was elected pope, coming under the immediate influence of Lambert, whose cause he supported. Lambert, encouraged by his equally spiteful mother, Ageltrude, finally wreaked his vengeance on Formosus, albeit posthumously, early the next year. Having stirred up anti-Formosan sentiment among the populace and nobility of Rome, Lambert commanded Stephen to convene a synod to try the dead pope on assorted charges such as perjury, canonical violations, and ambition in seeking the papacy. What made the proceeding so grotesque was Stephen's decision to have Formosus appear personally. The rotting corpse was taken out of the tomb, dressed in vestments, and propped up in a chair. A deacon, standing behind the body, answered on its behalf. To no one's surprise, Formosus was found guilty. His acts and ordinations were proclaimed null and void, his body was mutilated—three fingers on his right hand were cut off—and he was placed in a common grave. After a little while, the corpse was dragged out of the earth and hurled into the Tiber. A hermit retrieved the remains and gave the pope a decent burial. Pope John IX (898–900) declared the actions of the cadaver synod annulled. Its acts were burned, and a declaration made that no posthumous trials were ever to be held again. Stephen, meanwhile, had fallen from power, was stripped of his office and strangled while in prison.

❀ **CAIUS**   See *Gaius, St.*

❀ **CALIGULA, OBELISK OF**   See *Obelisk of Caligula.*

❀ **CALLISTUS I, ST.**   Pope from 217 to 222, also called Callixtus, he is mostly known through the writings of the antipope St. Hippolytus, a work that was often hostile toward him. According to Hippolytus, Callistus had been a slave in the household of a freedman named Carpophorus. This generous individual established Callistus with responsibility over a bank, including the money of widows and other Christians. Callistus soon lost the money, panicked, and tried to flee. Dragged back, he was put to work on a treadmill. The investors, hoping that he still had the money hidden somewhere, paid for his freedom. He supposedly then insulted the local Jews by fighting in their synagogue. The Prefect of the City sentenced him to labor in the dreaded mines of Sardinia, but he was freed through the intercession of Marcia, mistress to Emperor Commodus. When he reached Rome, Pope Victor I gave him a pension. Pope Zephyrinus ordained him a deacon in 216 and appointed him his chief counselor. The next year, having won the confidence of the Roman Christians, he was elected pope. His election was not accepted by all, however, and he was faced with a rival, Hippolytus, a presbyter, considered the first of the antipopes in Church history. His reign was to be troubled throughout by the presence of Hippolytus, who attacked him for being lax in matters of discipline, especially for readmitting into the Church those members who had committed adultery and fornication. Traditionally considered a martyr, Callistus possibly did in fact die as a martyr, but some doubt exists about this owing to the absence of any serious persecutions under Emperor Alexander Severus. He was buried in Trastevere on the Via Aurelia and not in the cemetery named after him, the Cemetery of San Callisto. Successor: St. Urban I.

❀ **CALLISTUS II**   Pope from 1119 to 1124. Born around 1050, he was the son of Count William I of Burgundy and was originally called Guido di Borgogne (of Burgundy). Through his family, he was related in some fashion to virtually every royal house in Christendom. In 1088 he was made Archbishop of Vienne and then served Paschal II as his legate in France (1106). He earned considerable notoriety by opposing the capitulation of Paschal to the demands of Emperor Henry V in the matter of lay investiture (the investing of prelates by lay or secular rulers). Guido participated in the Lateran Council of 1112 and presided over the Council of Vienne, which condemned lay investiture as heresy and excommunicated Emperor Henry. At Cluny, in France, when Pope Gelasius died on January 29, 1119, the small group of cardinals who were present wasted no time in electing a successor, a move necessary because of the crises facing the Church. At the urging of Cardinal Cuno, the conclave elected Guido pope on February 2, and he was consecrated on February 9 at Vienne. Immediately facing him was the very real problem of Emperor Henry V. It was the hope of many in the Church that Callistus's relations with various royal families might assist him in making peace with the emperor. Callistus and Henry both sought a peaceful resolution to the investiture question, but their agreement fell through and, at Reims, Callistus renewed the condemnation of Henry, whom he called a second Judas. The next year, he entered Rome and was able to lay his hands on Henry's antipope Gregory VIII. With much flourish, Gregory was humiliated and sent to a monastery. Callistus decided that the time was ripe for renewed negotiation. He was aided in this by the German princes, who were anxious to effect a peaceful resolution to the controversy. Weeks of bickering and negotiation culminated in the famous Concordat of Worms (1122). The agreement was ratified at the Lateran Council of 1123. Callistus also issued a bull granting some protection for Jews in the city of Rome. Successor: Honorius II.

CALLISTUS III Antipope from 1168 to 1178. Also Callixtus III, he was elected antipope to Alexander III through the wishes of Emperor Frederick I Barbarossa. Named originally Giovanni di Strumi, he was the successor of antipope Paschal III and was quite loyal to Frederick until 1176, when the emperor signed the Treaty of Anagni, which ended his conflict with the pope. As he no longer had need of an antipope, Frederick effectively ended his backing of Callistus. Instead of submitting, however, the antipope declined the offer of an abbacy and stood firm in his declaration that he was the legitimate pontiff. He finally surrendered in 1178, only after receiving assurances from Alexander that he would be well treated.

CALLISTUS III Pope from 1455 to 1458, the first pontiff to come from the house of Borgia. While not as notorious as his nephew, Pope Alexander VI (1492–1503), he was similiarly much devoted to advancing the fortunes of his ruthless family. Alfonso de Borja y Borja (or Borgia in Italian) was born in Jativa, near Valencia in 1378. The son of a landowner, he became a noted jurist and was a familiar figure in the court of King Alfonso V of Aragon and Sicily, earning much notoriety for playing a key role in the reconciliation effected between the king and Pope Martin V. Pope Martin named him bishop of Valencia in 1429 and in 1444 he was made a cardinal by Eugene IV. His period as a cardinal was conspicuous for its austerity, but he was rather undistinguished going into the conclave to choose a successor to the great Renaissance pontiff Nicholas V. To the surprise of many, he was elected pope on April 8, 1455. His election was considered at the time to have been a compromise between the two powerful families of the Orsini and the Colonna because they could not agree on a candidate from among their own ranks and Borja was not expected to live long. His brief three-year reign was mostly known for two aims, the aggrandizement of his family's fortunes and the calling for a crusade against the Turks. The latter was only partially successful; some islands in the Aegean were captured, as was Belgrade in 1457. Personally pious and abstemious, he was a devoted nepotist, granting honors and preferments to several relatives, most notably his nephew Rodrigo Borgia, the future pope. His greedy Aragonese relatives were the source of much discontent among the Romans, and the Spaniards were swept out of Rome after Callistus died on August 6, 1458. He also reopened the trial of Joan of Arc (d. 1431) who had been burned at the stake, finding her innocent of all charges. Successor: Pius II.

❀ **CAMAURO** A type of cap made of red velvet and trimmed with ermine or some other white fur that was long worn by popes, normally in conjunction with the mozzetta and rochet. It has no liturgical function and was worn most often to keep the head warm, especially during the chilly and damp Roman winters when the halls of the Apostolic Palace were freezing. Unique to the popes, it was akin to the zucchetto that was worn by clerics to cover the tonsure. The camauro was routinely worn by popes during the Middle Ages, the Renaissance, and beyond, and is routinely seen in the portraits of numerous popes. The camauro fell out of fashion to some degree as the typical headdress of the Supreme Pontiff from the time of Pius VI (1775–1799). He opted for the white zucchetto, an adornment adopted by most of his successors on a regular basis. The camauro was still used as a practical headdress during the winter, and even Paul VI (1963–1978) was known to wear it in the Vatican. Until recent times, popes were also dressed in the camauro, with mozzetta and rochet, when lying in state in the Sistine

Chapel. Pope John Paul II has not worn the camauro in public and it is perhaps likely that it will not be used regularly by his successors. During Easter week, the popes used to wear a white brocade camauro instead of their red one. (See also *Papal Dress,* pages 120–21.)

❁ **CAMERLENGO** Known in Latin as the *Camerarius,* the Chamberlain of the Holy Roman Church, a position in the papal court that is always held by a cardinal. The camerlengo was once a very important official in the papal government, having the task of administering the properties and all revenues of the Holy See and the revenues of the entire Catholic Church during a *sede vacante,* the period of an interregnum between popes. Today the camerlengo has a much reduced function, namely the administration of the Holy See after the death of a pope and until the canonical election of a successor. His duties are both real and highly ceremonial. It should not be thought that he acts as a kind of temporary pope; rather, he is charged with certain caretaker duties, functioning in cooperation with the collegial government of the Church undertaken by the College of Cardinals. As no significant administrative or governmental decisions are made during a *sede vacante* beyond the essential task of electing a new Supreme Pontiff, the period is devoted heavily to ceremony. The camerlengo must make certain that the pontiff is truly dead (traditionally tapping the pope on the forehead three times with a hammer, calling out the pope's Christian name with each tap), must deface the Ring of the Fisherman, seal the papal apartment, and summon the cardinals to Rome for the conclave. It is considered absolutely essential to have a camerlengo at every moment, and the pope, while allowed to appoint a new chamberlain, must do so immediately. A newly elected pope must reconfirm the cardinal camerlengo in his office or appoint a new one, but this is to be the first act of the pontificate. In the rare event that a camerlengo is actually elected pope—as occurred in 1878 with the elevation of Gioacchino Cardinal Pecci as Leo XIII and 1939 with Eugenio Cardinal Pacelli as Pius XII—the new pope will name someone without delay. The reconfirming of the camerlengo is customary, at least for the moment (as with the other cardinals in their positions), but this may be changed at the will of a pope. The Apostolic Camera, under the direction of the cardinal camerlengo, functions as the central office of administration for the property of the Holy See during the period of the *sede vacante.*

❁ **CANON LAW** The supreme and recognized body of laws that governs the Catholic Church. The term canon law is derived from the

Greek word *kanon,* meaning rule or measure. The laws of the Church developed very slowly over the centuries, but two main collections are noted as having been promulgated before the modern era. The first was organized by the canonist Gratian around 1140. The second was undertaken at the command of Pope St. Pius X (1903–1914) and was issued by Pope Benedict XV in 1917, coming into effect on May 19, 1918, Pentecost. It remained in effect for the Church until replaced in 1983 by the new Code of Canon Law, which was promulgated under Pope John Paul II. In 1991, a Code of Canon Law was issued for the Eastern Catholic Churches. For general purposes of law, the Vatican City State is governed by the Code of Canon Law, meaning that all who reside or work within its walls are subject to the laws of the Church. In those cases, however, where canon law does not obtain, the laws of the City of Rome do apply. (See *Vatican City, State of.*)

❀ **CANOSSA**   A castle situated in the area of Reggio, in northern Italy, that acquired considerable notoriety as a result of the meeting there in January 1077 between the then feuding Pope St. Gregory VII and Emperor Henry IV. It was distinguished by the abject humiliation of the emperor in seeking the forgiveness of the pope for his stubbornness during the controversy of lay investiture. Canossa was built by Azzo Adalbert and was the strategically placed possession of the counts of Canossa. By 1077, it belonged to Countess Matilda of Tuscany, an ally of the pope in his struggle with Henry. She invited him to stay at the castle while the pope was journeying to Germany to try to enforce the excommunication of the emperor. Henry, meanwhile, was fast losing the political support of his princes in Germany and had reached the political point that peace was necessary with the pope. He arrived at Canossa on January 25 on a snowy day seeking papal forgiveness. In a move that has reached nearly legendary status, Gregory left Henry literally standing in the snow for three days, forcing him to endure the biting cold as a humble penitent before his pontiff, finally relenting and granting him absolution on January 28. While Canossa was a memorable victory for the pope, Henry never forgave Gregory for humiliating him so severely, and he was able to win back the fidelity of his princes. He also wreaked his vengeance on Gregory in 1084, seizing Rome and driving his enemy into exile. A very colorful, if somewhat unreliable account of the event was written by the chronicler Lambert of Hersfeld. Canossa was destroyed in 1255 and is today a ruin.

❖ **CARAFA, HOUSE OF**   Also Caraffa, a Neapolitan noble family that came to exercise a brief influence over the papacy in the sixteenth century, largely through the election of Giampietro Carafa as Pope Paul IV (1555–1559). An earlier member of the family, Antonio Cardinal Carafa had distinguished himself as an admiral, commanding a fleet that had been paid for by Venice and Naples at the behest of Pope Sixtus IV (1471–1484) in the hope of waging war against the Ottoman Turks. Carafa proved a surprisingly good commander, using his ships to wreak death and destruction along the coast of Asia Minor, much to the consternation of the Turks. The most formidable of the Carafas, however, was surely Giampietro, Paul IV. Unfortunately, Paul proved a disappointment, relying on his own hard—and rather medieval—conception of the papacy to govern by decree and personal will. He also brought into the government his frequently reprehensible nephew Carlo, making him a cardinal and handing to him much of the say in political matters as his Cardinal Secretary of State. Carlo guided his uncle into a stern anti-Spanish policy that caused a war, a conflict in which papal forces were defeated, the Papal States were overrun, and a humiliating peace had to be signed at Cave in 1557. Carlo also introduced so many relatives and friends into lucrative papal service that the pope finally awoke to the lamentable state of his court and reputation, stripping Carlo and his own relatives of all offices and banishing them from Rome in January 1559. He died in August of that year, thus removing a shield that had protected Carlo and others of the Carafa clan from popular vengeance for their unscrupulous behavior in the service of the Church. Pope Pius IV had Carlo and another nephew of Paul IV, Giovanni, duke of Palino (Carlo's brother), arrested and put on trial for assorted crimes; the duke had apparently ordered his wife to be strangled on suspicion of adultery and had personally stabbed her supposed lover to death. As Carlo was considered a possible accomplice, he shared in his brother's fall, being found guilty of murder, abuse of power, and for illegally launching the calamitous war with Spain. Both were executed on March 5, 1561, to the delight of many in Rome. Another Carafa cardinal, Archbishop of Naples, was trapped in the shame that had eclipsed the house and died prematurely from abject mortification.

❖ **CARDINAL**   A high-ranking Church official, said to be second only to the pope himself, a cardinal has the responsibility of assisting the Supreme Pontiff in governing the Universal Church and takes part in the election of the successors of St. Peter. Each cardinal is a member of

Pope John Paul II places the red biretta upon the head of a new cardinal (William Keeler, Archbishop of Baltimore) at a consistory in 1994. (CATHOLIC NEWS SERVICE.)

the Sacred College of Cardinals and a duly ordained priest by the command of canon law (the last cardinal not ordained was Giacomo Antonelli who worked under Pope Pius IX). The rank of cardinal is bestowed upon a worthy individual entirely at the pleasure of the pope, who formally announces his choices at a consistory, at which time he asks the approval of the other members of the college with the question *"Quid vobis videtur?"* ("How does this seem to you?"). The rank confers no heightened theological or sacramental authority, but the cardinals are unquestionably the most powerful and influential figures in all of the Catholic world, and belonging to the select community is one of the significant achievements and honors that can be attained. (See also *Cardinals, Sacred College of.*)

The title cardinal is taken from the Latin *cardo* ("hinge"), a reference to the fact that early advisors to the pope in Rome were considered essential to the good governing of the Roman Church, the "hinges" upon which the Church turned. These predecessors of the later cardinals were initially chosen from among the bishops surrounding Rome and from among the priests and deacons of the city. Over time, they received the title cardinal, but the rank was not held by them exclusively until 1567. Each cardinal is considered a member of the clergy in Rome, in keeping with the origins of the office, and each belongs to one of three categories of cardinal: cardinal bishop, cardinal priest, and cardinal deacon. The cardinal bishops were long the actual bishops of the suffragan dioceses surrounding Rome. In 1962, however, Pope John XXIII decreed that henceforth their offices should be titular. The cardinal bishops today are the senior officials of the Roman Curia, holding key posts in the central administration of the Church. Cardinal priests were originally the pastors of the parishes of Rome and cardinal deacons the high officials who fulfilled a variety of tasks in the Roman churches, using one church as their base of work. From an early time, both cardinal priests and cardinal deacons were permitted to be bishops. Today, cardinal priests are bishops from around the world who head archdioceses; this is the largest category of cardinal. Cardinal deacons are titular bishops elevated to the cardinalate; they serve, like cardinal bishops, in the Curia.

The cardinals of the Church bear many special dignities and rights. They are designated Princes of the Church and are addressed as "Eminence." Their special color is scarlet, and they can be noted by their scarlet robes and the scarlet zucchetto and biretta. Their private coat of arms is decorated with a red hat and two sets of fifteen red tassels on each side. They are informed of their elevation through a special certficate called a *biglietto* and are invested into the cardinalate by the pope himself in the elaborate ceremony of the consistory. Each cardinal priest and deacon is assigned to a titular church; cardinal bishops are given one of the titular Suburbicarian sees. Traditionally, there was no age limit to the activities of the cardinals. This was changed in 1970 with the decree *Ingravescentem Aetatem* by Pope Paul VI, who ordered that at the age of eighty all members of the Sacred College should be ineligible to vote in papal elections and should step down from all Curial offices and posts, although they are still cardinals in all other senses. This reform was reportedly not greeted with delight in many Curial circles, as some cardinals courteously asked if the pope should retire at the same age. Beyond giving years of service and dedication to the Church, the cardinals can also shape its future in the most dramatic fashion possible through their choice in the papal elections. Since 1378 no man has been chosen pope who was not already a cardinal, a fact not lost on the reigning pontiff who knows that one of the persons he appoints to the Sacred College will very likely succeed him. (See also *Camerlengo; Cardinal nephew; Conclave; Consistories; Curia, Roman; Elections, Papal; Finances, Vatican; Petto, In; Secretariat of State;* and *Vicar General.*)

❀ **CARDINAL IN PECTORE**   See *Petto, In.*

❀ **CARDINAL NEPHEW**   The custom that flourished, especially during the sixteenth and seventeenth centuries, by which a pope would name as his chief minister and most important advisor a nephew or similar relative who was elevated to the rank of cardinal and thereafter oversaw many of the most vital elements of papal administration. The practice was not invented in the sixteenth century, as papal nepotism had long been an established part of the pontifical court. Pope Adrian IV (1154–1159), for example, named his nephew Boso (Breakspear) to the cardinalate and put him in charge of Castel Sant'Angelo. Throughout the Middle Ages, it was common for a pope from one of the leading noble families to promote the interests of his house, but nepotism began reaching absurd heights toward the end of the fifteenth century with the accession of Alfonso de Borja y Borja as Callistus III (1455–1458). He made two nephews cardinals and worked to assist other family members with such vigor that at his death, the Aragonese who had profited from his generosity were driven from Rome. One nephew, Rodrigo Borgia, became Pope Alexander VI (1492–1503). He made his son Cesare Borgia a cardinal and surrendered to him vast powers over papal policy. The cardinal nephew in later years developed out of the need for the pope, usually old at the time of his election, to be assisted in the demands of office by a younger and more energetic assistant. Given the climate of intrigue that often pervaded Roman society in the period, the pope regularly turned to a promising young nephew, as relatives were slightly more reliable than scheming prelates who might be anxious to replace the reigning pontiff. Among the most notable cardinal nephews were: Alessandro Cervini, to Paul III, (1534–1549); Carlo Carafa, to Paul IV (1555–1559); St. Charles Borromeo, to Pius IV (1559–1565); Scipione Borghese (adopted) to Paul V (1605-1621); Ludovico Ludovisi, to Gregory XV (1621–1623); and the nephews of Urban VIII (1623–1644). While the cardinals were often immature and at times quite incompetent, they also had a common fondness for amassing wealth and patronizing artists and architects. Thus, Scipione Borghese helped discover the genius of Bernini and built the immense and grandiose Villa Borghese near Rome. The most remarkable of the cardinal nephews was St. Charles Borromeo (1538–1584), one of the foremost saints of the age and a brilliant reformer of the Church. The reforms, in fact, that were wrought by the popes during the sixteenth and seventeenth centuries gradually took hold, especially after the pernicious corruption of the Barberini under Urban VIII. Innocent X (1644–1655), while dominated by his sister-in-law Donna Olimpia Maidalchini, refused to appoint her son as secretary of state, naming instead Cardinals Panciroli and, in 1651, Fabio Chigi (the future Alexander VII). Innocent XI (1676–1689) was determined to curb all nepotism, agreeing to accept election as pope only after the cardinals gave their support to his plan for reform, including a ban on nepotism. This unfortunately did not stop Alexander VIII (1691–1700) from appointing one grand-nephew, the twenty-year-old Pietro, his cardinal nephew, and placing another nephew, Giambattista, to the post of secretary of state. Innocent XIII (1721–1724) named a brother, Bernard, to the cardinalate, but the fears expressed at the time that a new wave of nepotism had struck were soon alleviated by Innocent's refusal to give him any meaningful power, faithfully adhering to Innocent XI's ban. Benedict XIII (1724–1730) did not rely upon a cardinal nephew, but rather left the reins of power largely in the hands of his corrupt minister Niccolo Cardinal Coscia. His sway was only ended at the death of the pope. From this time, the papacy was largely free of the custom of the cardinal nephew, the popes relying upon able secretaries of state who demonstrated ability and personal virtue and were generally free of ruthless ambition, avarice, and corruption.

❀ **CARDINAL PROTECTOR**   A title once used for a cardinal appointed by the pope or a congregation of the Curia with the duty of giving his protection or patronage to a certain religious order or congregation.

❀ **CARDINALS, SACRED COLLEGE OF**   The collective name given to the body of cardinals appointed by the pope to the high dignity of the cardinalate with the duties of serving as the Supreme Pontiff's chief assistants in governing the Church and gathering together when necessary to elect a new successor to St. Peter. The College of Cardinals is one of the most select bodies in the entire world, and its members are considered the most capable, gifted, and important leaders in the entire Church. They fulfill some of the crucial leadership positions in the administration of the Church, from heading or participating in the running of the various departments or dicasteries of the Roman Curia to the guiding of the major archdioceses of the world.

The college itself dates from 1150 when Pope Eugene III (1145–1153) formally constituted the body of advisors who had traditionally been used by the pope from among the bishops of the surrounding dioceses of Rome and the clergy of the city. By custom, the clerics who received designation as cardinals were required to reside in Rome, but this was changed in 1163 when Pope Alexander III permitted a recently appointed cardinal, the Archbishop of Mainz, to return to his see. To give him a legal residence in Rome, the pope named him to a church in the Eternal City, making him a titular pastor, a custom that has endured into the modern era. Further development came under Pope Alexander when he restricted the naming of cardinals to the pope's discretion alone. In 1567, Pope St. Pius V decreed that from that time all members of the college were to be considered cardinals, ending the ancient practice of having certain priests in Rome and even elsewhere called cardinals. This measure increased both the prestige and the exclusive nature of the college. Pope Sixtus V added to that selectivity in 1586 by limiting the number of cardinals to seventy. This rule remained in effect until 1959, when Pope John XXIII began to increase the size of the college. Further increases came under Pope Paul VI, but he added the provision that in all papal elections, the number of electors should never exceed 120 eligible voters, meaning cardinals under the age of eighty. Pope John Paul II has chosen not to reverse this regulation. The administrative needs of the college are fulfilled by the dean of the College of Cardinals, assisted by the sub-dean and a secretary.

The Sacred College from the time of John has become increasingly internationalized, most notably since the elevation of Laurean Cardinal Rugambwa of Tanzania, the first African cardinal. Today, there are cardinals found in more than fifty countries, a testament to the growth of the Church across the globe. More perhaps than at any time in papal history, the modern college is a reflection of the pope; John Paul II has appointed 100 of the 120 electors who will probably assemble to choose his successor. In this way, he has ensured that the Church will continue along the path he has set for it well into the next millennium. (See also *Cardinal; Conclave;* and *Elections, Papal.*)

❁ **CASTEL GANDOLFO**   The summer retreat of the popes, located in Romagna, thirteen miles southeast of Rome on the Appian Way, in the Alban Hills overlooking Lake Albano. Castel Gandolfo is the main place of rest for the pope away from the Vatican. It allows him to escape the often stifling heat of Rome in the summer, the constant demands of audiences and work, and the incessant hum of Rome's chaotic traffic, a distinctive sound caused by the city's construction on volcanic ash, called *tufo*. The residence is comprised of the papal palace, the Villa Barberini, the Cybo Villa, and the papal gardens. The surrounding town of Castel Gandolfo has a small population of under three thousand. The actual papal buildings, however, are not part of the town, but are formal possessions of the Holy See as stipulated by the Lateran Treaty of 1929; Castel Gandolfo is treated as an extraterritorial possession of the pope as sovereign of the Vatican City State.

Castel Gandolfo began as a castle owned in the twelfth century by the Gandolfo family. On the site of what were to become the papal gardens were the ruins of a first-century villa erected by Emperor Domitian. The entire property did not come into the actual possession of the papacy until the reign of Pope Clement VIII (1592–1605); in 1604 he was able to attach it to the Holy See. It was the fun-loving Pope Urban VIII, however, who recognized its potential value as a retreat from the often unhealthful air of the Roman summer. He chose as his architect the gifted Carlo Maderno (one of the architects of St. Peter's). The palace was not completed until the reign of Pope Alexander VII (1655–1667), with later work undertaken by Clement XIII (1758–1769). Built in nearly the shape of a fortress, the papal palace is not as architecturally attractive as the nearby Villa Barberini. The Villa Cybo was long the home of the Vatican Observatory (the *Specola Vaticana*).

The popes regularly spent their summers in the retreat until 1870 and the final loss of the Papal States under Pope Pius IX. From then until 1929 and the signing of the Lateran Accords, the estate was unoccupied and unattended. Extensive work was needed to refurbish and repair the neglected buildings under Pope Pius XI (1922–1939). Little used by Pope John XXIII, it was a favorite place of both Pius XII and Paul VI; both popes, in fact, died there in 1958 and 1978, respectively. Pope John Paul II has long spent his summers there and was responsible for bringing one of the most novel additions to the entire residence. He commanded that a swimming pool be installed to permit him to continue his well-known pursuit of physical exercise. When members of the Curia complained of the cost, he simply responded that it was cheaper than getting a new pope. The pope normally travels to Castel Gandolfo by helicopter. Castel Gandolfo also has a small farm, with fields and livestock, supplying the papal household with dairy products and vegetables. (See also *Gardens, Vatican.*)

�֍ **CASTEL SANT'ANGELO**   The massive fortress situated near the Vatican on the banks of the Tiber, at the foot of the Vatican Hill. Known as Castel Sant'Angelo from the statue of the Archangel Michael on the top of its battlements, it has served over the centuries as a tomb, a fort, and even a prison. The actual name was bestowed upon it by Pope St. Gregory I the Great (590–604), who, while leading a

Castel Sant'Angelo, from an early-twentieth-century photograph. (AP/WIDE WORLD PHOTOS.)

penitential procession through the streets of Rome in the hopes of bringing an end to a severe outbreak of plague in 590, beheld St. Michael descending upon its summit. A chapel was built at the top of the structure, later replaced in the eighteenth century with the present statue of St. Michael by the sculptor Pieter Verschaffelt.

Castel Sant'Angelo was first built in 136 to 139 as an extensive mausoleum for Emperor Hadrian (r. 117–138). It was constructed with Parian marble and statues of pagan gods and heroes. Later, in 271, it was incorporated into the Aurelian Wall, built to defend Rome from barbarian attack. During a siege of Rome in 537 by the Goths, these statues were hurled down upon the enemy by the desperate defenders. Used ever after as a formidable bastion, it was given added strength under Popes Urban VI and Boniface IX. Extensive improvements were made under Pope Alexander VI, the infamous Borgia pope (1492–1503), which proved fortuitous in 1527. In that year the city was sacked by imperial troops and Pope Clement VII found safety behind its walls. Crucial to his reaching safety was Alexander's earlier decision to restore the corridor, the *Passetto* (first built in 1277), connecting the Vatican with the castle.

The entire structure provides an interesting variety of decorations and styles. Of note are: the Sala Paolina, built for Pope Paul III from 1542 to 1549 and decorated with frescoes by Perin del Vaga and Pellegrino Tibaldi; the staircase of Alexander VI, which literally slices through the castle; the Hall of Justice with the fresco by Domenico

Zaga, *The Angel of Justice* (1545); and the Courtyard of Honor with its piles of stone cannonballs.

⚜ **CATAFALQUE** A stand on which a body is placed for purposes of allowing the deceased to lie in state; it is normally reserved for a person of exceptional rank; those of lesser rank and placed in a bier. The catafalque is also used as another name for the *castrumdoloris,* the second coffin of the three in which the pope is buried. The catafalque is seen by the crowds and viewing audience during the requiem mass held for the deceased Pontiff at St. Peter's. In the case of Pope John Paul I (1978), the catafalque was placed on a red carpet in St. Peter's Square, with a candle standing nearby and rain and wind setting a most somber tone to the solemn occasion. The term catafalque comes from the Latin *catafalicum,* or catapult, an allusion to its resemblance to a catapult. There is some indication that the word's etymological origins may have some connection to the oft-used saying that the dead pontiff may be besieging heaven.

⚜ **CATHEDRA** The Greek and Latin term meaning throne or church, used to designate the bishop's chair in the cathedral, a bishop's symbolic seat of authority. The bishop is said to speak and teach from his cathedra. The pope is Bishop of Rome and his cathedral church is not St. Peter's but St. John Lateran. In the Basilica of St. Peter's, however, is located the famed *Cathedra Petri* (the Chair of St. Peter), arguably the most magnificent cathedra anywhere. (See *Cathedra Petri* for details; see also *Ex cathedra.*)

⚜ **CATHEDRA PETRI** The Chair of Peter, a bronze altar encasing what was long revered as the actual throne of St. Peter, one of the greatest artistic monuments in St. Peter's Basilica, crafted in 1665–1666 by Gian Lorenzo Bernini (1598–1680). The *Cathedra Petri* is located in the apse of the basilica, past the papal altar and the baldacchino and next to the tomb of Pope Urban VIII. The throne was thought for many centuries to have been the very chair used by St. Peter when he delivered his sermons to the members of the young Christian community of Rome and was kept in the sacristy of the old St. Peter's as one of the most revered relics in all of Christendom and a prized possession of the popes as a symbol of their authority over the Church. Its authenticity was unquestioned right up until the time of Bernini and so Pope Alexander VII (1655–1667) commissioned the artist to create a grand reliquary. Bernini was confronted by the rather large impediment of a window at the second-floor level of the apse, and apparently he was forced twice to scrap design schemes because of it. Finally, he conceived a plan to include the window in his overall design. The result was a striking work in Baroque sculpture that stands out even in the splendor of the basilica. The chair is surrounded by a billowing golden cloud full of angels, leading to a stunning presentation of the window of the Holy Spirit (allowing sunlight to filter through the golden sunburst of the window). Holding up the entire edifice are statues of four Doctors of the Church: the Latin Fathers Augustine and Ambrose, and the Eastern Fathers Athanasius and John Chrysostom. Questions were finally raised as to the chair's actual age soon after Bernini completed his work. These would not be answered until 1968, when Paul VI ordered a careful examination. The ivory-paneled chair was found to date to around the time of Charlemagne in the ninth century (it may even have been used by him) with parts stretching to a much earlier period in the Church. The feast of the Chair of Peter was held on February 22, commemorating the primacy of Peter as founder of the sees of Antioch and Rome. (See *Peter's Chains, Feast of* and *Saint Peter, Basilica of.*)

❈ **CELESTINE I, ST.** Pope from 422 to 432. An ardent enemy of heresy, he was a deacon at the time of his election on September 10, 422, to succeed St. Boniface I. Little is known about his early days, but he supposedly came from Campania and his father was named Priscus. He also knew and had communications with such notable contemporaries as St. Augustine and St. Ambrose of Milan. Augustine, in fact, wrote to him in 418 in terms that make clear the high regard in which the demanding saint held him. Throughout his reign, Celestine apparently maintained a close, but long-distance friendship with Augustine (who lived in Africa), and at the death of that famed saint in 430, the pope wrote a long adulatory letter about him. Celestine combatted with much vigor the heresies of the time, but his methods were characterized by gentleness and dignity. He was an enemy of Pelagianism, Nestorianism, and Manichaeism, all unorthodox teachings then troubling the Church. He also consecrated St. Palladius at Rome and sent him in 431 on a short-lived mission to Ireland; Palladius would be succeeded by a more famous evangelist, St. Patrick. The sending of Patrick to the Irish in 432 was the last official act of the pope, who died on July 27, 432. The important Council of Ephesus (431) was held during his time and was attended by several of his legates. Successor: St. Sixtus III.

❀ **CELESTINE II**   Pope from 1143 to 1144, a Tuscan by birth, Guido di Città del Castello was from a noble family. He was a good and long-time friend of the controversial philosopher Peter Abelard (1142), remaining so even after his condemnation by the Council of Sens in 1140 for unorthodox doctrinal views. Guido was already quite old when elected to succeed Innocent II on September 25, 1143, surviving a mere six months. The main event of his reign was lifting an interdict of France that had been placed by his predecessor for King Louis VII's interference in the appointment of the Bishop of Bourges. At the time of his death on March 8, 1144, Celestine was on the verge of a major conflict with the Normans in southern Italy under their king Roger II. Successor: Lucius II.

❀ **CELESTINE II**   Antipope in 1124. The fate of this officially classified antipope is somewhat unfortunate because he was technically properly elected, but it was his lot to be recorded as a mere pretender. Known originally as Teobaldo Boccapecci, he was a member of the Boccapecorini family and was made a cardinal deacon by Paschal II and a cardinal priest in 1123 by Pope Callistus II. The next year, following Callistus's death, he was advanced as a candidate after the cardinals in the conclave chose not to elect the favorite, Cardinal Saxo of S. Stefano. Teobaldo was the choice of all of the cardinals and was already receiving their congratulations as Celestine (II) when the proceedings were rudely interrupted by a member of the Frangipani family who, with a troop of soldiers, demanded that Cardinal Lambert of Ostia be proclaimed pope. Some cardinals resisted, and in the ensuing violence, Teobaldo was severely beaten and possibly wounded. Under threat of more violence, Lambert was elected and installed as Honorius II. Celestine accepted the fait accompli and resigned, while Honorius went on to prove a fairly competent reformer. Teobaldo did not live long. Old and weak, he never recovered from the battering he took in the conclave, dying soon after. He is not considered a legitimate pope because he was neither consecrated nor enthroned.

❀ **CELESTINE III**   Pope from 1191 to 1198, the first pontiff to come from the House of Orsini, Giacinto Bobo (or Bobone) had enjoyed a very long career before his election as successor to Clement III. In fact, he had been a cardinal for forty-seven years and was eighty-five when chosen. Born around 1105, he had studied under Peter Abelard (d. 1142), the controversial philosopher at Paris, and even defended his old teacher at the Council of Sens in 1140, much to the consternation of St.

Bernard of Clairvaux, especially as Bobo was a mere subdeacon at the time. Made a cardinal by Celestine II (another student of Abelard), he proved a capable servant of Pope Alexander III and was a friend of St. Thomas Becket, who called him only one of two incorruptible cardinals. Elected probably on March 30, 1191, he was ordained on the night of April 13 (as he was only a deacon) and the next day consecrated pope, taking the name Celestine in honor of his old friend. His pontificate was largely concerned with relations with Emperor Henry VI (r. 1191–1197), the ambitious German heir to the Holy Roman Empire whom Celestine crowned on April 15 and toward whom the pope evinced a surprisingly conciliatory demeanor. Celestine did nothing to curtail Henry's ambitions in Italy, nor did he even punish him for imprisoning Richard the Lionhearted, King of England. Eager to ensure Celestine's continued passivity and desirous of securing the baptism of his young son Frederick (II), which would make the imperial crown hereditary, Henry vowed to undertake a crusade. Once again Celestine vacillated, delaying any decision on the deal being offered by Henry. As it was, Henry died on September 28, 1197. Celestine did not long survive him. As he lay ill at Christmas in 1197, he asked the cardinals permission to retire if they would accept his choice as successor, Cardinal Giovanni of Sta Prisca. This they would not do, so he remained on the throne until his death from sickness and old age on January 8, 1198. Historians have long debated his habit of vacillation. Celestine also gave recognition to the Templars, Teutonic Knights, and the Knights Hospitallers, military orders that would make lasting contributions to the Church and history. In the administration of his government, the pope was much aided by his chamberlain (camerlengo), Cencio Savelli (the future Honorius III). Successor: Innocent III.

CELESTINE IV Pope from October 25 to November 10, 1241, one of the briefest reigning of all popes. Originally known as Gofredo Castiglioni, he may have been a nephew of Urban III, receiving appointment as cardinal by Gregory IX, whom he succeeded. His election is quite memorable because of the conditions in which the cardinals were forced to deliberate. As there were a mere twelve cardinals still alive (with two in the dungeons of Emperor Frederick II) to choose a new pope, they fell into bickering in the conclave and could reach no conclusions because of disagreements over the policy the Church should adopt in dealing with the troublesome emperor. Frustrated and eager to have a new pope, the virtual dictator of the city Matteo Orsini had them locked up in a squalid, dank, ruined palace. Still the cardinals could not reach a majority, and their request to consider someone from outside their own ranks was furiously rejected by Orsini. One of the cardinals died from the terrible conditions, convincing the cardinals to make up their minds. This they finally did, after two months of unbearable food, unsanitary living quarters, and repeated threats of violence. Their choice, made perhaps to be a temporary measure, probably surprised even his electors with the brevity of his reign. Celestine died a few days after consecration, his poor health made terminal by the conclave. The cardinals returned to the task of finding a successor; this time they took a year and a half, albeit under more comfortable surroundings. Successor: Innocent IV.

CELESTINE V, ST. Pope in 1294, perhaps the most tragic figure in the long history of the papacy, one of only six pontiffs to resign. Pietro del Morrone was born around 1210 in the Neapolitan county of Molise to humble parents. Entering the Benedictines, he found that they could not offer him the kind of ascetic life he desired. So, receiving permission and after ordination, around 1231, he withdrew to Monte Morrone in Abruzzi. While there, he attracted a number of followers, similar simple souls eager to live a rigorous life of fasting and prayer. These were recognized by Urban IV in June 1263 and officially incorporated into the Benedictine Order, receiving the name Celestines in honor of their founder (after his election). His elevation as successor to Pope Nicholas IV came after the Church had endured an interregnum of over two years as the cardinals were bitterly divided by often petty squabbles and personal disagreements. The need for a decision only grew more acute in the summer of 1294 as Rome sank into anarchy. Finally, one of the cardinals, Latino Malabranca, declared that a holy monk had predicted dire consequences for the Church should the cardinals not elect someone. The cardinal pledged himself to this hermit, whom he revealed to be the well-known and deeply respected Pietro del Morrone. Deciding to accept the compromise, the other cardinals gradually agreed and Morrone was voted in as pope on July 5. There followed the peculiar scene of several cardinals and other dignitaries trudging up the slopes to the monastery of Monte Morrone, where they informed the dumbstruck ascetic of his election. He at first refused but was eventually convinced to accept. Taken by donkey to Aquila, he was consecrated Celestine V on August 29. The brief reign of Celestine was an unremitting disaster. He fell under the control of King Charles II of Naples, residing at Naples and duly naming twelve cardinals who were partisans and allies of the king. The pope was also completely ignorant of his duties as pontiff, allowing the Church's affairs to slide severely into confusion; he also shocked the Curia by displaying so feeble a grasp of Latin that Italian became the language of official business and at consistories. Unhappy and recognizing that he was harming the Church, he began considering abdication, finally doing so before the cardinals on December 13, 1294. While he desired only to retire to his monastery, his successor, Boniface VIII, could not permit this owing to the potential of having an enemy seize the former pope and use him against the Holy See. Celestine was taken and placed in the fortress of Fumone. He died there on May 19, 1296. He was reported as saying when taken to his cell, "I have desired nothing in my life save for a cell, and a cell they have given to me." He was canonized in 1313 by Pope Clement V. He was condemned by Dante, who put him at the entrance to Hell in the *Inferno* (3.59), writing of him as the one "who made, through cowardice, the great refusal." Successor: Boniface VIII.

✵ **CELLINI, BENVENUTO**   Florentine adventurer, goldsmith, and sculptor (1500–1571), whose memoirs record vivid if not somewhat unreliable details about the sack of Rome in 1527 and the siege of Pope Clement VII within the walls of Castel Sant'Angelo. Notorious as a swaggering swashbuckler and rapscallion, Cellini fled to the fortress as imperial troops descended on the city. He was soon joined by the pope, who had barely escaped with his life from the Vatican, 147 Swiss Guardsmen dying to buy him enough time to escape across the *passetto* connecting the papal palace with the fort. There Cellini took part in defending Castel Sant'Angelo from the siege of the imperial troops who had already begun systematically and cruelly sacking Rome. Cellini reports in his memoirs that he manned five cannon and was responsible for firing the gun that killed the Constable de Bourbon, commander of the enemy forces. Cellini then supposedly went down on bent knee and begged forgiveness for committing murder. The pope, however, was said to have "derived much pleasure" from the event. Cellini also used his skills as a goldsmith to melt down the pope's treasure to help prevent its capture and assisted in the hiding of the papal jewels. Cellini was later imprisoned in the fortress, escaping through a feat of great daring, but shattering his leg in the process. (See also *Castel Sant'Angelo; Clement VII;* and *Rome, Sack of.*)

✵ **CENTRAL STATISTICS OFFICE OF THE CHURCH**   A department of the Roman Curia that has the large task of compiling, organizing, and analyzing all of the relevant statistics on the current condition of the Catholic Church in the world, including the most up-to-date numbers of Catholics in each country, how many members in the clergy, and the effects of the work of the Church everywhere. It was first established on August 15, 1967, by Pope Paul VI and is attached to the Secretariat of State. It publishes the *Statistical Yearbook of the Church,* a compendium of all important data pertaining to the state of the Church. The *Yearbook* was first printed in 1972 under the title of *Collection of Statistical Tables, 1969.* For those interested in finding a copy, the reader should be advised that it is printed with two columns in corresponding Italian and Latin; there is some material in the introductory section in other languages. For those not fluent in one or the other language, it is suggested that the reader consult instead the *Official Catholic Directory* or the *Catholic Almanac;* the latter is especially helpful and is available at most Catholic bookstores.

❀ **CHAINS OF PETER** See *Peter's Chains, Feast of.*

❀ **CHAIR OF PETER** See *Cathedra Petri.*

❀ **CHANCERY OF THE DIOCESE OF ROME** See *Vicar General.*

❀ **CHAPELS** There are numerous chapels in St. Peter's Basilica, running along both sides of the church. Not counting the many altars (such as the Papal Altar and the Altars of St. Peter, the Cripple, the Crucifixion of St. Peter, and St. Wenceslas), the chapels include: Pietà, the Crucifix, Sacrament, Gregorian, St. Michael, the Column, Clementine, the Choir, Presentation, and the Baptismal Font. Each is of interest to the visitor and serves a practical purpose in its own right. The two largest are the Chapel of the Choir and the Chapel of the Sacrament. The pope has use of any chapel he might wish. Normally, however, he says mass every morning (when in Rome) in his private chapel within the Apostolic Palace. This small but beautifully decorated chapel has a stained-glass roof and a modern altar—with a frieze commemorating the martyrdoms of Sts. Peter and Paul, the two saints revered as the founders of the diocese of Rome. The mass is usually attended by his personal secretaries, the nuns who take care of the cooking and cleaning in the apartments, and various invited guests. The pope also uses the chapel for his private meditations, a rosary invariably in his hand. Arguably the best known of all chapels in the Vatican is the Sistine Chapel. (See *Sistine Chapel* for details.) Mention should also be made of the small room that is situated near the Sistine Chapel. It comes into prominence at the time of a conclave, for it used to house the tailors of Gammarelli's, the official papal tailor. The representative of the firm waits for the call from Vatican officials to hasten to the Chapel. He has with him white soutanes of varying sizes with which to outfit the newly elected pope. (See *Conclave*.) The room is called the Chapel of Tears.

❀ **CHAPLAIN**   A title of honor that is granted to certain secular priests at the request of a local bishop. The full title is Chaplain of His Holiness, although the individual is normally called a Monsignor. (See *Monsignor* for other details.)

❀ **CHOIR, PAPAL**   See *Sistine Choir.*

❀ **CHRISTINA OF SWEDEN, QUEEN**   (1626–1689) Queen of Sweden from 1632 to 1654 who abdicated from her throne and was converted to Catholicism. The only surviving child of the famed King Gustavus Adolphus of Sweden, Christina came to the Swedish throne after the death of her father from wounds received in the Battle of Lützen in 1632 in the Thirty Years' War. As she was still in her minority, the government was in the hands of her advisors until she turned eighteen in 1644. She was instrumental in bringing about the Treaty of Westphalia (1648), ending the war. As queen, she proved the source of much irritation to her advisors for two main reasons: she refused to marry and had a keen interest in Catholicism, a leaning that prompted her to form alliances with Catholic Spain and to infuriate her ardently Protestant court. Facing bitter complaints about her erratic rule, she began to discuss abdication in 1651, finally doing so on June 6, 1654, in favor of her cousin Charles X. The next year, she was formally received into the Catholic Church by Lucas Holste, the Vatican Librarian. She settled in Rome in the Palazzo Farnese and later the Palazzo Riario (modern Palazzo Corsini). A brilliant but somewhat eccentric individual, she studied philosophy, languages, and politics, making her court first in Sweden and then in Rome a center for intellectuals, including René Descartes. In Rome, she founded the Arcadia Academy. Her conversion was a considerable triumph for the Church and was proclaimed as such (even though it had come at the loss of the Swedish throne). Christina was welcomed into the Eternal City by Pope Alexander VII (1655–1667), who gave her a triumphant procession through the streets and a special audience in the Vatican. The room at the Vatican where she initially stayed was located far from the papal apartments, which appeared more seemly (today the room is in the complex housing the

Vatican Archives) and a Latin motto declaring that all troubles come from the north removed from it. Her antics and curious questions about the Catholic faith were the source of some embarrassment to Alexander and his successors, but she shared with him a love of art and letters. The queen supposedly fired off a cannon on the ramparts of Castel Sant'Angelo that sent a cannonball crashing into the garden of the Villa Medici; the cannonball still sits in the fountain of the villa. She died in a room in the Palazzo Riario overlooking her gardens on April 19, 1689. Her monument in St. Peter's Basilica depicts a bas relief of her reception into the Church at Innsbruck; it is located near the Chapel of the Crucifix. Many of her manuscripts are preserved in the Vatican collection.

❀ **CHRISTMAS** The feast celebrated on December 25. The Christmas holiday is celebrated by the pope with a number of important ceremonies. It is said that the midnight mass celebrating Christmas was first established by Pope St. Telesphorus (123–138). Since then, the popes have presided over what is now perhaps the year's most watched religious event, the Christmas Mass from St. Peter's Basilica, broadcast live to hundreds of countries and viewed by perhaps hundreds of millions of people. The pope also gives a special Christmas blessing to the throngs who pack St. Peter's Square beneath his window in the Apostolic Apartments. Pope John Paul II will regularly offer a blessing in over fifty languages, a small but respectful cheer rising from the nationalities in attendance when he speaks their language. The pope also gives what is called the Christmas message. This custom began in the early Church when the Roman clergy would gather and give greeting to their bishop. He would accept it and respond with his own words, often delivered as a sermon. It later became common for the pope to address his remarks to the assembled College of Cardinals. Pope Benedict XV (1914–1922) changed this significantly by speaking not just to the cardinals but to the entire world. From that time the message grew in fame and importance, being broadcast all over the world. One of the most famous was that of Pius XI (1922–1939) in 1937 when he spoke out against religious persecution in Nazi Germany. During the Christmas season, St. Peter's Square is normally decorated with a tall, lighted Christmas tree, near a shed housing a Nativity scene of life-size figures. Another scene is set up in the basilica, blessed by the pope himself.

❀ **CHRISTOPHER** Antipope from 903 to 904, although he has at times been listed as a legitimate pontiff. Christopher was a cardinal priest in Rome, head of the Roman parish of San Damaso (one of the twenty-five parishes of the city) when, in September 903, he instigated a coup against Pope Leo V. He had the pope placed in prison and was consecrated in his stead. His administration did not last long, for in January of 904, Pope Sergius III (who himself had been elected in 897 but had been forced to surrender to John IX) arrived with an army. Christopher was removed and imprisoned—with Leo V—and Sergius was consecrated pope. After languishing in prison for several months, Christopher was put to death (according to one source) or forced to spend his remaining days as a monk. Given the confused and chaotic circumstances of the era, the darkest in papal history, it is little surprise that in some lists he was counted as a real pope. The Church, however, today officially considers him an antipope.

❀ **CHRONOGRAPHER OF 354**   An important almanac that was compiled by an unknown writer in the middle of the fourth century; its name is from one given to it by the German historian of Rome Theodore Mommsen (1817–1903) who called the anonymous compiler *Chronographen vom Jahre 354.* The almanac provides a useful look at the life of the early Christian Church, with an especially detailed look at the Bishops of Rome. It has an examination of the calendar of Roman holidays; an Easter Table; a *"Depositio episcoporum,"* a list of the death dates of the Bishops of Rome from 255 to 352; a list of the Bishops of Rome to Pope Liberius (352–366); and a martyrology of Rome (the martyrs of the city). It also has lists of the Roman consuls up to 354 and a general history of the Eternal City to the start of the fourth century.

❀ **CIVICA SCELTA**   One of the old military units in the service of the popes, merged with the *Milizia Urbana* around 1850 to become the Palatine Guard of Honor.

❀ **CLEMENT I, ST.**   Pope from around 88 to 97, the third successor to St. Peter and one of the most significant of the early popes. While officially considered the successor to Pope St. Anacletus (76–88), he is listed by Tertullian and St. Jerome as the immediate follower of St. Peter. According to tradition, Clement was a one-time slave in the household of Titus Flavius Clemens, a cousin of the Emperor Domitian. He was also identified, by Origen and others, with the Clement mentioned by St. Paul in his letter to the Philippians (4:3).

Clement has been subject to a wide number of legends and stories, including the probably unreliable account of his martyrdom; he was supposedly banished to the Crimea and there put to death by having an anchor tied around his neck and hurled into the sea. He was also the reputed author of the so-called Clementine Literature, a body of apocryphal writings that includes homilies, the Apocalypse of Clement, the Second Epistle of Clement, and two Epistles to Virgins. He is known to be the author of the *First Epistle of Clement,* ranked as the most important Church document of the first century other than the New Testament and the *Didache.* Successor: St. Evaristus.

❀ **CLEMENT II** Pope from 1046 to 1047, a pontiff who owed his election to the German King Henry III. Originally called Suidger and of noble Saxon descent, he was Bishop of Bamberg in late 1046 when King Henry III launched a campaign into Italy to attempt a resolution of the state of affairs in Rome, which was currently occupied by three claimants to the Holy See: Benedict IX, Sylvester III, and Gregory VI. Through the Synod of Sutri (1046), the three popes were deposed. In their place, a new pope was to be elected, but since there were no obvious candidates Henry took it upon himself to supply one. His first choice was Adalbert, Archbishop of Bremen, but he absolutely refused, whereupon Henry, at Adalbert's suggestion, picked Suidger. He accepted only on condition that he be allowed to retain his see of Bamberg, a request born probably out of recognition that the Romans were quite likely to eject him from the papal throne within a short time. Elected at the nomination of the king on December 24 1046, he took the name Clement and was enthroned on Christmas Day. At the same time, he crowned his patron emperor. Clement wasted little time in launching a thoroughgoing reform of the Church, convening and presiding over a great synod in Rome in January 1047 at which simony was condemned. He then journeyed with the emperor through southern Italy. In the summer, he departed Rome for the Marches (to the north), possibly because of the usual social and political upheaval. October found him at the abbey of S. Tommaso, where he fell ill quite unexpectedly and died on October 9. The rumor spread immediately that he had been poisoned, seemingly confirmed by the return shortly thereafter of the reprehensible Benedict IX to Rome. Clement was buried in the cathedral of his beloved Bamberg, a city of which he never ceased thinking while pope. A careful study of his remains in 1942 revealed that the cause of death may have been lead poisoning. Successor: Damasus II.

�֎ **CLEMENT III**   Pope from 1187 to 1191, born Paolo Scolari, he was raised in Rome, spending much time in Santa Maria Maggiore, whose archpriest he later became. Eventually the cardinal bishop of Palestrina, he was among the cardinals who assembled in Pisa to elect a successor to Gregory VIII (d. December 17, 1187). Their first choice for pope declined, so the cardinals turned to Scolari. He accepted and was a popular choice with his fellow Romans. In fact, he was able to return to the Eternal City, the first time in six years that the commune of Rome was willing to permit their pontiff to reside there. Through negotiations, he entered Rome in February 1188, taking up residence in the Lateran, and settling a compact with the commune. The pope also focused on arranging a peace treaty with the Holy Roman Empire. This arrangement, while costly to the Holy See, freed up Clement to concentrate his energies on his dearest cause, the mounting of the Third Crusade (1189–1191) to recapture Jerusalem after its loss to the Muslim armies in 1187. Clement was to be disappointed in the undertaking, for while it had the support of Frederick I Barbarossa, King Richard the Lionhearted, and King Philip II Augustus of France, it failed in its objectives. Just as bad, Frederick died in Cilicia (drowning in his own armor after falling from his horse), freeing his ambitious heir, Henry VI (r. 1191–1197) to pursue an imperialist policy in Italy. Upon the death of William II, King of Sicily, Henry, who was married to Constance of Sicily, made swift moves to seize Sicily and unite it to the empire. He based his claims on his wife's position to the now empty throne of Sicily, William having died without male heir. This the Sicilians would not allow, and the pope perceived the disastrous situation that might result for the papacy should Henry possess both the empire and the Kingdom of Sicily. Clement thus permitted Tancred of Lecce, a grandson of King Roger II of Sicily (r. 1130–1154), to be crowned king at Palermo. Henry marched on Italy, but stopped near Lake Bracciano when word arrived that Clement was dead. The pope had died in March 1191, taking whatever plans he might have had with him. Successor: Celestine III.

✖ **CLEMENT III**   Antipope from 1080 to 1100. Known originally as Guibert, he was a native of Parma and was related to the Counts of Canossa. Guibert became an antipope through the backing of Emperor Henry IV (1056–1107) who was in the throes of a severe struggle with Pope Gregory VII (1073–1085). The ruler had Guibert elected pope on June 25, 1080. The antipope then journeyed with him to Rome in 1084, where on March 24, with imperial troops in charge and the real pope clinging to the fortress of Castel Sant'Angelo, he was consecrated in the Lateran under the name Clement III. He proved quite talented and successful as a rival to Gregory and his successors Victor III (1086–1087) and Urban II (1088–1099), actually controlling Rome throughout the 1090s. Finally, the Pierleoni family ejected him from Rome, Urban II claiming the city in August 1099. Undaunted, Clement was still planning new moves against the new pope Paschal II (1099–1118) when he died at Civita Castellana on September 8, 1100.

 CLEMENT IV   Pope from 1265 to 1268, elected as successor to Urban IV after a conclave lasting four months. Guido Fulcodi (or Guy Foulques) was born in France around 1195. Becoming a well-known lawyer in the service of King Louis IX of France, he married and had two daughters. After his wife's death in 1256, however, he was ordained, following in the footsteps of his father who after his mother's passing had entered the Carthusians. Pope Urban IV named him a cardinal in 1261, the first cardinal created by that pope. He served as a reliable legate for Urban, and was traveling through France after a mission to England when word reached him that the pope had died. He went straight to Perugia in answer to the summons of the cardinals who had entered the conclave. To his astonishment, he was told that the cardinals had unanimously elected him on February 5. At first tearfully refusing, he was convinced by the cardinals to accept the burdens of office. Crowned at Viterbo on February 22, he took the name Clement in honor of the saint of his birthday. He was soon confronted with the peculiar situation of having suitors arrive at Viterbo to ask for the hands of his daughters in marriage. He was careful in noting, however, that they were not marrying the children of the pope, but of Guy Foulques. (Both daughters entered convents, thus sparing Clement the task of being a father-in-law or a grandfather.) He was clear in his opposition to nepotism and noted for his asceticism. The overriding concern of his reign was the final liquidation of the Hohenstaufen dynasty that had for so long threatened the papacy. He crowned the adventurer Charles of Anjou (brother of King Louis IX) King of Naples and Sicily in 1266, thereafter using him as the principal weapon against the Hohenstaufen claimants Manfred and Conradin. The cost of his gamble against them was considerable; he secured loans from hard-bargaining Tuscan bankers to help keep Charles equipped with soldiers and weapons. Looking upon this as a crusade for the sake of the Holy See, Clement endured near bankruptcy to secure his ends. He proved victorious, for at the Battles of Benevento (1266) and

Tagliacozzo (1268) Manfred and Conradin were utterly beaten. Manfred died at Benevento and Conradin was beheaded by Charles on October 29 after being captured and tried. Clement had won for the papacy a great victory, but it was largely lost on the Romans (who liked Conradin) and resulted in Charles enjoying a dominant place in Italy, thereby posing yet another threat to the popes. Dante wrote of the struggle in the *Inferno* by describing it as a "war hard by the Lateran, and not with Saracens, nor Jews" (canto 28). Clement barely outlived the last Hohenstaufen, dying on November 29, 1268. He had done much to improve the condition of the papacy, but it had come at a fearful price in lives, money, and principles. Clement was buried in Viterbo, where he spent most of his reign, in the Dominican convent of Sta Maria in Gradi. The papal throne would be empty for three years, the interregnum ended by arguably the most unusual conclave ever. Successor: Gregory X.

 CLEMENT V   Pope from 1305 to 1314, the first pontiff of the Avignon Papacy, which would last from 1309 until 1377. A native of Villandraut in Gascony, France, Bertrand de Got was born in 1264. A member of a respected family (his brother had been Archbishop of Lyons, cardinal bishop of Albano, and papal legate), Bertrand studied law and served as vicar general to his brother. In 1295 he became Bishop of Comminges and in 1299 Archbishop of Bordeaux. As archbishop, he was technically a vassal of the King of England (owing to English possessions in France), but King Philip IV the Fair of France was a lifelong friend. Despite his association with Philip, he had given his support to Boniface VIII in the bitter struggle waged between the pope and king. In the conclave to find a new pope after the death of Benedict XI in 1304, the cardinals in attendance could not agree on a suitable name among themselves, so after eleven months of bickering among the various factions, they decided to look for someone other than their own number. Their choice on June 5, 1305, was Bertrand de Got, marking a victory for the French minority and signaling probably the influence of King Philip. They asked the new pope to come to Perugia and then go to Rome for his coronation. It was thus perhaps ominous that Clement declined this proposal, bowing instead to the pressure of the French court and being crowned at Lyons on November 15. He then failed to acquiesce to any pleas to journey to Rome and instead wandered for several years through Provence and Gascony until finally settling—at Philip's suggestion—at Avignon in March 1309. Few could have thought that the papacy would essentially remain there for the next seventy years. (See *Avignon* and *Babylonian Captivity*.) To this French location, Clement added a greater number of French cardinals, curbing the presence and influence of the Italians for many years to come. Clearly dominated by King Philip, Clement followed his request to rescind many of the acts of the ruler's great enemy Boniface, humiliatingly absolving the minister Guillaume de Nogaret of any wrongdoing in his brutal treatment of the pope at Anagni, and permitting the abuse of Boniface's memory. Far more unfortunate was Clement's role in the extirpation of the Knights Templar, the military order that had earned Philip's hatred and jealous desire for their wealth and property in France. Under threat, Clement allowed the Council of Vienne in 1311–1312 to serve as the backdrop for their condemnation and formal disbanding. The leadership, especially the last Grand Master, Jacques de Molay, was tortured and burned at the stake for assorted crimes such as sorcery, murder, and sodomy. On the more positive side, Clement founded the universities of Orleans and Perugia. A dedicated nepotist, he made five members of the family cardinals and spent so lavishly on gifts and legacies that the papal treasury was nearly wiped out. He died at Roquemaure, near Carpentras on April 20, 1314. Successor: John XXII.

 CLEMENT VI   Pope from 1342 to 1352, the fourth pontiff to reside at Avignon. Pierre Roger was born in 1291 in the castle of Maumont and entered the Benedictine order at the age of ten, subsequently studying at Paris and earning a doctorate. By 1326 he was an abbot and in 1328 Bishop of Arras. His advancement followed quickly: Archbishop of Sens (1329), Archbishop of Rouen (1330), and cardinal (1338). He owed his elevation to the cardinalate to Benedict XII, receiving election as his successor at Avignon on May 7, 1342. It was a choice almost universally desired; the French King Philip IV sent his son to Avignon to express his support for Pierre (he was elected even before the prince arrived), and the cardinals, tired of Benedict's austere government, looked to Pierre to reverse papal policy. The new pope wasted little time fulfilling their expectations, declaring that "My predecessor did not know how to be pope!" Easygoing, affable, and confident in his application of splendor, Clement seems to have labored to create a comfortable and grand French court, living more like a prince than the Supreme Pontiff of the Church. He purchased the city of Avignon directly from Queen Joanna of Naples for the large sum of 80,000 gold florins. He then enlarged the papal palace and staged lavish entertainments. Petrarch called him Nimrod and rumors circulated about his fondness for food, drink, and women (including his niece Cecile de Turenne), but these were almost certainly false as he was personally free of conspicuous moral decrepitude. His kind nature extended to a courageous episode in 1348 when the plague broke out in the city. Nearly eleven thousand people died, including seven cardinals, and Clement spent large amounts of money to ease the suffering, demanding at great personal risk that the papal Curia remain at work to provide example to the citizens of the stricken community. Even more remarkable was his bravery in suppressing the anti-Jewish riots that broke out in the city when wild stories spread that the Jews had poisoned the wells of Avignon. Concerned for the welfare of the Romans, Clement gave permission for the staging of a jubilee in 1350, bringing much-needed financial help to the increasingly impoverished city. He also sent the political adventurer Cola di Rienzo (d. 1354) to Rome in the hope that he might be able to restore order. A crusade against the Turks was hoped for, but it proved impractical and the pope contented himself with several naval expeditions. Genuinely popular with all classes, he died on December 6, 1352, after a short illness. In 1562, his grave at La Chaise-Dieu was desecrated and his remains burned by the Huguenots. Successor: Innocent VI.

 CLEMENT VII   Pope from 1523 to 1534, his reign was dominated by the spread of the Protestant Reformation, the divorce of King Henry VIII of England, and the savage sack of Rome in 1527. A member of the Medici family, Giulio de'Medici was the illegitimate son of Giuliano de'Medici, growing up in the household of the famed Lorenzo the Magnificent because his father was murdered soon after Giulio was born. His cousin Pope Leo X (1513–1521), refusing to accept the traditional impediment preventing an illegitimate person from becoming a bishop, named him Archbishop of Florence and a cardinal in 1513. He was one of the most important figures in Rome and the papal court during the reigns of both Leo X and Adrian VI (1522–1523). He was especially popular for his patronage of the arts, including Michelangelo. His election as pope on November 19, 1523, came after the death of the exceedingly unpopular Adrian and was hailed as the start of a potentially great pontificate on the basis of his shrewd leadership as a papal advisor. Clement VII proved unequal to the terrible challenges of the times, however, and too much a Renaissance pope in the traditions of his predecessors. While personally good and concerned for the welfare of the Church, he allowed himself to be distracted easily by the luxuries of the papal court, including banquets and art. In confronting the crises that were besetting the Church, he was to be weak and vacillating. This was most clear in his dealings with the two great rivals Emperor Charles V and King Francis I of France. He gravitated toward one and then the other, finally angering the emperor by joining the League of Cognac in 1526 with Francis. Charles sent an army of Spanish Catholics and Lutheran Germans (*Landsknechts*) against Rome, storming the Eternal City on May 6, 1527. For five months, Rome was sacked and brutalized, the treasures plundered, the people murdered, and nuns raped and tortured to death. Clement barely escaped with his life, literally running to the safety of Castel Sant'Angelo, his Swiss Guards sacrificing themselves to permit his escape. Finally surrendering, he sat a prisoner of the imperial troops until December 6, 1527. For the next two years he lived away from the ruined Rome at Orvieto and Viterbo. Making peace with Charles, he was able to secure the return of most of the lost temporal holdings of the papacy, but he remained under the influence of Charles. This had the most untimely consequences for the Church as the pope decided the difficult question of King Henry VIII's divorce with a keen awareness that Charles, the nephew of Queen Catherine of Aragon, had his eye on the situation. The result was Clement's declaration in 1533 against Henry's request for an annulment. The departure of England from the Church and the excommunication of the English king followed. Meanwhile, Clement was unable to stem the advance of Protestantism in Germany, Scandinavia, and elsewhere, his own political weakness matched by his personal failure to launch an effective program both to stem the Lutheran tide or to bring a meaningful reform of the Church, which was eagerly desired by many Catholic leaders. Of him the poet Francesco Berni satirically wrote: "His reign was rich in seeking every way,/In change of mind and trying to be wise,/In ifs and buts and nos and ayes,/With nothing ever done, but always much to say." Successor: Paul III.

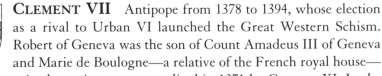 **CLEMENT VII** Antipope from 1378 to 1394, whose election as a rival to Urban VI launched the Great Western Schism. Robert of Geneva was the son of Count Amadeus III of Geneva and Marie de Boulogne—a relative of the French royal house— and received appointment to cardinal in 1371 by Gregory XI. In the conclave to find a successor to Gregory, Robert gave his vote to Bartolomeo Prignano, Archbishop of Bari as Urban VI, and was the first of the cardinals to do homage before him. Within a short time, however, he had turned against the erratic pontiff to become a leader of

the party seeking to have the pope deposed. On September 20, 1378, he was elected pope at Fondi by a group of rebellious cardinals. So began the Great Schism as Clement amassed the support of France, Burgundy, Naples, Scotland, and later Castile and Aragon. Settling at Avignon—from which the papacy had left in 1377—Clement organized a papal court in the style of the Avignon popes. Chronically troubled by financial concerns, he raised taxes and imposed levies on every possible source, including the heretofore exempt religious orders under his control. He hoped to be named pope by the conclave assembled in Rome following Urban's death in 1389, but he was soon disappointed. After the election of Boniface IX (1389–1404), he was pressured to step down in the interests of peace, but refused to do so, claiming the legitimacy of his claims right up to the moment of his death from a fit of apoplexy on September 16, 1394. He would be followed as antipope by Boniface XIII.

CLEMENT VIII   Pope from 1592 to 1605. Considered the last pope of the Catholic Reformation, his reign was quiet and tranquil, coming as it did on the heels of the incessantly busy pontificate of Sixtus V (1585–1590) and the three acutely brief reigns of Urban VII (1590), Gregory XIV (1590–1591), and Innocent IX (1591). Ippolito Aldobrandini was born on February 24, 1536, at Fano, the son of a renowned Florentine barrister. He was able to study at Padua, Perugia, and Bologna through the charity of Cardinal Alessandro Farnese and was brought into the Curia by his family's patron St. Pius V. After a long and distinguished career, he was made a cardinal by Sixtus V in 1585, taking part in the four conclaves from 1590–1592. In each, he was a leading candidate, finally gaining enough support to receive election in succession to Innocent IX on January 30, 1592. Crucial to his election was the determination of a minority group of cardinals to free the papacy from the domination of Spain, specifically King Philip II. Known for his purity, Clement had long been a friend and admirer of St. Philip Neri, whose charity had obviously left a deep impression on him. He thus made a point to visit every church and charitable institution in Rome to continue the last stages of the Catholic Reformation and to promote the labors of St. Francis de Sales. Much of his focus in matters of foreign policy was on fulfilling the hopes of the cardinals in the conclave. He reduced the number of Spanish cardinals and curbed Spanish influence in the papal court and policy. He fostered good relations with King Henry IV of France. With Henry's help, Clement added Ferrara to the Papal States, thereby increasing revenue for the Holy See. His concern for the welfare of his people in the States of the Church and Rome led him to conduct a campaign against brigands—in the tradition of the merciless Sixtus V. A brilliant administrator, he had a phenomenal capacity for work and involved himself in every aspect of papal and Church affairs. He thus presided over the the theological debate on the question of grace and free will between the Jesuits and Dominicans before a commission of cardinals. When he was unable to reach a decision on the matter after sixty-eight sessions, Clement was approached by the Jesuit cardinal St. Robert Bellarmine and told that while Clement might be a great lawyer, he was no theologian and should let the matter rest. Clement banished Bellarmine from the court, but the Jesuit saint was proven correct: no pronouncement was ever made. Clement died on March 5, 1605. Successor: Leo XI.

CLEMENT VIII Antipope from 1423 to 1429. The successor to antipope Benedict XIII, he was chosen by the three remaining cardinals appointed by Benedict who had charged them before his death to elect another pope. Known originally as Gil Sanchez Munoz, he was archpriest of Teruel when picked at Peñiscola in Spain, taking the name Clement in honor of Clement VII, the first antipope of the Great Schism. His claims to the papacy bordered on the comical, but Clement maintained the fiction of a papal court, with his own pitiful entourage and cardinals. Pope Martin V (1417–1431) greeted his election with generous terms for a settlement, and King Alfonso, after using him to leverage negotiations with the papacy, encouraged Clement to step down. This he did on July 26, 1429. He gave an oath of allegiance to Martin in August, the pope appointing him Bishop of Majorca as a sign of no ill will. He died on December 28, 1446. A key role in the settlement of the issue was played by Alfonso de Borja, the future Pope Callistus III.

CLEMENT IX Pope from 1667 to 1669. Giulio Rospigliosi was born on January 28, 1600, at Pistoia to a family from Lombardy. He studied in Rome and the University of Pisa, becoming a professor of philosophy at the age of twenty-three. A favorite of Urban VIII (who shared his fondness for poetry and literature), he was made a titular archbishop and dispatched as a trusted nuncio to Spain. Recalled by Alexander VII, he was made a cardinal and appointed Secretary of State in 1657. Ten years later he succeeded Alexander, receiving election by unanimous vote on June 20, 1667. The Romans were delighted with the choice, for he had cultivated their goodwill through his charity. As pope, he routinely heard confessions in St. Peter's and visited hospitals.

He was also relatively free of nepotism and refused to have his name inscribed on any building that was built through his generosity. Much of his time was taken up dealing with the cunning Louis XIV of France, who was working to curtail papal authority in France through the policy of Gallicanism. He was able to negotiate a compromise over the issue of Jansenism in France, the so-called Peace of Clement IX (1669). He also tried to help the Venetians in their struggle against the Ottoman Turks, expressing deep regret that no other Christian power would lift a finger to help the besieged Christians of Crete, which fell in September 1669. He died on December 9 still mourning the terrible loss of life on the island. The Romans expressed their sincere grief at his passing. Clement was a devotee of letters, composing a comic opera, *Chi soffre speri,* which premiered in 1639. Successor: Clement X.

 CLEMENT X Pope from 1670 to 1676, known originally as Emilio Altieri, he was a Roman, born on July 13, 1590. Studying at the Roman College, he earned a doctorate in 1611 and was ordained in 1624. He spent the next years in the service of the popes, holding the post of nuncio to Naples in 1644 at the command of Innocent X. Alexander VII, however, named him to high office in the Curia and Clement IX made him a cardinal a mere month before his death on December 9, 1669. In the conclave that followed, the cardinals were unable to find a suitable successor, their deliberations dragging on for four months; two candidates were rejected through the intrigue of the Spanish and French parties. So, in the custom of the cardinals, they sought an older, compromise candidate, Cardinal Altieri, officially electing him on April 29, 1670, assuming most likely that as he was nearly eighty years old, his would be a brief pontificate. The main concern of his reign was maintaining peace in Europe and promoting resistance to the advance of the Ottoman Turks. He also placed the famous statues of ten angels on the bridge leading to Castel Sant'Angelo. One dark spot on his reign was the overweening influence exercised by his cardinal nephew Cardinal Paluzzi degli Albertoni, related to Clement by the marriage of his nephew to the pope's niece. Among his many canonizations was Rose of Lima (d. 1617), the first saint of South America. Successor: Innocent XI.

 CLEMENT XI Pope from 1700 to 1721, Giovanni Francesco Albani was born in Rome on July 23, 1649, to the old Umbrian family of the Albani, a respected house of the Roman nobility. He earned a well-deserved name as one of the best educated and brilliant figures of the era, authoring a book at the age of eighteen and winning the attention of Queen Christina, the former ruler of Sweden. He mastered theology and canon law and was soon appointed to the papal court, where his intellectual abilities came to be matched by a reputation for piety and moral uprightness. After holding several posts in the administration of the Papal States, he was brought back to Rome and made vicar of St. Peter's before succeeding as secretary of papal briefs, an important position in the papal administration. In 1690, Alexander VIII made him a cardinal, and he was a major influence over that pontiff and his successor, Innocent XII (1691–1700). He was finally ordained a priest in 1700. On November 23 of that same year, he was elected to follow Innocent, accepting only after deep reflection. Word of his elevation was greeted with much enthusiasm around the courts of Europe, even in Protestant circles. His reign would be dominated by two main crises, war and Jansenism. The heretical Jansenists were condemned through the famous bull *Unigenitus* in 1713. Far more troubling was the War of the Spanish Succession (1701–1714), the conflict between the Habsburg and Bourbon claimants for the throne of Spain. The war demonstrated the inability of the papacy to deter violence when even Catholic rulers were determined to embark upon military ventures. Italy became a battleground, and in the negotiations leading to the treaties of Utrecht and Rastatt (1713–1714) bringing the fighting to a close, the pope was not permitted to have any say. Italian lands were parceled off without any consideration for the wishes or interests of the papacy. Duke Victor Amadeus II of Savoy (d. 1730), for example, was given Sicily, meaning that he controlled the Church there through the right called *Monarchia Sicula* (giving the King of Sicily authority over much of the Church in the area). Clement's protests were greeted by Victor's expulsion of three thousand priests and nuns whom Clement had to feed and shelter. Peace was arranged with Victor only in 1718. He also promoted missionary endeavors and decided against the Jesuits in their use of the so-called Chinese Rites (allowing converts in China to retain certain practices considered unorthodox or irregular). Clement died on March 19, 1721. Successor: Innocent XIII.

CLEMENT XII   Pope from 1730 to 1740. His reign was much concerned with bolstering the papacy in the face of the prevailing winds of monarchial absolutism and intellectual ferment. Lorenzo Corsini was born at Florence on April 7, 1652, a member of one of the noble houses of the city. He studied at the Roman College and then at the University of Pisa, earning a doctorate in law.

He then worked for a number of years for his uncle Neri Cardinal Corsini, but after his death and that of Lorenzo's father, he entered the clergy at the age of thirty-three. At first devoting himself to increasing the immense library of his uncle, he was named in 1691 a titular archbishop, and appointed nuncio to the court at Vienna. The emperor, however, would not accept him because of his unhappiness with the pope over his refusal to allow the emperor to submit a list of three names acceptable as papal representatives. Corsini thus remained in Rome, and in 1696 was given the difficult task of treasurer general and governor of Castel Sant'Angelo. In 1706, Clement XI made him a cardinal. He came to wield considerable power and influence under both Clement and Benedict XIII (1724–1730). Viewed as a potential pontiff in several conclaves, he was elected pope on July 12, 1730, taking the name Clement in honor of his patron, Clement XI. Clement lacked the vigor of youth—he was nearly eighty—to be a brilliant pontiff, and his weakness was aggravated by the onset of total blindness two years into his reign. He spent much of his final time as pope in bed, directing the affairs of state and Church and holding audiences from the bedchamber. Despite these infirmities, he was active in the resuscitation of papal finances, permitting the Roman lottery (a favorite pastime in the city) to be restored and sanctioning the prosecution of Niccolo Cardinal Coscia, the greedy minister who had dominated the reign of Benedict XIII. Other measures were taken to improve trade and commerce in the Papal States. Unfortunately, these positive developments were offset by the continued decline of papal influence in political affairs that had been so glaringly obvious in the time of Clement XI. The powers of Europe thus ignored him in their political and military moves, and he was unable to prevent the presence of Spanish troops in the territory of the Papal States. Spanish officials then forcibly recruited soldiers from among the population, causing riots in Rome and resulting in the sundering of relations between Spain and the Holy See. These were repaired by Clement only after making humiliating concessions. Clement also used some of his own money and funds brought in by the lottery to erect new buildings in Rome and was responsible for the famous Trevi Fountain (Fontana di Trevi) in the Piazza di Trevi. The Vatican Library was also enlarged. He died on February 6, 1740. Successor: Benedict XIV.

 CLEMENT XIII   Pope from 1758 to 1769. The pontificate of Clement was dominated, as would be that of Clement XIV, by the relentless efforts of many royal courts to destroy the Jesuit order, the Society of Jesus. Both popes would struggle to prevent the event, but their effort proved ultimately futile. Carlo della Torre Rezzonico was a native of Venice, born on March 7, 1693. His family owed its wealth to success in commerce and was able to buy its way into the nobility in 1687. Carlo studied under the Jesuits at Bologna, received a doctorate at Padua, and then attended the Academy of Noble Ecclesiastics, the school for training Vatican diplomats. Granted a position in the Curia in 1716, he embarked on a career that culminated with his appointment to the cardinalate by Pope Clement XII in 1737. In 1743, he was made bishop of Padua, earning renown for the intensely pastoral nature of his episcopal service, rebuilding the seminary with his own money. At the conclave in 1758 to choose a successor to Benedict XIV, Carlo was not the first choice of the cardinals, but that individual was vetoed by the French. He was subsequently elected on July 6, 1758, his elevation greeted happily by most courts but joyously embraced by the Venetians, who withdrew a series of antipapal enactments that had been passed in 1754. He soon ran right into the controversy of the Jesuits. Long hated by the ruling houses of Europe for their independence, talent, and devotion to the papacy, the Society of Jesus fell under attack first in Portugal and then elsewhere. The Portuguese hurled charges against them, such as illegal trade activities in South America and inciting rebellion in Paraguay. While false, the accusations gave the absolutist regime of the statesman Sebastiao José Pombal (d. 1782) all the cause it needed to expel the order and seize its assets in Portugal and the colonies in 1759. Portugal was followed by France in 1761 where demands were made for the Jesuits to make massive changes in their constitution. Clement responded with his famous declaration *"Sint ut sunt aut non sint"* ("Let them be as they are or not at all"). His bull of 1765 praising the Jesuits failed to stem the continued campaign of persecution in Spain, Naples and Sicily, and the duchy of Parma. Finally, in 1769, the representatives of the major crowns came before the pope and demanded the complete dissolution of the Jesuits. This Clement would not do, dying suddenly of a stroke on February 2, his death hastened by the constant stress of the crisis. While his passing spared the Jesuits, it proved only a temporary reprieve. Successor: Clement XIV.

CLEMENT XIV   Pope from 1769 to 1774, his pontificate was dominated by the final crisis of the Jesuits. Lorenzo Ganganelli (baptized Giovanni Vincenzo Antonio) was born on October 31, 1705, at Sant'Arcangelo, near Rimini, the son of a village doctor. At the age of seventeen, he entered the Franciscans, earning a doctorate in theology in 1731. He lectured for several years before receiving appointment as rector of St. Boniface's in Rome in 1740. Well known for his learning, he declined the office of master general of the Franciscan order in 1756, but accepted appointment as cardinal in 1759 by Clement XIII. A long supporter of the Jesuits, he gradually softened his position toward the order throughout the latter part of Clement XIII's pontificate. The question of the Jesuits had erupted into a full crisis by 1769 and was left unresolved at Clement's death on February 2, 1769. Thus when the cardinals assembled to find a new pope to follow Clement, they found themselves under the most intense pressure possible by the ambassadors of France and Spain, who made it abundantly clear that the cardinals were fully expected to elect a pontiff who would carry out the dissolution of the Jesuit order; the kings of France and Spain, the cardinals were told, would brook no opposition. The cardinals were outraged, but the ambassadors, most notably the French representative d'Aubeterre, were unyielding, whispering dire

Pope Clement XIV, the pontiff who suppressed the Jesuits.

threats and giving hints that there were only a few cardinals they might consider acceptable. One of them proved to be Cardinal Ganganelli. He possibly signed a promise to disband the Society of Jesus, but this has long been the subject of much debate, and no actual letter has ever been produced. Nevertheless, he clearly gave certain indications that he would not be averse to disbanding the order. On the basis of this, the courts stated that he was a tolerable candidate. The cardinals elected him on May 19, 1769. He immediately was confronted by the ambassadors pushing him to fulfill his pledge. Clement XIV resisted for as long as possible, but the pressure and threats proved too severe. On July 21, 1773, he issued the brief *Dominus ac Redemptor* officially dissolving the Jesuits. Its ostensible purpose was to bring peace to the relations between the Church and the kingdoms of France, Spain, and elsewhere by

Pope Clement XIV and Mozart

The following is a translation from the Latin of the Papal Patent sent on July 4, 1770, from Clement XIV to Mozart informing him of his induction into the ranks of the Knights of the Golden Order. It is a wonderful example of a papal document and the formal use of language by the papal establishment.

To Our Beloved Son
Joannes Amadeus Wolfgangus Mozart
of that City and Diocese of Salzburg.

Clement P.O. XIV.

To Our beloved Son greetings and apostolic benediction. Inasmuch as it behooves the beneficence of the Roman Pontiff and the Apostolic See that those who have shown them no small signs of faith and devotion and are graced with the merits of probity and virtue, shall be decorated with the honours and favors of the Roman Pontiff and said See: We, therefore, wishing to honour thee with fitting tokens of our grace and beneficence on account of thy sincere faith and devotion to us and the aforesaid See, together with thy other merits, hereby absolves thee, insofar as shall give effect and consequence to these presents, from any sentence of excommunication, suspension and interdict, or other censures and penalties of the Church, imposed by law or man for whatever occasion or cause, if in any way whatsoever thou art enmeshed in them: And deeming thee to be thus absolved, and hearkening to the supplications humbly submitted to us on thy behalf in this matter, we hereby make and create thee—whom we understand to have excelled since thy earliest youth in the sweetest sounding of the harpsichord—Knight of the Golden Order, by the Apostolic authority and the terms of these presents: Receiving thee favourably into the number of Knights of the said Order, especially that thou mayst in like manner freely and lawfully use and enjoy each and all of the privileges and prerogatives which the other Knights of the Order enjoy by law, usage, custom or in any other way, and shall in future enjoy (exceptions such as have been abolished by the Council of Trent), notwithstanding any apostolic or other constitutions or ordinances to the contrary whatsoever . . .

Given at Rome at S. Maria Maggiore under the Fisherman's Ring, the 4th day of July 1770, in the second year of our Pontificate.

—Otto Erich Deutsch,
Mozart: A Documentary Biography
(Stanford University Press, 1965, pp. 123–24)

removing the Jesuits from the struggle. The order would remain dissolved until 1814 when they were reconstituted by Pius VII. Interestingly, many Jesuits were given sanctuary by Queen Catherine the Great of Russia, and others were allowed to live unmolested in England because the Catholics there were not allowed to follow the commands of the pope and the Jesuits had to remain untouched, saved by anti-Catholic laws from liquidation orchestrated by Catholic sovereigns. Clement also started the Pio-Clementine Museum and attempted unsuccessfully to improve the economic life of the Papal States. His last years were occupied by a peculiar fear of assassination, an unmanageable depression brought on by illness, and a pervasive guilt for his treatment of the Jesuits. After his death on September 22, 1769, the rumor spread that he had been poisoned—the Spanish claimed by the Jesuits—a story seemingly confirmed by the rapid state of decomposition. An autopsy was performed confirming death by natural causes, but the event was a precedent that would be used by some vocal critics of the Vatican in 1978 following the sudden death of John Paul I; they argued that an autopsy should have been performed, on the basis of the fact that one had been performed on Clement. The unfortunate nature of his passing epitomized the sad quality of his reign. The papacy had fallen into difficult times. These would only continue under his successors as the Papal States were invaded and the popes themselves imprisoned. Successor: Pius VI.

❀ **COAT OF ARMS**   The heraldic arms borne by each pope, used as one of the important symbols of their pontificate and found in a variety of settings, including seals, pronouncements, official documents, and banners and art. The Church relies upon a long and honored tradition of what is termed ecclesiastical heraldry—the field of heraldry concerned with the insignia, emblems, charges, and terms relevant to the ranks of the Church—and the papacy is no exception. The Holy See is rich in its symbols and heraldic arms. The long-accepted emblem of the papacy, and the one found on the Vatican flag, is the tiara and the crossed keys of St. Peter, one gold and one silver, tied together with a cord. When combined with the private coat of arms of the reigning pontiff, they are placed behind the coat of arms, surmounted by the triple tiara. This custom was first begun in 1522 by Pope Adrian VI. The private coat of arms has been remarkably diverse over the centuries. The first pontiff to have officially recognized arms was Innocent III (1198–1216). For many if not most popes, the coats of arms used have been those of their families. That is why a number of popes have had the same arms, such as the Medici popes Leo X, Pius IV, Clement VII, and Leo XI. In those cases where the pope does not have his own family arms, one will be provided for him. Pope John Paul II, for example, had his remarkably simple and attractive arms, a gold cross on a blue field with an *M* for Mary, designed for him by the foremost expert in ecclesiastical heraldry, Archbishop Bruno Heim. The arms of a pope are often a matter of personal taste, reflecting the disposition and personality of the bearer. The arms of popes are seen everywhere in Rome and the Vatican, from the Barberini bees of Urban VIII (1623–1644), to the arms of Alexander VII (1655–1667) atop the colonnade of Bernini in St. Peter's Square.

❀ **CODE OF CANON LAW** See *Canon Law.*

❀ **COHORS HELVETICA** The Latin name given to the Swiss Guard. (See *Swiss Guard* for details.)

❀ **COINS, VATICAN** The official currency of the Vatican City State. In the years prior to the demise of the temporal power of the papacy in 1870, the monetary needs of the Holy See were filled by the mint of the Papal States. This mint was taken over by the new Italian government and made the official mint of the country, forcing the popes to use a makeshift mint located in the Vatican Gardens. The old Papal Mint was finally put back into partial use by the popes in 1930 after the signing of the Lateran Treaty. By the terms of this agreement, the Holy See is permitted to order a set amount of currency each year, with increases permitted for a *sede vacante* or some other major event,

Vatican coins from the reigns of Pius XII and Paul VI.

such as a council. The Vatican cannot use any other mint and the currency must correspond with Italian *lire* in its content, size, and basic denominations. While actually used as money—it is legal tender in Italy and San Marino—one of the main purposes of the coinage is to raise money through the sale of coins around the world to dealers and collectors.

❁ **COLLEGE OF CARDINALS** See *Cardinals, Sacred College of.*

❁ **COLLEGE OF CARDINALS, DEAN OF THE** See *Dean of the College of Cardinals.*

❁ **COLONNA, HOUSE OF** A noble family of Rome that became one of the most important political factions in Roman life during the Middle Ages. The Colonna first emerged during the eleventh century as a branch of the House of Tusculum. Their rise was greeted with apprehension by the other families, such as the Caetani and the Orsini, but they soon managed to secure the appointment of members to the Roman Senate and the College of Cardinals. Their first great patron was Pope Nicholas IV (1288–1292), who, relying upon his ties with the Colonna, used them to strengthen his papal rule. Colonna were appointed to high positions in the papal government, one was made a senator, and another became cardinal. Such was the close identification of Nicholas with their interests that contemporary critics caricatured him as being entirely wrapped in a column (the symbol of the Colonna), only his tiara-bedecked head peering pitifully over the top. After Nicholas's death, the family tried unsuccessfully to secure the election of a Colonna as pope. At first they accepted the elevation of Benedetto Caetani as Boniface VIII in 1294 as successor to the disastrous St. Celestine V. Relations between the Colonna and Boniface were never cordial, however, degenerating steadily over the first years of his reign. In May 1297, several Colonna soldiers plundered a wagonload of bullion intended for the papal treasury. Boniface, never one to take things meekly, ejected two Colonna cardinals from the Sacred College (Pietro and Giacomo) and then launched a crushing war against them. Papal forces captured and burned their fortresses, dispersed the family and seized their properties, granting most of the land to relatives of the pope. The family submitted in October 1298, but the two cardinals fled to France and the safety of the court of King Philip IV the Fair, who was himself increasingly at odds with the pope. The Colonna soon joined the cause of Philip against Boniface, one of their own, Sciarra Colonna (d. 1329), participating in the brutal kidnapping and brief incarceration of Boniface at Anagni in 1303. (See *Boniface VIII.*) The Colonna cardinals were excluded from the election of Boniface's successor, Benedict XI. While absolved by Benedict, they were not formally restored until Clement V, under the thumb of King Philip, was compelled to exonerate the two cardinals and pay restitution to the Colonna family. The Colonna next entered into a struggle with the Orsini, a feud that led to the crushing defeat of the Colonna at the Porta San Lorenzo in 1347 at the hands of the Roman dictator Cola di Rienzo. A recovery was made starting in 1417 when Oddone Colonna was elected as Martin V to end the Great Western Schism. The Colonna tried to win election to the papacy over the next years, but they faced too much opposition from the other families. Like the Orsini, the Colonna remain one of the families with rich historical ties to the papacy, so much so that a member traditionally serves as a Prince Assistant at the Pontifical Throne, an honorary position in the papal court; this title was changed in modern times to Lay Assistant to the Throne.

✸ CONCILIARISM   The theory that found wide acceptance in many quarters of the Church during the late Middle Ages that supreme power rested in the hands of a General Council that possessed authority greater even than the pope; the implication of the theory was that a General Council could, if it so decided, depose the pope and replace him with another. Also called the Conciliar Theory, the idea was first developed in the twelfth and thirteenth centuries through the speculation of certain theologians in examining the extent of papal rights and privileges. The early fifteenth century brought Conciliarism to the height of its popularity, owing to the upheaval brought about by the Great Western Schism and the division of the Church into camps supporting rival claimants to the papal throne. The Schism was finally resolved by the Council of Constance (1414–1418), which deposed or succeeded in removing all three papal rivals, including the legitimate pontiff, Gregory XII (1406–1415), replacing them with Martin V (1417–1431), the first universally recognized pope since 1378. Despite the success of the council, the efforts of some leaders to make Conciliarism a recognized element in the government of the Church were never widely accepted and were much opposed by the popes. The irretrievable decline of the movement was signaled by the contentious Council of Basle (1431–1449), which tried unsuccessfully to depose Pope Eugene IV (1431–1447). In the bull *Exacrabilis* (1460), Pope Pius II condemned any possible appeal against the pope to a council.

Conciliarism was condemned by Vatican Council I (1870) and in the revised Code of Canon Law it states that any attempt to make appeal against the pope to a council is subject to punishment by censure.

❀ **CONCILIAZIONE, VIA DELLA**   The main thoroughfare leading from the Tiber to St. Peter's Square and Vatican City; it connects to the square of St. Peter's through the Pius XII Square, formerly called the Piazza Rusticucci after a Cardinal Rusticucci who owned a palace there. The via itself actually dates only to the period after the signing of the Lateran Accords in 1929 between Pope Pius XI and Benito Mussolini. It was *Il Duce*'s intention to commemorate the agreement by tearing down the old ramshackle streets of the Spina dei Borghi between the Vatican and the Tiber and replacing them with a broad via called the *Conciliazione* (or Conciliation after the signing of the peace accord with the Holy See). Finished in 1950, it was designed by the Fascist architects Attilio Spaccarelli and Marcello Piacentini and completely replaced the two older lanes, the Borgo Vecchio and Borgo Nuovo. For old-timers who remembered the route to the Vatican before the via, the new, clear view of St. Peter's Square was actually a disappointment. The reasons for this are found in the fact that the old roads meandered through the Borgo in such a fashion that visitors would look up suddenly and, without warning, the beauty and majesty of St. Peter's Square would loom before them. To make up for the loss, the architects decorated the street with lamps perched atop modern-style obelisks—innovations never much appreciated by the Romans. On the via are situated the Palazzo dei Convertendi where the artist Raphael died, and the small Caffe San Pietro, an espresso bar where Mehmet Ali Agca drank a final cup of coffee before walking to St. Peter's to shoot Pope John Paul II in 1981.

❀ **CONCLAVE**   The name used for the lawful or canonical gathering of the Sacred College of Cardinals who fulfill their obligation by electing a new pope; the term can also denote the actual site used for the election. The conclave derives its name from the Latin *con* (with) and *clavis* (key), implying the central element of the election—that the cardinals are placed together in a locked chamber, remaining there without contact from the outside world until a pope has been duly elected. First established in 1274 under Pope Gregory X (1271–1276), the conclave system of elections has remained essentially unchanged into modern times. Pope Gregory introduced changes into the process of elections after the contentious and even absurd three-year interregnum that fol-

The stove used to burn the ballots during the election of a new pope by the cardinals in conclave. (CATHOLIC NEWS SERVICE.)

lowed the death of his predecessor Clement IV in 1268. On the basis of this terrible experience, the pope introduced conclaves.

The modern conclave is one of the most riveting of all events for Catholics and non-Catholics alike, capturing the imagination with its ancient mystique and traditions, its air of drama and mystery, and the great importance of its outcome, namely the election of the next leader of a faith that claims as members fully one fifth of the world's population. By custom, the conclave is held in the Sistine Chapel in the Vatican. The last election not held there occurred in 1846 when Pius IX (1846–1878) was elected in the Quirinal Palace.

The process of election begins immediately after the death of the pope and the holding of all solemn obsequies. The cardinal camerlengo summons to Rome all the eligible members of the Sacred College of Cardinals, who are canonically obligated under threat of dire excommunication to come, save for such inconveniences as imprisonment, serious illness, or death. The chapel is hastily prepared by the *sampietrini,* as are the rooms of the papal palace that are to serve as the living quarters for the cardinals during the conclave. Each Prince of the Church is provided a simple set of quarters with a small bed, a chair, a wash basin and pitcher, and a prie-dieu (a kneeling bench for prayers). The Spartan arrangements, coupled with the sealing of the apartments, perhaps in the stifling heat of the Roman summer, are intended to encourage the cardinals in their task at hand. Each elector may bring to Rome an assistant and is permitted small conveniences such as

Election Facts

The following are some of the curious facts related to the choosing of popes that have occurred over the centuries. The longest inter-regnum was from 1268 to 1271, between the death of Clement IV and the election of Gregory X on September 1, 1271, following a conclave marked by such frustration on the part of the people of Viterbo that the roof was torn off the papal palace and the cardinals were reduced to bread and water. There were many conclaves convened and completed in one day, the swift decision usually the result of either an obvious candidate presenting himself or because of some pressing potential disaster. Other facts include:

First person already a bishop at election: Marinus I (882)

First Roman elected pope: St. Anacletus (76)

Last Roman elected pope: Eugenio Pacelli as Pius XII (1939)

First Italian elected pope: St. Linus (67)

Last Italian elected pope: Albino Luciani, as John Paul I (1978)

Last non-Italian elected pope: Karol Wojtyla as John Paul II (1978); prior to this the last non-Italian was Adrian Florensz in 1522 as Adrian VI

Last person not a cardinal at election: Urban VI (1378)

Last conclave not held in Rome: 1800 in Venice, electing Pius VII

Last conclave not held in the Vatican: 1846, in the Quirinal Palace, electing Pius IX. The Quirinal also hosted the conclaves of 1823, 1829, and 1831

Last pope elected by acclamatio: Gregory XV (1621)

Last pope elected by compromise: John XXII (1316)

Last cardinal vetoed by a European power: Mariano Rampolla (1903)

Last Secretary of State elected pope: Eugenio Pacelli as Pius XII (1939); before that, Giulio Rospigliosi as Clement IX (1667)

Last camerlengo elected: Eugenio Pacelli as Pius XII (1939); before that, Giaocchino Pecci as Leo XIII (1878)

books, a bathroom kit, and other items of a personal nature. One American cardinal reportedly brought with him to one of the conclaves in 1978 a handful of chocolate bars.

The cardinals enter the chapel with great pomp after celebrating a Mass of the Holy Spirit in St. Peter's, at which they are exhorted to do their duty by the camerlengo. Their chambers having been examined for all possible means of sending out messages and swept for all possible electronic surveillance devices, the cry *"Extra Omnes!"* is now given, and all extraneous persons are ushered out. The camerlengo, assisted by other officials, seals the doors of the chapel. The cardinals are now alone, having become in that moment essentially the simple priests of Rome who have come together to choose a new bishop. In the past, when there were only seventy cardinals, each elector sat beneath his own canopy. When a new pope had been elected, the other cardinals lowered their canopies, leaving only one—the cardinal to whom they had entrusted the crushing burden of leading the Church. Owing to the costs involved and the size of the Sacred College, this custom was not followed in the two conclaves of 1978.

The cardinals vote twice a day, with three ballots per session, one set in the morning and another in the afternoon. Three methods of election are recognized as legal: secret ballot, compromise, or *acclamatio,* the latter a rare event as it is literally a sudden inspiration of the cardinals to choose someone unanimously without prior consultation amongst themselves. The most common method is by ballot. Voting goes on until a two-thirds-plus majority is reached. After three days, a one-day break is called for prayers and meditations (as well as some hard wrangling among the voters). If delays continue, the cardinals are addressed by the senior of the cardinal bishops. They may also change the required majority to secure election, decide on a run-off between the leading candidates, or shift to the process of compromise whereby the electors are represented by a chosen committee of cardinals empowered to vote on their behalf.

All ballots are supposed to be secret, with each cardinal instructed to disguise his handwriting and not to vote for himself. Should a vote be completely unanimous it is declared invalid, because either an error has occurred or the winner had committed the most serious of breaches of decorum in voting for himself, something which good taste and ecclesiastical humility forbids. Each ballot is carefully counted by the cardinal scrutineers who were chosen by lot. Karol Cardinal Wojtyla (the future Pope John Paul II) was a scrutineer in the conclave that elected John Paul I in 1978. The votes are carefully tabulated and called out to permit each voter to keep his own tally of the shifting fortunes of the leading candidates. If a majority is not reached, the ballots, bound and tied together, are burned, traditionally with wet straw, making the smoke dark so that the world knows no decision has been reached. In the event of an election, the ballots are burned with dry straw sending up white smoke. (See *Sfumata.*)

Once a person receives the necessary votes, he is either brought in great haste to the Vatican—if he is not a member of the conclave—or, as is more likely to occur, the camerlengo goes before the chosen cardinal and ceremonially intones in Latin the question: "Do you, Most Reverend Lord Cardinal, accept your election as Supreme Pontiff, which has been canonically carried out?" The cardinal is under no obligation to accept, and in fact, over the years several have turned down their election. The last-known time this occurred was supposedly in 1922 when Camillo Cardinal Laurenti declined the post and Achille Cardinal Ratti (Pius XI) was chosen instead. Once the cardinal utters the simple word *Accepto* ("I accept"), he is Bishop of Rome and his reign, long or short, great or mediocre, has begun. The camerlengo next asks, "By what name will you be known?" and the pontiff gives his chosen name, which can be his own if appropriate, although there is an unbroken custom that the name Peter is not to be used again. (See also *Malachy, Prophecies of.*) The joyous signal is received with a frenzy in the Square of St. Peter, confirmed by the announcement *"Habemus papam!"* ("We have a Pope!"). The current regulations governing the conclave were laid down by Pope Paul VI in 1975 with the document *Romano Pontifici Eligendo,* a set of rules left unchanged by John Paul II. **Conclave compacts** are agreements signed or sworn to by the cardinals entering a conclave that whoever of their number is elected pope that person will adhere to the program or oath taken by all the cardinals with respect to some action or kind of behavior. While irregular, compacts were agreed to on a number of occasions until Pope Pius IV finally outlawed them in 1562. **Conclave constitutions** are a set of specific rules that are issued by a pope to govern the election of his successor and to make certain that the next conclave functions smoothly, with a minimum of interference and delay. Pope Gregory X (1271–1276) issued the constitution *Ubi periculum* in 1274, requiring the cardinals to meet within ten days of a pope's death, to be locked away from contact with the outside world, and to endure greater austerities if the process continued for long without resolution. Although rescinded and then reinstituted by various popes, the Gregorian constitution continued to govern papal elections right up until 1975 when Paul VI promulgated the incredibly detailed constitution *Romano Pontifici Eligendo.* (See also *Elections, Papal.*)

✤ CONCORDAT   A type of agreement or treaty signed between the Holy See and a civil government or ruler. The concordat has long been one of the chief ways in which the papacy is able to advance and protect its rights and those of the Church in specific countries or regions. Such an agreement is normally concerned with matters of considerable importance to both the pope and the secular government, but it normally tends to focus on the parameters to be granted to the Church in the conduct of its affairs and, most important, in determining how far the Church can go in advancing its teachings. The first generally recognized concordat was signed in 1122 between Pope Callistus II and Emperor Henry V (the Concordat of Worms or the *Pactum Calixtinum*), although some scholars argue that the honor should go to a little-known agreement of 1107 reached between the English and the pope. Since that time there have been well over a hundred treaties between the Holy See and governments or regimes all over the world. Among the most famous are: the Concordat of 1801 between Pius VII and Napoleon Bonaparte; the Lateran Treaty of 1929 between Pius XI and Benito Mussolini (which was renewed and renegotiated in 1984); and the famous concordat reached in 1933 between Pius XI and Nazi Germany, a treaty for which the pope—who had acted in good faith— was much criticized and which Hitler soon violated. The popes also negotiated concordats with numerous Communist regimes in the hopes of protecting as best as they might the Church in such lands as Poland, Hungary, and elsewhere, agreements routinely abrogated by the Communists. Pope John Paul II has had the unique opportunity of signing concordats with the governments in Eastern Europe that replaced the Communists after the fall of the Soviet Union. A new concordat was signed, for example, with Poland in 1993.

✤ CONCORDAT OF WORMS   See *Worms, Concordat of.*

✤ CONON   Pope from 686 to 687, Conon was the son of a Thracian soldier, receiving education in Sicily and ordination in Rome. His election at an advanced age came about because the two main parties in the city could not reach a mutually acceptable agreement. He thus was consecrated on October 21 and quickly approved by Byzantine authorities. Conon, while popular with the military, proved constantly ill and quite feeble. He thus provided no real leadership or direction. At his passing on

September 21, 687, the factions in Rome resumed their squabbling. The result would be violence in the streets and the presence of two antipopes, Theodore and Paschal, within a short time. Successor: St. Sergius I.

CONSISTORIES The name given to assemblies of cardinals presided over by the pope. There are several types of consistories that can be held, including the private and the public. The private consistory can have several purposes. At one, the pope will announce to the assembled cardinals his choices for new appointments to the Sacred College of Cardinals. While the pope has complete authority over his choices, he asks the nominal blessing of the cardinals with the question, *"Quid vobis videtur?"* ("How does this seem to you?"). When the new cardinal appointees come to Rome, they are given a private ceremony of investiture into the college, including assignment to one of the parishes or churches of Rome. At the public consistory, the pope, most of the College of Cardinals, diplomats, press, and family gather to observe the formal universal declaration before the Church of the elevation of new members to the cardinalate. By custom, the newly created cardinals receive from the pope the kiss of peace after they have kissed his foot and hand in recognition of his place as Vicar of Christ. They then receive from him their scarlet zucchetto and biretta, the symbols of the Princes of the Church. After the public consistory, a final private one is held, attended only by the other cardinals. Other private consistories can be called by the pope for any reason. These might cover pressing financial matters or grave political or diplomatic crises. There is also a very special pre-conclave consistory held by the cardinals and presided over by the camerlengo. Here the cardinals who will take part in the election of the next pope are given the many rules governing the conclave and take an oath of secrecy not to reveal any details of the proceedings. (See also *Cardinal* and *Cardinals, Sacred College of.*)

CONSTANCE, COUNCIL OF The important council from 1414 to 1417 that brought an end to the Great Western Schism that divided the Church from 1378 and created at one point three different claimants to the papacy; the council also attempted to reform the Church and was the high point for conciliarism—the idea that a Church council has greater authority than the pope. (See *Conciliarism.*) The Council managed to secure the removal or abdication of all three rival popes, Pope Gregory XII and the antipopes Benedict XIII and John XXIII, and ended the Schism by electing the universally recognized Martin V (1417–1431).

CONSTANTINE Pope from 708 to 715, a Syrian by descent, he was described by a biographer as "a remarkably affable man" and his reign was said to have been divided into two parts, the first full of famines, the second great abundance. Succeeding Sissinius on March 25, he was confronted early the next year by the troublesome Felix, Archbishop of Ravenna, whom Constantine had himself consecrated. The prelate refused to give the customary oath of allegiance in an ill-advised attempt to revive the independence of his see from Rome. He was exiled by Byzantine Emperor Justinian II and was blinded by him for good measure. Returning in 712, Felix made obeisance to Constantine and would die in 723 at peace with the Holy See. Constantine, meanwhile, was summoned to Constantinople by Justinian to cement good relations with the papacy and secure his agreement on various canons and decrees that had been passed by a council (the Quinisext Council) in 692 but which Pope Sergius I had refused to endorse. Constantine was given great honors everywhere he went in the East, and was welcomed triumphantly in Constantinople. His trip (710–711) had as its highlights the kissing of his feet by the emperor and the reaching of a satisfactory accord between the papacy and the empire. This was broken almost immediately by the assassination of Justinian by the new emperor Philippicus Bardanes (711–713). His brief reign ended with another murder and the accession of Anastasius II (713–715), who sent assurances of his commitment to religious orthodoxy and the agreement with Justinian. Constantine died on April 9, 715. Successor: St. Gregory II.

CONSTANTINE Antipope from 767 to 768. The brother of Duke Toto of Nepi, he was installed on the papal throne after the death of the unpopular St. Paul I, thereby breaking the promise made by Toto to Christopher, the chief notary, that the next election would be entirely legal. Constantine was ordained a subdeacon and deacon, and then consecrated on July 5 in St. Peter's, a squad of hard-looking soldiers standing menacingly near to ensure that the bishops went through with the ceremony. Word was sent to King Pepin III of the Franks (d. 768), but he failed to respond. Meanwhile, the antipope was beset by domestic political troubles that were exploited by the ever watchful Lombards. Fighting broke out, and Toto was killed on July 30, 769. Shorn of his protection, Constantine fled to the Lateran where he was seized. A new pope was duly elected, Stephen III (IV). Constantine was tried, stripped of all rank and insignias, and imprisoned. A troop of guards gouged his eyes out. Blind and brutalized, he was taken back for a formal tribunal in April 769. He was sentenced to imprisonment in a monastery, presumably dying there at an unknown date.

❀ **CONSTANTINE, DONATION OF**   See *Donation of Constantine.*

❀ **CORNELIUS, ST.**   Pope from 251 to 253. A member of the Roman clergy, Cornelius was elected in March 251 as successor to St. Fabian, who had been martyred during the terrible persecutions of Emperor Decius. The papacy had been without a holder for over a year owing to the decision of the clergy in Rome to wait until the oppression subsided and because their favorite candidate, Moses, was in prison. By March 251, the terror had eased, but Moses was now dead. The expected bishop of Rome, Novatian, to everyone's surprise was not elected, the clergy having decided in favor of Cornelius. Novatian immediately contested the results and entered into schism over the issue of the so-called *lapsi,* those Christians who had given up the faith during the persecution and who were now the source of heated controversy as to whether or how they should be readmitted. Novatian led the rigorists in calling for their exclusion from the Christian community; Cornelius, however, favored a moderate view, seeing such harshness as undesirable, cruel, and impractical. After enduring a time of hardship in which Novatian seemed to have the upper hand (the antipope even had himself consecrated), Cornelius proved successful in securing the support of most of the bishops of the East, by synods in Rome and Carthage, and most of all by the influential St. Cyprian, Bishop of Carthage (d. 258), who rankled Cornelius by stipulating the need to make a personal investigation into the affair before deciding in one or the other's favor. His words on Cornelius's behalf did much to cement the pope's position in Rome and the wider Church. Several letters from the two to each other have survived and make for interesting reading. Cornelius was not destined to remain on the throne for long. In the middle of 252, a new wave of persecution was launched. Cornelius was arrested and shipped off to Centumcellae (modern Civitavecchia), where he died the following June. He was probably martyred, but the exact circumstances of his death are unclear. His body was taken back to Rome and placed in the cemetery of Callistus where so many other early popes were buried. Successor: St. Lucius I.

❀ **CORONATION OF A POPE**   The formal and ceremonial coronation of a newly elected pope. In the early days of the Church, the installation of a new bishop of Rome was a fairly simple affair, becoming more elaborate as the position of the papacy grew in prominence and influence. The two symbols of the coronation were traditionally the tiara and the pallium. The placing of the tiara on the head of the new pontiff was accompanied by great pomp, a ceremonial event that endured right into the late twentieth century, essentially unchanged from the sixteenth century until the reign of Pope John Paul I in 1978. By custom, the new pope was carried triumphantly into St. Peter's on the *sedia gestatoria,* surrounded by the ornately resplendent Papal Court and College of Cardinals. The crown was then placed upon the pope's head, the presiding cardinal pronouncing the words: "Receive this tiara adorned with three crowns; know that thou art the father of princes and kings, victor of the whole world under the earth, the vicar of our Lord, Jesus Christ, to whom be the glory and honor without end." This grand ceremony was last held in the traditional manner in 1963 at the coronation of Pope Paul VI. When Albino Luciani was installed as John Paul I in 1978, he chose to dispense with a formal coronation, adopting instead a simpler installation with only the pallium, thereby stressing the pastoral image he wished to project for his reign. (See also *Pallium.*)

❀ COUNCIL OF CARDINALS FOR THE STUDY OF ORGANIZATIONAL AND ECONOMIC PROBLEMS OF THE HOLY SEE   A council established in 1981 comprised of fifteen cardinals that was part of the extensive effort by Pope John Paul II to bring genuine reform to papal finances, especially after the scandal and irregularities that occurred in the 1970s. The council is comprised of fourteen cardinals from outside the Roman establishment, including Cardinals Roger Mahony of Los Angeles and John O'Connor of New York. It had a role in the successful reorganization of Vatican finances, so much so that the Holy See was finally able to remove itself from debt in 1993 for the first time in many years. (See *Finances, Vatican.*)

❀ COURTYARDS, VATICAN   The numerous courtyards found within the Vatican Museums and the Apostolic Palace. The courtyards were largely created over the centuries by the frequent building programs of the popes, who added palaces, loggias, and towers, coming into existence often where one part of the Vatican palace was joined to another part of the papal city, such as the spot where the papal residence is connected to the Sistine Chapel. Two of the most significant courts are those of Sixtus V and Saint Damase (San Damaso). The **Court of Sixtus V** is located in the Apostolic Apartments and named after Pope Sixtus

V (1585–1590), who completed the last important additions to the palace. The courtyard is surrounded by the papal apartments, especially the Pontifical Audience Apartments on the third floor. The **Court of Saint Damase** is located to the west of the Sixtus V Courtyard and is best known today as the main entrance spot to the Apostolic Apartments; it has been the site of numerous arrivals by monarchs, presidents, and diplomats, including the Israeli representatives in 1994, marking the establishing of formal relations between the Holy See and Israel. The court was also the touching scene of the return of John Paul II to the Vatican in 1981 after his recovery from the attempt on his life by Mehmet Ali Agca in St. Peter's Square. During the Middle Ages, the court was a secret garden used only by the popes. Farther to the west are four smaller courtyards, slicing across the papal palace and situated at the southern end of the Vatican Museums. These courtyards are the **Courts of the Marshal** (*Cortile del Maresciallo*), **Parrot** (*Cortile del Pappagallo*), **Borgia** (*Cortile Borgia*), and **Sentinel** (*Cortile della Sentinella*).

In the Vatican Museum are several very significant courtyards, namely the Courts of the Belvedere, Library, and Pine, part of the large complex of the Belvedere Palace in which are housed the Vatican Museums, Library, and Secret Archives. The **Court of the Belvedere** (*Cortile del Belvedere*) was the original site of the famed Statue Garden of Pope Julius II (1503–1513), started in 1503 and containing such works as the *Laocoön* and *Apollo Belvedere*. In the more profane era of the sixteenth century, the court was used for bullfights, jousting, and theatrical shows. An elephant that was presented to Pope Leo X (1513–1521) was supposedly buried in the court, but its remains have never been found in the various diggings, excavations, and modifications made in the court. The sensual enjoyments came to an end, however, under the frenetic builder Pope Sixtus V when he erected a new part for the Library. To make room, he cut the court in half. Today it is commonly used for parking by Vatican personnel or as a training ground for the Swiss Guard. The **Court of the Libary** (*Cortile della Biblioteca*) is situated between the Belvedere Courtyard to the south and the Pigna Courtyard (Court of the Pine) to the north. It was formed out of the building of two arms across the Belvedere Courtyard, which had stretched the full length occupied by the three present courts. One arm houses part of the Vatican Library and was completed toward the late 1580s by Pope Sixtus V. The other arm contains the **Braccio Nuovo** ("New Wing"), constructed under Pius VII (1800–1823) to house the numerous art treasures that had been stolen from all over the Papal States by the French under Napoleon and finally returned to papal ownership after Napoleon's fall. The Braccio Nuovo was especially used for the classical sculpture. It was renovated recently under Pope John Paul II. The **Court of the Pine** (*Cortile della Pigna*) is the most northerly of the three courts that had once comprised the Belvedere Courtyard, deriving its name from the immense bronze pinecone that stands in the Nicchione designed by Pirro Ligorio at the northern end. The pinecone once adorned a Roman fountain to the goddess Isis and later stood in the courtyard of Old St. Peter's, in the Garden of Paradise. Within the Vatican Museums is the famed **Octagonal Courtyard** (*Cortile Ottagonale*) that was originally built by Pope Innocent VIII (1484–1492) to serve as the inner cortile for the Belvedere Palace. The courtyard was taken over by Pope Julius II (1503–1513) to serve as the site of his famed sculpture garden, which came to house such masterpieces as the *Apollo Belvedere* and the *Laocoön* group. The courtyard thus served as a kind of ancestor to the Vatican Museum and is still one of the most imposing areas in the entire complex, anchoring the Pio-Clementine Museum, the Chiaramonti Museum, and the Egyptian Museum. Its octagonal shape was given to it in 1773 under Clement XIV (1769–1774). The cortile today continues to offer visitors glimpses of the *Apollo Belvedere* and the *Laocoön*.

❀ **CRESCENTII, HOUSE OF**   Also Crescenti, a noble Roman family that dominated the papacy and controlled the political life of the city throughout the late tenth century. Among the notable members were Crescentius, executed in 998 by emperor Otto III for instigating a revolt against Pope Gregory V; John II Crescentius (d. 1012), who controlled Rome as patrician from 1003, securing the election of such pliant pontiffs as John XVII, John XVIII, and Sergius IV. Following the deaths of both Sergius and John II Crescentius within weeks of each other, the House of Tusculum rose to power. When the Crescenti resisted, the Tusculans waged pitiless war, crushing their castles and driving them from the political field of Rome.

❀ **CURIA, ROMAN**   The *Curia Romana,* the central government of the Catholic Church comprised of the numerous congregations, offices, committees, tribunals, commissions, and support departments (all called dicasteries) that assist the pope in the massive task of running the affairs of the faith around the world. The Curia is centered in Rome, in and around the Vatican City State or in offices found throughout the city. It functions entirely at the will of the reigning pontiff, but the extensive bureaucracy that has performed its duties for centuries is one of the most important elements in the institutional life of the Catholic Church. The name Curia is from the Latin for court, and the term is useful in denoting the earliest nature of the papal administration, for it was a court at which officials received from the pontiff any duties he might wish to delegate. The ancestor of the Curia was the Apostolic Chancery, dated to the fourth century. The actual Curia was founded in 1588 by Pope Sixtus V (1585–1590) when he inaugurated the permanent congregations with specific areas of competence. The dicasteries represented the temporal and spiritual involvements of the popes, with such congregations as those of the Sacred Rites and Ceremonies, the Inquisition, the Papal Navy, and the maintaining of the Papal State's roads, bridges, and waters. Over the centuries many departments were abolished (the Papal Navy is rather unnecessary today) and others created. The three most memorable reforms were by Pope St. Pius X in 1908, Paul VI in 1967, and John Paul II in 1988 with the decree *Pastor Bonus,* which gave the Curia its present demeanor. The Curia was also given clearly delineated regulations in the *Regolamento Generale della Curia Romana* ("General Rules of the Roman Curia"), which was issued in March 1968 under Pope Paul. This small book, comprised of 130 different articles in rich and somber Italian, gave superb expression to the bureaucratic system of the Curia. It listed the ranks of Curial officials, including their educational, moral, and physical requirements for any and all appointments; the hours of work (thirty-three a week, and from nine o'clock to one-thirty, with provision for keeping the office open until four); holidays; suggested attire (the cassock or simar, although these have been increasingly replaced by the black suit, to the consternation of many old-timers); and the extensive protocol to be observed in the meetings of the Curial departments, such as the traditional custom of always having the presiding cardinal speak first.

❀ DAMASUS I, ST. Pope from 366 to 384, one of the longer-reigning pontiffs, he was born around 304, the son of a Spaniard who became a priest in Rome; his mother was named Laurentia. Damasus was probably born in Rome, certainly growing up there and serving as a deacon under Pope Liberius (352–366). He was elected pope on October 1, 366, but was almost immediately faced with an opposition group of adherents of Liberius who preferred the deacon Ursinus. Ursinus was consecrated in the Julian basilica while Damasus was installed in the Lateran. Violence erupted in the streets of Rome, bringing 137 dead, if the historian Ammianus Marcellinus is to be believed, as Damasus's followers, supported by armed bands of leg-breakers routed the Ursinians. What makes the event so remarkable, beyond the fact that people were killed in trying to install their own candidate, was Damasus's request for help from the prefect of the city, the first known instance of a pope asking civil authorities for assistance. The fighting continued for some weeks as the Ursinians were forced out of the city. While left in command of Rome, Damasus was forced to devote much time to repairing his tattered reputation with other ecclesiastical leaders in Italy and had to defeat repeated efforts by the Ursinians, who hurled assorted charges and accusations against him over the next years. In 371, for example, Damasus was wrongly accused of adultery, needing the emperor himself to clear his name. Despite these distractions, he worked to suppress the heresies that were plaguing the Church, such as Arianism, Macedonianism, and Donatism. He is also especially notable for being the first pontiff to consider Rome the primatial see of the Church and to press for the recognition of his office as being in direct succession to St. Peter. Damasus also met St. Jerome (d. 420), making him a secretary. At the pope's request, Jerome began work on revising the Latin translations of the Bible that would later be called the Vulgate, a lasting contribution to biblical history. The pope rebuilt old churches, built new ones, such as S. Lorenzo in Damaso, and provided new housing for the archives of the Roman Church. Successor: St. Siricius.

DAMASUS II Pope from July to August 1048, the second of the German pontiffs who were nominated (and not surprisingly elected) by Emperor Henry III (r. 1039–1056). Originally named Poppo, he was a Bavarian by descent and was serving as Bishop of Brixen (modern Bressanone, Italy) when he journeyed with Henry to Italy in autumn 1046 to settle the continuing difficulties in Rome where three different popes were claiming the papal throne (Benedict IX, Sylvester III, and Gregory VI). He took part in the proceedings that removed the three claimants and installed Clement II, going back to Germany in the spring of 1047. Following the death of Clement in October and the return of the odious Benedict IX, Poppo was nominated by Henry to be the next pope. After some delays, Poppo was finally installed in Rome and consecrated on July 17, 1048. He lasted only twenty-three days, dying on August 9, 1048. Given the peculiar circumstances of Clement's passing, it was widely rumored that Damasus had been poisoned; it was most likely malaria. Successor: St. Leo IX.

DEAN OF THE COLLEGE OF CARDINALS A cardinal who is elected among the cardinal bishops to serve as the head or highest-ranking member of the Sacred College of Cardinals, although his authority is considered to be that of *primus inter pares* (first among equals). As the dean is elected from among the cardinal bishops, he is already the holder of one of the so-called suburbicarian dioceses, but he is also always given the titular see of Ostia (one of the seven suburbicarian dioceses), this being the traditional see of the senior cardinal bishop. He is assisted by a subdean who has authority to act in his name during any time the dean might be absent. The subdean is also elected from among the ranks of the cardinal bishops. The dean oversees the many matters related to the College of Cardinals, all the while continuing in his duties within the Curia, such as the running of a Congregation. He also has important roles to play following the death of the pope and in electing his successor, as well as the honor of ordaining to the episcopacy a newly chosen pope should he not be a bishop at the time of his election. Assisting both the dean and subdean is a secretary, with a small staff. (See also *Cardinals, Sacred College of.*)

DEATH OF A POPE The inevitable event in every pontificate that is traditionally treated with important ceremony and protocol. By long-established custom, at the moment of the pope's passing or at the discovery of his remains, the first official summoned is the papal chamberlain, the camerlengo. It is his task to make certain that the pope is indeed deceased—the word of the attending physician, while medically accepted, being insufficient for the determination. In a somewhat grim ceremony, the camerlengo takes a hammer and taps the pontiff three times on the forehead. With each stroke, he calls out the pre-election name of the pope. (Thus, the camerlengo Jean Cardinal Villot would have called out "Albino! Albino! Albino!" after the shocking death of John Paul I on September 28, 1978.) This done without any response, the cardinal then defaces the Ring of the Fisherman and destroys all papal seals to avoid their misuse. The private papal apartments are sealed with tape and a wax seal. The cardinal then officially informs the members of the Curia that they have ceased to hold any office, communicates with all the members of the College of Cardinals summoning them to Rome, and then permits an announcement to the rest of the world, which by then has probably known for several hours. From this point, the complex and ritualized process begins of holding the funeral and burial of the pope and electing his successor. Nine days of masses follow, part of the formal obsequies. The deceased pope is placed in a coffin made of three layers—wood, lead, and marble—and is interred in the place appointed for him, normally within the confines of St. Peter's Basilica. At the conclusion of all ceremonies and rites, a *rogito* is compiled, the certification that the pope was formally and properly buried. The College of Cardinals then assembles in a conclave to elect a new successor of St. Peter. (See *Elections, Papal;* see also *Camerlengo, Conclave,* and *Rogito.*)

❀ **DECORATIONS, PAPAL**   Also called Pontifical Decorations, the broad name given to those honors bestowed by the Holy See upon laypeople for their loyalty and service to the Church. The decorations range from the high honors of papal knighthood to medals of honor. Papal decorations once included the conferring of nobility—in a legitimate sense—with the ranks ranging from count, to marquis, to prince; the pope also could make the title personal or hereditary. The papal nobility was an institution in Rome for centuries, but it gradually died out in the twentieth century and ceased to exist in any meaningful or traditional sense under Pope Paul VI (1963–1978). (See *Knighthood, Pontifical,* for details on the orders of knighthood and the military orders.)

The medals of honor granted by the Holy See are quite different from the Orders of knighthood in that they do not confer any membership in a knightly order nor do they ever offer noble status. Rather, they are given to men and women who have earned recognition for their service to the Church. While looked upon by some as anachronistic, the papal medals are still a deeply treasured award by many and often signify important service to the faith. The medals are normally not bestowed personally by the pope (he has better things to do with his time) but are awarded by a diploma signed by the cardinal secretary of state. The best known are the Pro Ecclesia and the Benemerenti. The Pro Ecclesia et Pontifice (For the Church and the Pontiff) was established by Pope Leo XIII in 1888 in honor of the fiftieth anniversary of his ordination to the priesthood. The Benemerenti (For Him Who Deserves It) is issued for services of a particular nature. It bears the name and likeness of the reigning pontiff on one side and a laurel with the letter *B* on the other; it comes in gold, silver, and bronze. Two other medals, not issued by the Holy See but fully approved by it, are the Lateran Cross, granted by the chapter of the Lateran Basilica, and the Medal of the Holy Land, given by the Franciscan Superior, who is Custodian of the Holy Land. (See also *Golden Rose*.)

The papal decorations bestowed upon the worthy by the Holy See. Top row, l. to r.: Supreme Order of Christ, Order of St. Gregory the Great, Order of the Holy Sepulchre; bottom row, l. to r.: Order of Pius IX, Order of St. Sylvester, Pro Ecclesia et Pontifice.

❀ DECRETALS A type of papal letter written in response to questions that may have been sent to the pope on a variety of matters. It is believed that the first known decretal was sent by Pope Siricius (384–399) to Himerus, Bishop of Tarragona. Over succeeding centuries, the decretal became one of the best ways for popes to make contributions to Church law and to extend their authority over the Universal Church, becoming the recognized authority to whom Church leaders could appeal on matters of doctrine, law, custom, and discipline. The decretals thus became quite important and were gathered together for preservation. The earliest collection was made by Dionysius Exiguus around 520. The collections of later popes, such as

Gregory IX (in 1234) and Boniface VIII (in 1298) were granted the status of being law. The most famous of all decretals were the **False Decretals,** a set of brilliant forgeries that were long considered a genuine compilation of canon law. Also called the "Decretals of Pseudo-Isidore," the collection included some legitimate papal letters, but the presence of numerous forged canons caused the entire collection to be labeled false. They were first organized in the ninth century by a forger, known by the name Isidore Mercator in France, with the apparent intention of advancing papal authority, promoting the rights and autonomy of bishops, and reducing secular interference in Church affairs. From their first appearance, the authenticity of the decretals was fully accepted. The popes themselves never declared the decretals to be genuine and chose not to exercise the prerogatives that were stipulated by the canons, even though the widespread acceptance of them made such a claim fully possible. A few canonists had doubts about the collection, but serious questions surfaced only in the Renaissance. Finally, in 1628, proof was given concerning the forged decretals. (See also *Papal Letters.*)

❀ **DEUSDEDIT, ST.**   Pope from 615 to 618, also called Adeodatus I or Deusdedit I, he was a Roman by birth and was apparently quite elderly when elected to succeed St. Boniface IV on October 19, 615. His election has been interpreted as an effort of certain parties in Rome to curtail the policies of Gregory I the Great and Boniface IV of promoting monks to all the prominent positions in the papal administration. Deusdedit was apparently careful to name regular members of the clergy instead of monks; the biography of popes, the *Liber Pontificalis,* observed that he "greatly loved the clergy." He was forced to give much of his time to assisting the poor and especially the victims of an earthquake that struck the area around Rome. He also gave support to a Byzantine force that was fighting the Lombards, who were a constant menace to Rome. His reign marked the first time that leaden seals (the *bullae*) were used on documents. (See *Bull, Apostolic* for details.) He died on November 8, 618. Successor: Boniface V.

❀ **DIONYSIUS, ST.**   Pope from 259 to 268. Dionysius was elected after an interregnum of over a year, following the martyrdom of St. Sixtus II in August 257 and the liquidation of most of the Roman ecclesiastical leadership by Emperor Valerian (r. 253–260). During that time, the Church was guided by a committee of presbyters who were reluctant to elect a new pope as long as Valerian remained in power. After word

Papal Dress

In his white robes and zucchetto (or skullcap), the Supreme Pontiff is today perhaps the most easily recognized religious and political figure in the entire world. The pope is by virtue of his office and his personality the central focus of attention and a commanding presence in any situation. His attire only makes him more so. The dress of the pope is so identifiable because it is normally so distinct. He customarily wears a white simar (a type of cassock), with white zucchetto and sash. The simar is made of regular woven wool (in the past, it was supposedly made of wool from virgin sheep); a linen version is used in warm weather. The trim is of white watered silk, while the sash has at its ends the papal coat of arms embroidered in gold and the colors of the pope's armorial bearings. A pectoral cross completes the attire. For shoes, the famed and ornate Shoes of the Fisherman have been replaced by red leather loafers. (See also *Shoes of the Fisherman.*) To this dress might be added a white double-breasted overcoat or the red *cappa,* a cloak. A red flat hat might also be worn. Beneath the simar are a Roman collar, a white shirt with French cuffs, and white socks. Minor touches might be added to this ensemble, such as the replacing of the loafers with hiking shoes or even sneakers, as occurred in 1993 when the pope visited Denver, Colorado, and went for a walk in the hills. For the occasion, he was presented white walking shoes, complete with laces in the appropriate pontifical gold color. The pope might also don some honorific headdress from the country he is visiting, to the delight of the crowds and usually with an entirely unembarrassed enthusiasm. In his travels, John Paul II has worn a sombrero, African tribal hats, and even hats from the Andes.

The popes did not always wear white. For many centuries, in fact, red was their primary color. They also regularly donned the *camauro,* a warm velvet hat, in the winter. The change came in 1566 with the election of the Dominican cardinal Michele Ghislieri. As Pope St. Pius V, he refused to give up his white robes as a member of the Order of Friar Preachers and so from that time white became reserved for the exclusive use of the popes. (See also *Gammarelli's* and *Papal Vestments,* pages 364–65.)

The pope, zucchetto in hand, walks in a white coat for cold weather, while on a trip to Poland.
(COURTESY L'OSSERVATORE ROMANO, CITTÁ DEL VATICANO.)

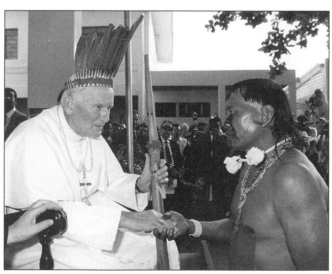

The pope in one of the variety of headdresses he has worn over the years, while on a visit to Brazil.
(CATHOLIC NEWS SERVICE.)

arrived that the emperor had died in the East, the committee gathered and chose Dionysius, a presbyter of Greek descent. He proved steady and confident, dealing with the two-fold difficulty of first rebuilding the shattered community in the wake of the persecutions and then trying his best to administer the extensive properties that had been seized by Valerian and were now returned at the command of the new emperor Gallienus (r. 260–268). He made a fairly extensive reorganization of the Roman Church and still found the time to send letters of concern to the afflicted in Caesarea after an invasion by the Persians and send money to ransom any Christians made captive. His main theological involvement was the so-called Affair of the Two Dionysii, in which he investigated the charges made against Bishop Dionysius of Alexandria concerning possible adherence to Tritheism (the heresy that the members of the Holy Trinity were three entirely different deities). In finding in favor of Dionysius of Alexandria, the pope won broad acceptance of papal authority in such matters, a significant step in winning wider recognition of the special position of the Holy See over the Church. Successor: St. Felix I.

✾ **DIOSCORUS** Antipope from September 22 to October 14, 530, against Pope Boniface II. (See *Boniface II* for details.) While technically an actual pope, Dioscorus was never recognized as such and is officially considered an antipope.

✾ **DIPLOMACY, PAPAL** See *Apostolic Delegate; Concordat; Curia, Roman; Legate, Papal; Nuncio; Pontifical Ecclesiastical Academy;* and *Secretariat of State.*

✾ **DISSIDIO** See *Lateran Treaty, Pius IX,* and *Roman Question.*

✾ **DONATION OF CONSTANTINE** One of the best-known forged documents in history, which supposedly granted to the popes spiritual authority over all of Christendom and temporal control over the Western Roman Empire. The donation, called in Latin the *Constitutum Constantini,* was said to have been given by Emperor Constantine the Great (d. 337) to Pope St. Sylvester (314–335) and used by the papacy to advance its position in temporal affairs throughout the Middle Ages. It was long accepted as completely genuine, even by the most ardent enemies of the popes, being added to most medieval collections of canon law, including the infamous False Decretals. The donation was probably first created in the eighth or ninth century somewhere in the lands of the Frankish Empire. Its purpose was to add weight to the claims of papal supremacy against the Byzantine Empire, and Pope Leo IX first used it in this capacity in 1054 as a legal document in his disagreement with Michael Cerularius, Patriarch of Constantinople, over the rights and powers of the papacy. Only in the fifteenth century did scholars begin to question seriously the authenticity of the donation; it was finally proven a forgery by such eminent figures as Nicholas of Cusa and Lorenzo Valla. (See also *Donation of Pepin.*)

❀ **DONATION OF PEPIN** A grant of land made by Pepin III the Short, father of Charlemagne and founder of the Carolingian Empire, to Pope Stephen II in 756 by which the papacy received the territories that would serve as the basis of the Papal States. The donation of land comprised the area of Rome and its surrounding territories, which were under the control of the Franks and had at one time been the holdings of the Byzantine Empire. Pepin had promised to give the land to the Church in 754 in return for papal recognition of the deposition of the last Merovingian king of the Franks and the dynasty's replacement by Pepin's own house. While the lands were under the protection of the Franks and were considered virtual dependencies, the reception by the popes of actual territories in Italy had momentous consequences for the region and the political ambitions of the papacy. (See also *Papal States.*)

❀ **DONUS** Pope from 676 to 678, also called Domus and Dommus, he was from Rome and was old at the time of his election in August 676 to succeed Adeodatus II. Confirmed by the Byzantines and consecrated on November 2, he had a rather obscure reign. He is best known for being generous to his clergy, rebuilding and restoring churches in Rome, and forcing the archbishop of Ravenna to back down in his attempt to make his see independent from Rome. He also put a marble pavement in front of St. Peter's Basilica. Successor: St. Agatho.

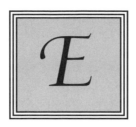

❀ **EASTER**   The most important feast of the Christian year, celebrating the resurrection of Christ and his triumph over death and the cross. The significance of the feast is made abundantly clear by the immense celebrations held in St. Peter's Basilica. The Easter Sunday mass and celebrations are naturally presided over by the pope, who also gives his annual Easter blessing, one of the most significant of the year. The blessing, with its annual address, is given in a variety of languages; Pope John Paul II regularly gives the greeting to the nations of the world in a staggering number of languages.

❀ **ECONOMIC AFFAIRS OF THE HOLY SEE, PREFECTURE FOR**   See *Prefecture for the Economic Affairs of the Holy See.*

❀ **ELECTIONS, PAPAL**   The process by which a new pontiff is lawfully and canonically elected. The election of a pope is seemingly a simple affair: the cardinals of the Church, collectively known under the title Sacred College of Cardinals, gather together as the symbolic clergy of Rome and use one of three methods to choose a new Bishop of Rome—secret ballot, compromise, or the suddenly inspired unanimous declaration of a person to be pope called *acclamatio.* Over the centuries, the rituals of papal elections and their wider implications for the Church and all nations have grown in complexity and significance. At the heart of the election, however, remains the proclaimed belief that each new pope is chosen through the guidance and even the inspiration of the Holy Spirit, a claim seemingly proven by the often stunning election surprises over the centuries.

   The history of elections dates back to the first century after the establishing of the see of Rome by Sts. Peter and Paul in the year 62. The earliest manner of picking a new bishop was in keeping with that of other dioceses in the fledgling Christian community. The clergy and laity of the Christian community assembled in the presence of the other bishops of the province and elected or simply proclaimed their new leader. This was a logical practice, so long as the community was small. Once the Church had grown in both size and social diversity (with members of both the lower and upper classes), strains developed as the various social groups put forward candidates who represented their interests. Disagreements finally erupted into violence, and the Eternal City in the fourth century was beset by rioting and fighting between the factions supporting their candidates, such as that occurring after the disputed elections of Pope St. Damasus (366–384) and antipope Ursinus in 366. So bloody was the upheaval that the prefect of the city was forced to restore order with imperial troops. As disputes became common, the Roman emperors began to arbitrate and, after the demise of the empire in the West in 476, the Germanic rulers of Italy also maintained a watch over the vote. When they were conquered by the Byzantine Empire in the sixth century, the emperors at Constantinople demanded the right to receive tribute from the new popes and the privilege of confirming the election. Each new bishop of Rome had to send word to the emperor (later his representative in Italy, the Exarch of Ravenna) and then wait, perhaps for many months, for the Byzantines to give their assent. Both inconvenient and insulting, the confirmation was last requested in 731, by Pope Gregory III. Thereafter, the popes sought the political protection of the Franks. This lasted only until the middle of the ninth century when the Frankish (or Carolingian) Empire broke apart, leaving the popes at the mercy of the ruthless Roman nobility, such as the Crescenti or the Tusculani, who regularly deposed and murdered pontiffs, and controlled the election process. What brought this lamentable state of affairs to an end were the reform elections and the rise of the College of Cardinals.

The first major reform actually came in 769 when Pope Stephen II confirmed a decree actually issued in 502 by Pope Symmachus that only the clergy should vote for the pope. In 1059, Pope Nicholas II introduced the important reform by which the cardinal bishops should elect the pope, with the subsequent approval of the cardinal priests and then the clergy and the people, although the latter groups were probably considered nominal. In 1179, the Lateran Council under Pope Alexander III ended the distinction between the cardinals and required a two-thirds majority of votes. This new need for a majority created a chronic problem: long, protracted interregnums while the often bitterly divided cardinals could not agree on a new pope. Three years would pass, for example, after the death of Clement IV in 1268. They failed to settle the election at Viterbo, despite having the roof torn off the palace and being reduced to bread and water by the exasperated inhabitants of the city; in their efforts to reach a final successful

Election Places

Popes today are elected in the Sistine Chapel in the Vatican, the newly chosen pontiff given his traditional greeting by his electors while seated upon a throne just below the overpowering fresco of the *Last Judgment* by Michelangelo. The Vatican, however, has not always been the site of papal elections; the first actually held there was in 1378, when Urban VI was chosen, soon after the return of the popes to Rome from Avignon. The Lateran Basilica and Palace were frequently used by the electors as were the basilica of Santa Maria Maggiore (Stephen II [III]), the basilica of San Martino (Sergius II), the church of Sta Maria in Pallara on the Palatine (Gelasius II), and the church of S. Gregorio (Innocent II). The Quirinal Palace was also adopted as a good election spot, housing the conclaves in 1823 (Leo XII), 1829 (Pius VIII), 1831 (Gregory XVI), and 1846 (Pius IX); the Quirinal was subsequently taken over by the Italian government of King Victor Emmanuel II, and all elections since then have been in the Vatican.

The popes spent extensive periods away from Rome and the list of cities where conclaves were held is a long one. Perhaps the oddest was Naples in 1254, when the mayor of the city, eager for the revenue and prestige of having a pope elected there, commanded that the city gates be closed and locked to force the cardinals to stay. They swiftly elected Alexander IV to get away from the place. Boniface VIII was later elected there as well, in 1294. Other cities have included the monastery of Cluny (Callistus II); Siena (Nicholas II); Verona (Urban III); Ferrara (Gregory VIII); Pisa (Clement III); Perugia (Honorius III, Honorius IV, Celestine V, and Clement V); Anagni (Innocent IV); Viterbo (Urban IV, Gregory X, John XXI, and Martin IV); Arezzo (Innocent V); Lyons (John XXII); Constance (Martin V); and Avignon (Benedict XII, Clement VI, Innocent VI, Urban V, and Gregory XI). The last election not held in Rome was in Venice in 1800 and was the stressful conclave that produced Pius VII. (See also *Conclave* and *Elections, Papal*.)

vote, the cardinals wasted no time in mourning the passing of their own fellow members of the college. When one old cardinal fell ill, they assumed he was at death's door and stuffed the Prince of the Church into a coffin. Only his protests that he was still very much alive prevented a most untimely burial. Finally, the eighteen surviving cardinals chose Gregory X (1271–1276). In 1274, he inaugurated the conclave system that has, with some modifications, remained in force to the present day. (See also *Conclave,* and box, *Election Places.*)

❀ **ELEUTHERIUS, ST.**
Pope from around 175 to 189, he reigned over the Christian community during a period of quiet in the persecution of the faith. Eleutherius was probably from Nicopolis, Greece, and was perhaps a deacon in the service of Popes Anicetus (*c.* 155–166) and Soter (*c.* 166–174). Elected to succeed Soter, he no doubt took comfort in the fact that while Christians were being persecuted in many

✝ ELEVThERIVS

Pope Eleutherius.

parts of the empire, the Roman officials under Emperor Marcus Aurelius (r. 161–180) did not press a violent anti-Christian program in Rome, a policy apparently maintained through much of the early period of the reign of Emperor Commodus (180–192). Eleutherius spent part of his pontificate trying to deal with the heretical followers of Montanism, a highly rigorist and pessimistic sect that stressed the sinfulness of humanity. The popes had been slow in confronting the sect, and Eleutherius most likely heeded the request of the Christians of Lyons who wrote him a now-lost letter for him to deal with the matter but not in too harsh a manner. He is traditionally said to have died in May 189. His burial spot was on Vatican Hill. Successor: St. Victor I.

❀ **ELIGENDO, ROMANI PONTIFICI**   The apostolic constitution ("On the Election of the Roman Pontiff"), issued by Pope Paul VI on October 1, 1975, that established the regulations covering the election of his successor as pope. The constitution, an extensive and comprehensive document that was over sixty pages long and written in magnificent Latin, replaced the rules governing papal elections that had been in force quite literally for centuries. While introducing a number of interesting innovations, the decree did not alter the time-honored custom of the conclave, attended by the members of the College of Cardinals and conducted in secret. In fact, Paul took several measures to increase the secrecy by making stern provisions for sworn confidentiality concerning the proceedings and the use of technical surveillance equipment to check for electronic bugs, listening devices, and cameras. *Eligendo* also stipulated: no cardinal over the age of eighty will be eligible to vote; there will be no more than 120 electors; all cardinal officeholders in the Curia will immediately resign their posts upon the death of the pope; the cardinals in conclave will not have any radios, tape recorders, or transmitters of any kind; and they are to be accompanied by only one assistant who is not allowed into the conclave itself save under highly unusual circumstances such as to assist an infirm Prince of the Church who may be in a wheelchair. The *Eligendo* remains in force and will probably serve as the basis for the next papal elections, unless Pope John Paul II or his immediate successors introduce changes into the process. (See also *Conclave* and *Elections, Papal.*)

❀ **ELIGO IN SUMMAM PONTIFICEM**   Latin phrase meaning "I elect as Supreme Pontiff" that is printed on each ballot cast by the cardinals during the conclave to elect a new pope. The phrase is placed on the top of the ballot card with space underneath for the cardinal to write the name of the person he believes to be worthy of election. The cardinal should not place his own name on the ballot (especially if he has a chance of winning, as it would be more than embarrassing to the pope-elect to win by a unanimous vote, including his own), and cardinals are instructed to alter their handwriting so that the scrutineers who read the ballots for the count should have no way of recognizing who has voted for whom (this is more logical than it sounds, as most of the cardinals know one another quite well and share private handwritten letters). After each session of voting, the ballots are burned and, no majority being achieved, new ballots are handed out. (See *Conclave; Elections, Papal;* and *Sfumata.*)

❀ **ENCYCLICAL**   A type of papal document that is normally concerned with an important issue or topic that relates to the general welfare of the Church. In advancing his position or expressing his view on some matter, the encyclical is one of the most significant papal documents and its release is surrounded by much fanfare and close scrutiny by analysts and observers. Customarily, an encyclical is addressed to all the bishops of the world, although on a number of occasions, the encyclicals have been granted to all of the faithful of the Church. The popes issue two types of encyclicals: letters and epistles. The epistle has a limited audience and is targeted by the pope to a specific country, being addressed to the bishops and people of that region. It has as its purpose to draw attention to some lamentable situation, to warn against some unfortunate development, or to celebrate or commemorate some historical event. An example of this type of encyclical was promulgated by Pope Pius XI (1922–1939) in 1932 to protest the severe persecution of the Church in Mexico. The most famous epistle was *Mit Brennender Sorge* ("With Burning Sadness") issued by Pius in 1937 and denouncing Nazi Germany. The second type of encyclical is the letter. This is more formal than the epistle and has a much broader audience. Both types of document are not considered infallible pronouncements by the pope, but they do fall under the heading of the Magisterium, or teaching authority of the Church, and are thus to be respected and granted internal assent by all Catholics. The encyclicals of Pope John Paul II have covered a wide variety of topics, from labor (*Laborem Exercens,* 1981), to social concerns (*Sollicitudo Rei Socialis,* 1987), to morality (*Splendor Veritatis,* 1993). **Social encyclicals** are concerned with important or pressing social issues, helping to form the basis of Catholic social teachings. The first so-called social encyclical was *Rerum Novarum* (1891) by Pope Leo XIII (1878–1903), called the magna carta of Catholic social doctrine. Other memorable social encyclicals include *Quadragesimo Anno* (1931) by Pope Pius XI, *Mater et Magistra* (1961) and *Pacem in Terris* (1963) by John XXIII, and *Populorum Progressio* (1967) by Paul VI. Pope John Paul II has written several very important social encyclicals: *Laborem Exercens, Sollicitudo Rei Socialis, Evangelium Vitae* (1995), and *Centessimus Annus* (1991).

❀ **EUGENE I, ST.**   Pope from 654 to 657, also called Eugenius and said by contemporaries to be kind and saintly, he was a Roman by birth, literally raised in the churches of the Eternal City and growing old in the service of its bishops. He succeeded to the papacy on August 10, 654, after Pope Martin I had been deposed and banished by the Byzantines for his steadfast opposition to Monothelitism, which was then being advanced by the Greeks (a theological position that Christ had only one will, instead of two, human and divine). For his stubbornness, Martin had been flogged, cruelly humiliated, and finally imprisoned, dying from starvation and abuse in June 653. Before his death, however, Martin wrote a letter stating that he recognized Eugene as a rightful pope; he had perhaps hoped that the Romans might wait until he was dead before naming a successor, but the Byzantines put considerable pressure on them to elect someone and Martin accepted this as unavoidable. Eugene was probably acceptable to the Greeks because they anticipated little trouble from him. The new pope quickly disappointed them. He picked up where Martin had left off, remaining adamant on the subject of Monothelitism and refusing to recognize the Patriarch of Constantinople, Peter, because of his heretical sympathies. The incensed Emperor Constans II (r. 641–668) promised to hand out the same treatment on Eugene if he did not give in, but the ruler's promised brutality was delayed by military campaigns, and by the time he was ready to vent his rage, Eugene had died (on June 2, 657). He was buried in St. Peter's. Some scholars prefer to date his reign from the actual death of Martin in September 655, in deference to the martyred pontiff. Successor: St. Vitalian.

❀ **EUGENE II** Pope from 824 to 827. According to the often unreliable *Liber Pontificalis,* Eugene was described as a lover of peace, learned and eloquent, and wholly devoted to doing what was pleasing to God. Little at all is known of his early days, but he was an archpriest in Rome at the death of St. Paschal I. In the days that followed the pope's passing, the Romans were in a state of severe disagreement as to who should follow him. One party desired to have a pontiff who would continue in Paschal's style. This was a most distressing prospect to the nobles of Rome, who had feuded with Paschal and were eager for someone more reliable. Their candidate was Eugene. He won election on June 6, 824, marking a victory for the Roman nobility and their Frankish patrons. Eugene recalled the nobles exiled by his predecessor and took steps to care for the widows and orphans made so through assassination and execution. He welcomed the co-emperor Lothair I to Rome and accepted the *Constitutio Romana* (Roman Constitution, November 11, 824), a decree acknowledging the supremacy of the emperors in Rome and their de facto mastery over the papacy. By the terms of the constitution, popes were to be elected by the vote of both the people and the clergy of Rome, but with the stipulation that such an election be approved by the emperor and that the new pope should take an oath of loyalty. The decree would have lasting implications for the papacy and for relations with the emperors. While surrendering papal authority in political matters, Eugene strove to maintain ecclesiastical independence, using a synod in Rome in November 826 to enact several reforming measures and disciplinary canons (such as a decree against simony). He displayed the same resolve in the matter of the veneration of images that had precipitated the famous Iconoclast Controversy in the Byzantine Empire and Frankish lands. Despite the findings of a theological commission established by Emperor Louis I the Pious (r. 814–840) and the suggestions of both the Frankish and Byzantine emperors, Eugene would not change his position, proclaiming that the veneration of images was permissible. In this, Louis did not try to press him. In 826, Eugene also commended to the entire Church the important missionary endeavor of St. Anskar (d. 865) the Apostle of the North, among the pagans of Denmark, a cause close to Eugene's heart. He died on August 27, 827. Successor: Valentine.

�֎ **EUGENE III** Pope from 1145 to 1153, the first pope from the Cistercian Order. Bernardo Pignatelli was born near Pisa to a family of humble origins, although some of Eugene's biographers insisted that he was of noble parentage. Educated in Pisa, he entered the Church and came to hold office in the diocese of Pisa. In 1130, however, he met the magnetic and overpowering St. Bernard of Clairvaux (1090–1153), falling completely under his saintly spell and entering the monastery of Clairvaux where he became his pupil. Earning the trust of the Cistercians, he was sent on several missions before receiving appointment as abbot of SS. Vincent and Anastasius outside Rome, a position he was still holding when Pope Lucius II died on February 15, 1145. His election came as an absolute surprise to the Church, most of all to St. Bernard, who expressed amazement that the cardinals should choose so inexperienced an individual. The circumstances of his election were far from ordinary.

Following Lucius's death, the cardinals hastily arranged his funeral and removed themselves from the city of Rome proper to avoid any possible interference from the Roman Senate, which they feared might demand that the next pope accept their supremacy. Settling at the isolated cloister of St. Caesarius on the Appian Way, they took the extremely unusual step of deciding to elect someone not in the conclave. Their choice, for some unknown reason, fell to the obscure Abbot Pignatelli. Elected on the same day of Lucius's death, he took the name Eugenius, was enthroned at the Lateran, and promptly fled the city to avoid being murdered by the Roman mob. He was consecrated at Farfa just to the north of Rome, and from there went to Viterbo, from where he managed to make a brief peace with the commune of the city. Christmas passed peacefully, but in January 1146 he was forced to flee back to Viterbo. One of his chief efforts was to organize the Second Crusade, the military campaign that he felt was necessary after the fall of the Crusader possession of Edessa in the Holy Land. To preach the crusade, Eugene appointed Bernard, but he traveled to France himself around 1147 to further his plea. The resulting expedition proved a crushing disappointment, both in terms of its failure in defeating the Muslims and also because it was useless in extending a dialogue with the Byzantines, who were increasingly drifting away from the West. Such was the sentiment against the Greeks, in fact, that Eugene himself had to reject an idea to attack Constantinople. (See *Innocent III.*)

Pope Eugene III.

Returning to Italy in 1148, Eugene excommunicated the radical social leader Arnold of Brescia, being denounced by Arnold as "a man of blood." In 1149, with the help of the Normans, Eugene was able to enter Rome once more, but the commune and Arnold made him reconsider and leave, another disappointment. Eager to improve relations with the Holy Roman Emperors, he negotiated the Treaty of Constance (1153) with Frederick I Barbarossa, and used his relationship with the German king to negotiate yet another peace with the Romans. He anticipated the arrival of Frederick in Rome in 1153, but the pope died before the ruler could arrive. Eugene passed away at Tivoli on July 8, 1153. Despite Bernard's fears, Eugene proved an able pontiff. The great saint had written for him a treatise, *De Consideratione,* detailing the duties of the pontiff, and was a frequent counselor to the pope, although his influence upon his one-time student has been somewhat exaggerated. Successor: Anastasius IV.

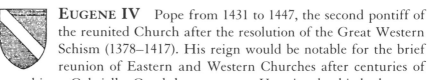 **EUGENE IV** Pope from 1431 to 1447, the second pontiff of the reunited Church after the resolution of the Great Western Schism (1378–1417). His reign would be notable for the brief reunion of Eastern and Western Churches after centuries of schism. Gabriello Condulmaro was a Venetian by birth, born to wealthy but not noble parents around 1383. His uncle was Gregory XII, a relative who was conspicuous in the favor shown to his nephew. Gabriello was made Bishop of Siena in 1407 and a cardinal in May 1408. As a cardinal, he participated in the Council of Constance (1414–1418) that brought an end to the division of the Church. Pope Martin V (1417–1431) named him governor of the March of Ancona and Bologna. In the conclave to find a successor to Martin V, Gabriello won election on March 3, 1431, because of the hope of many cardinals that he would be amenable to the continued key role of the council in running the affairs of the Church, the overall process called conciliarism. The test of this was to be the Council of Basle (1431–1449), which Martin had summoned and which Eugene had confirmed. The reforming council soon betrayed its intentions in asserting the rights of the council over the pope and thus earned Eugene's doubts and mistrust. He used the fact that the council was so poorly attended to dissolve it on December 18, 1431. The move seemed at first an inevitable cause of another division in the Church, but the pope's gamble paid off when Emperor Sigismund (r. 1410–1437)—whom Eugene wisely crowned at Rome in May 1433—agreed to negotiate a settlement between the pope and the council. The cardinals in Basle were undeterred, however, proceeding apace with their version of reform, namely a gradual reduction in papal influence and power and the sharp curtailing of the papal Curia. Eugene opposed its activities and convened a new council in Italy—Ferrara, later Florence. The rump council (those cardinals who refused to leave Basle) declared Eugene to be deposed, replacing him with the antipope Felix V (actually Amadeus VII, Duke of Savoy). Eugene refused to recognize the acts of the council, going ahead with his own plans. These were mainly focused on trying to effect a reunion with the Greek Church. He was aided in this by the increasingly desperate condition of the Byzantine Empire, which was on its last legs and being slowly overrun by the Ottoman Turks. A formal reunion was signed in early 1439, a triumph

for the pope but a reunion that unfortunately was brief. The Byzantines were soon disappointed that no help was forthcoming from the West and so repudiated their agreement, the last realistic hope for Christian unity. The city of Constantinople would fall on September 29, 1453. Through patience and diligence, Eugene was able to defeat the council in the end by winning the assent of his authority by the bulk of the cardinals. His victory signaled a distinct defeat for conciliarism and a formal restoration of unquestioned authority for the pope over the Church.

Eugene had troubles other than the council. Reversing the policy of his predecessor, he forced the cardinals belonging to the Colonna family to give up the wealth they had amassed under the pontificate of their own member, Martin V, and thus brought their vengeance. They instigated a revolt in Rome, driving Eugene out in May 1434. He could not return until 1443. He also was faced with the Pragmatic Sanction of Bourges issued by King Charles VII of France in 1438, a decree that sought to curtail papal power in the activities of the French Church. Another personal humiliation was the destruction of a crusader force of Christian knights at Varna in 1444 by the Ottoman Turks. This grand military venture had been organized by Eugene, and he staked much of his personal prestige on its success. Successor: Nicholas V.

❀ **EULALIUS** Antipope from 418 to 419, a Greek, he was an archdeacon in Rome when Pope St. Zosimus died on December 26, 417. Supported by a small group of presbyters, Eulalius was elected on December 27, the previous pope barely interred. The next day, ignoring these developments, the majority of the Roman clergy chose instead Boniface (I). Events became stranger the following day when both were duly consecrated, Eulalius in the Lateran and Boniface in the church of S. Marcello. Unlike other rival or contested elections, this one was relatively peaceful, with both sides appealing to the Roman emperor Honorius (393–423). On the basis of a report by the pagan prefect of the city, Symmachus, he found in favor of Eulalius, but then reversed himself when a full and contradictory report was sent by the Roman presbyters. The emperor ordered both claimants to withdraw from Rome to await a decision by a council to assemble at Spoleto in June 419. Boniface followed the command, but Eulalius ill-advisedly returned to Rome in the mistaken belief that his position could be improved by presiding at Easter services. Rioting broke out, and troops were used to throw him out of Rome. Honorius then decreed Boniface to be the legitimate pontiff. Eulalius accepted the decree with a certain aplomb, departing for Atium (modern Anzio). When Boniface died in September 422, it was feared that Eulalius might try to reclaim the see, but he declined, despite the urging of his followers, perhaps knowing what the imperial response would be and already failing in health. He died in 423.

❀ EUSEBIUS, ST.   Pope from April to August 309 or 310. This pope is best known through two main sources, the papal listings of the *Liberian Catalogue* and the epitaph for his tomb that was ordered by Pope St. Damasus and which survived through ancient transcripts. A fragment of the original, with a sixth-century marble copy (ordered to replace the original), was discovered by the archaeologist Giovanni De Rossi (1822–1894) in the crypt of Eusebius, in the Catacomb of Callistus. He was chosen to succeed Marcellus on April 18, 309 (or 310), but his reign would prove to be short because he was exiled to Sicily by Emperor Maxentius around August 17. He died there soon after; his body was brought back in 311. The main event of his reign, as noted in the epitaph, was a dispute that occurred in Rome over the so-called *lapsi,* those Christians who had turned away from the faith during the persecutions of the time and who sought forgiveness and readmission to the Christian community. Eusebius felt that they should be readmitted, but only after proper penance. He disagreed with some Christians, headed by one Heraclius, who argued against any punishment. Successor: St. Miltiades. (See also *Liberian Catalogue.*)

❀ EUTYCHIANUS, ST.   Pope from 275 to 283, also known as Eutychianos and simply Eutychian, he was perhaps from Tuscany and was the son of Marinus, if the *Liber Pontificalis* is to be believed. One of the more obscure pontiffs, he was the successor to Pope St. Felix I, probably reigning from January 4, 275, until December 7, 283. The lack of information about a reign that lasted nearly a decade was due to the unreliability of the *Liber Pontificalis* and probably the destruction of so many records during the brutal persecutions under Emperor Diocletian in the late third century. Eutychianus himself probably did not die a martyr as his particular period was relatively free of oppression. Successor: St. Gaius.

❀ EVARISTUS, ST.   Pope from 97 to 105, the fifth Bishop of Rome and the fourth successor to St. Peter, Evaristus was the successor to St. Clement I. Little reliable information is known about him, but sources such as the *Liber Pontificalis* state he was a Jew from Bethlehem. He may have died as a martyr, but this cannot be verified; neither can the tradition that he was buried on Vatican Hill near St. Peter. Successor: St. Alexander I.

❀ **EX CATHEDRA** Latin term meaning "from the throne" that is used for the formal pronouncement by the pope while exercising his rights of papal infallibility on matters of faith and morals. A pronouncement *ex cathedra* implies that he is speaking as head of the Universal Church and his words and teachings are official, solemn, and binding upon all Catholics. Such a pronouncement is without appeal and is considered unreformable. The pope needs the consent of no one in the Church to make his declaration, but it is made only on matters of grave importance. (See *Infallibility, Papal.*)

❀ **EXTRA OMNES!** The cry meaning "Everyone out!" that is made by the Papal Master of Ceremonies to announce the start of the conclave to elect a new pope. The command is given after the cardinals have assembled in the Sistine Chapel and signals that all others must depart the conclave area so that the Princes of the Church can be locked in the Chapel to begin their deliberations.

✿ **FABIAN, ST.** Pope from 236 to 250. A native of Rome, he was pontiff during a most welcomed peaceful period, the empire being spared large-scale persecutions by Roman officials against Christians. Fabian followed St. Anterus and was described as a remarkable individual, fulfilling the truly amazing event that supposedly occurred at the gathering to choose a new Bishop of Rome. Fabian had come to Rome from his farm nearby for the election and was not considered by anyone as a possible candidate. At the actual gathering, the crowd was stunned when a dove flew over their heads and landed on Fabian's head. Taking the event as a rather clear sign from God that he was to be their leader, the crowd chose Fabian and installed him on the Chair of Peter. The story, told by the historian Eusebius, is considered legendary, but Fabian was clearly a good leader to the community. The main acts of his reign included ordering extensive work done to improve the catacombs and the division of the diocese of Rome into seven districts, each one supervised by a deacon, with the help of subdeacons. This arrangement would later influence the formation of the College of Cardinals. Fabian's time as pope ended abruptly and tragically on January 20, 250. Emperor Trajanus Decius (r. 249–251), who once stated he would rather face a usurper supported by five legions than hear another pope had been elected, launched a terrible persecution, starting with Fabian. The pontiff was buried in the Crypt of the Popes in the Catacomb of Callistus. His body was later moved to the Church of San Sebastiano where his sarcophagus was found in 1915. Successor: St. Cornelius.

✿ **FABRIC OF ST. PETER'S** Also *fabbrica,* the name given to the branch of the papal government that has authority over the care of St. Peter's Basilica. A "fabric" in general terms refers to the church building and all of the possessions found within it; in a more narrow sense it denotes the office or institution that has authority over the fabric, the terms becoming interchangeable and synonymous. The Fabric of St. Peter's has been in existence since the reign of Pope Julius II (1503–1513), roughly from the time that he laid the cornerstone for the new St. Peter's Basilica. Since that time, the *fabbrica* has been in continuous existence, with the enormous task of caring for the largest church in the world and everything related to it. Overall authority is placed in the hands of the President of the Fabric of St. Peter's; he is always a cardinal and is assisted by an archbishop. (See also *Saint Peter, Basilica of.*)

✿ **FELIX I, ST.**   Pope from 269 to 274. One of the most obscure of all the popes, he was the successor to St. Dionysius, reigning from January 5, 269, until December 30, 274, although these dates are often considered unreliable. Next to nothing is known with certainty about him, save for his writing a letter on the Church's teaching about the Holy Trinity that found wide circulation among the bishops of the East. According to the *Liber Pontificalis,* he died a martyr, a statement not supported by other sources. The *Liber* also claims that he built a basilica on the Via Aurelia, the same church in which he was buried. Another source, the *Liberian Catalogue,* has him buried in the Crypt of the Popes in the cemetery of Callistus on the Appian Way. Successor: St. Eutychianus.

✿ **FELIX II**   Antipope from 355 to 365. The rise of Felix as an antipope was made possible by the banishment of Pope Liberius from Rome by Emperor Constantius II (r. 337–361) for his refusal to adopt the creed of Arianism. The clergy of Rome took an oath not to elect a successor to Liberius as long as he lived, but they soon came under pressure from the emperor to do so; Felix, an archdeacon, took the oath as well. He was summoned, however, to Milan and the imperial court and was consecrated pope by several Arian bishops. Because the act was undertaken by the emperor (known for his volatile temper) the Roman clergy accepted the consecration despite its severe irregularities. The Roman people had another opinion on the matter. They steadfastly refused to recognize Felix, going so far as to confront Constantius during a visit on May 357 and demand angrily that he bring Liberius back to them. When Liberius was at last returned in 358, the jubilant crowd gave him a thunderous greeting and promptly tossed Felix out of the city. When he returned with the help of some followers and established himself in the Basilica Julia, an angry mob stormed it and forcibly expelled him again. Taking the hint, he retreated to the suburbs and built a church there. It seems that for a time there was an urban pope and a suburban one, Liberius residing in the Lateran and Felix in his little church outside the city. This peculiar situation was the source of irritation to the prefect of the city, who had the duty of preventing bloodshed while spirits in both camps ran high. The situation may well have deteriorated had Felix not died on November 22, 365. Ironically, he was remembered with more fondness than Liberius. Indeed, in many lists, he was considered one of the popes.

�֍ **FELIX III, ST.**   Pope from 483 to 492, he is also numbered Felix III (II) owing to the fact that in some lists Felix II was considered a pope and in others an antipope. Felix was a Roman and an ancestor of Pope St. Gregory I the Great through the family he raised before entering the religious life after the death of his wife. He was elected to succeed St. Simplicius through the involvement of an official named Basilius, a servant of King Odoacer, a German who had come to rule Italy and whose claim to fame was overthrowing the last Roman Emperor in the West in 476. Basilius was active in the election at the request of Simplicius, who wanted to ensure a smooth transition. His reign was much preoccupied with matters in the Eastern Empire, most notably the unorthodox activities of the Patriarch of Constantinople, Acacius. On the grounds that Acacius was supporting the heretical cause of Monophysitism, Felix sent him a declaration of excommunication; it was announced to the whole world when a group of overzealous monks actually pinned it to his vestments while the patriarch was saying a mass. The excommunication sparked off the Acacian Schism, which divided the Eastern and Western Churches from 484 until 519. The attitude displayed by Felix in this and other matters points to a pontiff who was both certain of authority but rather stubborn and harsh in its execution. Successor: St. Gelasius I.

✖ **FELIX IV**   Pope from 526 to 530. Also Felix IV (III), he owed his election largely to the influence of Theodoric, King of the Ostrogoths and master of Italy, and the genuine fear that the Germanic king justifiably earned among the people of Rome. He was consecrated on July 12, 526, to succeed John I who had died in prison at Ravenna as the rather unpleasantly treated guest of Theodoric. The king, probably seeking a reliable person to serve as pope, stepped in and suggested very firmly that Felix be elected. As it was, he proved a competent pope, using his good relations with Theodoric and then his heir and grandson Athalaric (under the regency of the lad's mother, Amalasuntha, daughter of Theodoric) to further the cause of the Church. He received from Amalasuntha the gift of two pieces of property in the Roman Forum (*Forum Romanum*), one of which was a pagan temple, the other an office for land registry. The temple was converted into the Church of SS. Cosmas and Damian which still stands. In Church matters, Felix convened the second Council of Orange in 529 to bring an end to the ongoing controversy over grace and gave his full approval to the teachings of St. Augustine on both original sin and grace. To provide for an orderly succession, Felix took the highly unusual step of placing the pallium (or symbol of his office; see *Pallium*) on the shoulders of his trusted archdeacon, Boniface, thereby making clear his desire that Boniface should follow him. After his death on September 22, 530, these wishes were not executed without protest and a schism soon broke out, precisely what he had hoped to avoid. Successor: Boniface II.

FELIX V Antipope from 1439 to 1449. Amadeus VIII, Duke of Savoy came to be antipope Felix V through the actions of the rump council of Basle (1431–1439) which was feuding with Pope Eugene IV (1431–1447). Born in 1383, he became Count of Savoy in 1391, remaining effective ruler of his territory until 1440, although he abdicated in name only in 1434 in favor of his son Ludovico. At the time of his inheritance, Savoy was ruled by a count, but through his diplomatic skill, he added so many new holdings that Emperor Sigismund elevated him to the rank of duke in 1416. He was profoundly saddened by the death of his wife in 1422 and his son in 1431, and became deeply spiritual, retiring in 1434 to Ripaille on Lake Geneva to lead a life of prayer and contemplation with a group of knights who had formed with him the Order of St. Maurice. He was a close observer of the activities of the Council of Basle and when that body deposed Pope Eugene in 1439, it also elected him pope (on November 5, 1439), sending a delegation to inform him. He hesitated for some time before accepting their offer, but on January 6, 1440, he formally abdicated as duke; on June 24, 1440, he was consecrated and crowned as Felix V at Basle, having previously been ordained. He was elected by an assortment of clerics, including one cardinal, seven abbots, and eleven bishops. His rise as a claimant to the Holy See was not greeted with thunderous applause in Christendom, and he never could rouse much support beyond his own lands. Further, his relations were frequently poor with the very council members who had elected him. Eugene excommunicated him in March. Quickly sick of the complaints about and whining of his electors, he left Basle and settled back in Savoy, where his attempts at organizing a Curia were fruitless. He was aided most ably by Aeneas Sylvius Piccolomini (the future Pope Pius II) as his private secretary, but it was increasingly obvious that Eugene was supported by nearly the full weight of Europe's political powers. He thus entered into negotiations with Eugene, and on April

7, 1449, he stepped down as self-declared pope. Generously, Eugene made him a cardinal and appointed him apostolic vicar general of Savoy and several other dioceses. Amadeus died on January 7, 1451, the last of the antipopes.

❀ **FIESOLE, FRA GIOVANNI DA**   See *Fra Angelico.*

❀ **FINANCES, VATICAN**   See under the following: *Administration of the Patrimony of the Holy See; Bank, Vatican; Council of Cardinals for the Study of Organizational and Economic Problems of the Holy See; Curia, Roman; Prefecture for the Economic Affairs of the Holy See;* and *Secretariat of State.*

❀ **FISHERMAN, RING OF THE**   See *Ring of the Fisherman.*

❀ **FISHERMAN, SHOES OF THE**   See *Shoes of the Fisherman.*

❀ **FLABELLUM**   Also flabella in plural, a type of long-handled fan that was used during a mass to keep insects away from the sacred species and the priest. It is best known, however, for its long use in solemn papal processions whenever the pope was carried on the *sedia gestatoria,* the portable papal throne. One of the most lavish elements in the pomp and circumstance that surrounded the pontiff right up until the reign of Pope Paul VI (1963–1978), the flabellum was made of leather, decorated with superb red velvet and gold embroidery; the papal coat of arms was worked onto the scarlet field in gold, the tiara regularly decorated with rubies and emeralds. On top of the spread (the body of the fan) was an array of ostrich plumes tipped with peacock feathers. During the papal procession, the flabella moved behind the throne, and during papal ceremonies were always in view, gently swaying to provide air to the pontiff and to keep flies and mosquitoes away. Increasingly viewed as a relic of a bygone age, the flabellum was slowly edged out of processions, its final demise ensured by the cessation of the use of the *sedia gestatoria* and the numerous reforms of papal court ceremonial. Were a pope so disposed, the fan could be brought back, but this today seems more than unlikely. (See also *Sedia gestatoria.*)

❀ **FLAG, PAPAL**   The official flag of the Vatican City State that was officially authorized in 1929 by Pope Pius XI. The flag is divided vertically into two equal fields of yellow and white, the white field bearing the papal insignia of the tiara, superimposed on a pair of crossed keys of gold and silver. The tiara is said to represent the triple character of the papacy, namely as teacher, ruler, and Vicar of Christ. The keys portray the power of the pope on earth and in heaven to bind and to loose from the power of sin. The flag is said to be the same as the one adopted by Pope Benedict XII in 1342 while at Avignon, taken supposedly from the yellow and white flag used by the crusader Godfrey de Bouillon; over this flag, Benedict superimposed the papal insignia.

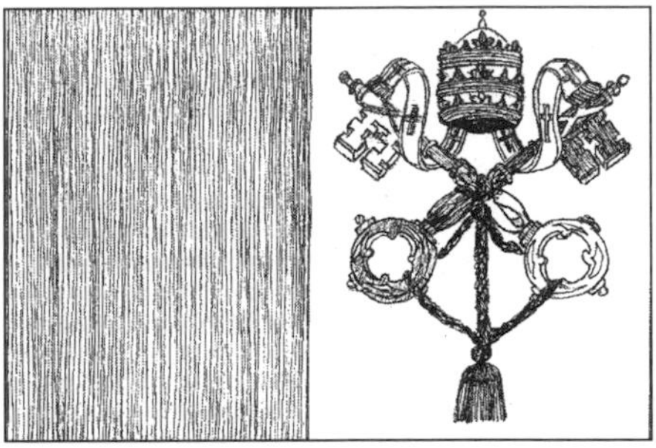

The papal flag.

FLAT HAT Also called the *capello Romano* (or Roman hat), the hat that was traditionally worn by ecclesiastics whenever they were outside in a cassock. Customarily, the flat hat has a round shaped crown, with a brim approximately three inches wide. It is normally of beaver, but can be made of felt. The color varies according to the wearer. Priests, bishops, and cardinals wear a black hat tied with different colored cord: black for priests, green and gold for bishops, and red and gold for cardinals. The pope also can wear the flat hat. His is red, with a red and gold band, the brim held up by small gold strings. John Paul II has worn the hat on his many travels, but he has also donned sombreros, Indian bonnets, and even African tribal headwear, much to the delight of the throngs in attendance. (See also *Papal Dress,* pages 120–21.)

FONTANA, DOMENICO Roman architect (d. 1607) of the Late Renaissance who was responsible for a number of important contributions to the Vatican and St. John Lateran. Fontana was born at Merli on the Lake of Lugano, journeying to Rome where he undertook an intensive study of the ancient and contemporary masters in art and architecture. His early work won the confidence of Cardinal Montalto (the future Pope Sixtus V) and earned for him the commission to erect a chapel in the church of Santa Maria Maggiore (the Chapel of the Manger). After completing another project for the cardinal, Fontana had the pleasure of seeing his patron elected pope in 1585. Sixtus named him the architect for the ongoing construction of St. Peter's, a massive project that already had taxed the talents of Bramante and Michelangelo. Armed with the symbol of papal approval—the title Knight of the Golden Spur—Fontana added a lantern to the dome of the basilica and proposed to increase the length of the interior through a more developed nave. His alterations of the church of St. John Lateran included the north facade with the loggia from which the popes give a blessing at various times. He also designed the building that came to house two surviving elements of the old Lateran Palace (the principal residence of the pope until 1309), the *Scala Sancta* and the *Sancta Sanctorum* (the private papal chapel). Particularly notable was the establishing in 1586 of the obelisk in the square of St. Peter's, an event so remarkable at the time that he erected three more in the Piazza del Popolo, Piazza di S. Maria Maggiore, and the Piazza di S. Giovanni Laterano. Fontana remained in the service of Sixtus's successor, Clement VIII, but eventually fell out of favor and moved to Naples, dying there. (See also *Obelisk of Caligula* and *Saint Peter, Basilica of.*)

❀ **FORMOSUS**   Pope from 891 to 896, who in death earned lasting fame for his participation in the gruesome Cadaver Synod. Born around 816, Formosus was probably a native of Rome, first receiving mention in history when he was appointed bishop of Porto in 864 by Pope Nicholas I. Winning the confidence of the pope, he was sent to Bulgaria as a legate. His association with the ruler of Bulgaria, King Boris I (r. 852–889) proved so amicable that the king petitioned Nicholas and then Adrian II to appoint Formosus the archbishop of Bulgaria. Neither pope was willing to acquiesce, and Formosus remained in Rome as a servant of the popes. Under Pope John VIII, he was ordered to offer the imperial crown to Charles II the Bald (r. 875–877), but this move was opposed by many servants in the court of the pope. Fearing possible reprisals, some officials in Rome fled from the city. For this act, and per- haps owing to some personal dislike, John excommunicated Formosus and deposed him as bishop in April 876. In 878, Formosus was par- doned, in return for his promise to remain in exile (he lived in Sens) and not to pursue his old see. This peculiar set of circumstances ended with the accession of Pope Marinus I (882–884) who recalled him to Rome and reappointed him as bishop of Porto. He remained in Rome and served both Marinus and Stephen V (VI) (885–891) without apparent incident. On October 6, 891, he succeeded Stephen as pope.

While advanced in years, he proved quite active in two main areas: dealing with the Eastern Church and attempting to destroy the ruthless Guido (or Guy) III of Spoleto. His efforts at healing the poor relations with the Byzantines came to nothing, his hopes for a peaceful end to the schism that had developed failing to find appeal with the

Greeks. Far more troublesome was his relationship with Guido. This nobleman had forced Stephen to crown him emperor and in 892 compelled Formosus to crown his son Lambert co-emperor. The Spoletans, however, proved so violently unpredictable that Formosus appealed to the king of the East Franks, Arnulf, for help. After the death of Guido in 894, Arnulf invaded Italy, seizing Rome in 896 and receiving coronation by Formosus as emperor. His hopes of finishing off the Spoletans were wrecked by the sudden bout of paralysis that struck Arnulf. The emperor departed Italy, leaving the ailing Formosus to his own devices. The pontiff soon fell seriously ill, dying on April 4, 896. His immediate successor, Boniface VI, lasted only fifteen days. The next pope, Stephen VI (VII), was a supporter of Lambert of Spoleto. He executed the grotesque revenge of the Spoletans upon the deceased pontiff by convening the Cadaver Synod in January 897—arguably the lowest point in the history of the papacy—by exhuming Formosus's rotting body and placing it on trial. Condemned on various charges, Formosus's corpse was abused and thrown into the Tiber. A hermit gathered the remains out of the water and placed it back in its proper tomb in St. Peter's. Successor: Boniface VI. (See also *Cadaver Synod.*)

❀ **FOUNTAINS, VATICAN** Over the centuries, the Vatican City State has been the recipient of a large number of fountains through the munificence of its papal rulers. The two most visible fountains are those located in St. Peter's Square, positioned on either side of the great obelisk. The oldest of the two fountains is on the right, dating to 1613 and the reign of Pope Paul V (1605–1621); the second was completed by the ubiqui-

Five Vatican fountains commemorated on Vatican stamps; note the Galleon Fountain.

tous artisan Gian Lorenzo Bernini during the reign of Pope Alexander VII (1655–1667), patron of the magnificent colonnade encircling the square. Other fountains are placed throughout the papal city, especially in the Vatican Gardens. Three are considered especially notable, each the result of the artistic generosity of Paul V, the Borghese pontiff. They are the Eagle Fountain (*Fontana dell'Aquilone*) and the Fountain of the Sacrament (*Fontana del Sacrament*) in the gardens, and the Fountain of the Galley (*Fontana della Galera*), located near the Belevedere Palace. The Galley Fountain is a delightful miniature ship made of lead, complete with masts, sails, oars, flags, and cannon; water pours out of the cannon, giving expression to the inscription placed on the upper right of the fountain and coined by the future Pope Urban VIII, Maffeo Barberini: *Bellica pontificum non fundit machina flammas, sed dulcem belliqua perit ignis quam* ("The papal fleet does not pour out flames, but sweet water that quenches the fires of war").

❀ **FRA ANGELICO**   Early Renaissance painter and Dominican monk (d. 1455). Born Guido di Pietro, he took the name Fra Giovanni da Fiesole when he entered the Dominican order (*c.* 1420), but earned the title *angelico* (angelic) for his devout daily regimen and his magnificent abilities as a painter. Fra Angelico's contribution to the long and glorious tradition of papal art came under the patronage of Pope Nicholas V (1447–1455), the first of the great Renaissance pontiffs. For the pope, he decorated a private chapel from 1447 to 1451 with frescoes on the lives of St. Stephen and St. Laurence. The frescoes display the delicacy and the profound Christian humanism of the friar and foreshadow the brilliant age of Renaissance painting that was to follow him.

❀ **FUNERAL OF A POPE**   See *Death of a Pope*.

❀ **GAIUS, ST.** Pope from 283 to 296, also called St. Caius, he was the successor to Pope St. Eutychianus and possibly came from Dalmatia, although the reliability of this as reported in the *Liber Pontificalis* is considered dubious. Almost nothing is known with certainty about him, but he was clearly bishop of Rome during a period of relatively little persecution by Roman authorities. He died on April 22, 296, almost certainly not as a martyr. He was buried in the cemetery of Callistus; interestingly, he was not buried in the Crypt of the Popes in the cemetery, most likely because there was no more room. Successor: St. Marcellinus.

❀ **GALERRO ROSSO** Italian term meaning "red hat," which was long considered the most important symbol of the cardinalate; it is still customary to say of someone that he has "received the red hat" when referring to the decision of the pope to appoint the person a Prince of the Church. The *galerro rosso* is shaped like a regular flat hat, although it is entirely of scarlet. In the public consistories at which new cardinals were formally invested with their cardinalatial dignity, it was standing custom to bestow upon the new cardinal a great scarlet hooded cloak and the *galerro rosso*. The hat actually sat upon his head for only a brief moment, thereafter remaining unused and carefully preserved. After the death of the cardinal, it was removed from safekeeping and placed with solemnity upon the bier of the deceased. It was then hung over the altar of the cardinal's cathedral church until it literally disintegrated with age. The custom of cardinalation investiture is much more simplified today. (See *Cardinal* for other details.)

❀ **GAMMARELLI'S** An Italian tailoring company in Rome that has served as the official tailor of the popes for nearly two hundred years. Gammarelli's also serves as the main source for ecclesiastical wear for most of the members of the higher ranks of the Curia and the hierarchy in and around Rome. They are able to provide an extensive catalog for any cleric, but the quality of their workmanship places their costs at the higher end of the scale, so they cater mostly to prelates. While assisting monsignori, bishops, archbishops, and cardinals, their proudest client has always been the pope. Representatives of Gammarelli's are summoned to the Vatican at the moment of a new election of a pope in order to dress the pontiff in his white simar, the attire he will wear on a regular basis for the rest of his life. In a small room near the Sistine Chapel called the Chapel of Tears, three sizes of white simar are kept during a conclave, one for the three basic sizes of any possible pope. At times, the fit has not been exact. Pope John XXIII in 1958, for example, barely managed his enormous girth into the largest simar available, and John Paul I in 1978 found his so big (the smallest available) that it nearly covered his arms and hands. Gammarelli's is located on the Via Santa Chiara.

❀ **GARDENS, VATICAN**   The extensive and highly variegated garden and natural areas within the Vatican City State. Long the private retreat of the popes, away from the incessant noise and traffic of Rome and the Vatican, the gardens occupy nearly half the total acreage of the papal city and include an interesting and historical array of buildings, fountains, monuments, statues, and rest areas. What makes the gardens especially significant and enticing is the fact that they have always been the personal area of the popes—with the members of the court and important guests—so that one may imagine the numerous pontiffs who walked the winding pathways, perhaps praying, reflecting, and saying the rosary, or pondering the high affairs of the Church or matters more mundane. One might reflect upon the warrior Pope Julius II (1503–1513); or the meditations of the mystic Pius XII (1939–1958), who was reportedly so concerned for his own privacy that he forbade even the gardeners from working while he was taking his daily walk; or the ailing John XXIII (1959–1963) who went to his favorite spot, a Chinese pavilion, to weep over the terrible burdens of his office.

The Vatican Gardens had their beginnings at least as early as the reign of Pope Nicholas III (1277–1280), who commanded that a vegetable garden and fruit trees be planted near his palace at the Vatican. The gardens of today, however, were largely organized under Pope Leo XIII (1878–1903). There are to be found within its confines large patches of wild growth, sprawling woods affectionately called the Boschetto (small wood), and gardens in the finest traditions of elevated European palace life: French gardens of expertly manicured flower beds; Italian gardens in their characteristic geometric shapes; and English gardens, boasting a naturalistic and open composition. Once, there was even a zoo. There is also a small vegetable garden, providing for the table of the pontiff.

Among the notable buildings or offices that are located within the boundary of the gardens are: the Governatorate (the Government Palace), Vatican Radio, the Ethiopian College, the Casina of Pius IV (a minor masterpiece of architecture), the St. John Tower, and the Casa del Giardiniere, situated halfway down the slope from St. Peter's, which serves as the headquarters of the Directorate of Archaeological Studies and Research and which was probably once part of a tower attached to a defensive wall erected by Pope Innocent III (1198–1216). The fountains, fed by the waters of Lake Bracciano—thanks to the rebuilding of an aqueduct, dating to the time of Emperor Hadrian in the second century, by Pope Paul V (1603–1621)—boast the Fountain of the Rock and the Fountain of the Sacrament. The monuments and statuary include St. Peter, Our Lady of Guadalupe and the Indian Juan Diego to whom she appeared, a representation of the famed grotto at Lourdes, and a curious 1930s art deco bust of Hermes, messenger of the gods, placed within the Vatican Radio building.

�֍ **GELASIUS I** Pope from 493 to 496. Despite a reign of only four years, Gelasius made lasting contributions to the strengthening of the papacy's ecclesiastical supremacy over the Church. Perhaps of African descent, he was probably born in Rome, succeeding St. Felix III (II) on March 1, 492. He quickly demonstrated his own view of the Roman Church by asserting his authority in the ongoing difficulties with the Eastern Church over the Acacian Schism (the schism that erupted over the unorthodox activities of Acacius, Patriarch of Constantinople). Gelasius maintained the position of his predecessor concerning the supremacy of the Roman see, so the schism was not resolved. In so doing, however, he made an important contribution to the conception of papal authority. He sent to Byzantine Emperor Anastasius a letter in which he detailed his view on the relations of church and state. Gelasius argued that the two institutions were divinely created, but he saw a natural superiority of the Church—the pope in particular—over the secular government. This would have a profound influence on thinking during the Middle Ages and would reach its height under Popes Innocent III (1198–1216) and Boniface VIII (1294–1303). Gelasius was also the first pontiff to use the title Vicar of Christ. While seemingly a tyrant and arrogant in asserting his views, Gelasius was in fact revered by his contemporaries for his humility, prayerful nature, and sincere concern for the Church. He died with virtually no money, having given it away to the poor. A writer with a strong and vigorous style, he wrote many letters and treatises and was the reputed author of the *Decretum Gelasianum* and *Gelasian Sacramentary* (neither was actually by his pen). Much of his reign was also taken up dealing with the Ostrogoths under their ruler King Theodoric, who had taken control of Italy in 493. He was fortunate in that Theodoric, while a devoted Arian, did not interfere in Church affairs and was even willing to be put upon by the pope for assistance in relieving famine. Gelasius is one of the remarkable popes in the first centuries of the Church, but he is largely unknown because of the greater fame and renown of Pope St. Leo I (440–461). Successor: St. Anastasius.

❀ **GELASIUS II** Pope from 1118 to 1119, born John of Gaeta, he entered at a young age the famed monastery of Monte Cassino. There he authored several lives of saints. In 1088, Pope Urban II named him to the cardinalate and the next year appointed him chancellor, supposedly because his Latin was superb. His work in this post would last for nearly thirty years and would be distinguished for widening the scope and efficiency of papal administration. Under Pope Paschal II (1099–1118), he was a trusted advisor, sharing with him the period of harsh imprisonment at the hands of Emperor Henry V in 1111 over the Investiture Controversy. After Paschal's death, he was summoned to Rome from Monte Cassino and, at the conclave held in Santa Maria in Pallara on the Palatine Hill, he was unanimously elected pope on January 24, 1118, much to his own surprise and personal grief. Brooking no refusal, the cardinals gave him their homage. His election, however, was an insult to Emperor Henry V as it had taken place without seeking the approval of the imperial party. Henry's client in Rome, Cencio Frangipani, attacked the monastery and arrested the new pope. Gelasius was beaten and dragged by his hair to a dungeon in a nearby castle where he was placed in heavy chains and left to rot. The Romans, angered at the interference of the imperial forces in their affairs, gathered outside the castle and threatened to burn it down unless the pope was released. Frangipani was obviously impressed by their resolve. He brought Gelasius forward and groveled at his feet begging for forgiveness. The pope was then escorted to the Lateran and enthroned. Henry was not so easily intimidated. He rode to Rome with troops and was soon ensconced in St. Peter's. Gelasius fled the city and, in a memorable scene, escaped by rowing down the Tiber with his court in two galleys. As they sped along the water, imperial forces and their followers hurled stones, arrows, and foul abuse at the retreating pope. He reached Gaeta and there waited for developments. Henry, frustrated in his effort to capture the pope, left Rome, leaving behind the pitifully senile antipope Gregory (VIII). Gelasius returned briefly to the Eternal City in secret before setting out for France, where he was warmly greeted. At the monastery of Cluny, where he was the guest of the renowned Abbot Suger, Gelasius fell ill and died of pleurisy on January 29, 1119. He was buried in the monastery without coming close to settling the conflict with the empire over investiture. Successor: Callistus II.

❀ **GENDARMES, PONTIFICAL** The *Gendarmeria Pontifica,* the police corps of the Papal States and ancestors of the modern Vigilanza, the current security and police authority in the Vatican. The Gendarmes were first organized in 1816 under Pope Pius VII (1800–1823) with the name Pontifical Carabineers. They were reorganized in 1850 and given the name *Gendarmeria Pontificia.* The unit's function was to provide a kind of police force for the Papal States and Rome, being shorn of most of its duties with the demise of the States of the Church in 1860 and then the seizure of Rome itself by the troops of King Victor Emmanuel II in 1870. In subsequent years, the Gendarmes maintained order in the Vatican (after 1929 the Vatican City State), enforced the laws, and directed the ubiquitous traffic in and out of the tiny state. It also provided an honor guard for the pope on certain special occasions. The Gendarmes were not intended to defend the actual person of the Supreme Pontiff, but could if needed fight on behalf of both their pope and his territories. They thus valiantly defended the Papal States in 1860 and 1870, but to little avail. In its final years, the corps numbered approximately 150 to 200 men. During the reign of Pope Paul VI (1963–1978), the Gendarmes had their name changed to the Vigilanza, the Civil Guard, under the authority of the Central Security Office of the Vatican. Gone is the splendid formal garb of the Gendarmes— complete with sword and Italian bicorn hat—replaced by the more efficient, practical, but distinctly less attractive uniform of police officers. (See *Vigilance, Office of the* for other details.)

❀ **GHIBELLINES** See *Guelphs and Ghibellines.*

❀ **GOLDEN ROSE** One of the most beautiful of all tokens of special papal favor that was traditionally granted to a worthy individual or community. The Golden Rose was a delicately made ornament of gold and precious gems, crafted into the shape of a spray of roses, with a container or ampule of musk or balsam in the middle of the largest and most impressive flower; it is blessed by the pope on the fourth Sunday of Lent (called Rose Sunday or Laetare Sunday). The Golden Rose was long a deeply desired reward and could be won through very special service to the Church or for conspicuous devotion. Its origins are obscure, but it dates to some time before the reign of Pope Leo IX who, in 1049, referred to it as being an old custom. In this century, the granting of the Golden Rose has been limited to queens of Catholic countries, the last being Grand Duchess Charlotte of Luxembourg; it is also bestowed upon certain shrines, especially those dedicated to the Blessed Virgin Mary. The rose is kept in the Vatican until such time that it can be given to a suitable recipient. (See also *Decorations, Papal.*)

꙰ **GOOD FRIDAY** The Friday of Holy Week that commemorates the Crucifixion and death of Christ. It is considered one of the most essential elements of the Easter triduum (Good Friday, Holy Saturday, and the Easter Vigil) and is the only day of the year on which the mass is not said. The liturgy of Good Friday consists of the reading of the passion account (according to John), the recitation of prayers for the Church and all people, the veneration of the Cross, and a communion service (but not a mass). Beyond the liturgy celebrated in St. Peter's Basilica, Good Friday is distinguished in Rome by a solemn, impressive, and moving torchlight ceremony. Carrying a simple wooden cross, the pope guides a large procession of torch-bearing faithful through the streets of the ancient quarter of Rome along the Via Crucis (the Way of the Cross), through the Colosseum, the traditional site of so many martyrdoms in the early Church. There he leads the congregation in prayers at each of the traditional fourteen stations of the cross, the commemoration of the passion and

The pope, carrying a wooden cross, presides over Good Friday Services in the Colosseum.
(COURTESY L'OSSERVATORE ROMANO, CITTÁ DEL VATICANO.)

death of Christ. Pope John Paul II also hears confessions in St. Peter's Basilica, a custom he began in 1979 in his effort to stress the importance of the sacrament of penance (or reconciliation). In this he ceases to be pope and becomes a simple priest, exercising his function to hear confessions as he did so many years before in the tiny town of Niegowice in Poland. Many visitors, going to confession in the basilica perhaps for the first time in many years, are completely unaware that the priest hearing their sins is in fact the Vicar of Christ.

❀ **GOVERNATORATE, PALAZZO DEL** The Palace of the Governorate, the headquarters of the civil administration of the Vatican City State. The largest building in the Vatican Gardens, the palazzo houses the offices of the city-state's administration and bureaucracy and is the place where the Council of the Vatican State holds its meetings. The building itself was erected at the order of Pope Pius XI (1922–1939), who used some of the enormous financial grants from the Lateran Treaty of 1929 to fund it. The architect was Giuseppe Momo, a friend of Pius, and it was intended to serve as a Roman seminary and a possible place to provide state apartments for visiting dignitaries. Constructed from 1928 to 1931, it soon proved impractical for its original purpose because of the unexpected need for extra space to accommodate the administrative offices for the recently established city-state government. The palazzo is located behind the apse of the basilica. It is a large wedding cake–like structure in salmon pink with a semiclassical temple perched at the top, crowned by a statue of the Virgin Mary. One of its most distinctive marks is the flower bed placed before it in its sloping yard. Here the staff of the gardens maintains a bed of flowers arranged in the shape of the coat of arms of the reigning pope. (See also *Vatican City, State of.*)

❀ **GREGORIAN REFORM** See *Alexander II, Gregory VII, Leo IX, Stephen IX (X),* and *Victor II.*

❀ **GREGORY I THE GREAT, ST.** Pope from 590 to 604, one of only two popes, with St. Leo I, to be granted the title "the Great." Gregory has been called the last of the Romans, the last of the Latin Fathers of the Church, and the initiator of what has been termed the "Medieval Papacy," the prominent place of the Holy See in the life of the Church and the West. A member of the Roman nobility and the son of a senator, Gregory initially pursued a purely secular career, receiving appointment as prefect of the city of Rome in 573. After the death of his father, however, he was drawn toward a strict ascetic life, renouncing his worldly pursuits and converting his own estate in Rome into a monastery; with his inheritance he also founded six other monastic institutions in Sicily. He joined his own Roman community in 574 and spent the next years in constant prayer. By 578 he was so revered in Rome that the popes pressed him into their service. Benedict I made him a deacon and Pelagius II sent him as an ambassador to the Byzantine court at Constantinople in 579. Returning to Rome in 585, he served as abbot of his monastery until 590 and the death of Pelagius II. To his genuine horror, he was unanimously elected pope, struggling for months to avoid the terrible burden of the papacy because he desired to remain in his contemplative community. Despite his protests to anyone who might listen, Gregory was consecrated on September 3, 590.

Once resolved that his place as pope was the will of God, Gregory proved an amazingly active and forceful pontiff, overcoming his often severe bouts of poor health. The work before him was truly daunting since Italy and Rome were in dire trouble from plagues, famines, and the constant menace of war because of the presence of the Lombards. As there was no central government, Gregory assumed the main task of civil administration, reorganizing the territorial possessions of the Holy See—the *Patrimonium Petri* (Patrimony of Peter)—to use their financial value to feed the starving and care for the sick. While acknowledging the political supremacy of the Byzantine emperors, Gregory essentially ignored the presence of the exarch of Ravenna (the Byzantine representative in Italy) and personally negotiated peace with the Lombards. He also took steps to resist the increasing claims by the Patriarch of Constantinople to an equal status with the Bishop of Rome, an egregious violation of papal rights.

Beyond his temporal labors, Gregory also brought a variety of reforms to the Church. The first monk to be elected pope, he gave much favor to monasteries and appointed monks to numerous posts in the papal government. He also wrote a guide to proper religious practices (the *Liber Regulae Pastoralis,* "Book of Pastoral Rules") and promoted missionary activities, especially in England. A prolific writer, he authored the *Dialogues,* an account of the lives of early Latin saints; homilies on the Gospel; over 850 letters; and a work on the Book of Job. He is given credit for launching the long revered form of music called Gregorian chant and for making contributions to the Gregorian sacramentary. Soon after his death on March 12, 604, he was canonized a saint by popular demand. His last days had been full of profound physical suffering. He is honored as a Doctor of the Church and his epitaph declared him God's Consul. Successor: Sabinian. (See also *Servus Servorum Dei*.)

✿ **GREGORY II, ST.**   Pope from 715 to 731, Gregory was born in 669 in Rome to a well-placed family. At an early age, he was entered into the *schola cantorum* (the papal school for singers) and later became a subdeacon and almoner (or keeper of the purse) for the Roman Church. He is noted for being the first papal librarian and almoner to be known by name. He took part in the delegation of Pope Constantine to the Byzantine capital of Constantinople in 710–711, proving most adroit in negotiating with Emperor Justinian II (r. 685–695, 705–711). Much respected, he was elected to succeed Constantine on May 19, 715, the first Roman pope in seven reigns. He subsequently proved a gifted pontiff, one of the best of the entire eighth century. His reign marked the beginnings of the iconoclast controversy in the Eastern Empire (the struggle over whether icons could be venerated) under Emperor Leo III the Isaurian, when he decreed the destruction of images all over the empire. Gregory steadfastly opposed these enactments, thus causing a marked breakdown in the relations between the papacy and the imperial court. While nominally still loyal to the Byzantines, he used every opportunity to resist his participation in the oppressive tax program of Emperor Leo. The emperor connived to have him deposed or even assassinated, but the popularity of the pope prevented any serious steps toward the fulfillment of his plans. Gregory was able to use his keen diplomatic sense to convince the Lombards in Italy to surrender extensive properties to the Holy See, and then saved Rome from possible invasion by Liutprand, King of the Lombards, by appearing quite suddenly and most unexpectedly in the Lombard camp to make a personal appeal. His calculated gamble paid off as Liutprand made obeisance before the tomb of St. Peter. Concerned for the program of evangelizing Northern Europe, the pope consecrated the famed St. Boniface (d. 754) and other missionaries, sending them to bring the gospel among the peoples of Frisia, Bavaria, Thuringia, and Hesse. Gregory also rebuilt the walls of Rome and restored many churches. Successor: St. Gregory III.

✿ **GREGORY III, ST.**   Pope from 731 to 741, the successor to Pope St. Gregory II, he was a Syrian by birth and was so esteemed by the Romans for his learning and holiness that a crowd surrounded him during the funeral procession of Gregory II and declared him their bishop. He was then carried by the jubilant Romans to the place of the vote, where he was elected by acclamation. On March 18 he was consecrated, seeking immediately the approval of the Byzantine exarch (or governor) of Ravenna, the last time that a pope would ask for such approbation. He was to face throughout his reign the ongoing iconoclast controversy, opposing the policies of Emperor Leo III the Isaurian, who had decreed that all icons or images should be destroyed. Since the pontiff was adamant in resisting the decrees, the emperor punished the Holy See by stripping away some of its territories. Shrewdly, Gregory did not assist the Lombards in their capture of the Byzantine Ravenna and even helped the Byzantines in their efforts to recapture what had been their capital in Italy. This paid off for Gregory, because he won an end to Leo's hostility without having to capitulate on the matter of the controversy. The Lombards were now a major threat, however, and Gregory was forced himself to pay for the rebuilding of Rome's walls and other defensive measures. He also made alliances with the various enemies of the Lombard King Liutprand and made the important decision of appealing for aid from the Franks under Charles Martel, the Frankish mayor of the palace from 716 to 741. While the Franks sent no troops to Italy, Gregory had begun a relationship between the popes and the Franks that was to have momentous consequences over the next years. Successor: St. Zacharias.

🕸 **GREGORY IV**   Pope from 827 to 844. A Roman by birth and belonging to the nobility of Rome, he was elected in the latter part of 827 but was not consecrated until March 29, 828, owing to the need to have the election approved by the imperial legate, the representative of Emperor Louis the Pious (r. 814–840). Ordained a priest by Pope Paschal I, he had been serving as cardinal priest of the Basilica of St. Mark in Rome at the time of his election. He owed his elevation to the papacy to the Roman nobility, but was apparently quite reluctant to accept. He devoted much time and personal credibility to intervening in the rancorous dispute between Emperor Louis and his sons Lothair I (r. 840–855), Pepin (d. 838), and Louis the German (d. 876), which would prove a major cause in the demise of the Frankish Empire. Gregory supported Lothair and traveled with him to meet with the Frankish bishops. The bishops angrily denounced him as a traitor to Louis, reminding him of his oath of loyalty to the emperor, which all popes then had to take. Gregory responded by asserting the authority of the Holy See, reiterating his singular desire for peace in the empire. At Rotfield in 833, he tried to negotiate a settlement, realizing too late that Lothair had merely used him as a pawn in the wider scheme to depose Louis bloodlessly. On June 30, 833, Louis was forced to step down in humiliating circumstances after his army deserted him. Gregory returned to Rome deeply saddened by Lothair's perfidious schemes. Louis managed to secure restoration in 834, renewing his association with the pope several years later. The emperor died in 840 and the empire sank into civil war. Gregory fruitlessly tried to stop the carnage. In other matters, Gregory was compelled to strengthen his defenses in the face of the chronic threat of the Saracens. He also decorated churches and instituted the observance of the Feast of All Saints. Successor: Sergius II.

⚜ **GREGORY V**   Pope from 996 to 999, the first German pontiff, he was born around 972 and was named Bruno of Carinthia, the son of Duke Otto of Carinthia and Judith; he was a grandson of Emperor Otto I the Great and a cousin of the German king Otto III (r. 996–1002). He was serving as chaplain to Otto III when the ruler, who had marched on Italy to assist Pope John XV against the Crescenti, learned that John had died. Soon after, a delegation arrived from Rome asking him to provide a name for a possible successor. He suggested Bruno as his candidate, despite the fact that Bruno was only in his twenties. He nevertheless had much to recommend him, including a keen mind, an excellent education, and considerable experience in the court of his cousin. The Roman nobility were happy to have a member of the imperial family as their pope, although the Romans themselves soon resented a foreign pontiff. Escorted to Rome, he was officially elected and consecrated on May 3, 996, under the name Gregory V in honor of Gregory I the Great, whom he hoped to emulate. On May 21 he crowned Otto emperor and the two initially worked well together. Relations slowly chilled, however, over a number of issues, and Otto left Rome in October. Gregory was now faced with a growing problem. He had unwisely secured a pardon for the dictator Crescentius II Nomentanus, who had caused difficulties for John, and no sooner was Otto gone than Crescentius launched an attack on Gregory's position, assisted by the Roman mob, which disliked having a German on the throne of Peter. Gregory fled, and Crescentius secured the elevation of an antipope, John XVI in 997. The pope was soon rescued by Otto, who marched on Rome, capturing John XVI and humiliating him in a most terrible fashion. Crescentius was besieged in Castel Sant'Angelo and reduced to surrender. Otto had him hanged on the castle walls (998) as a warning. Gregory did not live long after his restoration, dying on February 4, 999. Successor: Sylvester II.

❀ **GREGORY VI**   Pope 1045 to 1046, the godfather to the infamous Pope Benedict IX, John Gratian (or Giovanni Graziano) was a participant in the reprehensible effort of Benedict to sell the papacy in 1045. John possessed a reputation for virtue and was known in some circles for his reforming zeal. He was consulted by his godson as to whether it was possible to resign the papacy because Benedict had become infatuated with a woman and was anxious to wed. John replied in the affirmative, and was suddenly offered the throne himself in return for a large payment of money. While technically paying the pope to step down, John in effect purchased the throne of St. Peter. His action was not apparently motivated by the self-serving ambition, and greed of the times but was a sincere effort to rid the Holy See of such a corrupt, dissolute, and violent master. Taking the name Gregory VI, he was elected on May 1, 1045, immediately upon Benedict's abdication, and with the irregular gesture of being named by Benedict as his desired successor. The elevation of John Gratian as pope was greeted in many quarters with joy; even St. Peter Damian (d. 1072), an ardent reformer and Doctor of the Church, was all in favor of it, although he was not aware at the time that John had paid money to Benedict (ironically, Peter Damian had proclaimed that the election was a blow to corruption). The situation did not long remain harmonious. The claimant Pope Sylvester III refused to surrender his hopes of becoming the sole pope, and Benedict, disappointed in the marriage, soon reappeared announcing his claim to the papacy. Both rivals to Gregory controlled parts of Rome, so the Church was faced with three different popes. King Henry III of Germany, determined to end this ridiculous state of affairs, marched across the Alps and convoked the Synod of Sutri in December 1046, commanding all three popes to attend. It is possible that Gregory himself summoned the council, an event perhaps declared by later authors to make up for the awkward situation of having a secular ruler solve such a crisis in the Church. Regardless, Gregory voluntarily stepped down after being convinced by the council participants that he had acquired the throne by illegal and irregular means, and the other two popes were removed. Suidger, a German bishop, was elected to replace them as Clement II, and Gregory then went to Germany with Henry. With him traveled his secretary, Hildebrand, the future Pope St. Gregory VII. Gregory VI died at Cologne in late 1047. Successor: Clement II.

❀ **GREGORY VII, ST.**   Pope from 1073 to 1085, one of the foremost pontiffs of the Middle Ages and one of the greatest reformers in the history of the Church. Originally called Hildebrand, he was born in

Tuscany; his parents were reportedly humble, the story long told that his father was a carpenter. Educated at Rome, including the papal palace of the Lateran, he received appointment as chaplain to Pope Gregory VI (1045–1046). He first came to prominence in 1046 when he chose to accompany Gregory into exile at Cologne. Following Gregory's death the next year, Hildebrand entered a monastery and most likely would have remained there had Pope St. Leo IX (1049–1054) not summoned him to Rome, or-dained him a subdeacon, and given him charge of the *Patrimonium Petri* (the Patrimony of Peter). He subsequently emerged as one of the most powerful and influential figures in the Church throughout the reigns of Leo, Victor II (1055–1057), Nicholas II (1058–1061), and Alexander II (1061–1073). Having been considered for some years an obvious choice to be pope, he had resisted all considera-tion of his elevation. On April 22, 1073, however, a mere day after Alexander's death, he was elected pope. Convinced to accept, he was consecrated on June 29, the feast of Sts. Peter and Paul, taking the name Gregory in remembrance of St. Gregory I the Great.

Pope Gregory VII accepts the penitent Emperor Henry IV at Canossa in 1077. The pope traditionally was said to have left Henry standing in the snow for three days. (CATHOLIC NEWS SERVICE.)

In the previous years, Hilde-brand had worked tirelessly to pro-mote reforms in the Church by ending simony, clerical abuses, concu-binage, and ecclesiastical irregularities. As pope, he made the reforms a central focus of his reign, giving his name to the movement. He appointed sober papal legates who went out across Christendom and convinced or cajoled the reluctant bishops in France, Germany, and elsewhere to participate. Gregory also used the so-called Lenten Synods—councils convened every Lent in Rome—to issue decrees and

condemnations. The most famous was held in 1075 at which he outlawed lay investiture. (See *Investiture Controversy*.)

Gregory's declaration brought him into conflict with the
German king and future emperor Henry IV (1056–1106), an obstinate supporter of investiture. The young ruler convened two synods
in 1076, at Worms and Piacenza, proclaiming Gregory to be
deposed. The pope wasted no time in excommunicating and deposing Henry, going further to free Henry's subjects from any obligations of fealty. In early 1077 Henry made peace by enduring a
humiliating penance before Gregory in the snows at Canossa. By
1080, relations had once again deteriorated and Gregory reimposed
his excommunication. Henry secured the elevation of the antipope
Clement III, but still sought a mediated settlement. This was
unthinkable to the unyielding Gregory, whose obstinacy first lost
him the support of a group of cardinals and then Rome itself, which
fell to Henry's troops in March 1084. The pope was rescued by the
Normans under Robert Guiscard, but the Romans became so
incensed at the looting, pillaging, and burning perpetrated by the
gruff Norman knights that they rose up in revolt and ejected
Gregory from the city. Disheartened, Gregory journeyed to Monte
Cassino and then Salerno where he died on May 25, 1085. His dying
words were: "I have loved justice and so die in exile." Gregory was
canonized in 1606 by Pope Paul V. Successor: Victor III.

❋ **GREGORY VIII**   Pope from October 21 to December 17, 1187.
Originally called Alberto de Morra, he was born around 1110 in
Benevento to a noble family. At a young age he became a Cistercian
monk (or perhaps a Benedictine) and was later a canon regular in Laon
and a professor of law in Bologna. Made a cardinal by Pope Adrian IV,
he was appointed chancellor of the Roman Church in 1172 or 1178. He
was also one of two legates sent to England to investigate the murder
of St. Thomas Becket in Canterbury Cathedral in 1170. Alberto was
elected to succeed Urban III at Ferrara after the pope had died from a
broken heart due to the capture of Jerusalem by the Muslims under
their general, Saladin. Crucial to his being chosen by the cardinals,
despite his advanced years, was the fact that he was known to be on
good terms with the German king Frederick I Barbarossa (d. 1190), as
the cardinals were quite unhappy with the direction taken by Urban
III in dealing with the ruler. Gregory seemed to confirm their hopes,
taking a conciliatory posture toward Frederick, which resulted in an
immediate improvement in relations. Gregory took as his main

enterprise the organizing of another crusade to rescue Jerusalem, insisting upon the dress of penance for all taking part, the reflection of his belief that the Holy City had fallen because of God's punishment of Christians for their sins. To make the launching of ships easier, Gregory traveled to Pisa in December, hoping to negotiate peace between the Pisans and their rivals, the Genoese. In Pisa, he fell ill, died, and was buried in the city's cathedral. Successor: Clement III.

GREGORY VIII   Antipope from 1118 to 1121. Originally Maurice Bourdin, he was born in Limoges, studied at Cluny, and became a member of the Benedictines. In 1098 he was appointed Bishop of Coimbra and in 1111 archbishop of Braga. Meeting Pope Paschal II, he so thoroughly impressed the pontiff (who was also a one-time student at Cluny) that the pope kept him in Rome and used him as a reliable agent in assorted matters of great import. In 1117, he was sent by Paschal to meet with Emperor Henry V in Rome (the pope residing in Benevento) over the controversy of lay investiture. To the pope's surprise and deep anger, he threw himself completely into Henry's cause, crowning Henry on Easter Day. Paschal excommunicated Bourdin, but he never wavered in his new commitment. When, after Paschal died and Henry learned to his own frustration that the cardinals had swiftly elected Gelasius II, he had Bourdin proclaimed pope on March 8, 1118. He took the name Gregory VIII. He was never able to win recognition from the crowned heads of Christendom, Gelasius having wrecked any ambitions in that quarter by a series of pointed letters and because of Gregory's increasing senility. Gelasius died on January 29, 1119, and Henry found it possible to enter into negotiations with the new pope, Callistus II, which effectively ended Gregory's usefulness to the emperor. Gregory retreated from Rome to Sutri in 1119, but was soon abandoned by Henry and besieged by Callistus. Handed over to Callistus's troops by the residents of Sutri, Gregory was paraded through the streets of Rome seated backward on a camel while the crowd pelted him with food, rocks, and verbal crudities. Imprisoned in several monasteries, he died around 1140. Of him, the chronicler William of Malmesbury wrote that all would have been obliged to honor him because of his achievements, "had he not preferred to seek glory by so notorious a crime."

GREGORY IX   Pope from 1227 to 1241 whose pontificate was devoted to the struggle of the papacy with Emperor Frederick II. Born Ugolino of Segni, he was the son of the count of Segni and a nephew of Innocent III (1198–1216). Studying at the

University of Paris, he became a highly respected theologian and lawyer, receiving elevation to the cardinalate in 1198 by his uncle. He later distinguished himself as a papal legate. Elected on March 19, 1227, to succeed Pope Honorius III, he proved a pontiff much in the mold of Innocent III, a forceful personality who was willing to fight for the principles in which he believed. Deeply committed to the crusading effort, he wasted little time in demanding that Emperor Frederick fulfill his vow to sail to the Holy Land. As the emperor temporized, Gregory excommunicated him, going so far as to work against Frederick even after the ruler had negotiated a brilliant treaty that won control of Jerusalem.

A reconciliation was reached in 1230 through the Treaty of San Germano, but relations soon deteriorated again. War erupted in 1239, ending two years later with Frederick's siege of Rome. With the imperial troops at the gates of the city, Gregory died on August 22, 1241. While his wars with Frederick overshadowed his other acts, Gregory also promoted the Franciscan order and the founding of the Court of Inquisition, control of which he gave to the Dominicans. Successor: Celestine IV.

GREGORY X   Pope from 1271 to 1276. Known originally as Teobaldo Visconti, he was a native of Piacenza, born sometime around 1210. A remarkable personality, he had studied at the University of Paris, 1248–1252, becoming an associate of both Sts. Thomas Aquinas and Bonaventure. Prior to that, he had played a major role in the organizing of the Council of Lyons in 1245. In 1271, he was serving as archdeacon of Liege and was in the Holy Land on a crusade with the future King Edward I of England when word reached him at Acre that he had been elected pope. The absolute stunning surprise of his elevation on September 1, 1271, as pope came about at Viterbo where the cardinals, hopelessly deadlocked in their efforts to choose a successor to Clement IV, ended the three-year interregnum by permitting a compromise committee of six cardinals to choose on their behalf. Their choice was of a Church figure well known in the royal courts of the time, but still only a layman. Reaching Viterbo on February 10, 1272, Visconti journeyed to Rome where he was consecrated on March 27, 1272. His pontificate of five years revealed him to be committed to mounting a crusade to the Holy Land, bringing reform to the papacy, and improving relations with both the Holy Roman Empire and the Eastern Church. These ambitions were to be only partially fulfilled. At the Council of Lyons (1274–1275), he negotiated a fleeting reunion with the Eastern Church, and his call for another military effort to capture Jerusalem from the Muslims came to nothing. His most significant act was the issuing of the decree *Ubi periculum* (1274) by which he introduced the conclave system in the election of popes. He was beatified in 1713. Successor: Innocent V.

GREGORY XI   Pope from 1370 to 1378, who brought an end to the Avignon Papacy by returning the papal court to Rome in 1377. Called originally Pierre Roger de Beaufort, he was born in 1329 at the Chateau of Maumont, outside of Limoges, the son of a noble family and a nephew of Pope Clement VI. Appointed by his uncle to the ranks of the cardinalate in 1348, he studied at the University of Perugia, was considered a leading canonist, and was a major figure in the pontificate of Pope Urban V. At Urban's death in December 1370, de Beaufort was considered the clear favorite to succeed him, receiving unanimous election as pope on December 30, a mere two days after Urban's passing. Deeply religious, he was of the belief that the papacy belonged in Rome, but any serious thoughts of moving from Avignon proved impractical owing to more urgent affairs. From 1375 to 1378 he directed the War of the Eight Saints— with Florence over the Papal States, ending the struggle with the Peace of Tivoli; he also labored without success to negotiate an end to the Hundred Years' War between France and England and promoted assorted changes within the Dominican order.

The return to Rome, however, was the main event of his reign, to which the Romans had looked with increasing agitation. Receiving the constant urging of St. Catherine of Siena, Gregory finally entered the city on January 17, 1377. The stay proved regrettably brief as upheaval in Rome upset the pope; he finally departed to Anagni after violence broke out in the wake of the massacre perpetrated in Cesena in February 1377 by his legate Robert of Geneva. Catherine of Siena loudly assured him of disaster should he leave the city, her predictions coming true on March 27, 1378, when Gregory died from exhaustion. Successor: Urban VI.

GREGORY XII   Pope from 1406 to 1415 who helped to resolve the Great Western Schism that had divided the Church since 1378. Angelo Correr was born to a noble family of Venice, serving as a bishop and the Latin patriarch of Constantinople before receiving elevation to the cardinalate in 1405 by Pope Innocent VII. He succeeded Innocent on November 30, 1406, making him the next legitimate pontiff during the schism; his rival at the time of his election was antipope Benedict XIII. As part of the conclave that chose him, Gregory agreed to work toward a resolution of the crisis, a promise made by all participating cardinals. As negotiations proved unproductive, however, Gregory hardened his position, coming to oppose the work of the Council of Pisa (1409), which condemned both the pope and Benedict and elected as "pope" Alexander V. A final means of ending the schism came starting in 1414 with the Council of Constance (1414–1418), which Gregory was convinced to recognize. The pontiff subsequently agreed to abdicate in the interests of the Church, resigning on July 4, 1415, but his pontifical acts were formally ratified and he was named cardinal bishop of Porto. He died at Porto on October 18, 1417. Successor: Martin V.

GREGORIVS·XII·PAPA·VENETVS

Pope Gregory XII.

GREGORY XIII Pope from 1572 to 1585, best known for his monumental reforms of the calendar. From Bologna, Ugo Boncampagni was born in 1502, the son of a merchant. He studied at the University of Bologna and earned a doctorate in law before teaching there for a number of years. During this time, he enjoyed life, fathering a son who would later receive appointment as governor of Castel Sant'Angelo. In 1539, however, he underwent a kind of personal reform that led away from the pleasures of the Renaissance to a full appreciation of the stern needs of revitalizing the Church. Ordained a priest in 1542, he swiftly won the trust of Popes Paul III and Paul IV for his legal acumen. Paul IV made him Bishop of Vieste in 1558; Pope Pius IV named him to the cardinalate in 1565. Appointed legate to Spain, he so impressed King Philip II that the king helped secure his election as successor to Pope St. Pius V on May 14, 1572.

Famous for his kindly and easygoing nature, Gregory was nevertheless very determined to continue advancing the full implementation of the Council of Trent in reforming the Church. Toward that end, he founded many seminaries, promoted education (including the funding of twenty-three colleges in Rome), and encouraged missionary activities in the Far East. His most memorable achievement was, of course, the calendar. Seeking to resolve the mounting calendrical errors in the Julian calendar, in place since 46 B.C., Gregory commanded that a committee look into possible reforms. On the basis of their work, the pope issued the encyclical *Inter gravissimas* (February 24, 1582) changing the calendar to match the more precise calculations of his astronomers. Unfortunately, Gregory's education program and other building efforts in Rome severely drained papal monies. The Papal States also fell into disorder, terrorized by bands of brigands who would not be extirpated until the next pope's reign. He died on April 10, 1585. Successor: Sixtus V.

GREGORY XIV Pope from 1590 to 1591, Niccolo Sfondrato was born in 1535 at Somma, near Milan. He studied at Perugia and Pavia, receiving a doctorate in law. Named Bishop of Cremona at the age of twenty-five by Pope Pius IV, he took part in the Council of Trent from 1562 to 1563, receiving elevation to the cardinalate in 1583 by Gregory XIII. While not considered one of the most formidable figures in the Curia, his election on December 5, 1590, came about in part because of his personal piety and despite his rather poor health. His main achievement was to bring relief to the Romans from the chronic outbreaks of unrest, famine, and plague. He also passed a decree forbidding all betting on papal elections. Successor: Innocent IX.

GREGORY XV Pope from 1621 to 1623, originally known as Alessandro Ludovisi, he was a native of Bologna, studying in the university there and earning a doctorate in law; he had earlier studied under the Jesuits. After a swift career in the Curia, he was named Archbishop of Bologna in 1612 and, after negotiating a peace treaty between Savoy and Spain, he was made a cardinal. On February 9, 1521, he was elected pope by *acclamatio* (acclaim), despite his delicate health, to succeed Paul V. The main support of his pontificate was provided by his nephew Ludovico Cardinal Ludovisi. His reign, although brief, was not without achievement. He canonized Francis Xavier, Teresa of Ávila, Ignatius Loyola, and Philip Neri, and founded the Sacred Congregation of the Propagation of the Faith, the central office for directing the Church's overseas missions. He is also notable in the history of papal elections for his decrees *Aeterni Patris Filius* (1621) and *Decet Romanum Pontificem* (1622) requiring that all voting in a conclave should be by secret ballot, a tradition that is essentially unchanged into modern times. Successor: Urban VIII.

GREGORY XVI Pope from 1831 to 1846. Born in 1765 in Belluno, Italy, Bartolomeo Alberto Cappellari was the son of an aristocratic lawyer. At the age of eighteen, he entered the Camaldolese monastery of S. Michele at Murano, Venice, receiving ordination in 1787. After teaching for several years, he went to Rome in 1795 and four years later wrote the book *Il Trionfo della Santa Sede contro gli Assalti dei Novatori* (*Triumph of the Holy See Against the Attacks of the Innovators*), which aggressively supported papal infallibility and papal rights against the state. An abbot in 1805 and procurator-general of the Camaldolese in 1807, he fled Rome in 1808 to escape the harsh persecutions of Napoleon, returning only in 1814. Made a cardinal in 1826, he was appointed head of the Congregation for the Propagation of the Faith that same year. Known to be opposed to theological and political liberalism, he was elected to succeed Pius VIII on February 2, 1831, by the *zelanti,* similar-minded and conservative cardinals. His reign would very much reflect this outlook and would be plagued with political upheaval in the Papal States, with violence erupting shortly after his election. Austrian troops were called in to restore order, but no

Pope Gregory XVI.

meaningful solution to the crisis was forthcoming because Gregory was unwilling to compromise in the face of complaints in Rome and the States of the Church among both the clergy and laity. These complaints contended that the papal administration was corrupt, arbitrary, and blindly unrepresentative of the lay people it governed. More insurrections flared up, Austrian troops returned, and, suspicious of Austrian motives, France sent forces into the papal territory of

Ancona. In matters of doctrine, he was equally determined, denouncing the entire spectrum of liberal ideas in the encyclical *Mirari Vos* (1832). Nevertheless, Gregory enthusiastically promoted the missions around the world, reorganized the Church's hierarchy, and helped return the Dominicans and Franciscans to France. He also founded the Gregorian-Egyptian and Gregorian-Etruscan museums in the Vatican. Despite these positive accomplishments, he left behind him the Papal States severely debilitated and the papal treasury dangerously depleted. Successor: Pius IX.

❀ **GROTTOES, SACRED VATICAN** One of the two subterranean areas beneath St. Peter's Basilica to which the public is allowed; the second is the Scavi, the excavations below the grottoes. The Sacred Vatican Grottoes are situated directly below the apse of St. Peter's, reaching to approximately half the length of the nave, and entered—without charge—through a door located under Bernini's grand baldacchino on the side of the huge pier of St. Longinus. Aside from the attractions of the grottoes themselves, the entire subterranean complex gives the visitor an excellent idea as to the approximate dimensions of the original basilica—for its length matches the layout of that church replaced in the sixteenth century.

There are two main sections to the grottoes, the Grotte Vecchie and the Grotte Nuove; the former dates to the late sixteenth century and the latter, a semicircular ambulatory, was added in the early seventeenth century. The grottoes were long overlooked and neglected, notorious for their poor lighting, dampness, and the inconvenience of trying to visit with lamps or candles. Women were forbidden from entering because of the claustrophobic conditions, save for one day a year, Whitmonday (the Monday following Pentecost), or with the express, written permission of the archpriest of St. Peter's and then only after a formal petition to the pope. Extensive changes were begun in 1935 under Pope Pius XI and largely completed under Pius XII. Electricity was brought down into the area, the walls were redone with marble, many of the sarcophagi (the traditional attraction of the grottoes) were removed, and ten rooms were added. The main sites are St. Peter's Chapel and the tombs of many popes, including Pius XII, John XXIII, John Paul I (the Smiling Pope), and Adrian IV.

❀ **GUELPHS AND GHIBELLINES** The names given to the two main Italian political factions in the thirteenth and fourteenth centuries, supporting the papal and imperial causes, respectively, during the period of intense conflict between the papacy and the Holy Roman Empire. The Ghibellines gave their loyalties to the rulers of the empire, in particular the Hohenstaufen dynasty. They took their name from the Hohenstaufen Castle of Waiblingen that was the center of opposition in Germany to the Welf family of Bavaria, which tried to win the imperial throne in the twelfth and thirteenth centuries. The Guelphs (or Guelfs) received their name from the Welf dynasty, emerging as devoted adherents of the popes. The two parties first became distinct and inveterately hostile during the tumultuous reign of Emperor Frederick I Barbarossa (1155–1190) with the onset of often severe military and political struggles in Italy. The actual names came into common usage during the time of Frederick II's conflict with the papacy, from around 1227 until his death in 1250. The Guelph and Ghibelline struggle was most pronounced in Florence. Here the victors in the political maneuverings routinely drove the vanquished into exile or put them to death with considerable gusto, the survivors plotting their return to power and the inflicting of brutal reprisals. The Ghibelline cause suffered a catastrophic blow in 1268 with the defeat and extermination of the Hohenstaufen dynasty. Bereft of their formidable imperial patrons, the Ghibellines fell into eclipse and suffered savage liquidation throughout Italy where pro-papal forces had a free hand against them.

❀ **HABEMUS PAPAM!** The joyous declaration made by the senior member of the College of Cardinals to proclaim the election of a new pope. Meaning "We have a pope!," the proclamation is made from the loggia of St. Peter's Basilica. After making the announcement, which is much anticipated by the crowd in the square, the cardinal then gives the name of the cardinal (or individual-elect) and his choice of papal name, both in flowing Latin. The full announcement begins with the booming voice of the papal master of ceremonies, who calls out over the loudspeaker, *"Attenzione!"* The senior cardinal then steps forward and states: *"Annuntio vobis gaudium magnum! . . . Habemus papam!"* ("I announce to you great joy! . . . We have a pope!"), followed by the name of the person elected, normally *"Eminentissimum ac reverendissimum Dominum Cardinalem N. Cardinalem Sanctae Romanae Ecclesiae N."* Next comes *"Qui sibi Imposuit Nomen—"* stating the chosen name, such as "Joannem Paulum Secundum" (John Paul II). A little later, the new pope steps out to address the jubilant crowd in the square and an audience of perhaps a billion people, launching another pontificate.

❀ **HADRIAN**   See under *Adrian.*

❀ **HILARUS, ST.**   Pope from 461 to 468, also called Hilary and Hilarius, he was a native of Sardinia, the son of Crispinus. Under Pope St. Leo the Great, he served as an archdeacon, representing the pontiff as one of his legates, with Julius, Archbishop of Puteoli, at the so-called Robber Council of Ephesus (the Latrocinium) in 449. While at the council, he was an outspoken defender of papal rights. When violence erupted in the city of Ephesus over the doctrinal issues being discussed, Hilarus barely escaped with his life, hiding himself for a time in the tomb of St. John the Evangelist to avoid an angry mob. He thereafter attributed his escape to St. John. In November 461, he was elected to succeed Pope Leo, remaining faithful to the policies of his renowned predecessor. Hilarus was particularly active in advancing the privileges and rights of the Holy See, devoting much attention to the Church in

Spain and France (Gaul). The synod he held in Rome in 465 is the earliest in Church history for which minutes were preserved in detail. Successor: St. Simplicius.

❀ **HIPPOLYTUS, ST.** A profound theologian and an antipope from 217 to 235. Of Greek descent, he was born around 170 and studied under the great theologian Irenaeus of Lyons. Going to Rome, he was ordained and became a leading figure in the city's Christian intellectual community. He was a prolific writer, a list of his works preserved on a statue of him, probably made during his lifetime and rediscovered in Rome in 1551. His chief work was the *Refutation of All the Heresies* (after 222) of which books 4 to 10 have survived. Willful, obstinate, and extremely devoted to strict religious discipline, he was adamantly opposed to the elevation of St. Callistus I (217–222) because of his checkered background, going so far as to establish himself as the head of an opposition party in Rome. As such, he is counted as the first of the antipopes who would trouble the Church over the centuries. His opposition to the bishops of Rome continued under Urban I (222–230) and Pontian (230–235), ended only in 235 when both he and Pontian were exiled to Sardinia by the Christian-hating Emperor Maximinus Thrax. Apparently he was reconciled to the Church because after his death from the brutal conditions on the isle he was brought back to Rome and solemnly interred. His statue was placed in the Vatican Library by Pope John XXIII in 1959.

❀ **HIS HOLINESS** The title of honor that is bestowed upon the pope. It is used in addressing the pontiff in several ways. One addresses him as "His Holiness, Pope N." or in speaking to him directly, such as "Your Holiness." (See also *Titles of the Pope.*)

❀ **HOLY FATHER** A title of respect and reverence that is used for the pope. It is taken from the Latin *Beatissimus Pater* (Most Holy Father) and first came into usage in English during the fourteenth century. The term is derived from the position of the pope as spiritual father of the Universal Church and all the Christian faithful. It can be used by members of the papal household when speaking to the pope, although they normally use the Latin version. (See also *Titles of the Pope.*)

❀ **HOLY OFFICE, PALACE OF THE** A somber-looking building, situated just below St. Peter's Square, jutting technically outside the territory of the Vatican City State into Italy but considered an extraterritorial possession of the Holy See. The Palazzo Sant'Uffizio is the headquarters of the very important Congregation for the Doctrine of the Faith, which has competence over the safeguarding of the teachings of the Catholic Church in matters of faith and morals. The palace was long the heart in Rome and Christendom of the Congregation of the Holy Office of the Inquisition. It was the site of the dread Inquisition under Pope Paul IV (1555–1559). Upon the death of this grim pontiff, a large and angry mob of Romans, fed up with his harsh rule, stormed the Holy Office, burned it, and freed the prisoners who had been incarcerated within its walls. Today, the palace is far from the site of dungeons and torture, but is the very sensitive territory of learned theologians who attempt to safeguard the teachings of the faith at a time of considerable social, religious, and doctrinal upheaval. The palace is also the residence of the cardinal prefect of the congregation. One side of the palace faces the window of the pope in the Apostolic Palace across St. Peter's Square, a symbolic view that epitomizes the very close relationship between the pontiff and the congregation. The entire complex is generally off limits to the public and is visited only by individuals with legitimate purposes and appointments with the staff. The palace is also next to a hospice that was built in 1989 at the command of Pope John Paul II to assist the poor, sick, and homeless of Rome in response to the request of Mother Teresa of Calcutta. It is staffed by members of the Missionaries of Charity, the order founded by Mother Teresa. Her nuns give food and shelter to the homeless, offer beds to elderly women in need, and say prayers in their private chapel. The hospice opens onto a Roman street and is open to all who need help.

❁ **HOLY SEE** Known also as the Apostolic See, the name given to the authority, sovereignty, and jurisdiction wielded over the Universal Church by the Supreme Pontiff by virtue of his election as Bishop of Rome. Holy See refers also to the central administration of the Church—both spiritual and temporal—which is entirely under the authority of the pontiff and which is given form by the Roman Curia. The Holy See is also synonymous with the diocese or see of Rome, situated in the

The coat of arms of John Paul II, bearing the symbols of the Holy See: the triple tiara and the crossed keys, gold and silver. (CATHOLIC NEWS SERVICE.)

Eternal City in and around the Vatican City State. Two points should be remembered, however. First, the Holy See should not be thought of as being the same as the Vatican City State (Città del Vaticano), which is a purely territorial possession of the pope as established and guaranteed by the Lateran Accords of 1929. Second, the Holy See derives its unique status, its holiness, from the fact that it was founded by St. Peter; the pope as his successor is Supreme Pontiff because he is elected Bishop of Rome, not the other way around.

The Holy See is also the world's oldest sovereign state, represented for countless years in international affairs by a variety of diplomatic officials such as legates, apostolic delegates, nuncios, pro-nuncios, and inter-nuncios. The popes, in fact, maintained relations with states of the world even during the period from 1870 to 1929 when they had no territorial possessions to claim as their own. The Holy See itself is considered the sovereign state and not any properties or holdings it may control. For this reason, diplomats are accredited to the Holy See and not to the Vatican, although in common language, it is often said that someone is ambassador to the Vatican, a descriptive but not altogether accurate statement. Beyond its formal relations with literally hundreds of countries, the Holy See has representatives or observer status in a host of international organizations—such as the United Nations—a reflection of the global interests and concerns of the papacy.

❀ **HOLY THURSDAY WASH-ING OF FEET**   Also known as the *mandatum* and in England as Maundy Thursday, the Thursday of Holy Week leading to Easter and the start of the so-called Easter triduum. Holy Thursday is significant as the day on which all masses without a congregation are strictly forbidden, and, ideally, the only mass celebrated in parish churches should be the evening mass of the Lord's Supper. The memorial of Christ's love finds expression in the unique cer-

The pope washes the feet of his priests on Holy Thursday at the Lateran Basilica.
(Courtesy L'Osservatore Romano, Città del Vaticano.)

emony of the washing of feet, remembering that Christ did this for his disciples at the Last Supper. The pope also performs this act of humility, following the example of Christ, whose vicar he is. Each year, on Maundy Thursday, he washes the feet of twelve priests in the Basilica of St. John Lateran. The feet are held over a silver basin, water is poured upon them, and the pope washes and kisses them.

❀ **HOLY YEAR** A year in which the pope grants a special indulgence to any persons who visit Rome and make a pilgrimage to one of the patriarchal basilicas of the city. Also called the Jubilee, it is proclaimed by the reigning pontiff and officially begun by opening the great Holy Doors of St. Peter's Basilica. These doors, designed by Carlo Maderno and kept closed and bricked up during off-years, are swung open, allowing one-way traffic into the basilica for the throngs of tourists and pilgrims eager to traverse its threshold. The Holy Year was established in 1300 by Pope Boniface VIII, with the original intention that it be celebrated every hundred years. In 1343, however, Pope Clement VI changed the interval to fifty years. This was changed again by Urban VI in 1389 to thirty-three years (in keeping with Christ's time on earth), and by Paul II in 1470 to twenty-five years. It has largely remained at this time interval ever since. Exceptions have included 1933, when Pope Pius XI commemorated the nineteenth centennial of Christ's crucifixion, resurrection, and ascension; and 1983 when John Paul II celebrated the Year of Redemption and the 1,950th anniversary of the Passion. The Jubilee has long had an important benefit for the Romans in that it routinely attracts many thousands of pilgrims and visitors, thereby filling the coffers of shops, hotels, restaurants, and the Vatican itself through the sale of commemorative coins and memorabilia. It is believed that the Jubilee of 1983 was a special gift from the pope to the Italian government, a way of compensating it for the considerable financial losses it had accrued through the irregularities and scandal caused by the Vatican Bank; the Holy Year brought in a financial bonanza to the city of Rome.

❀ **HONORIUS I** Pope from 625 to 638, he was born in Campagna to noble parents and was a one-time student of Pope St. Gregory I the Great (590–604), whom he took as a model when he was himself elected to succeed Boniface V. Like St. Gregory, Honorius converted his residence into a house for monks, preferring to appoint members of the monastic orders to papal offices. He also gave his enthusiastic endorsement and encouragement to missionary endeavors in England among the Anglo-Saxons, working to help spread the acceptance of the Roman rite in place of the long-established Celtic rite. His pontificate, however, would be dominated by the controversy of Monophysitism, the heresy that proposed that Christ had only one nature instead of the usually accepted two, human and divine. Honorius became embroiled in the controversy over the heresy when he chose to respond to a letter on the nature of Christ sent by Sergius, Patriarch of Constantinople. The pope quoted the Council of Chalcedon (451), which was strictly orthodox, but he also used the unfortunate term "one-will" in Christ. This caused severe controversy in both the Eastern and Western Churches and Honorius was subsequently anathematized by the Council of Constantinople (680–681) and was actually condemned by his successors—Pope Leo II upheld the condemnation by the council in 682. Honorius's actions have long been the source of study by scholars and debates as to his actual intent. It is thought that the pope did not mean to advance a dubious theological position, probably hoping instead to work for religious unity and so accept a formula that would return the Monophysites to the Church. Honorius was used by opponents of papal infallibility in the nineteenth century as an example of the inappropriateness of granting the pope so sweeping a mandate. Successor: Severinus.

⚜ **HONORIUS II**   Pope from 1124 to 1130, originally named Lamberto Scanabecchi, he came from a poor family in Imola, Italy, receiving elevation to the rank of cardinal by Pope Paschal II in 1117. Under Pope Callistus II, he took an important part in the negotiations that led to the Concordat of Worms that ended the investiture controversy. In the election following the death of Callistus, Lamberto was elevated in December 1124 through the insistence of the Frangipani family, backed by a troop of soldiers. The cardinals, who had already chosen but not completely installed Cardinal Teobaldo as Celestine II, accepted the newly elected cardinal's resignation and chose Lamberto. Recognizing the unusual circumstances of his elevation, the new pope offered to step down, but was instead reaffirmed and enthroned. As pope, Honorius made the most of improved relations with the empire to promote Church reforms. He was less successful in opposing the rise of the Normans in southern Italy; an army raised by the pope was defeated by Roger II of Sicily and the pope was forced to recognize him as Duke of Apulia. Falling terminally ill in early 1130, the pope was moved by the formidable papal chancellor Aimeric to a monastery in Rome. Here he died on February 13. Aimeric had him buried in a common grave to permit an immediate election that would be under his control and that of the Frangipani. This being done, the dead pontiff was exhumed and carted off for proper interment in the Lateran. Successor: Innocent II.

❀ **HONORIUS II**   Antipope from 1061 to 1064 and a rival to Pope Alexander II (1061–1073). Originally named Peter Cadalus, he owed his designation as pope on October 28, 1061, to an assembly of bishops and imperial officials at Basle, under the influence of Empress Agnes, regent for the young German King Henry IV. The decision was the result of Roman nobles sending a delegation to the imperial court requesting that Henry name someone to succeed Nicholas II. In September 1061, however, there had already been the election of Anselm of Lucca as Alexander II, the claimant who was recognized as legitimate pope. Taking the name Honorius II, Peter fought his way into Rome, but was forced to withdraw by imperial troops under the Duke of Lorraine, who declared that the matter was to be solved by the imperial court. This soon worked against Honorius because Agnes had been replaced as regent by Anno, Archbishop of Cologne. He found in Alexander's favor in October 1062. Undeterred, Honorius attacked Rome and was officially condemned in May 1064 by a synod of bishops in Mantua. He died around 1071 still claiming to be pope.

HONORIUS III   Pope from 1216 to 1227, Cencio Savelli was born to a well-established Roman family. He received appointment to a number of posts in the papal government and was made a cardinal deacon in 1193 and later cardinal priest. He also served as a tutor to the future Emperor Frederick II (who would be so devoted an enemy of the papacy). Savelli became a highly respected papal official, earning considerable notoriety as the compiler of the *Liber Censuum,* an important register of the Roman Church. Already old and in poor health when unanimously elected to succeed Innocent III, he soon demonstrated vigor and enthusiasm, emerging as one of the greatest of all papal administrators. His actual election was by compromise, in which two cardinals were delegated to pick the next pope. He took as his main aims the reform of the Church and the promotion of the crusade that Innocent called for through the Fourth Lateran Council in 1215. In his effort to mount the crusade, Honorius called upon the young Frederick to fulfill his vow and embark upon the military effort. Frederick was twice crowned German king by Honorius, but a dispute between them over the disposition of Sicily allowed the ruler to avoid setting sail. Honorius crowned him emperor in 1220, in the hopes of giving him encouragement. This proved to be an error, since Frederick continued to vacillate, to the detriment of his long-standing friendship with the pope. In frustration, Honorius threatened to excommunicate him. A major conflict was avoided only by the pope's death. Honorius was a committed patron of the reform of the Church and the recently established mendicant orders such as the Dominicans and Franciscans. Renowned for his learning, he authored a number of important works, including the first compilation of canon law (the *Compilatio Quinta* or Fifth Compilation), a life of Pope St. Gregory VII, an extension of the *Liber Pontificalis,* and numerous letters and sermons. He was also a reputed sorcerer in popular legend, the supposed but fictitious creator of the *Grimoire of Honorius III,* a book on sorcery. Successor: Gregory IX.

HONORIUS IV   Pope from 1285 to 1287, of noble Roman birth, Giacomo Savelli was a grand-nephew of Honorius III. He studied in Paris and had a long career before receiving elevation to cardinal by Pope Urban IV in 1261. His election to succeed Martin IV on April 2, 1285, was swift and unanimous; in honor of his grand-uncle he adopted the name Honorius. His brief reign was noted for his patronage of the mendicant orders—which his relative had also undertaken—giving numerous benefits to the Dominicans and Franciscans, including control over the Inquisition. The main conflict of his reign was with King Pedro III of Aragon over papal rights in Sicily, which had been effectively ended in 1282 when the Aragonese took control of the island after the bloody massacre of the French on the island in the so-called War of the Sicilian Vespers that ended the reign of the Angevins. He also promoted the study of Oriental languages at the University of Paris in the hopes of furthering the possible reunion between the Eastern and Western Churches. In his two years as pope, he created only one cardinal, John of Tusculum. After his death on April 3, 1287, nearly a year would pass before the cardinals could choose a new pope. Successor: Nicholas IV.

HORMISDAS, ST.   Pope from 514 to 523, a member of the Roman aristocracy and an Italian despite his Persian name, Hormisdas had been married prior to his ordination. His son, Silverius, would become pope himself in 536. Elected to succeed Pope St. Symmachus on July 20, 514, he strove to maintain good relations with the Ostrogothic king Thoedoric, ruler of Italy. This permitted him the freedom to deal with the Byzantines and so he sought an end to the Acacian Schism that had divided the Eastern and Western Churches since 484, the result of the excommunication of Acacius, Patriarch of Constantinople (d. 489) for heresy. The pope was rebuffed by the hard-line Emperor Anastasius I (r. 491–518), but he found Emperor Justin I (r. 518–527) to be more accommodating, along with John of Cappadocia, the Patriarch of Constantinople. The schism was brought to a close in 519 and a reunion, albeit a brief one, was affected. He died on August 6, 523, and was buried in St. Peter's, his son composing his epitaph. Successor: St. John I.

❀ **HOUSEHOLD, PONTIFICAL** See *Papal Household, Prefecture of the.*

❀ **HYGINUS, ST.** Pope from around 137 to 140, ranked as the ninth pope and the eighth successor to St. Peter as Bishop of Rome. According to the *Liber Pontificalis,* he was a Greek, probably from Athens, working previously as a philosopher. His reign is considered noteworthy for the fact that during it there first came to Rome adherents of the heresy of Gnosticism, which would trouble the Church over the next years. The actual length of his reign varies among sources. The *Liber Pontificalis* and the historian Eusebius of Caesarea both state it to be of four years duration; the *Liberian Catalogue,* however, places it at the improbable length of twelve years. Successor: St. Pius I.

❀ **INFALLIBILITY, PAPAL** The special freedom from all error in teaching that is possessed by the Pope when he makes a formal proclamation on a matter concerning faith or morals. The infallibility of the Supreme Pontiff was first officially defined by Vatican Council I (1869–1870) under Pope Pius IX. One of the most misunderstood and even exaggerated rights of the Holy Father, infallibility is actually governed by specific requirements and areas of competence. The pontiff can only speak infallibly when he does so ex cathedra, meaning that he formally declares some teaching to be unchangeably correct and that he stands as shepherd of the Church and not as a private theologian giving his opinion; further, he may only speak infallibly on matters of faith and morals. Thus, the old charge that the pope tried to speak infallibly about the nature of the solar system in the time of Galileo is not correct. The popes use their power of infallibility with much care and only after extended study, reflection, and prayer.

❀ **INNOCENT I, ST.** Pope from December 21, 401, to March 12, 417, whose reign was overshadowed by the terrible sack of Rome by the Visigoths in 410. A native of Albano, Italy, he was perhaps the son of Pope Anastasius I, serving as his deacon and receiving election as his successor. He became pope in one of the grim periods in Roman history, when the empire in the West was falling to pieces, shaken by Germanic inroads and invasions and deteriorating political and economic stability. In the face of mounting turmoil, he used his considerable intellectual and spiritual gifts to advance the primacy of the Holy See over the entire Church. When, in 410, the Visigoths entered Italy, the pope traveled to Ravenna (the political capital) to negotiate a truce. His efforts failed, and the Visigoths under Alaric stormed the city while Innocent was still away, an event that shocked the entire Roman world. His absence from Rome was seen by contemporaries as providential, declaring him spared, like Lot, from the wrath of God. While he refused to countenance any public sacrifices to the now defunct pagan gods, he did allow—by ignoring them—the activities of old pagan Romans in making supplication to the gods in the desperate hope they might spare the city from pillage. While not returning to Rome until 412, Innocent gave much attention to relieving the famine and the suffering of the Romans, who long remained in a state of shock. Successor: St. Zosimus.

INNOCENT II   Pope from February 14, 1130, to September 24, 1143. Gregorio Papareschi Dei Guidoni was a native of Rome. He was made a cardinal by Pope Callistus II in 1122, taking part in the negotiations that led to the Concordat of Worms in 1122. His election as successor to Honorius II was hastily arranged and swiftly carried out by the Frangipani family and the powerful papal chamberlain Aimeric (Honorius had been buried in a makeshift grave, to make it legal). It soon aroused the anger of other factions in Rome and among the cardinals who opposed what they saw as a papal coup. Led by the Pierleone family, the opposition party elected Peter Cardinal Pierleone as antipope Anacletus II. Innocent, properly installed in the Lateran, soon had to flee Italy for the safety of France. There he found the help of St. Bernard of Clairvaux, the German king Lothair II, and King Louis VI of France. With Lothair and an imperial army, Innocent returned to Rome in 1133, but the Anacletan party made it impossible for him to remain for long once Lothair, having been crowned emperor in the Lateran, departed for Germany. A resolution of the crisis would not be possible until 1138 and Anacletus's death. The antipope's ally, Roger II of Sicily, soon sponsored another rival, antipope Victor IV, who eventually resigned at the behest of the most persuasive St. Bernard. Innocent's problems did not end, however, for in 1139, his papal army was routed and he himself was captured. He was released after acknowledging Roger as King of Sicily in the Treaty of Migniano (July 1139). Successor: Celestine II.

INNOCENT III   Pope from 1198 to 1216, one of the most important popes during the Middle Ages. Born in Gavignano Castle in Campagna di Roma, Lothair of Segni was a member of the family of the Count of Segni and a nephew of Pope Clement III. After studying in Paris and Bologna, he was appointed cardinal deacon by his uncle in 1190. Owing to a feud between his family and that of Pope Celestine III, he was far from one of the leading cardinals in Rome, devoting most of his time to studying and writing various theological treatises. Known for his intellect, he was unanimously elected to succeed Celestine on January 8, 1198, on the same day as the old pontiff's passing. At the time of his election, he was only thirty-seven years old and needed both ordination to the priesthood and consecration as pope. A truly formidable personality, with a broad conception of the powers of the papacy, Innocent proclaimed himself Vicar of Christ, commanding a position between man and God, above man but below God. In this, however, he chose almost always to stress his spiritual authority, restricting his concerns in temporal affairs to the troubled conditions in Rome and the Papal States. In this he was eminently successful, restoring control over the States of the Church by the Holy See. In other Church matters, he reformed the papal Curia, reluctantly launched a bloody crusade against the Albigensian heretics in France after they murdered one of his legates, and gave his enthusiastic support to the new mendicant orders, the Dominicans and Franciscans. Concerned deeply with launching another Crusade to the Holy Land, Innocent authorized the Fourth Crusade (1202–1204), but was then appalled when the soldiers, at the connivance of the Venetians, sailed not to Palestine but to Constantinople. There the Christian knights overthrew the Byzantine Empire and mercilessly sacked Constantinople. Forced to accept this development, he appointed a Latin Patriarch of Constantinople and acknowledged the so-called Latin Empire of Constantinople in the sincere hope that it might hasten a reunion of the Eastern and Western Churches. Unfortunately, his decision outraged the already deeply offended Byzantines and clouded relations over the next years. While averse to temporal matters, Innocent was drawn into numerous political squabbles, proving himself quite adroit at the political gambit, using his powers to punish certain kings on the basis that they were committing sins and that he, as a good pastor, was pointing out their shortcomings. His most interesting political move was to declare the Magna Carta to be void by virtue that it had been extracted from King John by the English barons under duress. His action was influenced by the agreement reached just before the event in 1215 by which the Holy See received a favorable fiefdom over the king's lands. He also summoned the Fourth Lateran Council in 1215, and commanded all Jews and Muslims to wear dress that might set them apart from the rest of society. His death on July 16, 1216, came quite unexpectedly at Perugia while he was making another appeal for a crusade. Successor: Honorius III.

⚜ **INNOCENT III**   Antipope from 1179 to 1180, the fourth rival who was established against Pope Alexander III during his struggle with Emperor Frederick I Barbarossa. He was handed over to the pope who imprisoned him; he died sometime later.

INNOCENT IV Pope from 1243 to 1254, a Genoese and the son of Count Hugo of Lavagna, Sinibaldo Fieschi studied at Bologna and then taught there. His career in the Church was impressive: Bishop of Albenga, vice-chancellor of the Roman Church, cardinal, and rector of the March of Ancona in the Papal States. He was elected to succeed Celestine IV on June 25, 1243, at Anagni after an interregnum of nearly two years marked by intrigue. Influencing his elevation by the cardinals was Fieschi`s friendship with the troublesome Emperor Frederick II. Any hopes for improved relations between the Holy See and Holy Roman Empire were soon dashed, however, when Frederick declared: "My friendship with a cardinal is ever possible; with a pope, never!" Innocent's reign was thus filled with more bitter conflict. Driven from Rome, he fled to France where, at the Council of Lyons in 1245, he excommunicated Frederick. He also gave his backing to the noble Henry Raspe, Landgrave of Thuringia, in the fight for the imperial crown against the emperor. The death of Frederick in 1250 was not the source of much relief, since Innocent was soon involved in the complex struggle for the imperial succession. He would continue to be plagued by Frederick's dynasty, the Hohenstaufens, in a blood feud that was not to be resolved until the reign of Clement IV (1265–1268). Innocent was much criticized by chroniclers for his rapacious taxation, his devious nature, and his unabashed nepotism and favoritism. He died in Naples on December 7, 1254. Successor: Alexander IV.

INNOCENT V Pope from January 21 to June 22, 1276, he was the first pope elected from the Dominican order. Born Peter of Tarentaise around 1224, he was French, entering the Dominicans in 1240 at Lyons. He subsequently studied at Paris and was later a teacher of theology at the university. In 1259 he had the special opportunity to work with Sts. Albertus Magnus and Thomas Aquinas on the program of study for the order. He also authored a well-known commentary on the *Sentences* of Peter Lombard, one of the main theological textbooks during the Middle Ages. Twice serving as provincial of the Dominicans (from around 1264–1267 and 1269–1272), he was appointed Archbishop of Lyons in 1271 and then cardinal (*c.* 1273), by Pope Gregory X. His election in Arezzo in Savoy, under the rules carefully laid down by Gregory, made him the first Dominican chosen as successor to St. Peter. His brief reign was preoccupied with continuing efforts to maintain the tenuous reunion between the Eastern and Western Churches negotiated at Lyons, mediating the differences between France and Germany, and organizing another crusade. He died suddenly of a fever. Successor: Adrian IV.

INNOCENT VI Pope from 1352 to 1362, the fifth pope to reside at Avignon, Etienne Aubert was born at Monts, in France, serving as a professor of law at Toulouse and then a judge before he entered the clergy. His ecclesiastical career was impressive: Bishop of Noyon (1338), Bishop of Clermont (1340), and cardinal priest (1342) at the hand of Pope Clement VI; in 1352 he became cardinal bishop and then was named a high official in the Avignon-based government of the popes. His election on December 16, 1352, to succeed Clement VI came after a two-day conclave following Clement's death. As part of the conclave, he had agreed with his fellow cardinals to place a variety of limitations on the next pope (such as the prohibition of creating new cardinals until their number had dropped below twenty). Once elevated, however, he refused to accept these conditions because they were a severe impediment to his powers. Innocent was determined and serious, ending the luxurious court of Clement and instituting a broad reform of the Curia at Avignon. He also had genuine hopes of returning to Rome, but he perceived that conditions there were far from safe because the Papal States had deteriorated severely in the absence of the papal government. To restore some kind of order, he appointed the warrior cardinal Gil de Albornoz as vicar general of the Papal States, launching a campaign that would last for many years. Innocent also tried unsuccessfully to end the Hundred Years' War between England and France, although he did negotiate the Treaty of Bretigny in 1360, which brought a halt to the fighting for a decade. Successor: Urban V.

INNOCENT VII Pope from 1404 to 1406. One of the legitimate pontiffs elected during the Great Western Schism that divided the Church from 1378 to 1417, Cosimo Gentili de'Migliorati was born at Sulmona in Italy. After studying law at Bologna, he taught at Perugia and Padua and then received appointment to the papal administration by Pope Urban VI. In 1378 he was made archbishop of Ravenna; two years later, he became bishop of Bologna and then cardinal in 1389 through Pope Boniface IX. Following Boniface's death on October 1, 1404, Migliorati was one of only eight cardinals who gathered to choose the next pope, accepting the preelection condition with his fellow cardinals that whoever was chosen should pledge to do everything possible to end the schism.

Elected pope on October 17, he was unwilling to meet with antipope Benedict XIII, and the council at Rome he tried to convene was a failure, owing to the chronic social and political upheaval in the Eternal City. The Romans extracted from the new pope a variety of concessions, and soon demanded more, compelling him to rely upon his nephew, the intemperate Ludovico Migliorati to restore order. Migliorati launched a massacre of nearly a dozen local leaders, causing a general uprising and forcing Innocent to flee with his court to Viterbo. The pope returned only in March 1406, dying on November 6 that same year. Quiet, unassuming, and unfortunately ineffectual, Innocent had taken as his main ambition the founding of a university in Rome; he did not live to see it, nor was any progress made toward resolving the schism. Successor: Gregory XII.

INNOCENT VIII Pope from 1484 to 1492, the pontiff between the active Sixtus IV and the infamous Alexander VI. Giovanni Battista Cibo was born in Genoa to a wealthy senatorial family, studying in Rome and Padua, becoming bishop of Savona in 1467 and cardinal in 1473 under Sixtus. After that pontiff's death in August 1484, the conclave that followed was steeped in intrigue and conspiracy as two main factions schemed to secure the election of their favorite; one supported Cardinal Giuliano della Rovere and the other wanted Cardinal Rodrigo Borgia (both would later become pope as Julius II and Alexander VI respectively). Cibo proved a compromise candidate, ensuring his election on August 29, 1484, in large measure because of numerous promises he made to other cardinals in his cell the night before and the financial backing of della Rovere. His pontificate was well in keeping with that of his predecessor. The papal court was often dissolute, profligate, and decidedly secular, made only more so by the poor moral example set by the pontiff himself. While kind, he suffered from indecision and poor health, made only worse by the financial troubles left to him by Sixtus. These were exacerbated by his own extravagances and his participation in several ill-conceived and frightfully expensive wars. Facing financial ruin, he was spared the further indignity of selling even more indulgences and offices by the sudden opportunity presented by the arrival of Prince Jem, the refugee brother of Sultan Bayezid II of the Ottoman Turks. The prince had lost out in a power struggle with Bayezid and had fled to Rhodes and the Knights of St. John. They gave him to the pope, who entered into negotiations with the Turks. Innocent kept the prince in appropriate luxury in the Vatican—safe from assassins and far from those who might scheme with him—in return for 40,000 ducats a year. Innocent was thrilled to have both a partial solution to his money troubles and one of the most impressive guests in the history of the Vatican. The prince was regularly observed in Rome, accompanied by his ornate and dangerous-looking retinue, earning the quizzical stares of the pilgrims who had come to Rome to give their prayers at the tomb of St. Peter. Innocent also issued the bull *Summis Desiderantes* (1484) against witches, sparking brutal activities by officials in Germany. His worldly and ineffective reign brought a decline in the papal administration and control over the Papal States; following his death, trouble would appear from a variety of directions. Successor: Alexander VI.

INNOCENT IX Pope for a mere two months in 1591. A native of Bologna, Giovanni Antonio Fachinetti studied at the University of Bologna and served as Bishop of Nicastro and was a papal nuncio to Venice from 1566 to 1572. While serving in Venice, he helped negotiate the league that won the immense triumph over the Turks at the Battle of Lepanto in 1571. Pope Gregory XIII made him patriarch of Jerusalem in 1576 and cardinal in 1583. He was a clear favorite, entering several conclaves between 1585 and 1591, finally winning election on October 29, 1591, to succeed Gregory XIV. His extremely brief reign accomplished little save for efforts to curb the raids of bandits in the Papal States and improving the sanitation of the Borgo. Already ill in the middle of December, he ignored the wishes of his doctors and went on a pilgrimage to several churches; while traveling he grew worse and died on December 30, 1591. Successor: Clement VIII.

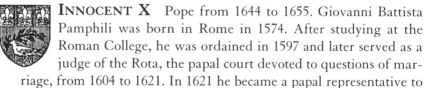

INNOCENT X Pope from 1644 to 1655. Giovanni Battista Pamphili was born in Rome in 1574. After studying at the Roman College, he was ordained in 1597 and later served as a judge of the Rota, the papal court devoted to questions of marriage, from 1604 to 1621. In 1621 he became a papal representative to Naples. Five years later, he was named patriarch of Antioch and then papal nuncio to Spain. Elevated to the cardinalate in 1627, he was actually invested with the office only in 1630. A well-known figure in the pontificate of Urban VIII (1623–1644), Pamphili was considered a serious candidate for the papal throne in 1644, receiving election by the seriously divided cardinals on September 15, 1644, in large measure because the majority of electors wanted to reverse Urban's policy of conciliation toward the French. As Innocent X, he adopted a generally pro-Spanish outlook, thus damaging relations with France. The degree of hostility was made manifest by the decision of Jules Cardinal Mazarin, minister of King Louis XIII, who gave refuge to two cardinals of the now discredited Barberini family, who had fled to France to escape prosecution by the new pope for corruption under the Barberini pope, Urban VIII. While a reconciliation was later effected, Innocent responded to Mazarin's move by offering sanctuary to Mazarin's enemy, the dissolute Jean Cardinal de Retz. The chief foreign policy event of his reign was the signing of the Treaty of Westphalia in 1648, bringing to a final end the Thirty Years' War (1618–1648), which had left whole parts of Europe in ruins. While he welcomed peace, Innocent found himself in the difficult position of opposing the treaty on the grounds that Catholic interests had not been addressed, that the papacy had not been given a leading role in the negotiations, and that the Protestant position was granted too much recognition; he confirmed his protests in the bull *Zelus Domus Meae* (The Zeal of My House, 1648). In a testament to the declining international prestige of the papacy, the princes of Europe, weary of war, ignored the complaints of the Holy See. Innocent also condemned the heretical movement of Janseninsm with the bull *Cum Occasione* in 1653.

The reign of Innocent began with the repudiation of the pernicious rapacity of the Barberinis, but he, too, soon fell prey to the dangers of nepotism. He was dominated in policymaking by his relatives, most especially the truly imperious Donna Olimpia Maidalchini-Pamphili, his brother's widow. She exercised an altogether unhealthy control over the papal court, convincing the pope to grant honors to several nephews. Significantly, however, he refused to appoint the traditional cardinal nephew, naming instead a reliable set of cardinals to the office of secretary of state. He first gave the office to Giovanni Cardinal Panciroli, and then after his death in 1651, granted it to the very able Fabio Cardinal Chigi (the future Pope Alexander VII). Within the court, however, Donna Olimpia was supreme, running the entire household, down to the kitchens. As death approached the eighty-two-year-old pontiff, the Donna abruptly departed the papal palace to avoid reprisals from the incoming papal administration. Unfortunately, chaos ensued in the palace, and the deceased Innocent (he died on January 7, 1655) was supposedly left unattended for three days in his chambers; when officials called upon wealthy Donna Olimpia to organize the funeral, she responded that there was no way she could pay for the obsequies as she was but a poor widow. Successor: Alexander VII.

INNOCENT XI   Pope from 1676 to 1689. Born in Como, Italy, in 1611, Benedetto Odescalchi studied with the Jesuits and earned doctorates in law in 1639. After holding a variety of posts, he was appointed a cardinal under Innocent X in 1645, legate to Ferrara in 1648, and Bishop of Novara in 1650. In 1654, he retired owing to poor health, and was thus flabbergasted at his election on September 21, 1676, to succeed Clement X. He would accept his unanimous elevation only after the cardinals gave their acquiescence to a fourteen-point plan of reform. This initial measure made clear his determination to introduce reforms and defend the rights of the Church. Renowned for his piety and charitable nature, he sent aid to the Poles and Austrians, who were suffering under the invasions of the Ottoman Turks. Closer to home, he demanded social changes, closing down the infamous Roman gambling dens and prohibiting women from wearing gaudy clothing. Papal finances were also restored by means of austerities and careful taxation. Innocent also resisted the Gallicanist tendencies of King Louis XIV of France, especially opposing the Gallican Articles, which had been issued in 1682 and sought to curtail papal rights in France. The pope also disagreed with Louis on the revocation of the Edict of Nantes in 1685 (which brought oppression of the Protestants) since Innocent had reached the realistic conclusion that the Protestants would have to be dealt with and that repression was unacceptable. The pope also made as his great ambition the expulsion of the Ottoman Turks from Europe, organizing the Holy League against them and contributing large amounts of money to its success; he had the satisfaction of learning of the liberation of Hungary in 1686 and the capture of Belgrade in 1688. After his death, he was deeply respected and revered, even by the Romans, whose gambling fun he had done much to curb. Beatified in 1956 by Pope Pius XII, he is considered one of the foremost pontiffs of the seventeenth century. Successor: Alexander VIII.

INNOCENT XII   Pope from 1691 to 1700, Antonio Pignatelli was born near Spinazzola, Italy, in 1615, studying under the Jesuits in Rome. Entering the papal government of Pope Urban VIII, he subsequently held a variety of posts, including papal governor of Viterbo and papal ambassador to Tuscany, Poland, and Austria. Appointed cardinal in 1681 by Innocent XI, he was made

Archbishop of Naples in 1687. In 1691, after the death of Alexander VIII, an interregnum of some five months followed, ended only after the Romans announced their displeasure by riots; the cardinals in conclave were also probably influenced by the unbearable Roman heat. Pignatelli was elected on July 12, 1691, and immediately fulfilled his reputation for being devout and honest by taking the name Innocent in honor of the reforming pontiff Innocent XI. He then launched a reform of the Curia and the Papal States, insisting upon fairness for the citizens of the States of the Church and an end to papal nepotism through the decree *Romanum Decet Pontificem* (1692), by which he required that only one relative should be made a prelate—and then with a limited income—and the family of the pope should not profit with lands and titles. His view on the matter was summed up with the statement: "If the leader of the Church has poor relations, let him give them the same charity as he gives other needy people." Innocent also reached an agreement with King Louis XIV of France that effectively ended the long-standing tensions between the Holy See and France over the Gallican Articles, which had sought to curtail papal influence in France. He also reiterated the declaration of Alexander VII (1655–1667) against the Jansenists and issued the brief *Cum Alias* condemning the mystical propositions of Quietism. Innocent died on September 27, 1700. Successor: Clement XI.

INNOCENT XIII   Pope from 1721 to 1724. Michelangelo Conti was born in 1655 near Palestrina, the son of the Duke of Poli. He studied at Ancona and in Rome received appointment to the papal administration. Named a governor in the Papal States, he served as nuncio in Switzerland from 1695 to 1698 and Portugal from 1698 to 1709. In 1706, he received elevation to the cardinalate under Clement XI. He was Bishop of Osimo from 1709 to 1712 and Viterbo from 1712 to 1719. In 1719 he resigned owing to poor health, but was still a candidate for election as pope in the conclave that followed the death of Clement XI. In that assembly, the favorite, Fabrizio Cardinal Paolucci (Clement's secretary of state), was vetoed by the Holy Roman Emperor, whereupon the cardinals unanimously chose Pignatelli on May 8, 1721. He took the name Innocent in honor of his distant relative Innocent III (1198–1216). The main thrust of his pontificate was to restore the Holy See's relations with the major powers of Europe. He recognized Emperor Charles VI as ruler of Naples, reversing Clement's refusal to do so after the kingdom had passed to Charles in 1720. Innocent also elevated the dissolute and corrupt

French minister Guillaume Dubois (1656–1723) to the cardinalate as a means of placating the French. Long suspicious of the Jesuits, he commanded that they obey Pope Clement XI's ban on their use of the so-called Chinese Rites, the practice of allowing Chinese converts to adhere to certain traditional Chinese religious customs. When he raised his brother Bernard to the rank of cardinal, fears of a return of nepotism were expressed in Rome, but these were relieved when Innocent adhered carefully to the ban on nepotism issued by Innocent XI. Successor: Benedict XIII.

❀ **INVESTITURE CONTROVERSY**   The name used for the struggle between Church and state over the right claimed by a number of secular rulers to invest abbots and bishops with their rings and staffs, the symbols of their office, and receiving from them acts of personal homage prior to consecration. This privilege, a long-standing custom found in parts of Europe, was the continuation of secular domination of the Church that had routinely occurred in the fourth to the eleventh centuries. By the middle of the eleventh century, however, the popes were eager to render the Church independent from secular interference. They thus launched a thorough reform of the Church and condemned investiture as an unacceptable violation of the rights of the popes and the Church. The practice was specifically attacked by Pope Nicholas II in 1059, followed by a decree issued by Pope St. Gregory VII (1073–1085) forbidding any secular ruler to engage in investiture. He was soon opposed by the German kings, and so began the investiture controversy. The most pronounced dispute was between the popes and Emperors Henry IV and Henry V. A settlement was reached through the Concordat of Worms in 1122. While lay investiture was generally brought to an end in the twelfth century, secular interference in Church affairs would continue for centuries, especially in France and England.

❀ **ITALY**   The European republic with whom the Holy See has full diplomatic relations. For many centuries following the demise of the Roman Empire in the West, Italy was nonexistent as a unified country, and the name Italy was described rather derisively by the Austrian statesman Prince Metternich as being "a mere geographical designation." The Church, however, had a long period of successful development, its direction facilitated by the presence of the Bishop of Rome, the Pope, so much so that Catholicism has always been the overwhelmingly dominant faith. Much of the Italian peninsula was directly under the authority of the popes for centuries, in the shape of the Papal States, until 1870 when the process of Italian unification, called the Risorgimento, reached its climax with the takeover of Rome and the foundation of the Kingdom of Italy under King Victor Emmanuel II. From 1870 until 1929, the popes refused to acknowledge the Italian government, an impasse called the Roman Question (or *dissidio*) that was finally ended in 1929 with the Lateran Treaty. The relationship begun with the treaty was renewed in 1985, with the signing of a new concordat between the Italians and Pope John Paul II. The culture of the Vatican City State remains distinctly Italian, and Italian continues to be the lingua franca of the Holy See and the Curia. (See also *Papal States* and *Rome.*)

✾ **JOAN, POPE** A famous legend about a woman who supposedly was elected pope, reigning as Pope John VIII from around 855 to 858, between the pontificates of Leo IV (847–855) and Benedict III (855–858); another version has her winning election in 1100. The story of Pope Joan is almost universally discounted by scholars, but the legend was extremely popular during the Middle Ages, was mentioned by Petrarch and Boccaccio, and was used by leaders of the Protestant cause in the sixteenth century to stir up antipapal sentiment. While disproved in the seventeenth century by a Protestant scholar, Maurice Blondel (1590–1655), it was still repeated by anti-Catholic bigots and propagandists as late as the nineteenth century. Joan was supposedly a very talented scribe in Rome who disguised herself as a man and took a position in the service of the papacy. She was advanced steadily through the Curia and finally received election as pope in large part because of the brilliance of her lectures. Her reign proved brief, however, for she gave birth to a child in a narrow street near the Colosseum, during a procession to the Lateran. (Popes supposedly avoided the street ever after.) Once discovered, she was stoned to death.

✾ **JOHN I, ST.** Pope from August 13, 523, to May 18, 526. A native of Tuscany, Italy, he was born around 470 and was serving as senior deacon when elected to succeed Pope Hormisdas. Distinguished as the first pope to visit Constantinople, he had earlier represented Hormisdas to the Byzantines during the negotiations to end the Acacian Schism, which had long divided the Eastern and Western Churches. The reunion was not greeted with joy by the ruler of Italy, King Theodoric of the Ostrogoths, a devoted Arian who looked with suspicion on any rapprochement between Rome and Constantinople. Concerned that there might be a growing conspiracy aimed at restoring Byzantine power in Italy, Theodoric seized the pope at Ravenna upon the latter's return from Constantinople to Italy in 526. The pope remained in prison at Ravenna until his death, most likely from starvation. His body was taken to Rome and placed in St. Peter's Basilica; the epitaph declared him a "victim for Christ." Successor: St. Felix IV.

❀ **JOHN II** Pope from 533 to 535, the first pope to change his name after election. Born in Rome, he was a priest of S. Clemente and was quite elderly at the time of his elevation on January 2, 533, to succeed Boniface II. Most likely a compromise candidate, the choice of the electors was named Mercury. As this was the name of a pagan god, he changed it to John, after the martyred St. John I (523–526). John enjoyed sound relations with both the Byzantine Emperor Justinian I (r. 527–565) and Athelric, King of the Ostrogoths. His main doctrinal decision was to excommunicate a group of heretical Nestorian monks in Constantinople in March 534 at the request of Emperor Justinian. John did not begin a new fashion in changing his name, since the practice was not made common until the time of Pope Sergius IV (1009–1012). Successor: St. Agapitus I.

❀ **JOHN III** Pope from 561 to 574, his reign was dominated by invasion and tumult. A Roman, he was probably the son of a Roman senator and was originally named Catelinus. Elected to succeed Pope Pelagius, he was consecrated on July 17, 561, forced to wait some four months until formal approval of his election came from Emperor Justinian. His pontificate is rather obscure; it fell during a time of attack by the Lombards. Desperate for help against the onslaught, John traveled to Naples and won the help of the Byzantine general, Narses. The Byzantines arrived in Rome in 571, an event that was greeted by rioting because of the unpopularity of the Greeks and a rumor that Narses had been conniving with the Lombards. John thus found it necessary to flee the city. He settled in the church of SS. Tiburtius and Valeria on the Via Appia some miles distant from Rome. There he conducted all business until the general died in 573. John himself died on July 13, 573. Successor: Benedict I.

❀ **JOHN IV** Pope from 640 to 642, a Dalmatian by birth, he was serving as archdeacon of Rome when elected to succeed Severinus. Chosen in August of 640, he was consecrated only on December 24, 640, having decided to wait until given formal approval by the Byzantine emperor. His brief reign was centered on continuing the opposition of the Church against the heresy of Monothelitism, which claimed that Christ had only one will (rather than human and divine). He convened a synod in Rome in 641 that condemned the heresy and a profession of faith made along Monothelitist lines, called the *Ecthesis,* issued by Byzantine Emperor Heraclius (r. 610–641). John was also deeply concerned for his native Dalmatia, which had been overrun by the Slavs and Avars, and sent money to assist in the ransoming of enslaved Christians. He died in Rome on October 12, 642. Successor: Theodore I.

❈ JOHN V   Pope from 685 to 686, an obscure pontiff, he was a Syrian by birth, hailing from Antioch and coming to Rome to escape the invasion of his homeland by the Arabs. Eventually serving as a deacon in Rome, he was one of three representatives, or legates, sent by Pope Agatho to the Third Council of Constantinople (680–681). One of the most eminent members of the Roman clergy, he was unanimously elected to succeed St. Benedict II, but his reign lasted only from July 23, 685, to August 2, 686. He cared for the poor of Rome and was a strong advocate of papal supremacy. His effectiveness was hampered by his poor health. Successor: Conon.

❈ JOHN VI   Pope from 701 to 705, a Greek by birth, he is little known prior to his election to succeed St. Sergius I. His reign, beginning on October 30, 701, was noted for the political upheaval in Italy that was precipitated by the deposition of Byzantine Emperor Justinian II (695) and the subsequent deterioration of Byzantine authority in the peninsula. John gave protection to the Byzantine exarch (or governor) when the latter fled to the pope's safety after an uprising by the Italians. Soon after (*c.* 702), the region of Campania was invaded by Duke Gisulfo of Benevento, compelling John to pay massive bribes for the hostages taken by the duke and convince him to depart with his army. Successor: John VII.

❈ JOHN VII   Pope from 705 to 707, John was the first pontiff to be the son of a Byzantine official—his father, Plato, was overseer of the imperial palace located on the Palatine Hill in Rome. Elected to succeed John VI and reigning from March 1, 705, he used good relations with the Lombards to secure the restoration of papal possessions in the Cottian Alps. He also rebuilt the Benedictine monastery of Mt. Subiaco, which had been pillaged and burned by Saracen raiders. In dealing with the Byzantines, however, John displayed a caution that was sharply criticized as cowardice by his biographer in the *Liber Pontificalis.* The cause of this criticism was his refusal to convene a synod and condemn the canons issued by the so-called Quinisext Council (or Council of Trullo) of 692 convened by the violently unpredictable Emperor Justinian II and condemning Roman ecclesiastical practices. John bypassed an offer made by the emperor and instead chose to return the canons without comment. A patron of the arts, John was much influenced by Byzantine style, as seen in his decoration of churches. Known for his devotion to the Virgin Mary, he was buried in the chapel of the Blessed Virgin Mary in St. Peter's, which is preserved today as part of the Vatican Grottoes. Successor: Sisinnius.

�֎ **JOHN VIII**   Pope from 872 to 882, an active but at times decidedly political pontiff who involved himself in the affairs of empire. A Roman by birth, he long served as the leading archdeacon in Rome and was a trusted figure in the pontificates of both Nicholas I (858–867) and Adrian II (867–872). Around fifty-two when selected to succeed Adrian, he displayed much vigor and energy in confronting the crises facing Italy. The central and chronic crisis was that of the Saracens, who were such a menace to Rome and the Papal States from their bases in southern Italy. Of them, John wrote: "If every tree in the forest were changed into tongues they could not describe the cruelties of the impious pagans. The devout People of God are massacred by a continual slaughter. . . ." The pope built a strong defensive wall around St. Paul's Basilica, organized a papal fleet, and labored, unsuccessfully, to forge an alliance against the Muslims. In the end, he was forced to buy them off. On Christmas Day 875, John crowned Charles the Bald emperor, receiving from him added territories and political considerations. At Charles's death in 881, John gave his blessing to the claimant Charles the Fat, crowning him emperor in February 881. Charles, however, proved a major disappointment to the pope in failing to provide support against the Saracens and by demonstrating such egregious personal failings that he would later be deposed by his own princes. John was also vexed by the ambitious Roman nobles, excommunicating a number of them, including Formosus, Bishop of Porto, who would later be pope. He recognized the repentant Photius, Patriarch of Constantinople, and thereby brought peace between the Eastern and Western Churches. He also gave his support to the missionary endeavors of St. Methodius, eventually sanctioning the use of Slavonic in the liturgy in 880. The last years of his reign were filled with bitter disappointments. According to the *Annales Fuldenses* (*Annals of Fulda*), he was assassinated by members of his own court, who supposedly poisoned and then beat him to death. If the story is accurate, John holds the distinction of being the first assassinated pope. His death is placed at December 16, 882. Successor: Marinus I.

❀ **JOHN IX** Pope from 898 to 900. Born in Tivoli, Italy, he had been a member of the Benedictine Order and had been ordained by Pope Formosus. His election as pope came in January 898, after the death of Pope Theodore II in November 897. He owed his elevation to the so-called Formosan Party in Rome and the help of Lambert of Spoleto, King of Italy, who expelled the recently chosen Sergius (III). The papacy was still in the shadow of the infamous Cadaver Synod of 897, and John was determined to erase its unsavory memory. He convened synods in Rome and Ravenna condemning Stephen VI (VII) for holding the synod, destroying all of the synod's acts, and restoring all deposed clergy. John also confirmed the constitution issued by Emperor Lothair I in 824 concerning imperial privileges in papal elections. Successor: Benedict IV.

❀ **JOHN X** Pope from 914 to 928 who owed his elevation to the powerful Theophylact family, which dominated Roman life and politics. A native of Romagna, he had a distinguished ecclesiastical career and was serving as archbishop of Ravenna when, in March 914, he was elected to succeed Pope Lando at the behest of the Theophylacts, in particular the formidable matron Theodora (d. 916). The main focus of his reign was defeating the Saracens, who regularly raided southern Italy. Organizing an impressive alliance of Byzantines, the Roman nobles, the Theophylacts, and others, the pope smashed the Saracens in 915 at the river Garigliano. In other matters, he gave his blessing to the Order of Cluny, rebuilt the Lateran, and worked toward improving relations with the Byzantines. His dealings with the Romans gradually deteriorated, however, and in May 928 he was deposed at the order of Marozia, daughter of Theophylact and de facto ruler of Rome. His brother Peter was brutally murdered in front of him in the Lateran, and he was placed in a cell in Castel Sant'Angelo, dying soon after, probably suffocated under a pillow. Successor: Leo VI.

❀ **JOHN XI** Pope from 931 to 935, his reign came during a truly bleak period in papal history. A member of the House of Theophylact, he was the son of the much-feared Marozia (d. 932), who was ruler of Rome and almost certainly the illegitimate son of the infamous Pope Sergius III. Already a cardinal in his late twenties, John was elected pope in succession to Stephen VII (VIII) with the full expectation by Marozia that he would be a proper tool of her ambitions. This he was, even presiding over his mother's extremely noncanonical marriage to her brother-in-law Hugh of Provence in the summer of 932. The union, however, sparked an uprising in Rome led by Alberic II, John's half-brother. Hugh escaped from the city, but John and his mother were imprisoned. Marozia probably died in prison, but John was released and kept on as pope under the watchful eye of his contemptuous half-brother. John died in December 935 or January 936. Successor: Leo VII

JOHN XII Pope from 955 to 964. He was the illegitimate son of Alberic II (d. 954), princely ruler of Rome and the figure responsible for the election of four popes. John XII was born Octavian around 937. On his deathbed, Alberic compelled the Roman nobles to swear an oath that his son would succeed him as prince and would also be elected pontiff on the passing of Pope Agapitus II. This occurred on December 955 and the eighteen-year-old Octavian was duly elected pope as John XII. He was thus the second pope to change his name, the first being John II in 533. As pope, John displayed little interest in the spiritual well-being of the Church, succumbing to a series of scandals and debaucheries recounted by gossipers of the time. Most notorious were the tales that he used the Lateran as a brothel, called upon the pagan gods to help him win at dice, and once toasted the devil during a drinking binge. Despite these serious shortcomings, he displayed a certain talent for government and a desire to advance the cause of the papacy.

To protect the Papal States from the danger posed by the Italian king Berengar II (r. 950–961) and his son Adalbert, John allied himself with the German king Otto I the Great, whom he crowned emperor in 962; he also accepted the *Privilegium Ottonianum,* which established imperial rights in papal elections. The two allies, however, soon had a falling out. Otto marched on Rome, and John fled. The emperor replaced him with an antipope, Leo VIII. In February 964 John returned to Rome and ousted Leo. He then launched reprisals against his enemies. Otto stormed back toward Rome, and John died suddenly of a stroke in May 964 while in Campagna working toward a negotiated settlement. His death was mysterious, coming in his twenties. He supposedly died while in the embraces of a married woman or was killed by her outraged husband. Successor: Leo VIII.

JOHN XIII Pope from 965 to 972, a Roman by birth, he was raised in the papal court and served as papal librarian under John XII. He owed his election in succession to Leo VIII to the influence of Emperor Otto I the Great. Unfortunately, John was thus politically dependent upon the emperor and much disliked by the scheming Romans. In

December 965, a mere two months after the start of his reign, John was deposed, brutalized, and exiled from Rome by the nobles of the city. Escaping from his place of confinement in Campagna, he made his way to the emperor and was restored in November 966. His reign thereafter was generally peaceful, thanks to the presence of the emperor and his army. In 967, John crowned Otto II co-emperor and was gratified to receive from his imperial patron extensive territories that had been seized some time before from the control of the papacy. John also promoted the clerical reform of Cluny and established the see of Magdeburg as an important archbishopric. He was called "the Good" in recognition of his piety. Successor: Benedict VI.

❀ **JOHN XIV** Pope from 983 to 984, a native of Pavia, he was originally known as Peter Canepanova and served as chancellor of Italy for Emperor Otto II and as the bishop of Pavia. He was serving as bishop at the time of his election in December 983 to succeed Benedict VII, largely through the express wish of the emperor. Changing his name to John, as it was not considered fitting to retain the same name as the first pope and Prince of the Apostles, the new pontiff was bereft of any support in Rome, the nobles and clergy hating him because Otto had not even bothered to consult with them on his choice. John's position became precarious with the passing of Otto II—his protector had died in his arms—soon after his pontifical installation in the Lateran. The pope was soon seized by the Crescenti family when the exiled antipope Boniface VII returned to Rome. John was imprisoned in Castel Sant'Angelo, dying there on August 20, 984, from poison or, more likely, cruel starvation. Successor: John XV.

❀ **JOHN XV** Pope from 985 to 996, he was the pontiff who established the custom of solemn canonization. A Roman by birth, he was cardinal of S. Vitale at the time of his election to succeed John XIV. His elevation was through the influence of the powerful Crescenti family of Rome, in particular the patrician of the city, Crescentius. The move by the Crescenti marked a resurgence of their fortunes, coming after the death of the antipope Boniface VII in 985. John was limited in his role as pope to liturgical or ecclesiastical matters, but his long-time subservient status became increasingly unbearable under the rule of Crescentius's brother, Crescentius II. In 995, John fled from Rome to Sutri and from there sent an appeal to Emperor Otto III for aid. The emperor set out for Italy, but the pope died of a fever before Otto could arrive at Rome. The most notable event in his pontificate came in 993, when he canonized Bishop St. Ulrich of Augsburg, the first formal canonization. Successor: Gregory V.

❀ **JOHN XVI** There is no legitimate pontiff with this number.

❀ **JOHN XVI** Antipope from 997 to 998, a Greek from Calabria, Giovanni Filagato had a long career that was much assisted by the imperial court. In February 997, he was in Rome at a time when Pope Gregory V was in exile. Known to be a favorite of the emperor, he was elected as John XVI through the machinations of the Crescenti family and with the connivance of the Byzantine Emperor Leo. Their hopes were soon dashed, however, since Otto remained loyal to Pope Gregory and stormed into Italy in early 998. John was captured, mutilated, and blinded, and in May 998 he was formally deposed and condemned. Placed in a Roman monastery, he languished until his death on August 26, 1001. His brief reign also brought an end to the career of Crescentius II, the formidable patrician of Rome who was captured by Otto and decapitated. (See also *John XX.*)

❀ **JOHN XVII** Pope from June 16 to December 6, 1003. Born Giovanni Siccone, he was a native of Rome, but little is known of him. His elevation to pope as successor to Pope Sylvester II was almost certainly through the influence of the Crescenti family. Owing to the domination of the Crescenti, his brief pontificate was spent in almost total obscurity. The only notable event of his reign was the granting of approval for the missionary efforts among the Slavs. Successor: John XVIII.

❀ **JOHN XVIII** Pope from 1003 to 1009, his pontificate ended with his abdication. Giovanni Fasano was from Rome and was serving as cardinal priest of St. Peter's at the time of his election to succeed John XVII. His elevation, like his predecessor's, was through the influence of the powerful Crescenti family of Rome. It is possible that he himself was related to the Crescenti. Unlike John XVII, however, he was of a more independent mind and thus became involved in Church affairs. The end of his reign is shrouded in mystery, for he died as a monk in St. Paul's-Outside-the-Walls in June or July 1109. It is possible that he was forced by the Crescenti to step down and retire to a monastery. Successor: Sergius IV.

❀ **JOHN XIX** Pope from 1024 to 1032. Originally named Romanus and a member of the Tusculani family, which was in control of Rome, he was also the younger brother and successor to Pope Benedict VIII.

A layman at the time of his election, he was the cause of much scandal in Rome because of his swift rise to the Holy See from the lay state, the payments and bribes that were reportedly made to secure his election, and his objectionable habits. He was able to maintain peace in Rome among the ever troublesome nobility and, in the most important political act of his career, crowned Conrad II (r. 1024–1039) emperor on March 26, 1027. The emperor, however, held the pope in little regard. Successor: Benedict IX.

❀ JOHN XX   There is no pope by this number in the records. The absence of such dates to the time of Pope John XV and is attributed to a scribal error that was subsequently adopted by official record keepers. Further confusion would later be caused by the question of whether antipope John XXIII should be considered at all legitimate. The matter was effectively resolved by Pope John XXIII at the time of his election in 1958. A Church historian, he declared with certainty that he was to be styled John XXIII.

JOHN XXI   Pope from 1276 to 1277. A native of Lisbon, Portugal, Peter Juliani (Pedro Juliao or Peter of Spain) was the son of a doctor, later serving as personal physician to Pope Gregory X, who appointed him archbishop of Braga in 1272 and then cardinal bishop of Tusculum in 1273. A gifted scholar, he authored a number of treatises on the eye, logic, theology, and philosophy. His election as successor to the short-reigning Adrian V at Viterbo in September 1276 came after severe upheaval in the city over the proper procedure of electing a new pope. Once chosen, he was styled John XXI instead of the more proper number John XX, probably owing to a scribal error dating to the time of John XV. His reign was cut short abruptly on May 20, 1277, when he was crushed by the collapsed ceiling of the papal palace in Viterbo. In the *Divine Comedy* (*Paradiso,* 12.134) he was placed by Dante in Paradise. Successor: Nicholas III.

JOHN XXII   Pope from 1316 to 1334, the second pope of the Avignon Papacy (1309–1377). Born at Cahors, France, Jacques Duese was the son of a shoemaker. After studying law at Montpellier, he taught at the University of Paris before embarking upon an ecclesiastical career. Made bishop of Avignon in 1310, he was elevated to the cardinalate by Pope Clement V in 1312. Following Clement's death in 1314, the cardinals proved unable to find a successor, first at Carpentras and then at Lyons. Under growing pressure from Count Philip of Poitiers (soon to be King Philip V of France) and after an interregnum of two years, the divided cardinals finally chose the compromise candidate of Duese on August 7, 1316. He owed his election to the favor of Philip and King Robert of Naples and to his reputation for austerity; although a stunning nepotist, he remained personally abstemious and maintained a simple style of life. John was also perhaps the ugliest pontiff ever elected; no contemporary writer neglected to comment on his uncommonly gruesome appearance. Not expected to live long because of rotten health, he shocked his electors by his nearly miraculous energy.

Grim and determined, John proved an important figure in establishing the papacy in Avignon on a more permanent footing. Confident as pope, he brought extensive changes to the Curia, established new dioceses or reconfigured old ones, and revived papal finances by widening the taxes paid to the Holy See. He also promoted missionary endeavors around the globe and added a third layer to the papal tiara. Two controversies would trouble his reign: the first was over the question of whether the Franciscans should be permitted to own property and the second was his conflict with King Louis IV the Bavarian. The Franciscan order was divided on the issue, between the Conventuals who favored ownership and the Spirituals who felt that property went against the intentions of their founder, St. Francis. Pope John found in favor of the Conventuals, whereupon many Spiritual Franciscans fled to John's devoted enemy, King Louis, who hated John from way back and gave support and safe harbor to any who might have common cause against him. Louis captured Rome in 1328 and installed a Franciscan as antipope Nicholas V. The antipope soon submitted and John weathered the storm. He died on December 4, 1334. Successor: Benedict XII.

JOHN XXIII Antipope from 1410 to 1415 and one of the papal claimants during the Great Western Schism (1378–1417), Baldassare Cossa was born in Naples, studying at the University of Bologna and then entering into the service of the Church. Pope Boniface IX made him a cardinal in 1402, and from 1403 to 1408 Cossa held the post of papal representative to Bologna. The Council of Pisa in 1409, attempting to end the schism, declared that Pope Gregory XII and antipope Benedict XIII be deposed, electing in their place yet another claimant, antipope Alexander V. Upon Alexander's death in May 1410, Cossa was elected unanimously as his successor under the name John XXIII. He had been one of the most influential cardinals in the council and the leading advisor to antipope Alexander. There were considerable questions regarding his own moral qualifications; while legate to Bologna he had acquired a loathsome reputation as a profligate ladies' man. Rumors also floated that he had poisoned Alexander in order to secure his own election. John was able to control of Rome in 1411, but the reforming council of 1412–1413 in which he had placed much hope came to nothing in ending the ongoing schism. At the behest of the future Emperor Sigismund, John agreed to convene a general council, which assembled at Constance in 1414. The Council of Constance proved a disappointment to John, for it had reached the decision in early 1415 that all three claimants should abdicate. After temporizing, John accepted the council's decision and then fled Constance dressed as a layman with the aim of disrupting the proceedings. Captured and imprisoned, he collapsed completely, accepting all actions by the council, including his own deposition. The newly elected Pope Martin V ordered him to remain incarcerated in Germany until 1419, when the sympathetic Ludwig of Bavaria purchased his freedom. Martin named him cardinal bishop of Tusculum. He died in Florence on November 22, 1419.

JOHN XXIII   Pope from 1958 to 1963, one of the most popular and beloved pontiffs, best known for convening Vatican Council II (1962–1965). Angelo Giuseppe Roncalli was born at Sotto il Monte, near Bergamo, Italy, in 1881, the son of a peasant family. After studying at the seminary of Bergamo and in Rome, he was ordained in 1904. He served as secretary to the local bishop and as a teacher of Church history in the Bergamo seminary, subsequently serving as a chaplain during World War I. While working as national director in Italy of the Congregation for the Propagation of the Faith, he spent all available time in historical research, which is how he met the future pope Achille Ratti, director of the Ambrosian Library of Milan. After election as Pope Pius XI in 1922, Ratti named him a titular archbishop in 1925 and sent him as apostolic delegate to Bulgaria (this was not a punishment); he next served in Turkey and Greece and in 1944 was appointed nuncio to France. After holding the post of observer for the Holy See at UNESCO in 1952, Roncalli was made patriarch of Venice and a cardinal by Pope Pius XII. In the conclave following Pius's death in 1958, Roncalli was not ranked high among the *papabili,* but in a complete surprise, he was chosen on the

The representative of the highest spiritual authority of the earth is glad, indeed boasts, of being the son of a humble but robust and honest laborer. The social progress, order, security and peace of each country are necessarily connected with the social progress, order, security and peace of all other countries.

Christians must be generous enough to offer also to God voluntary mortification in the imitation of our Divine Redeemer, who, according to the Prince of Apostles, "died also for sins, the Just for the unjust, that He might bring us back to God."

Only if we desire peace, as we should, instead of war, and only if we all aspire sincerely to fraternal harmony among nations, shall it come to pass that public affairs and public questions are correctly understood and settled to the satisfaction of all.

If each one of you does his best courageously, it will necessarily help in no small measure to establish the kingdom of Christ on earth.

The various nations are simply communities of men; that is, of brothers. They are to work in brotherly cooperation for the common prosperity of human society, not simply for their particular needs.

Human society must primarily be considered something pertaining to the spiritual. Through it, in the bright light of truth, men should share their knowledge; be able to exercise their rights and fulfill their obligations; be inspired to seek spiritual values; mutually derive genuine pleasure from the beautiful, of whatever order it be; always be readily disposed to pass on to others the best of their own cultural heritage; and eagerly strive to make their own the spiritual achievements of others.

twelfth ballot, on October 28, 1958. He took the name John (see *John XX*) and was said to have been a definite compromise candidate; his age (77 years) and reputed poor health pointed to an inactive reign. Pope John, however, had other plans.

He began making changes right from the start. The number of cardinals, fixed at seventy since the time of Sixtus V (1585–1590), was increased and internationalized. He issued several notable encyclicals, including *Mater et Magistra* (1961) and *Pacem in Terris* (1963), the latter pleading for international peace. Toward that end, he reached out to

the other Christian denominations, appointed observers to the World Council of Churches, and was outspoken in his esteem and concern for the Jewish faith, greeting a Jewish delegation in 1960 with the words "I am Joseph, your brother." He also strove to open a dialogue with the Soviet Union and Communist bloc, reversing Pius XII's unyielding stand against Communism. Finally, and most important, John embraced what he called *aggiornamento* (renewal) for the Church, a process of active revitalization in which the faith was to be led through a broad and positive process of modernization. The heart of *aggiornamento* was, of

The ever-popular Pope John XXIII.
(CATHOLIC NEWS SERVICE.)

course, Vatican Council II, the inspiration for which John credited the Holy Spirit. The council opened on October 11, 1962, but John would not live to see the completion of its work; his spirit, though, was much felt in its deliberations, and John was thus responsible for one of the most pivotal events in the history of the Church. Honest, practical, and renowned for his humor, he captured goodwill with a rustic common sense and a deft peasant's touch—he once caught his reflection in a mirror and was heard to observe "*Sono fa brutto*" ("I am so ugly"). He died on June 3, 1963. Successor: Paul VI.

JOHN PAUL I   Pope from August 26 to September 28, 1978, called the September Pope and the Smiling Pope, he had one of the briefest but most memorable of all pontificates. Albino Luciani was born in Forno di Canala (modern Canale d'Agordo) on October 17, 1912, to a poor family. He received ordination on July 7, 1935, serving for a time as a simple curate in the diocese of Belluno before teaching at the local seminary. Following World War II, he studied at the Pontifical Gregorian University in Rome and earned a doctorate in theology. Returning to Belluno, he was appointed vicar-general for the diocese in 1947 and then bishop of the mountain diocese of Vittorio Venetto in 1958. On December 10, 1969, he was appointed patriarch of Venice by Pope Paul VI, and on March 5, 1973, was elevated to the cardinalate. Unassuming and warm, Luciani distinguished himself with his common touch. He was quite alarmed, for example, that there were more tourists than Venetians in the churches of the city. He became a familiar sight in the city, wearing a simple cassock and sandals and sharing time with students while enjoying his favorite seaweed pizza. He authored a book, *Illustrissimi,* in which he wrote letters to famous figures, including Pinocchio, a work of greater depth than might at first appear.

Entering the conclave to elect a successor to Paul VI, Cardinal Luciani was little known outside of Italy and was generally not considered *papabile.* His election on the third ballot of the first day (August 26) was thus entirely unanticipated. A clear pastoral choice by the cardinals, he did not disappoint. Laughing constantly, speaking from the heart and not the text prepared for him, and ever impatient with papal ceremony, he enchanted audiences and brought an end to many traditional papal customs, such as the coronation with the tiara (he was invested in a simple ceremony with the pallium on September 5). After a reign of only thirty-three days, he was found dead in the papal apartments. The date of death was placed on September 28, the night before he was found. The world was stricken by the news, the outpouring of grief equal to the euphoria with which his reign had begun. Attributed causes of death were a heart attack or even a blood clot in the lungs. He had given only nineteen addresses. Successor: John Paul II.

JOHN PAUL II   Pope from 1978, one of the most significant pontiffs of modern history and the first non-Italian pope since Adrian VI in 1522. Karol Wojtyla was born on May 18, 1920, at Wadowice, near Cracow, Poland. His father was a one-time army lieutenant who had retired on a pension; his mother had died while Karol was still a young boy. He was a gifted student and demonstrated a love of sports, as well as a fondness for poetry and acting. Entering the Jagiellonian University in Cracow in 1938, he initially studied literature and Polish language, earning repute for his participation in theatrics; many friends, in fact, thought that he had a career ahead of him in the theater. In 1939 the Germans invaded Poland, and Wojtyla continued his studies in secret, since the university had been shut down; he also worked as a laborer in a limestone quarry and then in the water purification section of a factory. Following his father's death in 1942 and after surviving two accidents that nearly cost him his life, Wojtyla declared a desire for the priesthood. He studied in the underground seminary and, following the liberation in 1945, returned to the university in Cracow, graduating in 1946 with honors. After ordination on November 1, 1946, he was sent to Rome, earning a doctorate in theology in June 1948.

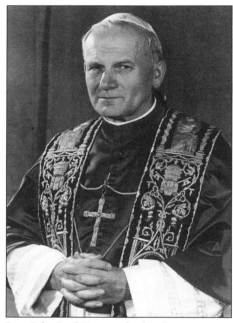

Pope John Paul II, soon after his election in 1978. (Catholic News Service.)

Returning to Poland, he served for three years as a parish priest, but was then permitted to resume his studies, earning another doctorate, this time in philosophy. In 1956 he was named a professor of ethics at Lublin. He continued his passions for outdoor sports, and it was jokingly said that a prerequisite for serving as one of his teaching assistants was an ability to canoe and ski. In 1958, to his surprise, he was appointed an auxiliary bishop to the see of Cracow. Five years later, Pope Paul VI named him archbishop of Cracow; on June 26, 1967, he was made a cardinal at the young age of forty-seven. As cardinal, he worked with the Polish primate Stefan Cardinal Wyszynski to resist Polish Communist oppression and was a well-known figure in the European and American Church. In 1976, he was given the great honor of delivering a series of Lenten sermons before the pope and the papal household. By 1978 he was quietly being advanced as a possible papal candidate, receiving election on October 16, 1978, to succeed the

Be Not Afraid!

To accept the Gospel's demands means to affirm all of our humanity, to see in it the beauty desired by God, while at the same time recognizing, in light of the power of God Himself, our weaknesses: "What is impossible for men is possible for God" (Lk 18:27).

These two dimensions cannot be separated: on the one hand, the moral demands God makes of man; on the other, the demands of His saving love—the gift of His grace—to which God in a certain sense has bound Himself. What else is the Redemption accomplished in Christ, if not precisely this? *God desires the salvation of man, He desires that humanity find that fulfillment to which He Himself has destined it,* and Christ has the right to say that His yoke is easy and His burden, in the end, light (cf. Mt 11:30).

It is very important to cross the threshold of hope, not to stop before it, but *to let oneself be led.* I believe that the great Polish poet Cyprian Norwid had this in mind when he expressed the ultimate meaning of the Christian life in these words: "Not with the Cross of the Savior behind you, but with your own cross behind the Savior."

There is every reason for the truth of the Cross to be called the Good News.

—John Paul II,
Crossing the Threshold of Peace (1994)

short-lived John Paul I. His election was an extraordinary development, ending four centuries of Italian domination of the papacy.

The youngest pope since Pius IX (1846–1878), John Paul made clear from the start a bold vision for the Church by declaring in his acceptance speech: "We will be at the service of the universal mission of the church, that is to say, at the service of the world . . . we will be at the service of truth, of justice, of peace, of harmony. . . ." With his ceaseless energy and desire to take the faith to the entire world, the pope quickly became the most traveled pontiff of all time, his journeys serving the purposes of fostering the faith in such blossoming regions as Asia, Africa, Oceania, and South America and making appeals on behalf of such issues as social, political, religious, and economic justice. The responses to his visits have been at times genuinely amazing, as demonstrated by the five million people who gathered to hear his mass in Manila in 1995.

While criticized by some for his unbending orthodoxy, John Paul has stressed an authentic interpretation of Vatican Council II's decrees, seeking to curb what he sees as potentially disastrous innovation while strengthening the Church after the troubled years of the reign of Pope Paul VI. John Paul brought extensive reforms to the Curia, fostered ecumenism and interfaith dialogue (especially with the Orthodox Churches and expressed in the encyclical *Ut Unum Sint,* 1995), and broadened even further the international nature of the College of Cardinals. He has authored a number of eloquent encyclicals, including *Laborem Exercens* (1981) and *Centessimus Annus* (1991), both profound documents on capitalism and labor; *Veritatis Splendor* (1993), on moral theology; and *Evangelium Vitae* (1995), a clear and powerful statement on the most important modern moral questions (abortion, euthanasia, capital punishment, and fetal research) and a call for the fostering of a "culture of life." His reign additionally has brought the revision of the Code of Canon Law and the issue of the first revised Catechism since the sixteenth century. Above all, the pope has striven to prepare the Church throughout the world for the opportunities and challenges of the approaching millennium.

John Paul's reign has witnessed some of the most significant events of the century. His election and subsequent policies were the source of deep consternation to the Kremlin, so much so that they may have motivated the attempted assassination of the pontiff on May 13, 1981, by Mehmet Ali Agca in St. Peter's Square. Recovering, the pope continued his work in resisting communism in Eastern Europe, and many scholars freely recognize the extensive role he played in the final collapse of the Soviet empire. He also launched formal relations with

Israel (1994), negotiated new agreements or diplomatic ties with Italy, Mexico, Spain, and the United States, and demonstrated his international influence in 1994 during the U.N.-sponsored Cairo conference on population growth.

A poet, playwright, philosopher, mystic, and theologian, John Paul is the author of numerous books and writings beyond his papal pronouncements. His poetry was well known, much of it published under a nom de plume, and his plays, such as *The Jeweler's Shop,* are noted for their close affinity to the thoughts and lives of ordinary people. Two of his most famous books are *Love and Responsibility,* a brilliant study on human sexuality written in close association with Europe's leading experts, and *Crossing the Threshold of Hope,* a 1994 international bestseller and the first work by a pope expressing his thoughts on the existence of God, human suffering, dignity, the nature of evil, the Church, and his own office. Always an active and athletic person, he was an avid skier, his passion curtailed only in 1994 (at seventy-four) after a hip injury. Rumors about his health soon surfaced, silenced by the immense success of his book, his triumph at the Cairo conference, his return to traveling in 1995, and being honored as *Time* magazine's Man of the Year. His motto has always been *"Totus Tuus"* ("Everything for You").

JULIUS I, ST.   Pope from 337 to 352, he devoted much of his reign to combatting the heresy of Arianism (which denied the divinity of Christ). A Roman by birth, he was elected to succeed Pope St. Mark on February 6, 337, after an interregnum of some four months. An ardent enemy of the Arians, he gave refuge and protection in Rome to St. Athanasius of Alexandria in 339 after the Arian party had expelled him from his see. Julius convened in Rome a council (340) to reaffirm the rights of Athanasius and then had summoned the Council of Sardica (342–343) to condemn Arian teachings and stamp out any possibility of its spreading to the lands of the Western Roman Empire. Through the legates he sent to the assembly, Julius won significant recognition of his papal rights and privileges. Successor: Liberius.

JULIUS II   Pope from 1503 to 1513, famous for his long wars and his patronage of the arts, Giuliano della Rovere was a native of Albissola, near Savona, born in 1443, the son of a poor family.

A nephew of Francesco della Rovere—the future Pope Sixtus IV—he was educated at his behest by the Franciscans at Perugia. After the election of his uncle as pope in 1471, Giuliano was quickly promoted, becoming Bishop of Carpentras, cardinal priest of S. Pietro in

Vincoli, and cardinal bishop of Santa Sabina. Deciding that the time was not ripe to work for his own election, he orchestrated the elevation in 1484 of Innocent VIII and, during his pontificate, Giuliano was one of the most important figures in Rome. At Innocent's death in 1492, Rodrigo Borgia, a sworn enemy, was elected as Alexander VI. Keenly aware of the often gruesome fate that awaited the foes of the Borgias, Giuliano fled to France and the safety of King Charles VIII. A reconciliation was arranged in 1498 with Alexander, but the cardinal stayed away from Rome. Finally, he went back to the Eternal City in 1503 and, after the brief reign of Pius III, used well-placed bribes and promises to ensure his own election in a conclave that lasted a single day. His reign is dated from November 1, 1503.

Pope Julius II, patron of Michelangelo and warrior pontiff.

As Pope Julius II, he set for himself a simple task: the restoration of the temporal power of the papacy, free from secular interference and once more in control of its own destiny. Toward that end he was largely successful, but it came at a frightful and bloody cost, and the ardor with which he pursued war prompted the Florentine historian Guicciardini to lament that save for the dress and the name, there was nothing of the priest in Julius; the Venetian ambassador to Rome observed, "It is impossible to describe how violent, headstrong, and difficult to manage he is. . . . Whatever is in his mind must be carried through, even if he himself were to perish in the attempt." From the start of his reign right up to the moment of his death from a fever on February 21, 1513, he was constantly in the field, driving his armies ever forward to recapture territories lost by the papacy in previous years and to reduce foreign ambitions toward papal lands.

While his Church reforms were minor—such as declaring papal elections by simony to be void and convening the Fifth Lateran

Council (1512–1517)—his patronage of Renaissance artists was on a grand scale. He was the enthusiastic patron of Bramante, Raphael, and Michelangelo, and in 1506 laid the cornerstone for the new St. Peter's Basilica. Intemperate, worldly, and irascible, Julius was given the well-deserved nickname *Il Terrible,* but he was also firmly convinced of the rightness of his cause. Critics called him too warlike (such as Desiderius Erasmus in *Praise of Folly*) and he was certainly far from a paragon of personal virtue, having fathered three children as a cardinal. Despite this, and perhaps because of it, he remains one of the most compelling of all pontiffs. The most famous portrait of the pope was done by Raphael, showing the pope with a beard; Julius had refused to shave until the Papal States were free of enemies. His beard grew very long. Successor: Leo X.

JULIUS III   Pope from 1550 to 1555, a Roman, Giovanni Maria Ciocchi del Monte was born in 1487. He studied law at Perugia and Siena and served as a chamberlain to Pope Julius II. Appointed archbishop of Siponto in 1511, he was rapidly advanced, becoming bishop of Pavia (1520), governor of Rome, vice-legate of Bologna, and cardinal in 1536. Under Paul III, he was co-president and papal legate to the opening of the Council of Trent in 1545. In the election to choose the successor to Paul, the cardinals were deadlocked in a contentious conclave. Finally, despite the known dislike of Emperor Charles V, del Monte was elected pope as a compromise on February 8, 1550. While typical in many ways of the Renaissance pontiffs of his time, Julius III was devoted to genuine ecclesiastical reform. He ordered the Council of Trent to reassemble on May 1, 1551, although he was forced because of political strife and war to suspend it after the sixteenth session in April 1552. Thereafter his reforms were on a much smaller scale and of much more limited effectiveness. Of lasting importance was his encouragement of the Jesuits (Society of Jesus). The high point of his reign came in 1553 with the accession of Mary Tudor as Queen of England, marking the return of England to the Church, albeit temporarily. As his ambitious program of reform proved a disappointment, the pope found solace in giving his enthusiastic patronage to the arts. Michelangelo was made chief architect of St. Peter's, and the famed composer Palestrina was appointed papal choirmaster. The sensual and fun-loving pontiff also gave himself over to hunting and banquets. Rome was scandalized for a time by Julius's relationship with a young man from Parma named Innocenzo, whom he appointed a cardinal. He died on March 23, 1555, from complications caused by chronic gout. Successor: Marcellus II.

❧ **KEYS, POWER OF THE**   Term used for the supreme authority and jurisdiction granted by Christ to St. Peter and his successors. The Power of the Keys refers to the special right of Peter and the popes both in heaven and on earth as recorded in the Gospel of St. Matthew: "Thou art Peter and on this rock I will build my Church. And the gates of Hell will not stand against it. I will give you the Keys of the Kingdom of Heaven: whatever you bind on earth will be bound in heaven; whatever you loose on earth will be loosed in heaven" (16:18–19). The **Keys of the Kingdom** are the keys to the kingdom of heaven and the earth, one gold, the other silver. They are seen in the rich symbolism of the Holy See, especially on the papal coat of arms and even on the papal flag.

❧ **KNIGHTHOOD, PONTIFICAL**   Known in full as the Pontifical Orders of Knighthood, these are the titles of honor that are bestowed upon lay people by the pope in recognition of significant or devoted service to the Church. Papal knights have several ranks; they are, in order of precedence: Supreme Order of Christ, Order of the Golden Spur, Order of Pius IX, Order of St. Gregory the Great, and Order of St. Sylvester. By custom, the **Order of Christ** is reserved exclusively for Catholic rulers or heads of state who have proven of great help to the Church. The **Golden Spur** was supposedly established by St. Sylvester I (314–335), later falling into disuse. Revived in 1905 by St. Pius X, it is distinguished by being a knighthood not restricted to Catholics. Also called the Golden Militia, the Golden Spur has been given to notable figures in the past, including Mozart (see *Clement XIV*), Mussolini, King Hussein of Jordan, and even the Shah of Iran. The **Order of Pius IX,** the *Ordine Piano,* is named after Popes Pius IV (who started it) and Pius IX (who reinstituted it) and was especially prized because until 1939 it actually conferred a noble status upon the recipient; this privilege was suppressed by Pius XII. The knighthood has four classes: Knight of the Golden Collar (for heads of state), Grand Cross Knight, Pian Grand Cross (reserved for ambassadors, of both sexes), and

Knights. This knighthood was the source of considerable controversy in 1994 when Pope John Paul II conferred it upon Kurt Waldheim. The **Order of St. Gregory the Great** was begun by Pope Gregory XVI (1831–1846) to give honor to those persons conspicuous in the defense of the temporal holdings of the Holy See. Later, the rank was widened to include anyone, not necessarily within the Papal States, who was devoted to the Holy See and obvious in their piety and loyalty. The order has two divisions, military and civil, with three ranks — Knights of the Grand Cross, Knight Commanders, and Knights. The **Order of St. Sylvester** was also begun by Pope Gregory XVI. It was later divided into two orders, the previously discussed Golden Militia and St. Sylvester. It is given to deserving lay people.

Two other orders of knights exist, both closely associated with the Holy See and boasting long and rich historical legacies. The first is the **Equestrian Order of the Most Holy Sepulchre of Jerusalem,** known commonly as the Knights of the Holy Sepulchre. Founded in 1099, soon after the fall of Jerusalem to the Crusader armies, the order was intended to protect the holy city of Jerusalem. From this beginning, the knights came to fight against the Muslims during the Crusades, to care for the pilgrims who traveled to the Holy Land, and to tend the sick. The knights were forced to leave Jerusalem after its capture in 1187, but the order survived over the succeeding centuries, and in the nineteenth century was twice reorganized, first by Pope Pius IX (1846–1878) and again by Leo XIII (1878–1903). It was the latter who opened its membership to women, the Ladies of the Holy Sepulchre, and today all five grades of knighthood are granted to the lady knights. In the modern Church, the order is one of the most prestigious of all organizations, existing under the protection of the Holy See, with its official headquarters in the Vatican. Its head, the Grand Master, is always a cardinal appointed by the pope. Its members, distinguished at ceremonial occasions by their white capes, decorated on the left breast by a five-cross emblem (signifying the five wounds of Christ), are involved in numerous charitable activities. They are also traditionally outspoken in defense of the Holy See.

The second order is the **Knights of Malta.** This order also dates to the late eleventh century (there is some dispute as to whether it is older than the Knights of the Holy Sepulchre) and was originally called the Knights Hospitallers, the Knights of Jerusalem, or the Order of the Hospital of St. John. Traditionally they are said to have started in 1070 in a hospital in the Holy Land, caring for pilgrims. Once the Crusades erupted, the members of the hospital took on a military hue and received formal papal approval as a military order in 1113. They fought in the Holy Land until 1291 when the last crusader fortress, Acre, fell to the Islamic Mamelukes. The knights fled to Cyprus and in 1310 captured Rhodes, which served as their headquarters. Known as the Knights of Rhodes, they proved one of the main enemies in the Mediterranean of the advancing Ottoman Turks. In 1522, after several bloody attempts, the Turks drove them from Rhodes. The knights received Malta from Holy Roman Emperor Charles V in 1530 and have been called the Knights of Malta ever since.

Today the order is one of the most unique institutions in the world and a genuinely prestigious body within the Church. It is formally recognized as a sovereign entity, meaning that despite the fact that it has no territory, it enjoys diplomatic relations with countries all over the globe and even has observer status in the United Nations. Its relations with the Holy See are quite peculiar, for as an independent state it is the equal of the Secretariat of State of the Holy See, but it is equally dependent upon the pope as a religious body; its professed knights (those who have taken a vow of chastity, poverty, and obedience), the Knights of Justice, fall under the auspices of the Congregation for Religious. At the same time, the knights have a formal ambassador to the Vatican. Members number around ten thousand and are found in fifty-three countries, organized into five grand priories and numerous national associations. They are actively engaged in charity work, relief for the sick, and the sending of medical aid across the globe. Technically, noble lineage is needed for admission, but one rank, Knight of Magistral Grace, permits those without illustrious ancestors to join. Among famous American knights are Alexander Haig, Lee Iacocca, and William F. Buckley, Jr. The knights were also quite active in the administration of President Ronald Reagan, fostering even further the cordial relations between the White House and John Paul II. The grand master, called Most Eminent Highness, has the rank of cardinal and must be of noble lineage. Since 1834, the headquarters have been in Rome, currently on the high-rent Via Condotti. (See also *Decorations, Papal.*)

LANDO   Pope from 913 to 914. Also called Landus, he was born near Rome to the family of a prosperous Lombard family. His is one of the most obscure of all papal reigns, said to have lasted six months and eleven days. Elected to succeed Pope Anastasius III in July 913, he most likely owed his elevation to the powerful House of Theophylact. He died probably in February 914. Successor: John X.

LATERAN **B**ASILICA   The Basilica of St. John Lateran or, as it is called in Italian, San Giovanni in Laterano, known officially as the Patriarchal Basilica of the Most Holy Savior and Saint John the Baptist at the Lateran. Located upon the Caelian Hill in the Eternal City, the Lateran is the formal cathedral church for Rome, meaning that the

The facade of the Lateran Basilica, the cathedral church of the pope as Bishop of Rome; from an early-twentieth-century photo.

pope, in his capacity as Bishop of Rome, has his seat of authority in this church, not at St. Peter's. (See *Cathedra.*) Here the popes were normally crowned, until 1870 and the seizure of Rome by the new Italian government. The basilica was first built in the fourth century and is honored as the first church publicly consecrated, in 324 (the feast is celebrated every year on November 9). It stands on land that once belonged to the noble Roman family of the Lateranii. They gave the real estate, including a palace, to Emperor Constantine the Great who in turn handed it to Pope Miltiades (311–314). The entire resulting complex of the Lateran Palace and Basilica became the residence of the popes from that time until 1309 and the start of the Avignon Papacy. The church has been the victim of fires and earthquakes over the years, and was even damaged by a bomb attack blamed on the Mafia in 1993. Repeatedly repaired and rebuilt during the Middle Ages, it fell into disuse during the Avignon Papacy (1309–1377) and was in dire need of repair—with the Lateran Palace—when the papacy returned to Rome. Pope Urban VI (1378–1389) oversaw its renovation. Another ambitious rebuilding was launched by Innocent X (1644–1655), receiving reconsecration by Benedict XIII in 1726. The basilica is much revered by the Romans and the Church at large. (See also *Basilica* and *Rome.*)

❀ **LATERAN PALACE**   The palace of the popes adjoining the Lateran Basilica, situated on the Caelian Hill in Rome that was the official residence of the Supreme Pontiffs from around 324 until 1309 and the moving of the papacy to Avignon. The Lateran Palace was originally the property of Plautius Lateranus of the old and distinguished noble Roman house of the Lateranii. Coming into the possession of Constantine the Great (d. 337), it was used briefly as a private house, but sometime around 313, he gave it to Pope Miltiades, who found it admirably suited to his need for an official residence. The palace remained the home of the popes throughout the Middle Ages. The Curia was headquartered here, so that the palace served essentially the same function then as the Vatican does today, namely the central administration for the entire Church.

When, however, Pope Clement V (1305–1314) took up residence in Avignon, the center of the papacy shifted to that French city. Soon the bureaucracy also moved to Avignon, leaving the palace in Rome abandoned. Such was its state when Gregory XI returned at last to Rome in 1377 that he decided—for health and safety reasons—that the palace was uninhabitable. He went instead to the Vatican, which henceforth was the papal residence. While repaired, and a new palace built by Sixtus V (1585–1590), the Lateran had a much reduced importance over succeeding centuries. In the 1960s, further refurbishing was undertaken under Pope Paul VI. Today, it is the headquarters of the Vicar of Rome, and is known as *Il Vicariato.*

♳ **LATERAN TREATY** The agreement signed on February 11, 1929, between Pope Pius XI (1922–1939) and Benito Mussolini that established the Vatican City State; it ended nearly sixty years of political and social tension caused by the seizure of Rome in 1870 by the forces of King Victor Emmanuel II of Italy and the declaration of Pius IX and his successors that they were "prisoners of the Vatican." It came about through the desire of Mussolini to reach an accord with the Holy See that might enhance his international standing and resolve the vexing social difficulties with Catholics in Italy over the self-imposed incarceration of the popes. Moving slowly, Pius accepted the offers of negotiating a settlement, and the Lateran Treaty's exceedingly favorable terms for the Church were a testament to both the hard-fisted skills of his negotiators (especially Pietro Cardinal Gasparri) and anxiousness on the part of Mussolini to have the Roman Question resolved. The treaty was actually comprised of three parts, the Lateran Treaty, the Lateran Concordat, and the Financial Convention. The treaty recognized the sovereign independence of the Holy See in international affairs as well as the complete jurisdiction of the pope within the constituted Vatican City State (*Stato della Città del Vaticano*). The pope was acknowledged as absolute sovereign of the tiny country (Pius deliberately wanted it kept small, because, as he put it, "We do not wish to be troubled with railroad strikes!"), with control as well over all extra-territorial possessions such as Castel Gandolfo and the basilicas of the Lateran, St. Mary Major, and St. Paul Outside-the-Walls. The Vatican territory was made inviolate, diplomatic relations were formalized between Italy and the Holy See, and all communication was guaranteed with foreign governments, even in wartime. In return, the Holy See recognized the Italian government, and Rome as the capitol. By the terms of the Concordat, Italy was confirmed as a Catholic country, a Catholic education was commanded for the schools, freedom was given for the activities of the social organization Catholic Action, and the pope was guaranteed full rights of spiritual authority. Bishops were required in return to take an oath of loyalty, and the geographical boundaries of the dioceses were changed to conform to the political provinces of Italy. Most felicitous for Pius was the financial convention. The Holy

See was paid 750 million lire in cash and another billion lire in five percent negotiable bonds. The salaries of priests were also paid by Italy. Formally retained by the Italian constitution of 1947, the Lateran Treaty remained in effect until the 1980s, when a new agreement was negotiated between the government and Pope John Paul II (represented by the brilliant Secretary of State Agostino Cardinal Casaroli). Ratified on June 3, 1985, it ended state payment of priests' salaries and mandatory Catholic education.

❊ **L'ATTIVITA DELLA SANTA SEDE**   See *Activities of the Holy See.*

❊ **LAWRENCE**   Antipope to Pope St. Symmachus from 498 to 499 and again from around 502 to 506. The archpriest of the Roman Church, Lawrence was elected as a rival to Symmachus on November 22, 498. His supporters were comprised of the minority of clergy in the city (most gave their backing to Symmachus) and a collection of the nobles. Violent outbursts took place in the city and eventually both sides petitioned that Theodoric, King of the Ostrogoths and ruler of Italy, should decide the issue. He found in Symmachus's favor, and Lawrence for a time accepted the verdict. Starting in 502, however, Lawrence's supporters seized the city of Rome, and the antipope became pontiff in all essentials, trapping Symmachus in St. Peter's. Fighting again broke out and the matter was only resolved in 506 with the final removal of Lawrence from the city.

❊ **LAY INVESTITURE**   See *Investiture Controversy.*

❊ **LEGATE, PAPAL**   The general name given to an officially designated representative of the pope. There are a number of different types of papal legates, their titles and authority varying according to the nature of the diplomatic assignment. By custom, they are superbly trained, normally graduates of the Pontifical Ecclesiastical Academy (Pontificia Academia Ecclesiastica) in Rome, and diplomats of long experience. The types of papal legates are: nuncios, inter-nuncios, pro-nuncios, apostolic delegates, and chargés d'affaires. A special kind of legate is the rare legate *a latere,* a cardinal sent by the pope to act on his behalf in some specific event or in some matter of great importance. Papal representatives date to at least 325, when Pope Sylvester I sent legates to the Council of Nicaea. From that time, it became common for popes to dispatch agents to uphold papal rights and interests, to protect the welfare of the Church, and perhaps to advance some important cause, such as human rights. Papal diplomats often have a dual role in their country of service. They must deal with the local government (when a nuncio or pro-nuncio) and serve as a vital liaison between the Holy See and the bishops of the country. In this capacity, they are an important participant in the appointing of new bishops, the advising of the so-called local Episcopal Conference, and in assisting the religious orders in the dioceses. Each legate, regardless of rank, receives advice and instructions from the secretary of state, who is answerable only to the pope. An important duty is also filled by the delegate for papal representatives, who travels the globe consulting with papal diplomats and coordinating their activities so as to foster a rapport with the central offices of the Secretariat of State in Rome. Legates are found all over the world. The current functioning of all legates was set down in the regulation of Pope Paul VI, in the document *Sollicitudo Omnium Ecclesiarum* (1969). (See also *Diplomacy, Papal.*)

🏵 **LEO I THE GREAT, ST.** Pope from 440 to 461, one of the two pontiffs, with St. Gregory I (590–604), to be granted the title "the Great." A native of Rome, he entered the clergy and was eventually promoted to the rank of deacon. Few details of his life, unfortunately, are known in any detail. He was a very prominent figure among the Roman clergy during the pontificate of St. Celestine I (422–432) and Sixtus III (432–440) and was elected to succeed Sixtus, receiving consecration on September 29, 440. Devoted to strengthening the place of the Holy See in the Church, Leo secured from Emperor Valentinian III (r. 425–455) recognition of his ecclesiastical jurisdiction over the West. While limited in the exercise of his influence in the East— where the heads of major sees such as Constantinople, Antioch, and Alexandria resisted his sway—Leo did play a major role in the final defeat of the heretical teachings then

Pope St. Leo I the Great.
(CATHOLIC NEWS SERVICE.)

finding currency in parts of the Eastern Empire that Christ possessed only one nature instead of the two, human and divine, taught by orthodox theologians. Leo wrote a famous work, called the *Tome of Leo*, elucidating and emphasizing orthodox teachings. After several years of setbacks and intrigue, the *Tome* was formally accepted by the Council of Chalcedon in 451. This declaration naturally did not keep the Byzantines from issuing a decree (canon 28 of the council) giving such patriarchal rights to the see of Constantinople that it stood nearly equal to the Bishop of Rome. Leo unavailingly protested.

Such was his moral authority within the Western Roman Empire that he twice came to the aid of the government. First, in 452, he courageously rode to Mantua and there met with Attila the Hun who was rampaging through Italy. He somehow convinced the dread ruler to depart the peninsula. Three years later, Leo stood at the very gates of Rome to plead with King Geiseric and the Vandals not to sack the city. Though he failed to prevent the fall of Rome, he was able to extract the promise of the barbarians not to massacre the inhabitants. Leo's surviving 96 sermons and 143 letters display both his penetrating mind and his abiding piety. He died in Rome on November 10, 461, and was buried in St. Peter's. Successor: St. Hilary.

❀ **LEO II, ST.**   Pope from 682 to 683, a Sicilian by birth, Leo was a student in the papal choir school, devoting part of his pontificate to the advancement of Church music. His election as successor to Pope St. Agatho was probably in December 681 or January 682, but he did not receive formal approval from the Byzantine Emperor Constantine IV; he was thus not consecrated until August 682. His most significant act was to give his formal ratification to the acts of the Council of Constantinople (682–681), which condemned the heretical teachings of the Monothelitists. He also accepted the censure of Pope Honorius I who had made the unfortunate unorthodox statement on the will of Christ. Successor: Benedict II.

❀ **LEO III**   Pope from 795 to 816, best known for his surprise coronation of Charlemagne as emperor. A native of Rome, Leo was long in the service of the popes, eventually becoming a cardinal priest of Santa Susanna. His election as successor to Adrian I on December 26, 795, was by unanimous vote, but the new pope was soon confronted by partisans of the dead pontiff and other Romans who disliked his style of government. The difficulties continued to simmer for several years and then erupted into violence on April 25, 799. An angry mob attacked Leo, brutalized him, and nearly cut out his tongue and gouged out his eyes; shut up in a monastery, he escaped and fled to the court of Charlemagne. With a Frankish army at his back, Charlemagne returned him to Rome and cleared him of all charges made against him by various usurpers. Anxious to repair his shattered image, Leo surprised Charlemagne on Christmas Day 800 by placing a crown upon his head while the ruler knelt in prayer in St. Peter's. Through this act, Leo established the custom of having all Holy Roman Emperors receive their crowns from the pope. Leo gave to the papacy a powerful privilege while allying it closely to the Western Roman Empire, thereby ending forever any reliance upon the Byzantines, long the protectors of the Holy See. Leo proved himself a capable administrator, although his reign was spent in the shadow of Charlemagne, whom he outlived by two years. Leo died on July 12, 816. Successor: Stephen IV (V).

❀ **LEO IV, ST.** Pope from 847 to 855, a Roman, Leo entered the Benedictine order at a young age and later worked in the papal government, receiving promotion to subdeacon and then cardinal priest. He was elected to succeed Sergius II on the same day of that pope's death, January 27, 847, and was consecrated on April 10, 847, without first requesting imperial ratification owing to what Leo claimed was the dire necessity of haste because of the threat of the Saracens, who had recently (846) sacked Rome and St. Peter's. The main focus of his pontificate was the defense of Rome from the Saracen raids. He constructed a set of strong walls along the Tiber, ringing St. Peter's and creating the redoubtable Leonine City. Leo also organized a military alliance of Naples, Amalfi, and the Holy See that launched a powerful fleet against the Saracens, defeating them in a sea battle in 849 just outside of Ostia. His stern nature against the raiders carried over into his other areas of rule. He put to death several imperial officials for murdering a legate, an act that strained relations with Emperor Louis II. He also advanced papal rights and privileges. Successor: Benedict III.

❀ **LEO V** Pope from August to September 903. A little-known pontiff, he was a humble priest at Priapi, near Rome, at the time of his election to succeed Pope Benedict IV. He was much respected by contemporaries for his goodness. His reign, however, ended abruptly with his deposition by antipope Christopher. Leo was hurled into a prison, but was soon joined by Christopher himself, the usurper having been removed by Pope Sergius III. Leo died probably in early 904. It is possible he was murdered by Christopher, although more likely he and Christopher were strangled at the command of Sergius. Successor: Sergius III.

✿ **LEO VI** Pope from May to December 928. A Roman, he was serving as cardinal priest of Santa Susanna at the time of his election to succeed Pope John X, who had recently been deposed and was still languishing in prison. Leo's election was secured by the will of the formidable Marozia, head of the house of Theophylact, which controlled Rome. Old when chosen, he died even before the imprisoned John. Successor: Stephen VII (VIII).

✿ **LEO VII** Pope from 936 to 939, one of the pontiffs who owed his election to Alberic II, ruler of Rome from 932 to 954. A native of Rome, he was serving as cardinal priest of San Sisto when Alberic chose him to succeed to the papal throne on January 3, 936. He followed the deposed and imprisoned John XI, half-brother of Alberic. While wielding no political power, Leo was permitted to pursue a fairly aggressive policy of religious reform. He thus supported the reformer Odo of Cluny (d. 942). Leo was opposed to the forced conversion of the Jews of Mainz under the local archbishop, although he did not place any ban on the expulsion of those Jews who declined the offer to convert. According to the chronicler Flodoard of Reims, Leo was both kind and wise. Successor: Stephen VIII (IX).

✿ **LEO VIII** Pope from 963 to 965. Originally a very respected layman who was serving as chief notary of the Church of Rome, he was elected pope at the recommendation of Emperor Otto I by the same synod that had just deposed the reprehensible Pope John XII. He was hastily ordained and consecrated on December 6, 963, beginning what was to prove a difficult pontificate. He was bitterly opposed by the partisans of the removed pontiff and, early in 964, was beset by an uprising organized by John XII. This was suppressed with considerable gusto by imperial troops, but it did little to reduce the spirits of Leo's enemies. When Otto departed Rome, another revolt broke out, driving Leo from the city. After the death of John in May 964, the Romans still refused to accept Leo, requesting instead that Benedict (V) be made pope. When Otto refused, they elected Benedict anyway, prompting a march on Rome by the exasperated emperor. Leo was restored in June 964, dying on March 1, 965. Successor: John XIII.

❀ **LEO IX, ST.**   Pope from 1049 to 1054, one of the originators of what came to be called the Gregorian Reform. Known originally as Bruno of Egisheim, he was from Alsace, the son of a count. After studying at Toul, he was made a canon of the city cathedral and then bishop in 1027. Known and much respected by Emperor Henry III, especially for his reforming zeal, Bruno was put forward by the emperor in December 1048 as the ideal candidate to succeed Damasus II. Bruno was swiftly elected, but he accepted only after the emperor agreed that the new pope should be ratified by the people and clergy of Rome. He entered the Eternal City dressed as a pilgrim and immediately won the hearts of the Romans. On February 12, 1049, he was crowned pope, formally taking the name Leo (IX). While somewhat overshadowed by his renowned contemporary Hildebrand (the future Gregory VII), Leo proved an able pontiff, devoted to the reform of the Church. In his labors, he was aided by Hildebrand and St. Peter Damian. His reign ended with two calamitous events. The first was his decision in 1053 to launch a campaign against the Normans in southern Italy. This military adventure ended with the rout of his army and his capture. Held prisoner for nine months, he was well treated and shown every respect by his captors, but his release was secured only after granting the Normans numerous concessions. Leo's campaign angered the Byzantines, who saw it as interference in their affairs in Italy. With relations thus already strained, the stage was set for the final break in 1054 between the Eastern and Western Churches, a schism that was never healed. He died on April 19, 1054. Successor: Victor II.

LEO X   Pope from 1513 to 1521, considered one of the Renaissance popes whose reign hastened the rise of Martin Luther and the Protestant Reformation. The second son of Lorenzo de'Medici the Magnificent, Giovanni de'Medici was born in Florence in 1475, growing up in the culturally resplendent court of the Medicis. Made a cardinal at the age of thirteen (although not officially invested until 1492) by Pope Alexander VI, he was taught by the foremost humanists of the time and later studied theology and canon law at Pisa (1489–1491). With the exile of the Medicis from Florence in 1494, Giovanni wandered across Europe, journeying to France, Germany, and Holland from 1494–1500. Returning to Rome in 1500, he became one of the leading figures in the pontificate of Julius II; Julius appointed him legate to Bologna in 1511 and commander of the oft-used papal army. In April 1512, Giovanni was captured at Ravenna, escaping a short time later. That same year he helped secure the return of his family to prominence in Florence, becoming de facto master of the city until 1513 and the summons to attend the conclave to choose a successor to Julius. Only thirty-eight years old, he was nevertheless elected pope on March 11, 1513, in a vote free of bribes and simony. The tone of his reign was set by his exclamation, "Let us enjoy the papacy which God has seen fit to bestow upon us!" The incomparably lavish inauguration festivities alone cost a staggering 100,000 ducats, one seventh of the vast wealth Julius had left for his successor. The rest was soon spent on hunting parties, dances, banquets, theatrical spectacles, and every form of excess and entertainment. Leo was personally generous, moral and free of any serious wickedness, but his court and enjoyments of the papacy were unprecedented. Artisans and writers flocked to Rome to share in the pope's patronage and cardinals vied to create palaces worthy of the golden age of culture in which they lived. Such was the appalling state to which papal finances were soon reduced that Leo turned to bankers for loans from such banking houses as the Gaddi, Salviati, and especially the Chigi, money secured at the usurious rate of 40 percent. To repay them, the pontiff sold offices and indulgences, creating in 1517 alone thirty new cardinals and so netting 500,000 desperately needed ducats. Other revenue was squeezed out of the survivors of an assassination plot orchestrated by Cardinal Petrucci in 1517; Petrucci was strangled, and the other members of the cabal pardoned after paying various ransoms, some around 50,000 ducats.

The shadow upon his reign was the rise of Martin Luther, whom Leo excommunicated in 1520 and whose tirades against the Church found fertile ground in Germany. In the political field, Leo was as vacillating in his alliances as he was disinterested in the reform of the Church. He at first concluded a concordat with King Francis I of France in 1516 to replace the long-standing Pragmatic Sanction of Bourges, but then, realizing he had alienated the Holy Roman Empire at a time when he very much needed its help against Luther, he supported the election of Charles (V) as emperor and concluded an anti-French alliance. This did little to stem the Lutheran tide, and his successors would bear the full brunt of the Reformation, the dangers of which Leo and his advisors, including Niccolo Machiavelli, had failed to recognize. Leo died on December 1, 1521. Successor: Adrian VI.

 LEO XI Pope from April 1 to April 27, 1605. Alessandro Ottaviano de'Medici was born in 1535 in Florence to a branch of the famed Medici family; through his mother he was a nephew of Pope Leo X. A favorite disciple of St. Philip Neri, he served for some years as the ambassador to Rome of Grand Duke Cosimo of Florence and there came to the attention of Pope Gregory XIII, who appointed him Bishop of Pistoia in 1573. He was named Archbishop of Florence in 1574 and a cardinal in 1583; he was also legate to France from 1596 to 1598. His election to succeed Clement XI came at the pleasure of the French, who were gladdened by the elevation of a relative of their queen, Marie de'Medici. His reign proved incredibly brief: he died after catching a cold at the Lateran. Successor: Paul V.

 LEO XII Pope from 1823 to 1829. Born near Spoleto, Annibale Sermattei della Genga belonged to a noble family, studied at Rome, and was ordained in 1783. He was soon appointed private secretary to Pope Pius VI and embarked upon a long albeit relatively undistinguished career as a diplomat. He was papal representative to Lucerne, Cologne, and various German royal courts, spending several years as the virtual captive of Napoleon in the abbey of Monticelli while the emperor held Pope Pius VII a prisoner. He served as nuncio to Paris after the release of the pope in 1814, but he earned the sharp rebuke of Ercole Cardinal Consalvi for failing to secure from the French the return of the papal property of Avignon. Pius, however, made him a cardinal in 1816 and in 1820 appointed him Vicar-General of Rome. In the conclave of 1823 to choose a successor to Pius, Genga certainly did not consider himself a likely candidate. Events proved him wrong. After several weeks of deliberations, the vote seemed to be heading toward the conservatives' choice, Cardinal Severoli, but a veto arrived from the Austrians. Severoli then led his fellow conservative cardinals, the *zelanti,* into a swift vote for Genga whom they felt represented their own views. On September 28, 1823, he was elected pope.

Leo was devout and personally mild, but quite without warmth or much of a sense of humor, reportedly a lifelong shortcoming. He did not disappoint the *zelanti,* turning the papacy away from broad political distractions to a more religious disposition. Toward this end, Consalvi was replaced as secretary of state and decrees were issued against liberalism, freemasonry, and indifferentism. His policies were especially stern in the matter of the Papal States. The Jews were ordered back to their ghetto in Rome, and the sale of wine was restricted in the taverns, choking off one of the few sources of merriment in the states. The pope also disapproved of realism in art, commanding that many statues or ornaments be removed from public gaze owing to their nakedness and others too heavy to move be covered over in strategic locations. Worst of all, the financial and political reforms introduced by Consalvi were reversed, replaced by a severe police regime. The Papal States thus became one of the most inefficient territories in Europe and economically stagnant, setting the stage for the severe social upheaval that would plague Gregory XVI (1831–1846). In matters of foreign policy, Leo learned the importance of fostering good relations with the courts of the time, negotiating a series of concordats. At his death on February 10, 1829, Leo was extremely unpopular. His passing was hastened by a botched operation. Successor: Pius VIII.

 LEO XIII Pope from 1878 to 1903, Gioacchino Vincenzo Pecci was born the son of a minor noble family in Carpineto, near Rome on March 2, 1810. His studies took him to Viterbo, the Roman College, and the Academy of Noble Ecclesiastics in Rome (the training ground for Vatican diplomats). Ordained in 1837, he was well known for his remarkable skills in Latin. In 1838, he was named governor of Perugia and in 1841 governor of Benevento. Pope Gregory XVI appointed him in 1843 to the post of nuncio to Belgium, with the rank of titular archbishop. In 1846, he was made Bishop of Perugia and was appointed a cardinal in 1853 by Pius IX, who made him camerlengo in 1877. The next year, he fulfilled his duties, convening the conclave to choose Pius's successor. He was elected pope after the third ballot, on February 20, 1878. His election almost certainly was a compromise. He was sixty-eight years old and rumored to be in poor health; he would thus have

Pope Leo XIII, the Worker's Pontiff.

been a short interregnum pope after the thirty-two-year reign of Pio Nono. None could have imagined that Leo would last for twenty-five very capable years.

The Quotable Leo XIII

Every man has by nature the right to possess property of his own.

It is one thing to have a right to the possession of money, and another to have a right to use money as one pleases.

Christ's mission is to save that which had perished, namely not some nation or people but the whole human race, without distinction of time or place.

. . . the Church is the city of the Living God, born of God Himself and established by His Authority, which is indeed a pilgrim here on earth, but is ever calling to men, teaching them and leading them on to eternal happiness in heaven.

. . . the State is bound to protect natural rights, not to destroy them.

When there is question of defending the rights of individuals, the defenseless and the poor have a claim to special consideration. The richer class has many ways of shielding itself, and stands less in need of help from the State; whereas the mass of the poor have no resources of their own to fall back on, and must chiefly depend on the assistance of the State. It is for this reason that wage earners, since they mostly belong to the latter class, should be specially cared for and protected by the government.

A scholar, poet, and expert on the writings of Dante, Leo XIII took as his main goals the fostering of improved relations with the states of Europe and the development of a coherent social doctrine for the Church. Remaining faithful to Pius, he would not deal with the Italian government, and his outreaches to the major states, especially England and France, were rebuffed. Progress was made to end the *Kulturkampf* (the anti-Catholic program of Otto von Bismarck) in Germany. In matters of doctrine, Leo turned his thought to social teaching, using a series of brilliant encyclicals to elucidate Christian social policy, especially *Rerum Novarum* (1891), called by John XXIII the Charter of Catholic Social Doctrine. He decried the dangers of socialism (accurately predicting its major failings), while stressing the problems of democratic societies and Christian responsibility in promoting human democracy. He also gave much encouragement to the study of St. Thomas Aquinas, missionary work around the world—new dioceses were established in Japan, India, Africa, and elsewhere, twenty-eight in the United States alone—and to scientific study. In a grand gesture, he opened the Vatican archives to scholars in 1883, declaring "the Church has no secrets." Finally, he restored much of the international respect for the papacy that had been dissipated under Pius IX. He remained vibrant right up until his sudden death at the age of ninety-three on July 20, 1903. Successor: St. Pius X.

�֍ **LEONINE CITY**   The name given to the extensive and formidable defenses established by the popes to protect St. Peter's Basilica and the Borgo from attack by raiders; the name was derived from the founder of the city, Pope St. Leo IV (847–855). The Leonine City became necessary after the brutal sack of St. Peter's by Saracens in 846. Using money donated by Emperor Lothair I (r. 840-855), and relying in part upon plans drawn up under Leo III (795–816), the pope erected new walls, forty feet high, with four gates and forty-eight towers. Finished and consecrated on June 27, 852, the Leonine walls extended from the Tiber around the Vatican Hill (enclosing St. Peter's) and the Borgo and winding its way back to the river. The heart of the stout defenses was the mausoleum of Emperor Hadrian sitting on the Tiber, the fort that had been christened by Pope St. Gregory I (590–604), the Castel Sant'Angelo. Popes over the years added to the walls and thereby increased the size of the Leonine City, which became a separate entity from Rome. The remains of the Leonine wall can still be seen along the Via del Corridori extending to the Borgo S. Angelo. (See also *Borgo, The; Castel Sant'Angelo; Passetto;* and *Vatican.*)

❀ **LIBER PONTIFICALIS** The Book of the Popes, the collection of papal biographies covering the reigns of the pontiffs from St. Peter to around 1464. The *Liber* is actually an initial collection of biographies, from St. Peter until Felix III (IV) (526–530), to which later additions were made. The earliest compilation was probably written during the reign of Boniface II (530–532) and relied heavily upon the *Liberian Catalogue,* with other historical sources and succession lists. These early biographies are characteristically brief, detailing the family and birthplace of the pope, his regnal dates, important decrees, churches built under his rule, notable gifts, the bishops he consecrated, significant events of the time, his burial place, and the time of the *sede vacante.* The length of the entries began to increase with later editions, new biographies being attached, in changing styles, down to the times of Pope Pius II (1458–1464). While considered historically accurate only from the reign of Pope Anastasius II (496–498), the *Liber* remains one of the foremost sources on the lives of the popes. (See also *Liberian Catalogue.*)

❀ **LIBERIAN CATALOGUE** A list of popes from St. Peter to the time of Pope Liberius (352–366); it is known through its presence in the collection of the writer then called Chronographer of 354. It can be divided into two parts, the first extending to the time of St. Pontianus (230–235), and the second to Liberius. Scholars consider this first part to be of dubious reliability. The *Liberian Catalogue* includes the first specific date in the history of the popes: September 28, 235, the abdication of St. Pontianus.

❀ **LIBERIUS** Pope from 352 to 366, the first pontiff not honored as a saint, Liberius was a deacon of Rome at the time of his elevation on May 17, 352, to succeed Pope St. Julius I. He was faced immediately with severe pressure from Emperor Constantius II to sign a condemnation of St. Athanasius that had been orchestrated by the pro-Arian party of the Church (those who espoused Arianism, the teaching that Christ was not divine). This Liberius refused to do, and so the emperor had him brought to Milan where he was threatened with banishment. Liberius supposedly responded by saying: "The laws of the Church are more important than residence in Rome. If you desire peace then you must annul what you have decreed against Athanasius. . . ." He was sent into exile in 355, and Rome witnessed the elevation of antipope Felix (II). Two years later Liberius returned, but it is unclear how this came about. It has been suggested that the emperor acquiesced to the pleas of Roman ladies and permitted his recall. The more likely event was that Liberius accepted some kind of a compromise and subscribed to a heretical formula of the faith, a possibility supported by both Sts. Athanasius and Jerome, who spoke of the pope granting his assent to the formula while under duress, rendering the papal approbation illegal. The pope's actions, however, have long been debated by scholars. Liberius's return to Rome was not a pleasant one, for he not only faced an antipope but was held in little regard by the people or the imperial regime. Nevertheless, his last years were distinguished by his careful orthodoxy, and it is acknowledged that he did not teach or support any heretical doctrines, although he has never been revered as a saint. He was also responsible for the erection of the Liberian Basilica in Rome, the basis for the modern basilica of Santa Maria Maggiore. Successor: St. Damasus.

❀ **LIBRARY, VATICAN**   The *Libreria Vaticana* (the Apostolic Vatican Library) holds the vast collection of books, manuscripts, and incunabula (books printed before 1501) preserved and maintained in the Vatican. The official library of the popes, it is ranked as one of the foremost such institutions in the world because of the immense value of its manuscripts and the incomparable artistic and literary legacies they represent. Its primary objective, and the one it fulfills brilliantly, is to preserve books and manuscripts for the benefit of future generations. Researchers and scholars must apply to the prefect of the library for admission and must have a justifiable purpose to their researches. A working knowledge of Italian is naturally essential, as is a genuine sense of decorum because the library makes its rules of conduct clear and its staff is not reluctant to eject any troublemakers.

The popes had naturally acquired books and manuscripts over the centuries, but these collections unfortunately did not survive in any large sense owing to war, sacks of Rome, and the wanderings of the popes. For example, the popes at Avignon organized their own impressive library, but most never reached the Eternal City upon their return to Rome in 1377. Initial efforts were begun to reconstitute the library under Popes Martin V (1417–1431) and Eugene IV (1431–1447), but credit for the founding of the current collection goes to the great humanist pontiff Nicholas V (1447–1455). Pope Sixtus IV (1471–1484) appointed the first prefect, the humanist Bartolomeo Platina (who had been imprisoned and tortured under Pope Pius II), on June 15, 1475, an event beautifully captured by the artist Melozzo da Forli in a painting now on display in the Pinacoteca section of the Vatican Museums.

Pope Sixtus V (1585–1590) constructed special buildings to house the growing collection, the building where it now resides. The darkest time for the library came in 1797 when the French invaded and plundered the Papal States. The books and manuscripts were returned only in 1815, after the fall of Napoleon Bonaparte. Over succeeding decades, the popes aggressively added to the collections, buying or acquiring libraries and manuscripts from all over Europe. Pope Leo XIII (1878–1903) then made the very enlightened decision to permit scholars access to the library, which had previously been off-limits to all but officials of the Church. When asked if he was certain about the decision, Leo responded that "the Church has no secrets." Modernization and extensive improvements were made by Popes Pius XI (1922–1939), who had once been prefect of the library, Pius XII (1939–1958), and John Paul II, who inaugurated an extensive underground vaulting system, called the Manuscript Depository, to house the rarest and most precious books in 1984. Currently, the library houses some 65,000 manuscripts and 700,000 volumes, with numbers increasing each year. Its chief officer is the cardinal librarian appointed by the pope, although administration is in the hands of the prefect, assisted by a small staff.

❀ **LIBRERIA EDITRICE VATICANA** The official Vatican publishing house, which serves as the publisher of all works of the Holy See, including the congregations of the Curia; it is, in effect, the pope's publisher. The publishing wing of the Vatican began as a means of advancing the distribution of the official documents and decrees of the Holy See, such as the *Acta Apostolica Sedis*. In 1926, it was made an independent body, separate from the Vatican Press (the official printing plant of the Holy See) and henceforth was a publisher of considerable note. While the books and materials it produces are geared exclusively toward promulgating the official documents and writings authorized by the Holy See, the quality of the work so produced is internationally recognized. The press, for example, played a leading role in the production of the Catechism, which was finally released in 1994. Among the books published each year by Libreria are *L'Attivita della Santa Sede* (*Activities of the Holy See*) and *Annuario Pontificio*. The press is extremely well run and is located in the Saint Anne district of the Vatican, next to the other Vatican printing offices.

❀ **LINUS, ST.** Bishop of Rome from 67 to 76, the acknowledged successor of St. Peter. Very little is known about his reign, although both historical sources Irenaeus and Hegesippus are clear in naming Linus as the bishop of Rome after Peter, having received his mantle of office by both Peter and St. Paul. According to custom, he was not a Jew but an Italian; if so, he is the first of the Italian popes (he would certainly not be the last). He may also be the Linus mentioned in St. Paul's writings (2 Tim. 4:21). The most traumatic event of his reign for Christians was the burning of Jerusalem in 70, during the siege of the city by the Romans under Titus. Successor: St. Anacletus.

❀ **L'OSSERVATORE DELLA DOMENICA** The supplemental Sunday issue of the daily edition of the Vatican daily *L'Osservatore Romano*. It is published only on Sundays, as its name would suggest, and is in Italian. It is different from the regular paper in that it is framed more in a tabloid style and has photographs. (See also *L'Osservatore Romano*.)

❀ **L'OSSERVATORE ROMANO** The daily newspaper of the Holy See. Meaning in English, "The Roman Observer," the newspaper is the single most important source of information on the daily activities, statements, and proclamations of the pontiff, fully justifying its status as the "official newspaper of the pope." It is published in Italian every day, except for Sunday, at three P.M., although there are also weekly editions, available in English, Spanish, German, Polish (naturally), French, and Portuguese, and an Italian Sunday edition called *L'Osservatore della Domenica*. The foreign language editions are available in Rome, but they usually are sent to subscribers all around the globe and are read with considerable interest by diplomats, Vaticanologists, political leaders (even the Kremlin had a subscription), and Church officials everywhere. Overall, the paper has a subscription list of some 50,000 and has a profound influence and reach. During World War II, it was the only free paper in Italy, and throughout its history it has been an important voice for the Holy See on such matters as war and peace, and human rights. It has technically only one "official" section, the column on the front page called *Nostre Informazioni*. Here are printed all formal announcements by the pope. Other valuable information might include schedules of upcoming trips, translations or transcripts of encyclicals, speeches and decrees, appointments around the world, and editorials on relevant subjects. That the pope himself takes an interest in the editorial content was amply demonstrated in the early 1980s, when the pope sacked the editor-in-chief over an editorial critical of Lech Walesa.

The paper began in 1861 when four Catholic laymen, including the grandfather of Pope Pius XII, Marcantonio Pacelli, started up an independent newspaper to supplement the official state newspaper in Rome, the *Giornale di Roma.* Immediately deemed useful by the papacy, it was bought by Pope Leo XIII in 1890 and has ceased printing only once, in 1870, during the takeover of Rome by the troops of King Victor Emmanuel II. Its very distinctive masthead boasts the crossed keys and tiara of the papacy and the two mottoes *Unicuique suum* ("To each his own") and *Non Praevalebunt* ("They will not prevail") in memory of the terrible events of 1870. It is run today by the members of the Salesian Congregation of Don Bosco under the direction of an editor-in-chief, a small editorial board, and a staff of reporters. There are no foreign correspondents, but the paper has access to the services of the bishops' conferences when desirable. Overall funding is provided by APSA (Administration of the Patrimony of the Holy See). Its offices are situated in the Via del Pellegrino, in the Saint Anne district of the Vatican, near the Porta Santa Anna; it has been there since 1929. (See also *L'Osservatore della Domenica.*)

❀ **LUCIUS I, ST.** Pope from 253 to 254, Lucius was a native of Rome, receiving election as successor to St. Cornelius on June 25, 253. He was soon banished from Rome by the Christian-hating Emperor Trebonianus Gallus, returning to the Eternal City at the accession of Emperor Valerian that same year. St. Cyprian then wrote him to offer his congratulations that Lucius was able to return, because then the Bishop of Rome could suffer martyrdom with his fellow Romans. Lucius opposed the presence of the antipope Novatian and permitted the readmission of lapsed Christians into the Church after they performed suitable penance. According to the *Liber Pontificalis,* the pope was given the honor of dying in Rome, martyred by decapitation; the Liberian Catalogue, however, says that he died of natural causes. Successor: St. Stephen I.

❀ **LUCIUS II** Pope from 1144 to 1145, a warrior pope. Gheraldo Cassianimici was from Bologna and served as a prominent canon lawyer in Lucca before entering into the papal service. Pope Callistus II named him a cardinal in 1124, and Innocent II appointed him chamberlain and librarian. Gheraldo was elected pope on March 12, 1144, to succeed Celestine II, and he immediately found the task daunting because ambitious social climbers had established a commune within Rome and named as their spokesman Giordano Pierleoni, brother of the antipope Anacletus II. To garner support for his effort in reducing the commune, Lucius turned to the Norman ruler, Roger II of Sicily

(d. 1154), but he was little disposed to assisting the Holy See. Lucius was also disappointed in his effort to win the help of the German King Conrad III. On his own, the pope declared war on his own flock in Rome. With all the troops he could muster, Lucius tried to storm the Capitol, but was repulsed with much loss of life. Wounded in the fray, he died from his injuries on February 15, 1145. Successor: Eugene III.

❀ **LUCIUS III** Pope from 1181 to 1185. A native of Lucca, Ubaldo Allucingoli entered the Cistercian order under the influence of the great saint Bernard of Clairvaux (d. 1153). Known to be an honest and upright person, he was appointed a cardinal by Pope Innocent II and then cardinal bishop of Ostia by Adrian IV. He received election as Alexander III's successor on September 1, 1181. Crowned at Velletri outside Rome owing to troubles in the city, the pope found it prudent to stay out of Rome for most of the early part of his pontificate. Lucius devoted much effort to negotiating a peace with the Holy Roman Emperor Frederick I Barbarossa (d. 1190). Progress was made on only a few of the issues between them, but the pope did manage to secure Frederick's promise to embark on a crusade to the Holy Land (the ill-fated Third Crusade, during which Frederick would die by drowning). In 1184, Lucius also convened the Synod of Verona, which ordered measures taken against heretics. Lucius died at Verona on November 25, 1185. Successor: Urban III.

❀ **MAGISTERIUM** The formal teaching office of the Church, established in Catholic teaching by Christ to safeguard the faith and held by the bishops as the successors of the Apostles, under the authority of the Supreme Pontiff as successor to St. Peter, Prince of the Apostles. The Magisterium is also vested in the pope as Vicar of Christ. It exists in two senses, the ordinary and extraordinary; the former is exercised by the Church hierarchy under the leadership of the pope and comprises the regular teaching or instruction of the faithful, while the latter is the formal proclamation of some teaching on the faith. When related to matters of faith and morals, the teaching is considered infallible. The Magisterium is one of the most important of all papal prerogatives. (See also *Infallibility, Papal.*)

❀ **MALACHY, PROPHECIES OF** A set of famous prophecies supposedly made by St. Malachy (1094–1148), the Archbishop of Armagh and a beloved Irish saint. No writings of St. Malachy are said to have survived, but a fascinating set of predictions related to the papacy are attributed to him. The prophecies consist of a series of mottoes, said to match in some way each pope from Celestine II (1143–1144) to the last pontiff, Peter II the Roman (Petrus Romanus), who will lead the Church in its final period of persecution. Scholars have long debated the authenticity of the prophecies, but the consensus is that they are a forgery, written sometime in the sixteenth century. According to the prophecies, however, there is only one more pope until the reign of Peter II. The pope after John Paul II will be *Gloria Olivae* (The Glory of the Olive), a motto that coincides curiously with the traditional claim of the Benedictines that one of their own will reign again before the end of the world. Another name for the order is the Olivetans.

❀ **MARCELLINUS, ST.** Pope from 296 to 304, a native of Rome, Marcellinus was elected to succeed St. Caius, his rule dating from June 30, 296. Little is known with absolute certainty about his reign, but it seems that the Christian community enjoyed a period of relative peace in the early part of it. This ended abruptly in 303 when a new wave of persecution descended on the Roman empire under Emperor Diocletian. It is highly possible that Marcellinus was guilty of apostasy, handing over copies of the Scriptures to the Roman authorities and perhaps even giving incense to the gods. As this was a scandalous action for a Christian, let alone a pope, Marcellinus was possibly deposed or, if the *Liber Pontificalis* is to be believed, was filled with grief and beheaded at the command of the emperor. The fact of his unfortunate action was apparently generally accepted, as seen in the long-time omission of his name from the official lists of popes. His deposition or death (traditionally on October 25, 304) caused much hardship for the Church, and a successor was not elected until 308. Despite his apparent actions, Marcellinus was revered as a saint because of his apparent martyrdom. Successor: Marcellus I.

❁ **MARCELLUS I, ST.**   Pope from May or June 308 to January 309, the successor to the unfortunate St. Marcellinus. Marcellus was a native of Rome, receiving election on May 27 or June 26, 308, after an interregnum of some four years following the death of Marcellinus. His election had in fact proven possible only because of the easing of the persecution of Christians with the accession of Emperor Maxentius (d. 312). The chief aim of his reign was to restore discipline in the Church by imposing demanding penances upon those Christians who had turned away from the faith during the years of oppression. His move was probably considered essential for the well-being of the Church, but it also removed any possible stain made by the apostasy of St. Marcellinus. Marcellus, however, encountered great resistance, and his decree was so unpopular that riots broke out in the streets of Rome. Emperor Maxentius himself was forced to use troops to suppress the fighting. Marcellus was banished by the emperor on the grounds that the bishop had promoted civil disorder. Marcellus died a short time later, but his body was returned to Rome. Successor: St. Eusebius.

MARCELLUS II   Pope from April 9 to May 1, 1555, a short reign most notable for his being one of only two modern popes (with Adrian VI) to retain his baptismal name after election. Born in Montepulciano, Italy, Marcello Cervini was the son of an official in the papal administration, studying in Siena and then Rome and emerging as a scholar of high repute. In 1534, the newly elected Pope Paul III (1534–1549) appointed him tutor to his young nephew, Cardinal Alessandro. Five years later, Paul made him a cardinal, and in 1545 named him a co-president of the Council of Trent (1545–1563). One of his co-presidents was the future Pope Julius III (1550–1555), whom he succeeded after a brief conclave. As pope, Marcellus was joyously welcomed by the reforming movement in the Church, fulfilling their expectations right from the start with his immediate indications of launching further reforms. Unfortunately, he was already ill at the time of his election and swiftly worked himself into the grave. On May 1, 1555, he died of a massive stroke, aborting a reign rich in promise. Successor: Paul IV.

❀ **MARINUS I**   Pope from 882 to 884. Also incorrectly called Martin II, he was from Tuscany, Italy, and was serving the papal administration at the age of twelve. He spent years working on behalf of the popes, being sent as a papal ambassador to Constantinople. Marinus succeeded John VIII (872–882) on December 16, 882. His reign is little known, although he apparently pardoned the future Pope Formosus and other individuals of any possible complicity in the murder of his predecessor. Successor: St. Adrian III.

❀ **MARINUS II**   Pope from 942 to 946. Also incorrectly listed as Martin III, he was from Rome, although next to nothing is known about his earlier days. On October 30, 942, he was elected to succeed Stephen VIII (IX), owing his elevation to the patronage of Alberic II (d. 954), the noble ruler of Rome, and spending his short reign under Alberic's control. He did introduce some reforms among the clergy. Successor: Agapitus II.

❀ **MARK, ST.**   Pope from January 18 to October 7, 336, the son of a Roman by the name of Priscus. He received election in succession to Pope St. Sylvester. It is possible that Emperor Constantine had mentioned Mark (then a member of the Roman clergy) in a letter to Pope Miltiades (311–314). His pontificate came in the closing period of Constantine's mighty reign, and, like Sylvester, he was very much in the shadow of the emperor. It is known that he founded two new churches and introduced the significant innovation of having the Bishop of Ostia consecrate each new Bishop of Rome. Successor: St. Julius I.

❀ **MARTIN I, ST.**   Pope from 649 to 655. From Todi, in Umbria, he served as an ambassador to the imperial court of Constantinople prior to his election as successor to Pope Theodore I on July 5, 649, proving an exceedingly determined and independent-minded pontiff. He made manifest his resolve to stand free of imperial domination by declining to seek formal approval of his election from the Byzantine Emperor Constans II Pogonatus (641–648) and by convening a Lateran council in Rome in 649 that condemned the heresy of Monothelitism in the face of the imperial edict forbidding any discussion of the subject. Angered by the pontiff's temerity in flouting his authority, Constans commanded that Martin be arrested and deposed. On June 17, 653, the already ailing Martin was dragged from his sickbed, put on a boat, and sent to Constantinople. Along the way, he was brutalized by the soldiers and arrived at the imperial capital suffering from a variety of severe ailments. Condemned as a traitor, he was publicly flogged and sentenced to death, but the emperor magnanimously commuted the death penalty to banishment. Sent to the Crimea in early 654, he died on September 16, 655, from cruel treatment and the unbearable cold. While eventually revered by the Church in Rome, Martin—as he himself lamented—was all but forgotten by his own diocese. Not only did they disregard his wishes and elect a successor after his banishment, the Romans neglected to send any food, blankets, or even warm greetings to their suffering bishop. Successor: St. Eugene I.

❀ **MARTIN II**   See *Marinus I.*

❀ **MARTIN III**   See *Marinus II.*

MARTIN IV   Pope from 1281 to 1285, whose reign was dominated by the French king of Naples, Charles of Anjou (1266–1285). Simon de Brie (or Brion) was born at Brie, in France. He served as archdeacon and chancellor at Rouen, and then chancellor and keeper of the seal under King St. Louis IX of France. Made a cardinal under Pope Urban IV, he served as papal legate to France under both Clement IV and Gregory X. On February 22, 1281, he was elected to succeed Nicholas III, owing his elevation largely to the influence of King Charles, who was increasingly in control of Italian and papal affairs. He took the name Martin IV even though he was technically only the second pope so named, because Popes Marinus I and II were inadvertently called Martin in official lists of the thirteenth century. As a sign of the times, the new pontiff was unable to enter Rome because of unrest and had to be crowned at Orvieto. He would remain there, the Romans never warming to the French pope, whom they felt had been forced upon them. Martin was a loyal and generally obedient client of Charles. Martin also agreed with the king that a reunion should be effected with the Greeks by

Martyred Pontiffs

The popes of the early Church recognized that not only were they the Bishops of Rome and heads of the rapidly growing Christian faith in their region, but they were as well the virtual physical embodiment of the Church. It is not surprising, then, that the Bishops of Rome were frequently singled out for arrest and execution by Roman officials during periods of persecution, often with obsessive hatred. Emperor Trajanus Decius, for example, was especially concerned about the popes, once remarking that he would rather hear of a usurper arrayed against him with five legions than to learn that another bishop had been elected in Rome. The first pope to suffer martyrdom was, in fact, the first pope, St. Peter, who was crucified upside down by the accommodating Romans after declaring that he was unworthy of dying in the same manner as his Master. The story is told that he departed Rome in 62, when Emperor Nero launched his famous persecution, but while on the Appian Way leading out of Rome, he suddenly encountered Christ walking toward Rome. Asking, "Where are you going, Lord?" (*Quo vadis, Domine?*), Peter was told "I am going to Rome to die in your place." Getting the message, Peter turned around and went to give the ultimate sacrifice for the faith. The event is commemorated by a chapel still standing on the Appian Way and the famous novel *Quo Vadis* (1895) by Henryk Sienkiewicz. The list of martyred popes includes the following, and all are saints:

Peter,	Soter*	Stephen I
Linus*	Eleutherius	Sixtus I*
Anacletus*	Victor I*	Eutychianus*
Clement I*	Zephyrinus*	Gaius
Evaristus*	Callistus I*	Marcellinus*
Alexander I*	Pontian,	Marcellus I
Sixtus I*	Fabian	Eusebius
Telesphorus	Cornelius	John I
Pius I Anicetus*	Lucius I*	Silverius

St. Vigilius (537–555) and Boniface VIII (1294–1303) are sometimes ranked as martyrs because they died for refusing to surrender their principles in matters of the faith.

*These popes are traditionally honored as having died in martyrdom, although specific evidence is lacking.

military force if necessary, a policy that not surprisingly was the cause of terrible relations with Constantinople. In 1282, Martin excommunicated Byzantine Emperor Michael VIII Palaeologus (1282–1328). The tenuous reunion that had been negotiated at the Council of Lyons in 1274 was now dead. Martin died outside of Rome, at Perugia, on March 28, 1285, only a few weeks after Charles's passing. Successor: Honorius IV.

MARTIN V Pope from 1417 to 1431, the first universally recognized pontiff following the resolution of the Great Western Schism, which had divided the Church since 1378. Oddone (or Oddo) Colonna was born at Gennazano and was a member of the long-powerful house of Colonna. He studied at Perugia and owed his elevation to the cardinalate to Pope Innocent VII (1404–1406). While initially loyal to the Roman popes during the schism, he turned against Gregory XII, helped organize the Council of Pisa (1409)— which elected a third claimant to the throne, Alexander V—and subsequently remained a faithful adherent of antipope John XXIII right up until the Council of Constance (1414–1418). At that council, Colonna was elected the sole pope, since all other papal rivals had removed themselves or been deposed (although two antipopes with small followings would endure, Benedict XIII and Clement VIII). His elevation on November 11, 1417, brought to a close the schism and signaled the first and only time that the Colonna, traditionally active in papal affairs, would produce a pope. Chosen because of his mildness and for what was believed to be his fairly pliant nature in matters of conciliarism and reform, Martin chagrined the cardinals by his determination to resurrect the fortunes and power of the papacy and to revive the Papal States, which were essential for the improvement of the finances of the Holy See. Toward that end, he returned the papacy to Rome and waged a brutal war in the States, defeating the ambitious *condottiere* (general) Braccio de Montone in 1424. To advance the international prestige of the Holy See, Martin sent his ambassadors to various countries and even proposed to the Byzantines the possibility of a future meeting to discuss reunion. While concerned about surrendering any privileges to the conciliarists and holding councils in disgust, the pope did convene, as promised, the Council of Pavia in 1423 and later, under pressure, the Council of Basle that would so trouble his successor. Other reforms were introduced within the Curia and in matters of clerical discipline. Strong-willed on behalf of the papacy, Martin has been called the second founder of the monarchial papacy. His methods at times were quite harsh, one contemporary noting that "he has crushed the cardinals so utterly that they turn red and pale when speaking in his presence." He died of a sudden apoplexy on February 20, 1431. Successor: Eugene IV.

❀ **MARTYR**   See box, *Martyred Pontiffs,* page 236.

❀ **MASTER OF PONTIFICAL CEREMONIES**   The title borne by the official appointed to head the Office of Liturgical Celebrations of the Supreme Pontiff. (See *Office for Liturgical Celebrations of the Supreme Pontiff* for other details.)

❀ **MASTER OF THE SACRED PALACE**   Called in Latin the *Magister Sacri Palatii,* this is the position held by the priest who acts as theological advisor to the pope. The office was first established by Pope Honorius III in 1218. His choice as master was St. Dominic (1170–1221), who began the unbroken tradition of having the theological advisors picked exclusively from the ranks of the Dominicans (the Order of Friars Preacher, O.P.). While always a Dominican, the magister must also be a friar of the deepest possible spiritual comportment and considered the most eminent of all candidates in theology and canon law. Prior to 1870, he resided in the Quirinal Palace in Rome, where was kept a series of frescoes of his predecessors, stretching all the way back to St. Dominic. Today, he has apartments in the Vatican.

❀ **MEDALS, PAPAL**   See *Decorations, Papal.*

❀ **MEDICI, HOUSE OF DE'**   One of the most famous of all Italian noble houses, best remembered as important patrons of Renaissance artists, but also producing four popes and securing marriage to several royal houses of Europe. The Medici popes were: Leo X (Giovanni de'Medici, 1513–1521), Clement VII (Giulio de'Medici, 1523–1534), Pius IV (Giovanni Angelo de'Medici, 1559–1565), and Leo XI (Alessandro de'Medici, April 1–27, 1605). Although the last pope came from a collateral branch of the house, he was a nephew of Leo X. (See under individual popes; see also *Christina of Sweden, Queen.*)

❀ **METROPOLITAN OF THE ROMAN PROVINCE**   One of the titles of the pope. The pope is Archbishop and Metropolitan of the Roman Province, the ecclesiastical region comprising Rome and its surrounding dioceses. (See also *Titles of the Pope.*)

❀ **MICHELANGELO** In full, Michelangelo Buonarroti (1475–1564), one of the greatest of all artists of the Renaissance. Born in Caprese, Tuscany, he was the son of Ludovici and Francesca Buonarroti Simoni. Apprenticed to the painter Domenico Ghirlandaio, he subsequently studied in the famed Medici Gardens and was raised in the enlightened environment of the house of Lorenzo de'Medici, where he was surrounded by scholars, artists, poets, and philosophers. These formative years had a profound effect upon him, making him a true Renaissance figure, although he also was deeply influenced by the religious fervor of the reforming zealot Savonarola. He was to labor over the next decades in sculpture, architecture, painting, and even poetry. Some of his greatest works were in the service of the papacy.

He first journeyed to Rome in June, 1496, where he was much inspired by the treasure of classical monuments. It is believed that during this period he created the renowned *Pietà* (1498–1499) as part of a commission for Cardinal Billiers de la Groslaye. (See box, *The Pietà.*) Returning to Florence for several years, Michelangelo was brought back to Rome in 1505 at the summons of Pope Julius II (1503–1513). The pontiff became his greatest patron and the two had a fascinating and complex relationship. The pope commissioned Michelangelo to sculpt his tomb, a project that would take thirty years to finish; the greatest piece was the Moses, completed in 1542 and now in the Church of St. Peter in Chains, Rome. Julius also commissioned him to paint the ceiling of the Sistine Chapel (1508–1512), arguably Michelangelo's foremost achievement, although he took to the job with great reluctance because he never considered himself a painter. The tale is told—among many—that during the long period of working on the ceiling Michelangelo grew tired of the public sneaking in to look upon his labors. One night he saw someone prowling around below the scaffolding and, with a roar, hurled the astonished visitor out the door. It turned out that the victim of the painter's ire was none other than his employer, Pope Julius. (See also *Sistine Chapel.*) Michelangelo also painted the *Last Judgment* in the Sistine Chapel (1534–1541) and the frescoes in the Pauline Chapel of *The Crucifixion of St. Peter* and *The Conversion of St. Paul* (1542); both commissions were for Pope Paul III and reflected the deepening religious devotion of Michelangelo, a brooding spiritual introspection that can be seen in the dark, apocalyptic images of the *Last Judgment* and the overpowering images of the Pauline frescoes. Michelangelo also served the popes in the capacity of architect, leaving his mark on St. Peter's Basilica. He succeeded Sangallo as chief architect in 1546 and embarked upon the

The Pietà

Arguably the most famous of all the treasures in the Vatican is the Pietà, completed by Michelangelo in 1499 when he was only twenty-five years old. It shows the grieving Virgin Mother holding her dead son in her arms after his Crucifixion, a common theme in Christian art, its name from the Italian pietà (pity), a depiction of the lamentation surrounding the death of Christ. The masterpiece is the only work of Michelangelo that he signed, the result of an unfortunate experience when the statue was on display. Michelangelo overheard a group of awed observers, but was appalled to hear them attribute the work to another artist. He immediately carved his name on a strip across the front of a portion of the Virgin Mary, the name still visible today. One of the most revered pieces in St. Peter's Basilica, the Pietà is located in the Chapel of the Pietà, just inside the church, beyond the Porta Sancta. For most of its history in the basilica, the statue was separated from visitors only by a rail, its details clearly visible to visitors who could stand only a few feet away. In 1972, however, a hammer-wielding lunatic Hungarian (later a naturalized Austrian) jumped over the rail, screamed, "I am Jesus Christ!" and began smashing the precious work. Before he could be wrestled to the ground, he had badly damaged the arm of the Virgin and marred her face. In a brilliant restoration, the Vatican's experts undertook a complete repair, completed in such a way that in the future should any of the new pieces become yellowed or discolored, they can be removed and replaced. Today, the statue sits behind bulletproof glass; it is still visible to the public, but at a distance. Nevertheless, it is still the cause of awe.

task with considerable enthusiasm; it would occupy most of his later life. To ensure his plans for the great dome of the basilica were not misunderstood after his death, he had his friend Giorgio Vasari carve a wooden model of the proposed dome, inspired by the cupola of the Duomo in Florence by Brunelleschi. The dome of St. Peter's was built in keeping with Michelangelo's vision. He died on February 18, 1564. His motto was that he had labored "not for money or fame, but solely for the love of God." (See also *Julius II; Paul III;* and *Saint Peter, Basilica of.*)

🏵 **MILIZIA URBANA**   One of the older elements of the papal armed forces, the Milizia Urbana was combined with the Civica Scelta around 1851 to create the Palatine Guard of Honor. As the name would suggest, the unit was originally a kind of urban militia for Rome. (See *Palatine Guard of Honor.*)

🏵 **MILTIADES, ST.**   Pope from 311 to 314. Known also as Melchiades, he was possibly from Africa, although scholars generally consider him to have been born in Rome. He had served as a presbyter under the controversial Pope Marcellinus and received election to succeed St. Eusebius on July 2, 311. His pontificate came at a most propitious time, for the Church was at long last able to breathe free thanks to the reluctant issue of the Edict of Toleration in 311 by the Christian-hating Emperor Galerius; henceforth the faith was to be accepted across the Roman Empire and in time would actually receive the favor of the imperial government. Added to this good news was the decision by Emperor Maxentius, in the hopes of winning the support of Christians, to restore to them all properties seized by officials during the darker periods of the past. Maxentius's magnanimity did little to save himself, for in 312 he was defeated and killed at the Battle of Milvian Bridge by Constantine the Great, a towering figure whom Miltiades almost certainly knew. The new master of Rome gave to the bishop of the city the palace of Empress Fausta; this was to become the Lateran Palace, home of the popes until the fifteenth century. The main trouble of his reign came from the Donatists, radical rigorists who felt that the sacraments (communion and marriage) were not valid if the priest was in a state of sin or had once been a lapsed Christian. They were condemned by the pope in 313 at a synod, although the controversy would continue after his death on January 10, 314. Because of the suffering he endured in the persecutions, he was revered as a martyr. Successor: St. Sylvester I.

❀ **MONSIGNOR**   A title of honor bestowed on and used by certain clerics in the Church. Meaning in Italian "My Lord," it is bestowed upon a priest as a symbol of his elevation above the rank of priest. It is technically borne by all bishops and archbishops, and in Europe and especially within the Vatican, prelates below the rank of cardinal are termed monsignors. This usage is not common in the United States, where it is used by priests who have received one of the titles of distinction appointing them to the papal household. There are basically two types of monsignori, the active and the honorary. Active monsignors actually are appointed to the papal household, meaning they serve the pope in some direct capacity; honorary monsignori are those priests around the world who are given recognition for their long service to the Church (instead of appointment as bishop) or are granted the title to facilitate their work. Different types of monsignori are Protonotary Apostolic, Chaplain of His Holiness, and Prelate of Honor of His Holiness.

❀ **MOTU PROPRIO**   A type of papal document meaning "of his own accord" that is issued by the pontiff under his own decision and his own hand and not with the advice of his cardinals and advisors. It is normally addressed to the entire Church, to a part of the Church, to a group of persons, or one person; its contents can range from matters of administration to the conferring of a favor by the pope upon someone. Written in Latin or Italian, the *motu proprio* begins with an explanation of the reasons for the decree, followed by the actual text, such as the regulation or matter in question, or the favor being granted. At the bottom is the pope's signature, by his hand, with the date; both are always in Latin.

❀ **MUSEUMS, VATICAN**   The vast collections of art that are preserved and displayed by the Holy See in the Vatican. The Vatican Museums, with their paintings, sculpture, bronzes, reliefs, glass, gold, maps, tapestries, and relics are a stunning record not merely of the Christian faith but of human culture and civilization. The museums are as well a testament to the patronage of the popes and their zeal in collecting art and promoting the finest sculptors, painters, and artisans in their own eras. Indeed, long before any pontiff considered establishing a museum, the Vatican had become in essence a museum, holding the collective history of the Church as it was expressed in art and architecture. The origins of the museum, however, date to the reign of Sixtus IV, who in 1471 gathered together some of his favorite sculpture pieces and opened the doors of the Capitoline Palace to the Romans. His nephew Julius II (1503–1513) made a similar gesture, organizing the famed sculpture garden in the courtyard of the Belvedere Palace with such pieces as the *Laocoön* and the *Apollo Belvedere,* two of the signature pieces of the Vatican Museum. In typical fashion, the pontiff declared all were welcome, but he had a sign posted at the entrance that read *"Procul este prophani"* (The Profane keep away). The real start of the museums, however, is credited to Pope Benedict XIV (1740–1758) who founded the Museum for Christian Antiquities (also called the Sacred Museum), bringing together a large group of antiquities—bronze, terra cotta, and glass—which had been uncovered in the catacombs of Rome. From that time, spurred on by new discoveries and the revival in interest in classical art, popes found it desirable to devote money to the start of new museums and to improve or embellish already existing ones. Some of the foremost patrons of the museums were: Clement XIV (1769–1775) and Pius VI (1775–1799), who gave their names to the extensive Museo Pio-Clementino; Pius VII (1800–1823), founder of the Museo Chiaramonti; Gregory XVI (1831–1846), namesake of the Gregorian Etruscan, Egyptian, and Profane museums; Pius IX (1846–1878); Leo XIII (1878–1903); Pius XII (1939–1958), and Paul VI (1963–1978), who founded the Collection of Modern Religious Art.

The entire institution defies complete comprehension, so enormous is its size, grandeur, and breadth. Its magnificence is heightened by the historical nature of the many buildings, loggias, galleries, and stairs used to house the collections, themselves the product of such minds as Canova, Raphael, and Bramante. The museums, not surprisingly, are visited by millions of tourists every year, and such is the demand that the schedule permits no more than a few days a year for the museums' doors to be closed. The museums employ hundreds of experts and scholars who maintain catalogs, administer the important restoration labs, and keep the collection up to date with new discoveries and acquisitions. Overall authority rests in the hands of the general administration of the Pontifical Monuments, Museums, and Galleries, a branch of the Pontifical Commission for the Vatican City State. (See also Appendix 3, *The Vatican Museums.*)

❀ **NEPOTISM** The granting of offices, preferments, and positions of influence to family members and relatives. The history of the papacy is replete with incidents of nepotism, since the practice became common custom in the Middle Ages when popes belonged to prominent families and noble houses and there were many relatives to reward. The institution of the so-called cardinal nephew became so pervasive, in fact, that the word *nepotism* is taken from the Italian *nepoti* (nephew). The nepotistic tendencies of the popes stemmed in large part from the need for a pontiff to appoint reliable individuals to posts in his administration without fear of scheming and ambitions by those outside his family. That the custom was a problem by the eleventh century can be seen in the denunciation of the practice by Pope Sylvester II (999–1003). It continued unabated throughout the medieval epoch and into the Renaissance, reaching a peak during the sixteenth and seventeenth centuries, when the cardinal nephew system was a fully accepted part of papal life. The reforms of the papacy gradually ended nepotism, culminating with the proclamation of Pope Innocent XII (1691–1700), *Romanum Decet Pontificem* (1692), in which he decreed that pontiffs should not grant offices or estates and only one relative should be permitted elevation to the purple.

❀ **NICHOLAS I, ST.** Pope from 858 to 867, who did much to enhance the prestige and influence of the papacy. A native of Rome, he was the son of a local official, emerging as one of the chief figures in the pontificates of Sergius II, Leo IV, and especially Benedict III. He succeeded Benedict on April 24, 858, owing his election to the fact that the future Pope Adrian (II) refused to accept his own elevation. While he received the approval of Emperor Louis II (855–875), Nicholas was not to be a pontiff weak and pliant to the will of the imperial court. On the contrary, he was one of the most forceful personalities and a formidable advocate of papal rights and authority, ever vigilant for ways to advance his cause and to defeat any hint of secular interference. When threatened for his actions by Emperor Louis, Nicholas holed himself up in St. Peter's and rode out the siege. Louis finally gave up when it was clear that in this the Romans were behind their bishop. The defeat of Louis brought Nicholas immense prestige and much heightened spiritual influence. His relations with the Byzantines proved equally inflammatory, and there soon began the so-called Photian Schism, which would continue for the next years. While his successors would dissipate much of the power he had amassed, Nicholas was one of the foremost figure of his era and an architect of the monarchial claims the papacy would assume in the next centuries. Successor: Adrian II.

❀ **NICHOLAS II** Pope from 1058 to 1061, one of the pontiffs devoted to the so-called Gregorian reform of the Church. Born perhaps in Lorraine, Gerard was appointed Bishop of Florence in 1045 and was still in this post at the death of Pope Stephen IX (X) in 1058. A minority of cardinals hastily elected Bishop John of Velletri as Benedict X on April 5, a move much opposed by the reforming cardinals, who were determined not to choose a new pontiff, as per the demand of Pope Stephen, until the much-respected Hildebrand (the future St. Gregory VII) could arrive from Germany, where he had been on a mission. Once Hildebrand was among them at Siena, the cardinals elected Gerard as Nicholas II on the basis of his reforming zeal, on December 6, 1058. He refused to recognize antipope Benedict and quickly pleased the reformers by convening the Synod of Sutri in January 1059, at which he condemned his rival. In April that year he summoned the Lateran Council, which promulgated an electoral decree in strict conformity with the wishes of the reformers; henceforth, the popes would initially be chosen by the cardinal bishops, after which the vote of the cardinal priests and deacons would be given and the assent of the clergy and people of Rome requested. He also condemned clerical marriage and lay investiture, a move that caused much controversy in Germany, where investiture was common practice. Nicholas shrewdly secured much independence for the papacy by entering into an alliance with the Normans of southern Italy, giving to them the extensive territories of Apulia and Calabria in return for their fealty; Nicholas thus secured feudal control of much of the peninsula and a powerful military ally against the Holy Roman emperors. The fruits of this new alliance were immediate: Benedict was captured by the Normans and given over to the pope. Unfortunately, his steps were greeted with little joy in Germany, and at his death on July 26, 1061, relations with the German bishops were severely hostile. Successor: Alexander II.

NICHOLAS III Pope from 1277 to 1280, Giovanni Gaetano was born in Rome and was a member of the Orsini, a noble family with long ties to the papacy. He served under eight pontiffs in an impressive career and was a cardinal for some thirty years before finally winning election on November 25, 1277, as successor to John XXI. The conclave that chose him was attended by a mere seven cardinals and remained deadlocked for six months. His elevation was taken as bad news by the king of Naples and Sicily, the Angevin Charles of Anjou, who had emerged as a dominating influence over the papacy. As a cardinal, Gaetano had worked to reduce Charles's influence. As Pope Nicholas III, he continued this policy, even disrupting Charles's hopes of invading Constantinople by meeting with representatives of Emperor Michael VIII Palaeologus (1259–1282). He tried to maintain the tenuous reunion that had been negotiated in 1274, but his terms for the actual implementation of the decrees of the Council of Lyons proved extremely demanding. Known to be upright and honest, he nevertheless raised many an eyebrow by his unabashed nepotism. Of the six cardinals he appointed, three of them came from the Orsini; he argued that he needed family members to curb foreign (read French) influence. Fond of Rome, he devoted large amounts of money to its repair, restoration, and beautification, especially the papal palace and St. Peter's. He also built a lavish summer palace for himself near Viterbo; here he died from a stroke on August 22, 1280. For his nepotism and avarice, Dante condemned the pope in the *Inferno,* placing him upside down in the eighth circle of Hell. Successor: Martin IV.

NICHOLAS IV Pope from 1288 to 1292, the first pope to come from the Franciscan order. Girolamo Masci was born in 1227 at Lisciano, Italy, entering the Franciscans as a young man. He rose through the ranks and in 1274 was elected successor to the great St. Bonaventure as general of the order. Used by several popes on missions, he was appointed a cardinal priest in 1278 by Nicholas III and a cardinal bishop of Palestrina by Honorius IV. In the conclave that followed Honorius's passing on April 3, 1287, the cardinals proved hopelessly deadlocked, the interregnum dragging on for nearly a year. Finally, on February 15, 1288, they unanimously elected the humblest from among them, the Franciscan Masci. He refused, but the cardinals were undaunted, electing him once more on February 22. This time he accepted. His pontificate would witness the conquest of the last crusader possession of Acre in the Holy Land, signaling the end of the crusading movement. To his deep disappointment, Nicholas could muster no response to the loss from among the Christian states; in desperation he made a fruitless attempt at securing an alliance with Kublai Khan, leader of the Mongol Empire. He was quite successful in missionary and educational fields, sending missions to China and Africa and establishing universities in Lisbon, Montpellier, and elsewhere. He died on April 4, 1292; two years would pass before a new pope could be chosen. Successor: St. Celestine V.

NICHOLAS V Pope from 1447 to 1455, considered the first of the so-called Renaissance pontiffs, Tommaso Parentucelli was born at Sarzana, Italy, on November 15, 1397, the son of a country doctor. He studied at Bologna and worked for a time as a tutor to the rich houses of Florence. As a trusted assistant to Bishop Niccolo Albergati of Bologna, he accompanied him to Rome in 1426 and soon after entered into papal service. Pope Eugene IV appointed him a papal legate and then cardinal in 1446; named bishop of Bologna the next year, he was prevented from assuming the post owing to the city being in revolt against the pope. In the conclave that followed Eugene's passing, he was elected pope, most likely because the cardinals could not choose a candidate from among the great families.

NICOLAVS . V. PAPA . SERGIANENSIS

Pope Nicholas V, the first great Renaissance pontiff.

An intellectual and an ardent lover of books, Nicholas was most comfortable in the company of scholars and humanists. He thus proved one of the first truly dedicated patrons of the Renaissance, extending his favor to artists, humanists, and the learned. He essentially founded the Vatican Library, made sumptuous additions to the Vatican palaces, and built or restored churches, buildings, and bridges throughout Rome. Chief among the artists he supported was Fra Angelico. Throughout his reign, however, he remained genuinely humble, deprecatingly calling himself a "mere bell-ringing priest," and noting his diminutive stature and ugly appearance. The Renaissance glory of his pontificate unfortunately did not extend to a full reform of the Church, but he did manage to end the schism caused by the stubborn rump council of Basle and to secure the submission of antipope Felix V in 1449. In 1452 he also crowned Frederick III as emperor, the last Holy Roman Emperor to be so inaugurated in Rome. His last years were darkened by two terrible events. The first was a plot in 1453 to assassinate him, led by a wild-eyed schemer named Stefano Porcaro, who hoped to create a republic in Rome. The pope reluctantly executed the would-be assassins, but never again did he feel welcome in his own city. The second calamity was the fall of Constantinople to the Ottoman Turks on May 29, 1453, ending the Byzantine Empire and wrecking forever any chance of religious unity between the East and West. Depressed, disappointed, and suffering from gout, he died on March 24, 1455; the last straw had been the total indifference of the Christian states to his plea to mount a crusade against the Turks. Successor: Callistus III.

❀ **NICHOLAS (V)** Antipope from 1328 to 1330. A relatively nondescript Franciscan friar, Pietro Rainalducci was chosen by Emperor Louis IV the Bavarian as antipope to serve as a rival to the legitimate pontiff John XXII with whom the ruler was feuding. Nicholas eventually submitted to John, appearing at Avignon before the pontiff dressed once more as a humble Franciscan friar.

❀ **NOBILITY, BLACK** The name given to those Roman nobles who refused to acknowledge the end to papal rule in the Papal States (1860) and Rome (1870), the birth of a unified Italy, and the establishing of the Italian monarchy under King Victor Emmanuel II. The noble families were fanatically loyal to the cause of Pope Pius IX (1846–1878), remaining in a permanent state of mourning for the loss of the temporal authority of the Holy See, and were conspicuous for their perpetually somber dress, hence the name Black Nobility. They were greatly honored by Pius and were a mainstay of papal court life under his successors, but their day came effectively to an end when Pope Pius XI ended the *dissidio* and the Roman Question and agreed to the Lateran Accords with Benito Mussolini in 1929.

❀ **NOBLE GUARD, PONTIFICAL** One of the now disbanded corps of honor that served the papacy from 1801 until 1970. The Pontifical Noble Guards were members of the Italian nobility, who formed a truly resplendent honor guard for the pope. The unit dated to the reign of Pope Pius VII (1800–1823) and was recruited exclusively from among the noble families of Italy; their commander was traditionally appointed from among the aristocracy of Rome. Not surprisingly, the Noble Guards made up the elite element of the papal armed forces. Each member was considered an officer and had the duty of protecting the pontiff during events and celebrations of great solemnity. Their uniform included a silver helmet and horse-hair plume. Pope Paul VI disbanded the unit on September 14, 1970, on the grounds that it was anachronistic. (See also *Palatine Guard of Honor.*)

NOVATIAN The founder of the schismatic sect called Novatianism and possibly serving as the first of the antipopes, from around 251 to 258. Novatian was perhaps a convert to Christianity, receiving appointment as a presbyter in Rome and penning a treatise on the Trinity that was noted for its orthodoxy. He was also an adherent of the rigorist position that those Christians who had lapsed should not be permitted to return to the community. Such was his position in Rome that during the fourteen months following the martyrdom of Pope St. Fabian, he acted as chief spokesman for the Roman Church, and not without cause did he probably fully expect to receive election as Bishop of Rome. When, however, the election was finally held in March 251, Cornelius was chosen. Not only had Novatian been denied the see, but Cornelius was of a sharply different mind on the matter of the lapsed Christians. Novatian thus allowed himself to be elected a rival Bishop of Rome, receiving consecration by several friendly bishops. Cornelius was able to win recognition from most of the Church, however, and Novatian was condemned by a synod at Rome. The antipope departed Rome during the persecution of the Church under Emperor Valerian. According to the fifth-century historian Socrates, Novatian died a martyr in 258. While condemned in 325 at the Council of Nicaea, the followers of Novatian clung to their beliefs over the next few centuries until finally dying out.

NUNCIO Properly apostolic nuncio, the highest ranking papal representative of the Holy See to a country. The nuncio is a senior diplomat, always of long experience and superb training, sent to a nation with formal diplomatic relations with the Holy See and a large or significant Catholic population. By virtue of his position as a senior diplomat, he is accorded the rank of dean of the diplomatic corps in the capital to which he is posted. (See also *Diplomacy, Papal* and *Legate, Papal.*)

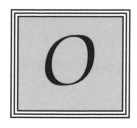

☘ **OBELISK OF CALIGULA** The 135-foot-high Egyptian obelisk that now stands in the center of St. Peter's Square. The obelisk was originally made in Heliopolis, Egypt, near modern Cairo, supposedly according to the specifications given by the lunatic Emperor Gaius Caligula in the year 37. It was to serve as a suitable decoration for the chariot-racing circus he was building upon the Vatican Hill (approximately where the square is today). Once in place, the obelisk stayed where it was even after the Basilica of St. Peter's was constructed, standing just inside the Arch of the Bells on the southern front of the church. Finally, Pope Sixtus V (1585–1590) decided that it would look better in the middle of the square, so, in 1586, he ordered it moved. Its weight at over 300 tons made this rather daunting challenge, needing 900 men, 140 horses, and 44 winches, but even these proved nearly insufficient. Concerned for the safety of his obelisk, Sixtus commanded that no one should speak during the operation so as not to distract the workers; any violators would be executed (and Sixtus always meant what he said). As the obelisk was being lifted, the ropes grew increasingly taut and showed signs of giving way. Luckily, a sailor from San Remo happened by and cried out, "Pour water on the ropes!" The workers followed his plea, and disaster was avoided. Taken before the pope for violating his order, the sailor was not only pardoned for his offense but was given a reward by the grateful pontiff. A golden ball, long reputed to contain the ashes of Julius Caesar, was taken off the top (and found empty, by the way) and replaced by an iron cross—with a splinter from the True Cross inside it. (See also *Saint Peter's Square.*)

☘ **OFFICE FOR LITURGICAL CELEBRATIONS OF THE SUPREME PONTIFF** The Vatican department that has authority over the preparation and conduct of all liturgical and sacred celebrations involving the pope. The office has responsibility, especially in ensuring that all such celebrations are carried out under the careful adherence to liturgical law. The members of the office are some of the most commonly seen Vatican officials at papal masses and ceremonies, carefully moving about and seeing that all elements proceed smoothly and properly as essential to the life and very existence of the pontiff in his place as the spiritual leader of the Church, a position rooted in the most profound sacramental activities. The office is under the authority of the master of pontifical ceremonies, who must be fully versed in every conceivable nuance of each liturgical activity. He is normally at the side of the pope during most of the ceremonies or services and travels everywhere with the pope. One of his most significant duties is to assist in sealing off the conclave in the Sistine Chapel to elect a new pope. (See *Habemus papam!*)

❀ **ORDINI EQUESTRI PONTIFICI** The broad title, meaning Pontifical Equestrian Orders, that is used for the orders of pontifical knighthood. (For details, see under *Knighthood, Pontifical.*)

❀ **ORSINI, HOUSE OF** A powerful Roman noble family that became one of the leading elements in the Guelph party that supported the papacy during the Middle Ages. The Orsini first arose to prominence in the late tenth century under the nobleman Ursus de Baro. In 1191, Giacinto Bobo-Orsini was elected as Celestine III (1191–1198). He used the papal office to reward his family with numerous positions and land, making inevitable their struggle with another Roman noble house, the Colonna. The Orsini joined the Guelph cause in the struggle between the popes and the Holy Roman Empire, while the Colonna threw themselves into the Ghibelline, or pro-imperial, cause. The strife between the families reached a bloody peak in 1241 when Matteo Rosso Orsini defeated the ambitions of Emperor Frederick II and his Colonna allies in their efforts to capture Rome. The next Orsini elected pope was Cardinal Giovanni Gaetano as Nicholas III (1277–1280). The Orsini were also quite prominent in coming to the aid of Pope Boniface VIII (1294–1303) in his bitter conflict with King Philip IV the Fair of France and the cardinals of the Colonna; singular in his betrayal of the pope was Cardinal Napoleone Orsini. Cardinal Orsini supported the election of Bertrand de Got as Clement V, the pontiff who began the Avignon residency of the popes. In later years, the house was one of the most important in Rome, becoming princes of the Holy Roman Empire in 1629 and princes of Rome in 1718. The last Orsini elected pope was Pierfrancesco Orsini, Benedict XIII (1724–1730). Having long ago made their peace with the Colonna, the Orsini, along with the Colonna, always provided the prince assistants to the pontifical throne, a post of high honor in the papal court.

❀ **OSSERVATORE ROMANO, L'** See *L'Osservatore Romano.*

❀ **PALATINE GUARD OF HONOR** The *Guardia Palatina Honoria,* the Palatine Guard, one of the honorary military bodies that was part of the old papal armed forces, ranking below the Swiss Guard in overall importance. The Palatine Guard of Honor was founded in 1850 by Pope Pius IX by merging two earlier units, the Milizia Urbana and the Civica Scelta. The recruits were drawn from among the Romans, like the Noble Guard, but unlike that unit, members hailed from all social classes. An unpaid, all-volunteer force, it supplied initially an actual martial function, but this was changed to exclusively ceremonial duties after the final loss of the temporal power of the papacy in 1870. The Guards took part in all formal papal ceremonies, also supplying a squad to watch over the conclave and the election of a new pope. Their uniform was dark blue, topped with a peaked cap, completed by a plume of feathers. Pope Pius XII (1939–1958) found the unit especially useful during the terminal period of fascist control in Italy under Benito Mussolini. Knowing that the fascists were forcibly recruiting all available young men for service at the front, the pope permitted hundreds of youths to be admitted into the Guard, preventing the possible deaths of many Romans while depriving the fascists of badly needed soldiers. Considered rather antiquated by the reign of Pope Paul VI (1963–1978), the Palatine Guard was formally disbanded on September 14, 1970.

❀ **PALLIUM** A circular band of white wool worn over the chasuble by all metropolitan archbishops and the pope himself; it is distinguished by the two hanging pendants, found on the front and back, approximately a foot long and tipped in black which give the front and back a Y-shaped appearance. The pallium is also decorated with six crosses, four in the quadrants of the round neck band fitting over the head and two—front and back—on the pendants. The pallium symbolizes the connection of the metropolitan archbishop (that is, an archbishop with jurisdiction over an ecclesiastical province) to St. Peter and the Holy See, demonstrates his share in the administration of the Church, and serves as a reminder of the yoke of office under which he labors. It is presented by the pope to each new residential archbishop, but not to titular archbishops, such as those who work in the Vatican. The pontiff is normally invested with the pallium at his coronation or installation, symbolizing his role as Bishop of Rome, bringing with it the terrible burden of primacy over the Universal Church as successor to Peter and Vicar of Christ, and can be worn by him anywhere. Pope John Paul I (1978) ended the actual coronation with the tiara and instead placed greater emphasis on his role as pastor by being invested only with the pallium. Pope John Paul II (1978–) upheld this precedent at his own installation. The pallium is made from the virgin wool of lambs that have been blessed on January 21 of each year, the feast of St. Agnes, in the church of Sant'Agnese fuori le Mura (St. Agnes Outside the Walls). The wool is then given to the Benedictine sisters of the convent of St. Cecilia in the Trastevere area of Rome who turn it into the pallia, which are then given to the pope. Once a year he takes the pallia into the *confessio* of St. Peter's Basilica and lowers them into the site of the grave accepted as that of the first Bishop of Rome beneath the church bearing his name. This special blessing is followed by the distribution of the pallia to the new archbishops around the world.

🕸 **PAPABILI**   Also *papabile* in the singular, the term used for those cardinals and possibly other prelates who are considered legitimate candidates for election as pope in an upcoming conclave. An old Roman motto that "He who enters the Conclave a Pope shall leave it a Cardinal" points to the frequent surprises that the cardinals may give to the world and the disappointment (or perhaps relief) encountered by those Princes of the Church considered favorites heading into the vote. On other occasions, however, a cardinal ranked as *papabile* is elected. The two most recent examples of this were in 1939 and 1963. In 1939, the cardinals turned to the favored Eugenio Cardinal Pacelli (Pope Pius XII) to lead the Church as the globe plunged into World War II, and in 1963 Giovanni Cardinal Montini (Pope Paul VI) was picked to guide the Church through the conclusion of Vatican Council II. Twice in 1978 the cardinals considered *papabili* failed to win election, losing first to the mildly surprising choice of Albino Cardinal Luciani, patriarch of Venice (John Paul I) and then, after his death, to the absolutely dumbfounding elevation of Karol Cardinal Wojtyla, Archbishop of Cracow (John Paul II). Neither Luciani nor Wojtyla were considered *papabili,* the press focusing on other eminent

Churchmen. (See also *Cardinals, Sacred College of; Conclave;* and *Elections, Papal.*)

❀ **PAPACY**   The term used for the various aspects of the office of pope as well as the name used for the period of a pope's reign. It refers to the authority and jurisdiction of the Holy See over the Universal Church, as well as the role of the Supreme Pontiff as a legitimate spiritual force in history—social, political, and religious—since the beginnings of the so-called Christian era. The powers of the papacy are magisterial (teaching the faith), legislative (interpreting divine laws), judicial (supreme authority over the Church), disciplinary (with corrective authority over the clergy and the faithful), and administrative (the right to bestow and withhold ecclesiastical benefices). Over the centuries, the papacy has enjoyed varying degrees of prestige, influence, and even respect. Today, the spiritual leadership of the Holy See is virtually at its peak around the world as demonstrated by the ability of one pontiff to command crowds in excess of four million people. (See also *Holy See; Infallibility, Papal;* and *Primacy of the Pope.*)

❀ **PAPAL DECORATIONS**   See *Decorations, Papal.*

❀ **PAPAL GUARDS**   See *Noble Guard, Pontifical; Palatine Guard of Honor;* and *Swiss Guard.*

❀ **PAPAL HOUSEHOLD, PREFECTURE OF THE**   Called the *Casa Pontifica,* the department of the Curia that has authority over the living arrangements of the pope as well as his nonliturgical ceremonies, papal audiences, his travels and visits, and all of the varied questions of protocol that may arise from them. It is comprised of the *Capella Pontificia* (Pontifical Chapel) and the *Famiglia Pontificia* (Pontifical Family). The Pontifical Family assists the pontiff in his capacity as a sovereign, organizing his daily routine and maintaining his living quarters; the Pontifical Chapel exists in the capacity of the household assisting the pope as spiritual head of the Church. The Papal Household today is still notable for its color and attention to ceremony and protocol, but it has been considerably reduced in its opulence and magnificence over the last decades. In the time right up to the reign of Pope John XXIII (1958–1963), the Papal Household was still very much the formal, grand court of the Supreme Pontiff, making its appearance in all of its glory during public processions and functions. It included such officials as the Capuchin Preacher to the Holy See, the Greek and Latin

Papal Grandeur

On Sunday, the Pope assisted in the performance of High Mass at St. Peter's. The effect of the Cathedral on my mind, on that second visit, was exactly what it was at first, and what it remains after many visits. It is not religiously impressive or affecting. It is an immense edifice with no one point for the mind to rest upon. . . . A large space behind the altar was fitted up with boxes, shaped like those at the Italian Opera in England, but in their decoration much more gaudy. In the center of the kind of theatre thus railed off, was a canopied dais with the Pope's chair upon it. The pavement was covered with a carpet of the brightest green; and what with this green, and the intolerable reds and crimsons, and gold borders of the hangings, the whole concern looked like a stupendous Bon-Bon. On either side of the altar, was a large box for lady strangers. These were filled with ladies in black dresses and black veils. The gentlemen of the Pope's guard, in red coats, leather breeches, and jack boots, guarded all this reserved space, with drawn swords, that were very flashy in every sense; and from the altar all down the nave, a broad lane was kept clear by the Pope's Swiss guard, who wear a quaint striped surcoat, and striped tight legs, and carry halberds like those which are usually shouldered by those theatrical supernumeraries, who never *can* get off the stage fast enough. . . . The singers were in a crib of wirework (like a large meat-safe or bird cage) in one corner; and sang most atrociously. . . . The next time I saw the cathedral, was some two or three weeks afterwards, when I climbed up into the ball; and then the hangings being taken down, and the carpet taken up, but all the framework left, the remnants of these decorations looked like an exploded cracker.

—Charles Dickens, *Pictures from Italy* (1846)

deacons, the Prince Assistants to the Holy Throne, the Privy Chamberlains (who held the flabella), the Noble Secret Antechamber, the Secret Chamberlains of the Cloak and Sword, the Macebearers, the Papal Servants and Attendants (the busolanti), and the Papal Majordomo. All were dressed in the most opulent robes and uniforms and each had an appointed place and function in the court. Reforms were launched by John to simplify the entire household and to reduce its medieval character, continued with some vigor by Pope Paul VI (1963–1978). Pope John Paul II thus inherited a much smaller and less monarchial household, although it still retains many of the central office-holders of the earlier court, including the Master of the Sacred Palace and Price Assistants to the Holy Throne. Monsignori around the world are considered members of the Papal Household. (See also *Monsignor.*) The head of the Prefecture of the Papal Household is customarily a titular bishop. He works closely with the Master of Ceremonies.

❀ **PAPAL KNIGHTS**   See *Knighthood, Pontifical.*

❀ **PAPAL LETTERS**   The collective name given to all decrees, letters, documents, and pronouncements sent out under the authority of the pope. The letters can be written for public reading or intended for private—sometimes extremely private—consumption. Aside from personal letters written by the very hand of the pontiff, the papal letters include such well-known declarations as encyclicals, constitutions, epistles, exhortations, and the motu proprio. (See under individual writings for details; for example, *Encyclical* and *Motu proprio.*)

❀ **PAPAL RESIDENCE**   See box, *Residences of the Popes,* page 23.

❀ **PAPAL RING**   See *Ring of the Fisherman.*

❀ **PAPAL STATES**   The territorial possessions of the Holy See, held by the popes as virtually absolute rulers from the eighth century until 1870. Also called the States of the Church or the Pontifical States, the Papal States long permitted the pontiffs to exist as temporal rulers and thus to wield political as well as spiritual authority. The states had their origins in the *Patrimonium Petri* (the Patrimony of Peter), the large land holdings that came to the popes in Italy, Africa, Corsica, and elsewhere through gifts, endowments, and outright seizure of fields that had been desolated following the collapse of the Roman Empire. These estates proved to be quite profitable, allowing the popes to make enough money to feed the starving, who frequently choked Rome and its environs during times of crisis and war. Even more territory fell to the popes as all vestiges of central government in Italy deteriorated in the sixth and seventh centuries.

The actual Papal States were created through the so-called Donation of Pepin, the granting of extensive lands in Italy in 756 to Pope Stephen II (III) by King Pepin III the Short. The popes thus emerged as powerful land holders in central Italy, giving them considerable influence with other rulers, but also forcing the Church to fight often bloody wars with the Holy Roman Empire and other Italian states. The Papal States were also often poorly run, inefficient, and subject to chronic economic and social stagnation. Unrest was quite common, bringing brigandage, crime, and rebellion. It had to be suppressed in the fourteenth century, the late sixteenth century, and then again in the mid-nineteenth century. The States were also seized in 1798 and 1808 by

Ercole Cardinal Consalvi, a remarkable statesman and an architect of the restoration of the Papal States after the fall of Napoleon in 1815; in an engraving of a portrait by Sir Thomas Lawrence.

the French, restored only after the end of the Napoleonic Wars in 1814–1815. There were those who felt sincerely that the States should not have been restored since they had filled their purpose and were now anachronistic. Pope Pius VII secured the return of the States, however, and in succeeding decades, the States of the Church were criticized in Europe for being the worst and often the most arbitrary administration in Europe. Finally, with the movement called Risorgimento, Italy was gradually but inevitably unified and the States were conquered by the Italian troops of King Victor Emmanuel II in 1860. Finally, Rome itself fell in 1870, ending the temporal power of the papacy. A restoration of temporal holdings would come in 1929 through the Lateran Treaty in the form of the Vatican City State. (See also *Holy See; Italy;* and *Vatican City, State of.*)

❀ **PASCHAL**   An antipope in 687. An archdeacon in Rome, Paschal harbored ambitions of election as pope in succession to Conon. As the pontiff declined in health, Paschal wrote to the Byzantine exarch (or imperial representative in Italy) and bribed him to ensure his election as the next pope. This the exarch, one John Platyn, did, but Paschal's plan went awry when the election was contested and resulted in a heated rivalry between himself and the antipope Theodore. Both sides claimed the Lateran Palace, cutting into two very tense halves. The city leaders soon grew tired of the dispute and so elected a third candidate, Pope St. Sergius I, legitimate because his elevation followed all legal requirements. Unrepentant, Paschal promised another bribe to the exarch, but the Byzantine official gave his blessing to Sergius when it was made clear that Sergius was, indeed, the legitimate pope. Theodore had already submitted, and finally, Paschal gave up. Deposed and imprisoned, he died in 692.

❀ **PASCHAL I**   Pope from 817 to 824. Paschal was from Rome, studying in the Lateran Palace and receiving ordination as a priest by Pope Leo III. At the time of his election to succeed Pope Stephen IV (V) on January 24, 817, he was serving as abbot of St. Stephen's monastery. After a hastily arranged consecration because of concerns that Emperor Louis the Pious might make trouble, Paschal sent formal announcement of his election and requested a continuation of the friendly relationship between the Holy See and the imperial court. Louis responded with the *Pactum Ludovicianum,* which established significant privileges for the popes. As a sign of the generally sound relations between the pope and emperor, Paschal crowned Lothair, Louis's son, as co-emperor in 823. Unfortunately, Lothair did not fully share his father's generous sentiment and several intemperate actions roused strong dislike of the Franks in Rome; soon after his departure, two Frankish officials were blinded and beheaded in the Lateran. Paschal was forced to submit to an oath of purgation to clear himself of any complicity and to execute the ringleaders of the murderous plot. These steps did little to garner the love of the Romans, nor did his often angry form of governing. So hated was he at the time of his death on February 11, 824, that the Roman mob would not permit his burial in St. Peter's. This proved possible only after the election of his successor several months later, and then in the church of Sta Prassede, not St. Peter's. Successor: Eugene II.

❀ **PASCHAL II** Pope from 1099 to 1118 whose pontificate was dominated by his struggle with Emperor Henry V over lay investiture. Rainerius was born in Bieda di Galeata, near Ravenna in 1050, entering one of the monastic orders at a young age. Sent to Rome around the age of twenty, he later attracted the favorable attention of Pope St. Gregory VII and in 1080 was appointed a cardinal. Under Urban II, he served as papal legate to Spain and, on August 13, 1099, succeeded Urban as pope. Taking the name Paschal, he immediately pledged himself to Urban's two main projects of continuing the reform of the Church and promoting the ongoing crusade, which had just captured Jerusalem from the Muslims. He unfortunately found most of his reign taken up by the bitter controversy over investiture, which had troubled Urban as well. Paschal first had to contend with Henry IV, whom he excommunicated at the Council of Rome in 1102. He then assisted Henry's son, Henry V, in overthrowing his father, but Paschal was soon disappointed when the new ruler proved just as determined and demanding as his father in the matter of investiture. Negotiations proved fruitless and the young ruler marched on Italy. Paschal sent representatives to Sutri in 1111, where an agreement was finally reached: Henry would cease granting Church offices and, in return, Paschal would surrender all feudal rights in the Holy Roman Empire, including the lucrative monies brought in from these temporal possessions. Paschal would also crown Henry emperor. Far more destructive than Henry's troops were his legal experts for they reasoned, correctly so, that when the agreement was read aloud at the coronation on February 2, 1111, it would create a firestorm of controversy, especially among the disenfranchised German bishops. Using the commotion at the gathering, Henry seized Paschal and sixteen of his cardinals, withdrew in bloody fashion, and went to work at snapping the pope's resolve. This he did through threat of torture and death. Paschal gave to Henry the right of investiture and crowned him at St. Peter's on April 13, 1111. Christendom was appalled at Paschal for giving in, and Henry for committing such an outrage upon the pope. The next year, the agreement was rescinded by the Lateran Council and the shamefaced pontiff, and Paschal finally excommunicated Henry in 1118. Paschal's last years were further troubled by the unrest in Rome. He left the city as an exile from his own flock, returning in early 1118 and taking up residence behind the stout walls of Castel Sant'Angelo.

There he died on January 21, 824, leaving the papacy in terrible condition. Successor: Gelasius II.

❁ **PASCHAL III** Antipope from 1164 to 1168, the first of the rivals to Pope Alexander III who would be set up by the pro-imperial party supporting the cause of Emperor Frederick I Barbarossa against the papacy. Entirely illegitimate as a papal claimant, he was able to secure a coronation in St. Peter's only on July 22, 1167, and then with the help of Frederick's troops in commanding the city; he crowned Frederick emperor on August 1 that same year. He died on September 20, 1168, generally discredited.

❁ **PASSETTO** The covered walkway, stretching along the top of an aqueduct connecting the Vatican and the fortress of Castel Sant'Angelo. Called also the Vatican corridor, it was built in 1277 to provide the pontiff with an emergency escape route when the chronically fiery situation in Rome made a hasty flight to the fortress desirable. It was added to a portion of the Leonine Wall, which had originally been constructed around 850. The Passeto proved useful in commanding the strategic area of the Borgo, since from its high position papal troops could rain down arrows, rocks, and missiles upon the neighborhoods below. Pope Alexander VI sought refuge in the fort in 1494 when French troops came into Rome. The most famous moment in the history of the Passetto came in 1527 when Pope Clement VII literally ran for his life from the invading mercenaries of the Holy Roman Emperor Charles V, who had stormed the Vatican. Today, the Passetto is unused and in a state of general disrepair, the popes no longer needing to escape from mobs or an imperial enemy. (See also *Castel Sant'Angelo* and *Rome, Sack of.*)

❁ **PASSPORT, VATICAN** The official passport carried by certain individuals who are in the service of the Holy See. Most of the passports issued by the Vatican are for diplomats, Curial cardinals, and other representatives who serve the Holy See around the world. The issue of a Vatican passport, however, does not automatically entitle a person to residential rights in Vatican City nor, in some cases, even the privilege of automatic admission into the inner areas of the Vatican. Those with the passport, especially cardinals, receive the privilege of exemption from the often crushing taxes found in Rome and the right to shop in the Vatican stores and therefore save considerably on household expenses. The Swiss Guard also receive passports, but theirs are not diplomatic; they carry service passports, as compared to the traditional diplomatic passport. (See also *Diplomacy, Papal.*)

❀ **PASTOR PASTORUM**   A title, meaning in Latin, "Pastor of Pastors" and used by the pope to designate his position as the foremost of all pastors over the Church. It is customarily seen on official documents in the signature of the pope in its abbreviated form, *P.P.,* such as in the signature of Pope John Paul II, whose name appears as *Joannes Paulus, P.P. II,* or *Paulus, P.P. VI.* (See also *Titles of the Pope.*)

❀ **PATRIARCH OF THE WEST**   One of the titles of the pope, which designates him as the patriarch of the Western Church. The title was initially granted to the Bishop of Rome as the first in prominence of the patriarchs of the other major sees of the Christian Church—Constantinople, Antioch, Jerusalem, and Alexandria. The position of Patriarch of the West does not in any way detract from the place of the pope as Supreme Pontiff of the Universal Church and Vicar of Christ, but is merely one of the ancillary or more limited positions that he holds in his capacity as head of the critical see of Rome. (See also *Titles of the Pope.*)

❀ **PATRIMONIES, PAPAL**   See *Papal States.*

❀ **PATRIMONY OF ST. PETER**   See *Papal States.*

❀ **PAUL I, ST.**   Pope from 757 to 767, the brother of Pope Stephen II (III). Paul was born in Rome and, like his brother, was educated in the Lateran Palace. Made a deacon by Pope Zachary, he was an important figure in the papal government under Stephen, succeeding him as pope on May 29, 757. The main concerns of his pontificate were the organizing of the papal territories, which had been given to his brother by King Pepin the Short of the Franks and the continuing threat of the Lombards. (See *Donation of Pepin* and *Papal States.*) Paul proved a competent administrator, installing the first elements of the papal government that would endure over the States of the Church for centuries. He also used with exceptional skill the dire threat of the Franks to keep the Lombards at bay. His relations with the Byzantine Empire were less than ebullient, however, owing to resentments of the papal alliance with the Franks and the strong protests of Paul about the iconoclast policies of the Eastern Church—icons and other images had been forbidden in the East. The nobles of Rome were uncommonly quiet during his pontificate, a testament to his strength of personality. One of Paul's most endearing habits was visiting prisoners in their cells at night to give comfort and to pray for their release. Successor: Stephen III (IV).

PAUL II Pope from 1464 to 1471, Pietro Barbo was born in Venice and was a nephew of Pope Eugene IV (1431–1447). Initially on a path for business, he had a rather abrupt change of career when his uncle was elected pope. Named an archdeacon of Bologna and then Bishop of Cervia and of Vincenza, he became a cardinal in 1440 at the age of twenty-three. A well-known figure in the papal government over the next years, he fell out of favor with Pius II, but then had the satisfaction of being elected his successor on August 30, 1464. A curious mixture of the secular prince and the devoted prude, he was much abused by the biased reporting of the times, which gossiped of his lustful nature; he was accused of spending excessively on luxury, banquets, and horse racing and attacked for hoarding art and treasure. Certainly vain—he had to be talked out of adopting the name Formosus, Greek for "handsome"—he was also rather peculiar in the matter of humanism. Opposed to paganism, he shut down the Roman Academy in 1468, arresting and imprisoning one of the members, Bartolomeo Platina, in Castel Sant'Angelo when he complained that Pius was a tyrant. Tyrannical he may have appeared, but he also was a patron of the arts and Renaissance achievement. The artisans and writers might laugh that the pontiff was inept at writing in Latin, but they appreciated his money, the restoration of the Arches of Titus and Septimius Severus, and the opening of the first printing presses in Rome. Paul also worked to promote a crusade against the Turks, but was disappointed by the lackluster response of Holy Roman Emperor Frederick III, whom he had sumptuously entertained during a visit to Rome in 1469. Paul died from a stroke after gorging himself on melons. Among the most acid-penned of his biographers was Platina, who later became papal librarian. Successor: Sixtus IV.

PAUL III Pope from 1534 to 1549, who is ranked as the first pontiff of the Catholic Reformation. Born in Farnese, in Canino, Italy, Alessandro Farnese was raised in the typical Renaissance environment of the age, studying at the Roman Academy, in the opulent environment of the palace of Lorenzo de'Medici in Florence, and then the University of Pisa. Returning to Rome in 1491, he was quickly advanced by Pope Alexander VI (1492–1503), the Borgia pope, who, as chance would have it, was enjoying the attentions of Farnese's sister Giulia as his mistress. Alessandro became papal treasurer and, in 1493, a cardinal, although he was still a layman. Long a cardinal in the Renaissance style (he had a mistress and fathered three sons and a daughter), under Leo X (1513–1521) he reformed his life completely. Ordained in 1519, he became a leader of the reform party within the Church and was a candidate to become pope in 1523. Throughout the ruinous reign of Clement VII (1523–1534), Farnese was one of his most loyal cardinals, sharing his grim seven-month period of imprisonment in Castel Sant'Angelo in 1527 during the sack of Rome and serving as dean of the College of Cardinals. On October 13, 1534, he was elected to succeed Clement.

Pope Paul III.

Paul's pontificate marked a significant turning point for the Church. Recognizing the towering danger of the Protestant Reformation, he set out to implement a massive effort to counter the spread of Protestantism and to reform the Church. His foremost achievement was to convene the Council of Trent (1545–1563), which opened on December 13, 1545, and brought genuine change and revitalization. Paul also promoted dedicated reformers to the cardinalate, including the Englishman Reginald Pole (who would come within one vote of election as pope in 1550), Marcello Cervini (the future Pope Marcellus II), and Gian Pietro Carafa (the future Pope Paul IV), and promoted the religious orders, especially the Jesuits. Paul felt compelled to excommunicate King Henry VIII of England in 1538, a move that hastened the departure of the English from the Church. A patron of the arts, he commissioned Michelangelo's painting of the *Last Judgment* in the Sistine Chapel and proceeded with the construction of the new St. Peter's, with Michelangelo as his architect. (See *Sistine Chapel*.) He repaired the terrible damage inflicted upon the Vatican Library in 1527 and completed the magnificent Farnese Palace through the architect Sangallo. A devoted nepotist, he was much pained in his last years by the death of one son and the malicious defection of a grandson to the cause of Emperor Charles V; worse than the absence of the grandson were the two papal duchies he took with him. Paul died of a fever on November 10, 1549; on his lips were prayers and forgiveness for his grandson. Successor: Julius III. (See also *Pauline Chapel.*)

 PAUL IV   Pope from 1555 to 1559, Giovanni Pietro Carafa was a member of the Carafa family of Naples and was born near Benevento on June 28, 1476. After completing his studies, he went to Rome, where he was given swift advancement in the papal government thanks to the patronage of his uncle Oliviero Cardinal Carafa. He served as Bishop of Theate from 1502 to 1524, papal legate to England from 1513 to 1514, and nuncio to Spain from 1515 to 1520. In 1524, however, he resigned from all offices and devoted himself to strict asceticism. He also founded the Congregation of the Clerks Regular with St. Cajetan, an order that came to be called the Theatines in honor of Carafa, who was their first general. Known henceforth as one of the foremost advocates of Church reform, he was made a cardinal in 1536 by Pope Paul III and named Archbishop of Naples in 1549. He was also appointed in 1542 to head the recently reconstituted Inquisition, earning a fearsome reputation for his absolutely unbending commitment to orthodoxy and his merciless zeal in rooting out heretics, once commenting that "were even my father a heretic, I would gather the wood to burn him." In 1553 Pope Julius III made him dean of the College of Cardinals. At the conclave to choose a successor to the short-lived Marcellus II in 1555, Carafa was not a particular favorite, and he was much opposed by the Spanish. Nevertheless, the cardinals entered into protracted negotiations and chose the seventy-nine-year-old Carafa, who took the name Paul IV.

One of the most severe of all popes, Paul was wholeheartedly devoted to reform, but he had little confidence in the Council of Trent, which had been suspended in 1552. Instead, he adopted a medieval style of ruling, relying upon his own decrees and power, supported by the omnipresent Inquisition. So ubiquitous did the dreaded institution become that no one, not even a cardinal, was safe: the respected Cardinal Morone was imprisoned in Castel Sant'Angelo for heresey. Rome became a much oppressed city as officials watched all conduct with ruthless vigilance. In 1558, Paul ordered out all so-called vagrant monks, clerics without a monastery, finally arresting over one hundred of them and sending them to languish on the galleys. The Jews of Rome were also ordered to wear distinctive clothing. At the same time,

the pope turned a blind eye to the industrious corruption of his relatives (see *Carafa, House of*), finally taking steps against them, but only
after he was led into a disastrous war and was forced to rely upon
Protestant mercenaries to protect papal lands. His foreign policy was
no more successful. He had no sway over the Spanish and his refusal
to work diplomatically toward a positive beginning with Queen
Elizabeth I (r. 1558–1603) ruined any hopes of a return of England to
the Church. Paul fell suddenly ill in 1559 and died on August 18, to the
delight of the Romans. They poured into the streets and tore down his
statue, proceeding to storm and burn the headquarters of the
Inquisition, breaking open the dungeons of Rome, which had been
filled by the pontiff. Successor: Pius IV.

 PAUL V   Pope from 1605 to 1621, a member of the famed
house of Borghese, Camillo Borghese was born in Rome in 1552.
He studied law at Perugia and Padua, subsequently entering
into papal service and becoming an eminent expert in canon
law; this background in law would temper his entire outlook as pope.
Slowly but steadily rising through the Curia, he was appointed cardinal in 1596 by Pope Clement VIII and Cardinal Vicar of Rome. In the
election of 1605 following the death of Leo XI, Borghese's reputation
for neutrality and his legal knowledge made him the preferred compromise candidate; he was elected on May 16, 1605. Devoted to continuing reform and the decrees of the Council of Trent (1545–1563), Paul
V ordered all bishops in Rome to return to their dioceses, ending the
habit of bishops remaining in Rome and lingering at the papal court.
He also canonized or beatified a large number of saints (such as
Francis Xavier, Ignatius Loyola, Charles Borromeo, and Philip Neri),
brought administrative reforms to the Curia, and promoted the reception of communion by the faithful. Paul founded as well the Secret
Vatican Archives. In foreign policy matters, he became embroiled in a
dispute with Venice and other Italian states over papal rights, but his
efforts to place the Venetians under censure were ultimately unsuccessful; Paul withdrew the papal ban after the mediating efforts of France
and Spain, effectively admitting that the old customs of wielding papal
authority were no longer practical. His final years were darkened by
the outbreak of the staggeringly destructive Thirty Years' War
(1618–1648), a conflict he could not prevent, and the start of the
famous Galileo case, in which Galileo Galilei (1564–1642) was censured for his theories on the solar system. A devoted nepotist, Paul is
distinguished for promoting generally competent relatives, but his

family also managed to amass vast wealth; most notable was his nephew Scipio Cardinal Borghese, who built the Villa Borghese. A patron of the arts, Paul commissioned Carlo Maderno to create a facade for St. Peter's Basilica on which the name of the pope was placed in very large letters: PAVLVS V BORGHESE. The family was much criticized at the time and over the centuries for such a boastful proclamation. Paul deserves additional mention for decorating the Vatican Gardens with so many of the magnificent fountains that continue to entice visitors. He died on January 28, 1621, after suffering a stroke. Successor: Gregory XV.

PAUL VI Pope from 1963 to 1978, whose reign was dominated by the implementation of the decrees of Vatican Council II. Giovanni Battista Montini was the son of the editor of the Catholic paper *Il Cittadina di Brescia* and a lawyer. He was born at Concesio, near Brescia, on September 26, 1897. While demonstrating a keen mind, he was plagued throughout childhood by poor health, actually spending much of his time during seminary studying at home; nevertheless, he graduated and received ordination on May 29, 1920. He then attended the Gregorian University in Rome and in 1922 was appointed to the Secretariat of State. After a short period of service in Warsaw in 1923, he returned to Rome and was thereafter a fixture in the Secretariat, also teaching diplomatic history in the Pontifical Ecclesiastical Academy, the training center for Vatican diplomats. Named an assistant to Eugenio Cardinal Pacelli (later Pope Pius XII), he accompanied him on many of his travels around the world. After the election of Pacelli in 1939, Montini spent much of his time working to provide help to refugees and to repair the damage caused by the war, a role he would continue to play in the postwar years. Considered a leading figure in the papal administration, he assisted Pius as prosecretary for the internal affairs of the Church from 1952, answering directly to the pope, who had appointed himself secretary of state. The next year Pius offered him the red hat, but Montini declined the honor of appointment to the cardinalate. Pius was never one to ask twice and in November 1954 Montini was appointed archbishop of Milan; the pontiff died in 1958 without ever naming Montini a cardinal. Montini was an energetic and dedicated archbishop, swiftly emerging as a genuine candidate to succeed Pius despite the fact that he was not a cardinal. In the ensuing conclave, however, Angelo Roncalli was elected as Pope John XXIII (1958–1963). John made Montini one of the first of his new cardinals and throughout the Vatican Council II (1962–1965), which the pope convened to modernize the Church, Montini played a leading role and John made clear the respect and regard he felt for the cardinal. Thus, when John died on June 3, 1963, Montini was immediately considered a favorite and, on June 21, 1963, was elected pope.

Pope Paul made immediate promises of continuing the Vatican Council, later observing to confidants that he felt obligated to John to continue the council as John had intended, remarking that the assembly was now on a track he could not reverse. He also confessed that had he been elected in 1958 he would not have had the courage to convene so sweeping an undertaking. The council proceeded on its program of reform and modernization, finally adjourning on December 8, 1965. He commanded that an extraordinary holy year (Jubilee) be celebrated to launch the reforms and changes in an environment of cheer and optimism. However, in the next years it grew swiftly apparent that there were great challenges in holding together the process of change within the council's intended framework while adhering to orthodox interpretation of its decrees. The Church was thus beset by a dual problem of some prelates holding firm against implementing the changes to the liturgy and Church life, while others were permitting wholesale reform on a scale far

Pope Paul VI. (Catholic News Service.)

wider and more innovational than the council—and certainly Paul— had intended. As it was, the pope struggled against tides of disorienting change, and many scholars have said that it was remarkable that Paul managed to prevent a serious schism within the Church. He also brought changes to the Curia and the entire papal administration, following up on the work of Pope John to reduce or even end many of the regal and medieval trappings of the papacy. Thus the old court ceremonial was much reduced and such bodies as the Pontifical Noble Guard were disbanded. Paul made 144 cardinals and continued the internationalization of the Sacred College of Cardinals. Stressing his pastoral role, Paul adopted the crosier (which had not been used by

The Quotable Paul VI

Every day you should put on Christ, an effort which is the beginning, end and whole of your life.

Freedom refers to the summing up of our duties in those supreme duties of love of God and our neighbor.

For every Christian the credential of his authenticity in the Church and in the world is this: "First make peace with yourself, so that when you have become peaceful you may bring peace to others."

We will say only that to be happy, one needs to learn "the art of loving." It is an art in which nature itself is a teacher, if it is listened to carefully and interpreted according to the great sovereign law of love which Christ has taught us.

When the rights of minorities are fostered, when the mentally or physically handicapped are assisted, when those on the margin of society are given a voice—in all these instances the dignity of human life, the fullness of human life, and the sacredness of human life are furthered.

We ask that families be strengthened in the great ideals of Christian living: faithful and generous love, mutual understanding, common prayer. Our encouragement goes likewise to the single people who through the effort and activities of their lives give witness to Christ, and to all groups of Christians dedicated to the Gospel of the Lord Jesus. Our special love is with the poor, the afflicted, the distressed.

popes for many centuries) and even sold a tiara that had been presented to him by the people of Milan. He also decreed that cardinals should retire at the age of eighty and bishops and priests at seventy-five. To oversee the election of his successor he issued the extremely detailed electoral decree *Eligendo Summam Pontificem,* which is still in effect.

Paul was the greatest traveling pontiff in history until the reign of John Paul II. Called the "Pilgrim Pope," he had adopted the name Paul as a reflection of his commitment to taking the Gospel to all nations, like his namesake St. Paul, and his journeys brought him to Jerusalem (where his visit caused a near riot from the jubilant crowds), India, Colombia, the United States, Australia, Turkey, and the Philippines—where he was saved from a knife-wielding assassin by the future Archbishop Paul Marcinckus, later head of the Vatican Bank. Paul also promoted ecumenism and Christian unity, including remarkable meetings with the Ecumenical Patriarch of Constantinople (separated from the Roman Church for centuries), the Archbishop of Canterbury, and representatives of Islam, Judaism, Hinduism, and Buddhism. He contributed important encyclicals and writings, such as *Populorum Progressio* (1967), which elucidated many social doctrines of the Church, and the eloquent "Creed of the People of God." These, however, were overshadowed by *Humanae Vitae* (1968) on the question of contraception. The harsh and controversial response to the encyclical, especially within the Church, left Paul demoralized and hesitant; it proved to be, in fact, his last encyclical.

Deeply spiritual and drawn toward asceticism—he reportedly wore a hair shirt and chains—he was also an active intellectual, a fact belied by his lack of an academic background. The effects of *Humanae Vitae,* the Vietnam War, the conflicts in the Middle East, and the chronic social and political struggles that characterized his era all took their toll; photographers, artists, and even casual observers noted the terrible pain in his eyes in his later years and his increasingly bad health, so much so that rumors were rife in the early 1970s that he might resign. His final public appearance was at the funeral of his good friend Aldo Moro, the leader of the Italian Christian Democrat Party, who had been murdered by terrorists. Profoundly saddened, he suffered a heart attack soon after and died at Castel Gandolfo on August 6, 1978. Successor: John Paul I.

❀ **PAULINE CHAPEL**   A chapel first erected during the pontificate of Pope Paul III (1534–1549), near the Sistine Chapel, it is reached through the Sala Regia, which serves as a kind of antechamber for the

Sistine and Pauline chapels, and is one of the most magnificent anywhere in the world. The chapel itself is rarely open to visitors and is
exceedingly difficult to see in any meaningful way, most tourists con-
tenting themselves with a glimpse of the Sala Regia and a distant view
of the chapel across its length. The chapel is the site of the assembly of
the cardinals as they make their ornate entry into the Sistine Chapel to
elect a new pope in a conclave. During the conclave, they use the
Pauline Chapel for prayers; it has been the site of the deep contemplation of a number of candidates who were aware of the tide of voting by
the cardinal electors and that their election as pope might be only a few
hours away. The Pauline Chapel is distinguished by two important
works of art: frescoes by Michelangelo, the *Martyrdom of St. Peter* (or
Crucifixion of St. Peter) and the *Conversion of St. Paul,* located on opposing walls. Both are unfinished, date to the 1540s, and are considered to
be examples of the deeply troubled final period of Michelangelo's brilliant career.

❀ **PECTORAL CROSS**   See box, *Papal Dress,* pages 120–21.

❀ **PELAGIUS I**   Pope from 556 to 561. A Roman by birth, he had a long
and distinguished career in the service of the papacy, and it can be
argued that his actual reign was not the equal to his earlier achievements. He traveled with Pope Agapitus I to Constantinople in 536,
receiving appointment by the pope as papal legate to the imperial
court. Soon thereafter Agapitus died and Pelagius returned to Rome
upon the deposition and banishment of Pope Silverius. Under the next
pope, Vigilius, he was sent back to Constantinople, winning the trust
of Emperor Justinian. In 546, he was Vicar of Rome while Vigilius
was away at Constantinople and proved extremely devoted in heading
the defense of the Eternal City during a siege by the Ostrogoths under
King Totila. After the capture of the city, Pelagius courageously
appealed to the Gothic king not to massacre the inhabitants. At
Constantinople he opposed Vigilius's surrender to Justinian on the
matter of the so-called Three Chapters Controversy (the condemnation of three theological writers who had opposed the heretical
Monophysites whom Justinian was trying to appease), but Pelagius
soon caved in to the pressure of the emperor and, like Vigilius, gave
his assent. Thus, after Vigilius died, Pelagius was fully supported by
Justinian as the next pope; he returned to Rome and was apparently
accepted by the Roman clergy. His consecration, however, was held

only on April 16, 556, owing to the passive opposition of many bishops in the West, who were upset about his surrendering to the emperor on the Three Chapters. Justinian, meanwhile, recognized Pelagius as virtual ruler of Rome, a move that greatly heightened the temporal power of the papacy. His pontificate was spent in two main areas: he labored incessantly to repair and rebuild Rome and bring relief to the suffering and starvation caused by the destructive Goths, and he strove to win back the support of the bishops, especially in Gaul (France). He was more successful in the former undertaking than the latter. Successor: John III.

❀ **PELAGIUS II**   Pope from 579 to 590. A Goth by descent, he was born in Rome and was elected to succeed Pope Benedict I in August 579, inheriting a desperate situation, since the Lombards were besieging Rome. Unable to make formal request of confirmation from the Byzantine emperor at Constantinople (as was then customary) owing to the Lombard blockade, Pelagius went ahead with his consecration on November 26, 579. After he convinced the Lombards to depart, however, he sent a delegation to Emperor Maurice to inform him of his election and to request badly needed military help. The Byzantines were not in a position to assist, so the pope cast about for other allies, unsuccessfully appealing to the Franks. Finally, the exarch of Ravenna, the Byzantine representative in Italy, negotiated an armistice in 585. Grateful for the respite, Pelagius undertook a building program in Rome and opened his own house as a hospital for the poor. He also promoted the conversion of the Visigoths in Spain, insisted on clerical celibacy, and protested quite vehemently the adoption by the Patriarch of Constantinople the title Ecumenical Patriarch, a name that implied patriarchal authority over the entire Church. His successor would be a more than worthy one. Successor: St. Gregory I the Great.

❀ **PEPIN, DONATION OF**   See *Donation of Pepin.*

❀ **PETER, ST.**   The first pope, the Prince of the Apostles, founder of the see of Rome, and the disciple of Jesus chosen to serve as Vicar of Christ, the Rock upon whom Christ built the Church. Peter is a figure of such importance in the history of the Church and the establishing of the papacy that it is easily forgotten that he lived as a simple fisherman for much of his life with his brother Andrew in the small community where he was born, Bethsaida, near Lake Tiberias in Galilee.

Throughout the accounts in the Gospel and the Acts of the Apostles, Peter appears as a fiery, strong, and even hotheaded individual. His call by Christ to be a disciple, as reported in the Gospel according to Luke, came about after he caught a miraculous amount of fish, so many that he collapsed at the knees of Christ, to which Jesus replied: "Do not be afraid; henceforth you shall be catching men." Simon (as he was originally known) was forever after the leading disciple, receiving from Christ the important new name of Cephas, meaning "rock." In Greek this was translated as Petros, from which Peter is derived. Christ also gave to Peter the so-called Power of the Keys after the disciple proclaimed, "You are Christ, the Son of the living God." One of the inner circle of Christ with John and James, Peter was involved in virtually all of the major events in the years of Christ's ministry. He also was quite prominent in the Passion accounts. For example, when Christ was arrested, he lopped off the right ear of a servant of the high priest, and that same night he denied Christ three times, as the Master had predicted. After the Resurrection, however, he was unquestionably the foremost of the Apostles, performing miracles, the first of Christ's followers to do so; his powers were so formidable as a healer that he was able to restore the sick with his shadow.

St. Peter, the Apostle and first pope, a statue probably by Arnolfo di Cambio in St. Peter's Basilica; note the front foot worn away by the kisses of pilgrims. (CATHOLIC NEWS SERVICE.)

In the years that followed, Peter was the unquestioned head of the fledgling Church, traveling extensively across much of the Roman world. It was inevitable, then, that he should come to Rome, noting in his first Epistle that he was writing from Babylon, the name customarily used for Rome. While his activities are quite obscure, it is clear that he was put to death in the Eternal City during the persecution launched by Emperor Nero around 64. As founder of the see of Rome, Peter was naturally singled out for arrest, reportedly begging the Romans to crucify him upside down because he was unworthy of dying in the same manner as his Master. His work in Rome was recognized even in the Early Church as establishing a religious primacy, with the Petrine See (as the diocese of Rome is called) enjoying a position of primacy over the Universal Church. Peter's successors as Bishops of Rome thus were holders of the same authority as Peter himself, a central pillar of their claims to primacy over the entire Church. His symbols are the crossed keys, for the Keys of the Kingdom; a cock for the triple denial of Christ (the cock crowed after his denials); and the boat (hence the term Barque of Peter). Successor: St. Linus. (See also *Holy See;* box, *Martyred Pontiffs,* page 236; *Peter's Chains, Feast of; Primacy of the Pope; Rome; Saint Peter, Basilica of;* and *Tomb of Peter.*)

❀ **PETER'S CHAINS, FEAST OF**   A feast previously celebrated in the Church liturgy on August 1, commemorating the release of St. Peter from the chains of bondage as recorded in the Acts of the Apostles (12:1–25) and honoring the only Old Testament persons listed on the Catholic calendar, the Seven Holy Maccabees (from 2 Maccabees, 7). The feast was known during the Middle Ages as Lammas Day, from the custom of consecrating baked bread made from the grain of the first harvest, or when the annual tribute of lambs was paid. The church of San Pietro in Vincoli on the Esquiline Hill in Rome contains the famed two chains (vincoli), which supposedly miraculously joined together and are traditionally said to have bound St. Peter in the Mamertine Prison, where, according to legend, the saint caused a spring to bubble forth in his cell so as to have water with which to baptize two of his guards. The chains are still on display in the church in a reliquary located below the high altar.

❀ **PETER'S CHAIR**   See *Cathedra Petri.*

❀ **PETER'S PENCE**   Called in the Latin *"Denarii S. Petri,"* the annual collection that is taken from among the world's Catholics intended to assist the Holy See in its maintenance. The collection of Peter's Pence was begun around the eighth century in England and was comprised of a tax of one penny on each household in the kingdom, collected on St. Peter's Day. Called the Romfeoh in the Anglo-Saxon, it was confirmed as a gift of funds to the papal legates in attendance at the Synod of Chelsea in 787. It was abolished in England in 1534 under King Henry VIII (1509–1547) and gradually died out in most of Europe as a result of the Protestant Reformation. In the nineteenth century the collection was started up again in order to provide support to Pope Pius

IX (1846–1878) after he was driven from Rome in 1848 by revolutionaries and forced to flee to Gaeta. Money poured in from Germany, England, Ireland, and elsewhere to help the pontiff defray the costs of living away from Rome and to express their solidarity with the pope in exile. The presence of Peter's Pence was to prove extremely important in keeping the Holy See solvent after the loss of the Papal States and the final demise of papal temporal power in 1870. The collection continues today in an entirely voluntary capacity. Customarily, bishops in each diocese make an annual appeal for Catholics to contribute; the funds are then sent to Rome. Peter's Pence remains a leading source of papal revenue, assisting in the maintaining of the Holy See, but also providing useful funds for the innumerable papal charities and aid for the poor. Observers note that the size of the collection is often a reliable barometer of the current popularity of the pope; a new pontiff is the source of enthusiasm and hence a larger than normal collection.

❀ **PETTO, IN**   A special way in which the pope is able to elevate a person to membership in the Sacred College of Cardinals. *In petto* means "in secret," denoting that the pope names the new cardinal in secret, customarily done so because of sensitive political considerations. *In petto* cardinals might have been found in Communist countries or in regions under the control of oppressive regimes where the appointment of a priest or bishop to the cardinalate could be considered highly inflammatory; the pope thus designates the cardinal in secret, naming the prelate a cardinal *in petto,* or a cardinal *in pectore* ("in the breast," or hidden). Normally, the cleric is not aware of the immense honor bestowed upon him, but he is officially a cardinal from the very moment of the pope's decision and his seniority as a cardinal dates from the day he was chosen and not from the time that the pope decides to make the appointment public. Should, however, the pope die before he makes the *in petto* cardinals known publicly, the promotions are considered void, in large measure because no one knew about them anyway. Any formal appointment to the cardinalate must be made by the next pope.

❀ **PHILIP**   An extremely briefly reigning papal claimant whose entire career lasted the one night of July 31, 768. He was proclaimed the occupant of the Holy See through the connivance of the priest Waldipert, who, on instructions from the cunning Lombard King Desiderius (r. 757–774), went to the monastery of S. Vito in Rome, seized the befuddled priest Philip, took him to the Lateran, and had him consecrated in some fashion. When, however, it was clear that no one in Rome would accept him, Waldipert took Philip back to his monastery, told him that he was no longer pope, and simply departed. The poor monk was left in peace by the factions in Rome since they were aware that he had been a mere pawn in the game to control the papacy.

❀ **PIUS I, ST.**   Pope from around 140 to 155, he is generally counted as the ninth successor to St. Peter and the tenth pope overall. It is possible that he was born into slavery and was the brother of Hermas, the author of the well-known book on penance, *The Shepherd.* As Bishop of Rome, he was forced to deal with a number of heretical groups, including the Gnostics and Marcion; he also dealt with the controversy of using Greek philosophical methods in the study of Christian theology. It is possible, but unlikely, that he died a martyr. Successor: St. Anicetus.

 PIUS II   Pope from 1458 to 1464. Enea Silvio Piccolomini was born in 1405 at Corsignano, near Siena. He studied at Siena and was at first inspired to enter a monastery through the inspiration of sermons by St. Bernardino of Siena. Convinced to continue his academic progress, he went to Florence in 1425 and there received instruction from the noted humanist Francesco Filelfo (d. 1481). Starting in 1432, he participated in the Council of Basle, serving as secretary to the bishop of Fermo and later acting as master of ceremonies in the conclave that produced the antipope Felix V (1439–1449). Felix disappointed him by naming him only his secretary, and so he departed the council for the bright court of Emperor Frederick III. Here Aeneas Sylvius—as he was known in humanist circles— earned the title Poet Laureate of the Holy Roman Empire. Finally reconciled with the legitimate pontiff, Eugene IV,

Pope Pius II, a gifted humanist scholar.

and undergoing a personal conversion, he expressed to a friend in a letter in 1446: "I have come to myself, but oh, that it is not too late." That same year he was ordained. Serving several popes in a variety of capacities, he was appointed a cardinal by Callistus III in 1456. In the conclave that followed Callistus's passing two years later, Aeneas was chosen his successor, taking the name Pius (the first since the second century) in honor of Pius Aeneas, the hero of the epic *Aeneid* by the Roman writer Virgil.

As pope, he was confronted with the pressing crisis of the advance of the Ottoman Turks who, in 1453, had captured Constantinople. He worked, albeit with little success, to organize a Christian crusade against the Turks. His other chief concern was the decline of papal authority, epitomized by his failure over the Turkish question, to which he attributed the evils of Conciliarism. He thus issued the bull *Execrabilis* in 1460, forbidding any appeals from the pope to an ecumenical council. A genuine intellectual in the traditions of the Renaissance, Pius was a patron of humanism, although once elected pope he distanced himself from many of his antipapal declarations, proclaiming that his earlier writings be ignored; he asked that all should "Believe the old man and not the youth ... reject Aeneas and accept Pius." His writings included poems, orations, a novel, *De Duobus Amantibus Eurialo et Lucresia* (*Concerning the Two Lovers Eurialis and Lucretia*), and a play. While pope he authored an ambitious geographical and ethnological treatise on the known world and the only public memoir ever assembled by a pope. Successor: Paul II.

PIUS III   Pope from September 22 to October 18, 1503, one of the briefest reigning of all pontiffs, he was born Francesco Todeschini Piccolomini at Siena in 1439, a nephew of Pope Pius II. Named Archbishop of Siena in 1460, he became cardinal the same year at the age of twenty-one. After a relatively distinguished career as a legate and cardinal protector of England and Germany, and after being considered a possible pope in several conclaves, he was elected to succeed Alexander VI, the Borgia Pope, almost certainly as a compromise candidate whom no one thought would live long owing to the affliction of gout. He probably surprised even the most optimistic elector by the brevity of his reign. So ill was he at the coronation that a number of ceremonies were omitted to make sure he lived through them. As it was, he survived a mere ten days after his coronation. Successor: Julius II.

PIUS IV   Pope from 1559 to 1565, the pontiff responsible for concluding the important work of the Council of Trent (1545–1563) in reforming the Church. Giovanni Angelo Medici was born in Milan in 1499 to a family with no connection to the famed house of de'Medici; his father, in fact, was a notary and a tax collector. After studying medicine and law in Pavia and Bologna, he received appointment in 1527 as prothonotary (a leading secretary) in the papal service. Gradually promoted, he was made Archbishop of Ragusa in 1545 by Pope Paul III after Giovanni's brother married into the family of the pontiff. Four years later he was appointed a cardinal, also serving as Bishop of Cassano (1553) and Foligno (1556) at the urging of Emperor Charles V. He departed Rome in 1558 after disagreeing with Pope Paul IV's policy toward Spain and perhaps out of disgust with his harsh and severe rule. The conclave that followed Paul's death in August 1559 proved protracted and bitterly divided. It finally ended on December 26 with Medici's election as pope as a compromise candidate. He took the name Pius because he intended "to be what the name signified."

In every way he was different from the stern and cheerless Paul. Easygoing, affable, and immediately endearing to the Romans, he blew away the gloom of the previous pontificate. Quite corpulent from years of overindulgence, he took to walking as a means of losing weight, his long treks through the city positively frustrating to a court used to the somber inactivity of Paul and mindful of traditional papal decorum. He also delighted the Romans by finally permitting justice to fall upon the hated nephews of Paul, Carlo Cardinal Carafa and Giovanni Carafa, Duke of Paliano, for a heavy list of crimes. They were executed on March 5, 1561. Guilty himself of nepotism, Pius nevertheless actually brought much good to the Church because of it, for the nephew he made a cardinal was the brilliant reformer and saint Charles Borromeo (d. 1584). As pope, Pius improved relations with Spain, brought reforms to the papal government, and released many prisoners of the previous pontificate, including Cardinal Morone, who had been sent to Castel Sant'Angelo. His main achievement, of course, was finishing the work of the Council of Trent, which he closed officially on December 4, 1563, confirming its decrees in January of the next year and devoting his remaining time to beginning the difficult task of implementing the reform throughout the Church. One of his most lasting decrees was the so-called Creed of Pius IV (the *Professio Fidei*

Tridentinae) issued in 1564, requiring a profession of faith by all ecclesiastical officeholders and remaining in use until 1967. In his later years he was less popular because of the need to raise taxes on the inhabitants of the Papal States and was nearly assassinated. He died on December 9, 1565. Successor: St. Pius V.

PIUS V, ST.   Pope from 1566 to 1572. Antonio Ghislieri was born in Bosco, Italy, to a poor family, working as a shepherd until around the age of fourteen. He then joined the Dominicans and studied in Bologna and Genoa. Called Brother Michele, he held the post of lecturer in theology and philosophy for sixteen years, receiving appointment as master of novices and then prior of several convents. Owing to his knowledge and piety, he was named Inquisitor for Como and Bergamo, so impressing then Cardinal Carafa (the future Paul IV) that Pope Julius III was convinced to promote him to commissary general of the Inquisition. In 1555, Carafa was elected pope and Ghislieri was one of his favorite advisors, receiving swift promotion to cardinal in 1557 and Grand Inquisitor in 1558. During the reign of Pius IV (1559–1565), Ghislieri was largely out of favor and had reduced responsibilities in keeping with the less stern policies of the pope. After Pius died, however, he was supported as a candidate for election by the deceased pontiff's nephew, St. Charles Borromeo. Unanimously elected pope on January 7, 1566, he took the name Pius and was greeted by the Romans with considerable wariness. His reputation as an inquisitor and ally of Paul IV caused many to fear a recrudescence of the grim social and religious policies of the Carafa pope. Pius surprised them by his evenhanded rule; certainly all immoral and decadent activities were curbed, the Curia was extensively examined, cardinals probed for their moral fitness (one found wanting spent his remaining days shut up in a monastery under the spiritual care of the Jesuits), and nepotism was strictly forbidden, but Pius was conspicuously fair and led an exemplary life, even wearing his coarse Dominican robes beneath the papal finery.

With the help of Borromeo and the other great reformers, he made his central focus the full implementation of the decrees of the recently concluded Council of Trent (1545–1563). The decrees were published across the entire Church—even in India, the New World, and China—and a Roman Catechism was published in 1566, the version that would stay in effect until the new Catechism was published in 1994 under John Paul II. Concerned about the advance of the Ottoman Turks, he crafted a formidable alliance between Spain, Venice, and the

Holy See that culminated in the triumph over the Turks at the Battle of Lepanto in 1571, which ended the Ottoman threat to the Mediterranean. Less positive aspects of this generally excellent pontificate were his decision in 1570 to excommunicate and declare deposed Queen Elizabeth I of England, an act that only demonstrated the reduced power of the papacy in the new order created by the Reformation, and his harsh treatment of the Jews, who were restricted in their activities and finally expelled in large numbers from papal territory. Personally devout and canonized a saint in 1712, he was one of the foremost popes of the movement known as the Catholic Reformation. Successor: Gregory XIII.

PIUS VI   Pope from 1775 to 1799, whose reign would stretch from the period of American independence to the rise of Napoleon Bonaparte. Giovanni Braschi was born in 1717 in Cesena, northern Italy, to a noble but impoverished family. He earned a doctorate in civil and canon law at the age of seventeen after studying under the Jesuits. In 1740 he was appointed the secretary to Antonio Cardinal Ruffo, then legate to Ferrara. After a distinguished period of service, he was named a papal secretary in 1750 and received ordination in 1758. Ranked as one of the most capable figures in the papal government, he was raised to the cardinalate in 1773 by Pope Clement XIV. Following Clement's death, the conclave chose Braschi, on February 15, 1775, despite the opposition of the Portuguese minister, the Marquis de Pombal, who feared the new pope might attempt to revive the hated Jesuits who had been suppressed by Clement XIV.

Pope Pius VI, pope during the French Revolution.

Ranked as one of the handsomest and most deeply cultured of all pontiffs, and said by a contemporary to have been born to be a sovereign, Pius would witness the collapse of the old order in Europe and would ultimately be a victim of the social and political storm brought by the French Revolution. The early part of his reign began in relative peace, and the pope was able to please the Romans by acting as a patron of the arts, including expensive improvements to the Pio-Clementine Museum and the Vatican; he also launched an ambitious program to drain the Pontine Marshes of Rome, something even the old Roman emperors had tried to accomplish. In the disasters that would overtake the Holy See over the next years, the Romans would remain devoted to their pontiff.

Pius was first challenged by the rampant spread of secularism and such anti-Church movements as Febronianism and Josephism, which sought to reduce the powers of the papacy and bring the Church under state control. Josephism was named after Emperor Josef II, the ruler of the Holy Roman Empire who was so energetic in crushing the Church under his imperial foot that Pius took the drastic step of visiting Vienna in 1782. Despite huge crowds on the way, the pontiff returned home empty-handed. He was soon confronted by another attack on his authority, from the Synod of Pistoia in 1786, which he condemned vigorously in the bull *Auctorem fidei* (1794). By then the French Revolution was well under way, having erupted in 1789. Pius tried to maintain stable relations with the anti-Catholic Revolutionary government, but this soon proved impossible. Adding to his troubles was the seizure of the Papal States in 1796 by the brilliant young General Napoleon Bonaparte. Pius negotiated peace with the French, but the Peace of Tolentino was arbitrary and deliberately cruel; much of the Papal States was left in French hands and enemy troops loomed at the gates of Rome waiting for any provocation. That came in late 1797 when the French general Duphot was killed in a riot in Rome. Urged on by Italian revolutionaries, the French sent in troops on February 15, 1798. The pope was deposed and a Roman Republic proclaimed. To ensure that his deposition was not challenged, the French ordered Pius removed from his city. Already old and ill, Pius defiantly refused to hand over the Ring of the Fisherman and faced his captors with such equanimity that the Spanish ambassador, an avowed atheist, expressed his deepest respect. As the pontiff left Rome, throngs of Romans knelt silently in the rain while he passed in his carriage. Pius died virtually alone in exile on August 29, 1799. Many thought it was the end of the papacy, but the wily pontiff had left provision for a conclave under these difficult circumstances. Through his forethought, the Church was not long without a pope. Successor: Pius VII.

PIUS VII   Pope from 1800 to 1823, his reign was dominated by Napoleon Bonaparte. Luigi Barnaba Chiaramonti was born in Cesena, Italy, on August 14, 1742, to a noble family. At the age of fourteen he entered the Benedictine order, adopting the name Gregorio, as was custom. He studied at Padua and Rome, serving as a professor of theology in Parma. In 1775 he was made the abbot of San Calisto in Rome by Pope Pius VI, subsequently holding the post of Bishop of Tivoli and Imola; in 1785 he was named a cardinal. Considered exceedingly progressive in thought and not entirely unsympathetic to the ideals of democracy being advocated by the French Revolution, he suggested a policy of nonresistance when the French invaded the Papal States in 1796. He was appalled, however, by the seizure and deportation of Pius VI, who died in captivity at Valence in August 1799. The cardinals assembled at Venice to elect a successor, and the conclave was long and stormy, lasting three contentious months. Two choices, Cardinals Bellisomi and Gerdil, were vetoed by the Austrians, who favored Cardinal Mattei. He was unacceptable to the cardinals who feared electing someone who would be a mere chaplain in the service of the Holy Roman Emperor, recognizing the need to find someone able to deal with Napoleon Bonaparte. At the quiet recommendation of the highly respected cleric Ercole Consalvi, the Princes of the Church finally settled on Chiaramonti; he was elected on March 14, 1800.

Pius VII was to prove devout and steadfastly courageous in the face of the crushing misfortunes that were to strike the papacy over the next years. His abiding faith and his gentle nature gave him forbearance and the patience to deal with Napoleon and to maintain his dignity even in the worst days of humiliation and captivity. As the cardinals accurately predicted, the new pope was immediately faced by Bonaparte who, in 1800, seized power in France as first consul. Appointing Consalvi his secretary of state, Pius negotiated a concordat in 1801; the ink was barely dry when Napoleon violated it with his Organic Articles (1802), through which he asserted his domination of the French Church. In the hopes of improving relations, Pius journeyed to Paris in 1804 to crown Napoleon emperor. The French ruler subjected him to repeated snubs and then degraded the pope on December 1 by crowning himself and his wife, Josephine. War erupted across Europe the next year and the succeeding period brought triumphs for Napoleon on such a scale that by 1809 he was master of the continent.

Conditions for the Church deteriorated steadily throughout the countries under Napoleon's control, and Pius, resisting the oppression and striving to maintain neutrality as Catholic nations embraced in bloody conflict, could not but watch relations with the emperor fall apart. He acquiesced to Napoleon's demand to remove Consalvi in June 1806, but his refusal to bend utterly to the will of the emperor led to the occupation of Rome in February 1808; the next year, the Papal States were annexed to the French Empire. Pius excommunicated Napoleon and on July 5 was arrested, taken from Rome, and banished, first to Grenoble and then to Savona. Ill from abuse, he was transferred to Fontainebleau in 1812. There, under grinding pressure, he signed the Concordat of Fontainebleau, an agreement full of extreme demands, on January 25, 1813. He retracted it two months later and, with the fall of Napoleon, was at last freed in March 1814, returning to Rome on March 24. Hailed throughout Europe as a champion against tyranny, Pius used his prestige to secure the full restoration of the Papal States by the Congress of Vienna (1814–1815) and to repair the severe damage done to the Church. He reinstituted the Jesuits in 1814, negotiated concordats with several countries, and, with Consalvi, brought numerous reforms to the Papal States. In a remarkable gesture, he not only entreated the English to spare Napoleon from cruel imprisonment on the island of St. Helena, but magnanimously allowed Napoleon's mother, Lucrezia, an uncle, and two brothers to live quietly in Rome when they were political and social outcasts everywhere else. Successor: Leo XII.

 PIUS VIII Pope from 1829 to 1830. Born to a noble family in Cingoli, near Ancona, Francesco Saverio Castiglione studied under the Jesuits at Osimo and then at Bologna and Rome. An expert on canon law, he was ordained in 1785, held several posts, and in 1800 was appointed bishop of Montalto. When in 1808 the Papal States were seized by the French, Castiglione, whose diocese was within the territory, refused to swear allegiance to Napoleon. Arrested, he was taken as a prisoner to France. Released after the fall of Napoleon, he was rewarded for his fidelity with the red hat, becoming a cardinal in 1816. A favorite of Pope Pius VII, he was made Bishop of Frascati and then prefect of the Congregation of the Index (the department that watched over all forbidden books) in 1823. It was widely recognized that Pius hoped for Castiglione to succeed him, once saying to the cardinal about some matter, "Your Holiness Pius VIII may one day have to settle this affair." In the conclave that followed Pius's passing, however, he was not elected; instead the stern Leo XII (1823–1829) was chosen. Finally, on March 31, 1829, he was elected to succeed Leo, taking the name Pius (VIII) to no one's surprise. His reign proved short, but he temporarily reversed Leo's hard rule over the Papal States and joyously received the Roman Catholic Relief Acts, which were issued in England in April 1829. His time also witnessed the first eruption of the revolutionary spirit that was to trouble Europe in the coming decades. Successor: Gregory XVI.

 PIUS IX   Pope from 1846 to 1878, the longest reigning pontiff of all time and one of the most memorable, he would witness the demise of the Papal States and the rise of a unified Italy. Born in Senigallia in the March of Ancona within the Papal States on May 13, 1792, Giovanni Maria Mastai-Ferretti was the fourth son of a count. Surviving a difficult child-hood, including bouts of epilepsy, he attended school in Viterbo and then Rome, and was ordained in 1819. Assigned to the papal diplo-matic corps, he served in Chile from 1823 to 1825 before receiv-ing appointment as archbishop of Spoleto in 1827 and bishop of Imola in 1832. During this time he was well known for his receptiv-ity to new ideas and was said to possess certain nationalist notions with regard to the then hot ques-tion of Italian unification. Despite this reputation, which ran counter to the views and temperament of Pope Gregory XVI, he was made a cardinal in 1840 and was con-sidered a genuinely favorite can-didate as his successor in the conclave of 1846. To no one's

Pope Pius IX, the longest-reigning pontiff in the history of the Church.

amazement he was elected pope after only two days, on June 16, 1846. Few could imagine that his pontificate would be one of the stormiest in the history of the Church.

In a grand gesture, he started his reign by granting a general amnesty for all political prisoners and ordered extensive reforms for the States of the Church, including a series of democratic measures that began to reverse much of the authoritarian atmosphere of his predecessors. His expression of sympathy for Italian unification and his democratic overtures were badly misinterpreted by the reactionaries, and even revolutionaries, who were stunned and angered by his comments that he had no intention of surrendering political and temporal control of the states, and especially by his neutral position in the bloody war that was foolishly begun in hopes of driving the Austrians from Italy. Matters in Rome soon deteriorated, and the last hope of a peaceful accord with the radicals died with the assassination of Pius's prime minister, Count Rossi, on November 15, 1848. Rioting broke out and a republic was soon declared, deposing Pius and trapping him in the Quirinal Palace. He escaped on November 24, dressed as a simple priest, to Gaeta, outside Rome, where he remained with much of his court until Rome was restored in 1850 with the help of the French. Having learned his lesson, he adopted stern measures to curb the unrest in the States and became a dedicated opponent of the relentless process of Italian unification called the Risorgimento, which he accurately predicted would spell the doom of the temporal power of the popes. The crisis came in 1860 when the troops of King Victor Emmanuel II stormed the Papal States and defeated the pope's troops at the Battle of Castelfidardo. Pius was left only with Rome, safe for the moment only because of the French troops stationed there by Emperor Napoleon III. When, however, France declared war on Germany in 1870 at the start of the Franco-Prussian War, the garrison was withdrawn. On September 20, 1870, Rome fell, to the absolute horror of Pius, who nevertheless commanded that there should be no resistance. From that day until the time of his death, Pius refused to acknowledge the existence of the Italian government, ignoring the Law of Guarantees (May 13, 1871), which declared the Vatican and his person utterly inviolable, proclaiming himself a "prisoner of the Vatican." In the decree *Non expedit* (1868) he placed a prohibition on Catholic participation in Italian elections and politics, thus beginning the so-called Roman Question or the *dissidio,* a perpetual state of tension that would not end until 1929 and the Lateran Treaty.

While definitely overshadowed by the disasters of 1848, 1860, and 1870, the rest of his reign was also significant and quite successful, assisted throughout until 1870 by the able secretary of state Giacomo Cardinal Antonelli. The pope was much concerned with fostering orthodoxy in the Church and reducing liberalism, issuing the encyclical *Quanta Cura* in 1864 that was best known for the document he attached to it, the *Syllabus of Errors,* a listing of eighty heretical propositions ranging from communism and socialism to indifferentism, to liberalism in all its forms; each of the condemned propositions had been censured before at varying times. He also proclaimed the definition of the Immaculate Conception (1854) and managed to restore the hierarchy of the Church in England (1850) and the Netherlands (1853), no mean feat given the long animosity toward the faith in the two lands. Above all, Pius gave vital direction to the Church and the papacy through his efforts to rebuild the papacy after the catastrophes of the era. In this he was greatly aided by Vatican Council I (1869–1870), which was a complete triumph for his hopes, with decrees against materialism, socialism, and atheism, and most of all, the solemn decree of Papal Infallibility, which emerged as one of the cornerstones of the resurrection of the papacy.

Renowned for his affability, kindness, and charm (despite the liberals' dislike of him for his unbending character), especially in his early years, he was the object of deep hostility by nationalists and the anticlerical party in the new Italian regime, a hatred he bore with a mixture of resoluteness and dogged faith. His stubbornness cost much support in Europe, but, in a statement of his charity, he commanded a priest be sent to the bedside of King Victor Emmanuel II to permit the ruler to die in the arms of the Church. Pius died on February 7, 1878, having reigned as a major transitional figure for the papacy between the medieval conception of a religious and temporal power and the modern understanding of the papal role as the pastor of the Church and the world. At his funeral an angry mob of anticlericals tried to grab his coffin and hurl him into the Tiber. Much to the chagrin of liberals in the Church, Pio Nono's cause for sainthood was opened in 1985 by Pope John Paul II. Successor: Leo XIII.

PIUS X, ST.   Pope from 1903 to 1914, the last of the popes to be canonized and the first since Pius V in 1712. Born in Riese, Venetia, on June 2, 1835, Giuseppe Melchior Sarto was the son of a seamstress and a postman. After studying at Riese and Castelfranco, he entered the seminary of Padua and received ordination in 1858. His next years were spent as a simple parish priest in Tombolo and the Salzano, embarking upon a long career that would distinguish him as arguably the most pastoral figure elected to the throne of St. Peter in this century. Sarto next served as rector and spiritual director of the Treviso seminary, chancellor of the Treviso diocese, and then bishop of Mantua in 1884. As bishop he earned the respect of the Italian Church and especially the Vatican for his work in revitalizing the faith in his diocese, so much so that he was made a cardinal in 1893 by Pope Leo XIII and was appointed patriarch of Venice, a post he held for ten years. In the conclave that assembled to choose a successor to Leo XIII, Sarto was not considered a leading *papabile* (favorite), and he probably would not have been elected had Emperor Franz Josef I not vetoed any possible vote for Mariano Cardinal Rampolla. The cardinals protested this interference in their affairs and resumed voting; interestingly, the veto did not stir sympathies in favor of Rampolla and he apparently faded as the balloting proceeded. Sarto was opposed to the votes he received, but in vain, and on August 4, 1903, his protests were overcome and he was chosen. He was to prove a champion of Church rights and orthodoxy and was a pastoral pontiff, his reign exemplified by his motto *"Instaurare omnia in Christo"* ("To restore all things in Christ").

Pope St. Pius X, the last pope to be canonized.

Immediately upon his election, he decreed that henceforth there should be no secular interference in papal elections. He then worked with his talented secretary of state, Rafael Cardinal Merry del Val, to resist all anti-Catholic measures introduced by the governments of France and Portugal. In matters of doctrine, he was sternly conservative, condemning the movement within the Church called Modernism (which promoted the radical interpretation of Church teachings to bring them into line with contemporary philosophical thought and science). Pius called it "the synthesis of all heresies" using the decree *Lamentabili* (1907), the encyclical *Pascendi* (1907), and the motu proprio *Sacrorum antistitum* to stamp it out; the latter decree required an anti-Modernist oath be taken by all the clergy. At the same time, however, Pius reorganized the Curia in 1908, began a revision of the Code of Canon Law, reformed church music, helped establish the pro-Church organization called Catholic Action, and was so dedicated to the fostering of daily communion by the faithful that he was given the name "Pope of Frequent Communion." Troubled profoundly by the headlong rush by Europe toward war, he tried desperately to stop it, but failed. He died partly from deep sadness on August 20, 1914, only days after the start of World War I; he predicted the horrors it would bring. Presented after his election with a magnificent bed for personal use, he looked at it, sighed, and said, "It is beautiful, but I shall die in it!" He was canonized by Pope Pius XII on May 29, 1954. Successor: Benedict XV.

 PIUS XI   Pope from 1922 to 1939, he negotiated the Lateran Treaty in 1929, creating the Vatican City State. Achille Ambrogio Damiano Ratti was born at Desio, near Milan, the son of the manager of a silk factory, on May 31, 1857. He entered the seminary at the age of ten, later studying in Milan and Rome and receiving ordination in the Lateran on December 27, 1879. In 1882 he earned three different doctorates, in theology, philosophy, and canon law. He returned to Milan from Rome, worked for a time as a curate in a local parish, and then taught at the seminary of Milan from 1883 to 1888. Elected to the staff of the famed Ambrosian Library in 1888, he so distinguished himself through his work as a scholar and paleographer that the King of Italy honored him with the Knighthood of the Order of Sts. Maurice and Lazarus. In 1907 he became prefect of the Ambrosian, also proving an able advisor to the Archbishop of Milan. Pope Pius X appointed him vice-

Pope Pius XI. (CATHOLIC NEWS SERVICE.)

prefect (1910–1911) and then Prefect (1914) of the Vatican Library. There he worked to catalog its vast collections and organize its manuscripts and books. Benedict XV chose to use him in other matters, sending him to Warsaw in 1918 as Apostolic Visitor (or delegate), and at the request of the much impressed Poles, he was appointed nuncio, receiving from them the prestigious order of the White Eagle for his courage in staying in Warsaw during the Bolshevik invasion of 1920.

Brought back to Rome in 1921, he was named archbishop of Milan and then elevated to the cardinalate on June 13, 1921. Amazingly, within seven months he was pope as successor to Benedict, receiving election on February 6, 1922.

As Pius XI, he took as his motto "To seek the peace of Christ in the reign of Christ," dedicating himself to the promotion of peace at a time when titanic forces were leading the world toward cataclysm. In his labors, he was much assisted by two able secretaries of state: first Cardinal Gasparri and then, from 1930, the brilliant Eugenio Pacelli (the future Pius XII). Pius negotiated the Lateran Treaty in 1929 with the Italian government of Benito Mussolini, thereby ending the *dissidio* and forging the Vatican City State. (See *Lateran Treaty* and *Vatican City, State of.*) A devoted enemy of communism, the pope swiftly recognized the oppressive nature of the Stalin regime in Russia and condemned communism in the encyclical *Divini Redemptoris* (1937). Partly to curb its spread and to protect the Church in Germany, Pius entered into the well-known and much criticized concordat with the Nazi regime in 1933, a treaty soon violated by the Nazis and manipulated for propaganda purposes. Within a short time, Pius was aghast at Nazi policies and in 1937 issued the encyclical *Mit Brennender Sorge* ("With Burning Sadness"), attacking Nazi Germany for its violations of the concordat and its anti-Christian program; smuggled into Germany, it was read from every pulpit in the land. His relations with Mussolini also deteriorated, and Pius was working on a speech even clearer in its denunciations of Fascism when he died; the speech was never given.

The pontiff also settled a bitter struggle with Mexico in 1930, issued twenty-three encyclicals, promoted the Catholic missions, encouraged the work of the Pontifical Academy of Sciences and the Vatican Observatory, and used every opportunity to strengthen the Church for the war he knew was coming. He also renovated St. Peter's Basilica and set the Vatican State on a sure footing. Indomitable, imperious, steeped in papal majesty, and fully aware of his power, he was unafraid to use his authority on behalf of the Church as he saw fit, once stripping a French cardinal of his title and dignity when the Prince of the Church spoke out on behalf of the condemned ultra-conservative group *Action Française*. Pius's own family had to petition the papal chamberlain for an audience when they wished to visit him. Long proud of his good health, he fell ill in early 1939 and died on February 10. He was the first pope to be heard on radio and had been a dedicated alpinist. Successor: Pius XII.

Pope Pius XII greeting reporters following the liberation of Rome in 1944; the future Pope Paul VI appears in the far middle left. (CATHOLIC NEWS SERVICE.)

PIUS XII   Pope from 1939 to 1958, his reign stretched through the dark years of World War II. A Roman and member of the much esteemed Pacelli family, Eugenio Maria Giuseppe Giovanni Pacelli was born on March 2, 1876. He was superbly educated at the Gregorian University, Capranica College, and the S. Apollonaire Institute in Rome, receiving ordination in April 1899. Noted for his keen intelligence, he was enlisted in the papal service in 1901 by Cardinal Gasparri, assisting with his mammoth codification of canon law. In 1914 he was appointed to a high office in the Secretariat of State and was made a titular archbishop in 1917 by Pope Benedict XV, who dispatched him as nuncio to Bavaria. This was expanded to the post of nuncio to the German Republic. In this capacity he negotiated a concordat with Bavaria in 1924 and with Prussia in 1930, developing a respect and even fondness for the German people. Made a cardinal in 1929 by Pius XI, he was soon named replacement to Cardinal Gasparri as secretary of state, on February 7, 1930. The next years would find him all over the world serving as the extremely gifted representative of Pius. His most famous act was to negotiate the Concordat with Nazi Germany in 1933. With Pius's death in February 1939, the cardinals recognized that war was coming and so looked for the foremost diplomat among them. They naturally selected Pacelli; he was elected on the third ballot on March 2, 1939.

The Quotable Pius XII

... the Church and her faithful are in time and in years of trial such as have never been known in her history of struggle and suffering. But in such times, especially, he who remains strong in his faith and strong at heart knows that Christ the King is never so near as in the hour of trial, which is the hour of fidelity.

In every age of the Church history, the mind of man, enlightened by faith, has aimed at the greatest possible knowledge of things divine.

If a laborer is deprived of hope to acquire some personal property, what other natural stimulus can be offered him that will inspire him to hard work, labor, saving, and sobriety today, when so many nations and men have lost everything and all they have left is their capacity for work.

O wondrous vision, which makes us contemplate the human race in the unity of its origin in God ... in the unity of its nature, composed equally in all men of a material body and a spiritual soul; in the unity of its immediate end and its mission in the world; in the unity of its dwelling, the earth, whose benefits all men, by right of nature, may use to sustain and develop life; in the unity of its supernatural end: God himself, to whom all ought to tend; in the unity of the means for attaining this end.

Though human reason is, strictly speaking, truly capable by its own natural power and light of attaining to a true and certain knowledge of the one personal God, who watches over and controls the world by his providence, and of the natural law written in our hearts by the Creator; yet there are many obstacles which prevent reason from the effective and fruitful use of this inborn faculty.

He took as his chief object the preventing of the war that was about to descend on the world, speaking out against the Nazi invasion of Poland on September 1, 1939, and using his Christmas allocution for the year to proclaim his so-called Five Peace Points: the Christian Spirit that should exist among nations; the recognizing of the rights of all nations; genuine disarmament; the recognition of minority rights; and the founding of an international court to ensure peace. These fell on deaf ears, of course, and throughout the long war Pius maintained assiduously the neutrality of the Holy See, devoting all available resources to war relief through the Pontifical Aid Commission. He also went to great lengths to give safety and comfort to the refugees, including many Jews.

Criticized severely for not doing enough to aid the Jews—even slandered by the play *The Representative* by Rolf Hochhuth—Pius supposedly did little if anything to help save Jewish lives or to protest their suffering. While his speeches might have been bolder, he recognized that German troops were on the verge of invading the Vatican, had learned from sources within the Nazi regime that Hitler had plans to exile the pope and establish a kind of antipope in his place, and that all Catholics in German lands might be arrested and imprisoned in retribution. As it was, several million Catholics would die in the Holocaust, joining the six million Jews. Pius, however, did so much for the Jews in Rome that after the liberation of the city, the chief rabbi of the city, Dr. Israel Zolli, declared his gratitude to Pius for having saved so many of his people. The Vatican, Castel Gandolfo, and two hundred churches and convents all over the city were opened as havens for Jews. In 1943 Pius ordered that sacred vessels be melted to help the Jews of Rome pay a Nazi extortion of one million lire and one hundred pounds of gold. Perhaps the most memorable event of his entire pontificate came in the summer of 1944 when, following the liberation, soldiers and ecstatic Romans gathered in St. Peter's Square and received the papal blessing.

In the following years, Pius devoted himself to assisting in the huge task of rebuilding the shattered world and repairing the damage done to the Church. After the death of his secretary of state, Cardinal Maglione, Pius assumed the office himself, receiving valuable assistance from two monsignori, Domenico Tardini and Giovanni Montini (the future Paul VI). His final years were noted for his memorable encyclicals, his promotion of the Church around the world, and various reforms that anticipated the changes brought by Vatican Council II, called by his successor. Ranked as one of the greatest popes, Pius is also considered the last pope of the pre–Vatican II Church. He died at Castel Gandolfo on October 9, 1958. Successor: John XXIII.

※ **POLYGLOT PRESS, VATICAN** The Tipografia Poliglotta Vaticana, the official printing house of the Vatican, located on the Street of the Pilgrim, and closely associated with the Libreria Editrice Vaticana and *L'Osservatore Romano*. Called the Polyglot Press because of its work in printing works in a wide variety of languages, it is capable of turning out books in over two dozen tongues. It principal purpose today is to print the official writings of various Church authors, along with religious texts and various official documents. It is run by the Salesian Fathers, S.D.B.

※ **PONTIAN, ST.** Pope from 230 to 235 who holds the distinction of being the first pontiff to abdicate from the throne of St. Peter. He may have been a Roman by birth, the son of one Calpurnius. Elected to succeed St. Urban I on July 21, 230, his activities are not known in any great detail. He almost certainly convened a synod in Rome that upheld the earlier condemnation of the heretical teachings of Origenism. He also grappled with the schismatic movement established in the city by the writer Hippolytus, but his pontificate was generally peaceful until 235 when a new wave of persecutions began under Emperor Maximinus I Thrax. Both Pontian and Hippolytus were arrested and banished to the infamous mines of Sardinia. In order for the Roman Church to have a leader, Pontian took the unprecedented step of abdicating on September 28, 235. Pontian died on the island with Hippolytus; both of their remains were returned to Rome under Pope St. Fabian. Successor: St. Anterus.

※ **PONTIFEX MAXIMUS** A title meaning in Latin "Supreme Pontiff" that is today limited in use exclusively to the pope. The term originated in pagan Rome for the priest who headed the college of priests in the city, an office of enormous power and prestige. Scholars point out that the etymological origins of the term *pontifex* are rooted in the Latin *pontem facere* ("to build a bridge"), implying that the original priest in Ancient Rome was responsible for building a bridge between humanity and the gods. Under Julius Caesar, the office was united with that of dictator, marking the quasi-religious significance of the emperors within the Roman religious system. Roman emperors thus served as Pontifex Maximus, even after the adoption of Christianity as the accepted faith of the empire. The last emperor to serve as Pontifex was Gratian (r. 367–383), who stepped down and gave the symbolic office to Pope St. Damasus in 375 as part of recognizing that the Bishops of Rome had supreme authority over the entire Church. The title Pontifex Maximus, also styled simply Pontiff, was subsequently adopted by the popes, although its common usage dates only to the end of the Middle Ages. Abbreviations for the title are *P.M.* or *Pont. Max.* They are found quite often on artwork and inscriptions bearing the name of the pope, such as on the facade designed for St. Peter's Basilica by Carlo Maderno, with its inscription honoring Pope Paul V Borghese. It usually follows the name of the pope. (See also *Pontiff, Pope,* and *Titles of the Pope.*)

❀ **PONTIFF**   Also properly, Roman Pontiff or Supreme Pontiff, one of the titles of the pope, derived from the appellation Pontifex Maximus. The pope is Pontiff in that he wields supreme authority over the Church. (See also *Titles of the Pope.*)

❀ **PONTIFICAL ACADEMY OF SCIENCES**   See *Academy of Sciences, Pontifical.*

❀ **PONTIFICAL ASTRONOMICAL OBSERVATORY**   The observatory traditionally run by the Jesuits that was long located in the Cybo Villa, part of the papal estates at Castel Gandolfo in the Alban Hills just outside of Rome. The administrative offices were in the Villa Barberini on the same estate. Owing to the age of the scientific equipment and the increasingly polluted air from Rome that interfered with the "seeing," the observatory received permission from Pope John Paul II to move its scientific equipment to the University of Arizona.

❀ **PONTIFICAL ECCLESIASTICAL ACADEMY**   One of the most important of the Pontifical Academies—the various schools established by the Holy See—which has the task of training the diplomats sent out by the Holy See to represent it around the world. The academy was first founded in 1701 by Clement XI under the title Academy of Ecclesiastical Nobles, the name derived from the fact that its members were required to come from noble families. The school is today one of the most exclusive of all pontifical academies, limited to specially chosen priests possessing degrees in canon law. The course of study lasts two years, at the end of which the student is given a posting to one of the papal nunciatures around the world as a low-ranking diplomat or assigned to some department in the Secretariat of State. The school is located in Rome, near the Pantheon. The academy has produced numerous popes over the years, including Clement XIII (1758–1769), Leo XII (1823–1829), Leo XIII (1878–1903), Benedict XV (1914–1922), and Paul VI (1963–1978).

❀ **POPE**   The popular title borne by the Bishop of Rome and the name among the many he bears by which he is best known to the people of the world. The term is derived from the Greek *pappias* (father) and was actually first used by St. Ennodius (d. 521); it has been in common use only since the eleventh century. While also given to certain bishops and clerics in the Orthodox Church, especially the Coptic patriarch of Alexandria, in the Western Church, the provenance of the title is exclusively that of the Bishop of Rome, Successor to St. Peter, the Supreme Pontiff, and Vicar of Christ. It should be remembered, however, that the reigning pontiff is pope (with all that this implies) by virtue of his election as Bishop of Rome. (See also *Titles of the Pope.*)

❀ **POPEMOBILE**   The special automobile used by the pope when traveling through crowds or large assemblies. The popemobile was introduced as the result of the near-fatal assassination attempt on the pope in 1981 by Mehmet Ali Agca in St. Peter's Square. Prior to this terrible event, the pope regularly was driven through crowds in an open Jeep, reaching out and touching the faithful. After the assassination try, the pope was convinced to use a new means of transport. The popemobile, normally a Mercedes-Benz 230-G station wagon, has room beneath its bulletproof shielding for the pope to sit or stand with other passengers and to address the crowd. It can race at speeds of 80 mph and has emergency kits should the pontiff have need. It is now one of the mainstays

The **Popemobile.** (CATHOLIC NEWS SERVICE.)

of any papal visit. In some places, the popemobile might be a converted truck or some other heavy form of transport, depending upon the environment of a visit and the size of crowds.

🏵 **POPES, FALSE** See *Antipope*.

🏵 **Pope Speaks, The** A quarterly journal first launched in 1954 that provides English translations of the most important papal documents, pronouncements, and letters; the journal also provides translations of Curial decrees. Customarily, the documents are presented with their official title, along with the English title, a complete English version of the texts, and the dates of the issuing. There is also a complete listing of papal addresses, including those not published in the journal itself. *The Pope Speaks* is published by Our Sunday Visitor, Inc., and is available by subscription.

🏵 **POPESSA, LA** The nickname given to Sister Pasqualina, the imperious and well-known—in Vatican circles—housekeeper of Pope Pius XII (1939–1958). After Pius's death, she worked at the North American College, placing flowers in the rooms of students on their birthdays. There was never any suspicion, rumor, or even whispered suggestion of any improper friendship between Pacelli and Pasqualina, and their relationship remained entirely chaste, one of the most interesting in the history of the papacy.

🏵 **POST OFFICE, VATICAN** The department in the Vatican that handles all mail for the Holy See and the Vatican City State. The Vatican Post Office is responsible for organizing the vast number of letters, packages, and assorted communications passing through its doors. Each day, it receives around a thousand pieces of mail for the Holy Father, the number increasing during holidays, papal anniversaries, and the birthday of the reigning pontiff. The office also works in conjunction with the Italian government in the issuing of the Vatican stamps, which are used on all letters sent from the Vatican. The postmark of the Vatican is highly prized, especially by visitors who send postcards from St. Peter's. The central post office is located in the St. Anne district, near the Vatican Printing Press and the Tower of Nicholas V. (See also *Stamps, Vatican*.)

🏵 **P.P.** The initials meaning *Pastor Pastorum* ("Pastor of Pastors") that is used frequently in the signature of the pontiff. For example, Pope John

Paul II will sign many documents *Joannes Paulus, P.P. II*. It is also taken to mean, simply, Pope.

🕸 **PREFECTURE FOR THE ECONOMIC AFFAIRS OF THE HOLY SEE** A department of the Roman Curia that has authority over the so-called temporalities of the Holy See, meaning all of its goods and possessions. The prefecture was established in 1967 and is now one of the most important economic offices of the Holy See, with the Vatican Bank and the Administration of the Patrimony of the Apostolic See (APSA). Always under the direction of a cardinal, it is the rough papal equivalent of the Treasury Department of a secular government, with the difficult task of organizing the complex budget of the Curia and the Holy See. The work has been made even more important under the extensive financial reforms launched by Pope John Paul II.

🕸 **PRIMACY OF THE POPE** The supreme, universal authority wielded by the pope over the Church as successor to St. Peter and Vicar of Christ. This primacy makes the pope the possessor of supreme jurisdictional authority through his office, entailing his role as teacher, legislator, and head of the Roman Catholic Church. According to Church teaching, this primacy was granted to St. Peter by Christ, as recorded in the passage in the Gospel of St. Matthew (16:18) when Christ declared to Peter that he would be the rock upon which Christ would build his Church. Peter was head of the Apostles, superior even to St. Paul, receiving his powers directly from Christ; he was also the historically recognized Bishop of Rome, working and finally dying in the Eternal City. The popes, as his successors in the see of Rome, receive his authority over the whole of the Church as granted by Christ. The symbol of his primacy is the two keys, one silver, the other gold. The primacy is also reiterated in the drum of the cupola of St. Peter's Basilica, where is written: TV ES PETRVS, SVPER HANC PETRAM OEDIFICABO ECCLESIAM MEAM, TIBIDABO CLAVES REGNI COELORVM ("Thou art Peter, Over this rock I shall build my Church, I will give to thee the Keys of the Kingdom of Heaven"). (See also *Rome, Bishop of; Keys, Power of the;* and *Pope.*)

🕸 **PRIMATE OF ITALY** One of the titles borne by the pope, it is a statement of his jurisdiction over the dioceses of Italy, by virtue of his being the Bishop of Rome and his supreme authority as the successor to St. Peter. The pope also holds the title of primate over the entire Roman Catholic Church. (See also *Titles of the Pope.*)

❀ **PRINCE OF THE APOSTLES**   One of the honorific names bestowed upon St. Peter, it denotes the elevated status of Peter as having been chosen by Christ as the rock upon which the Church would be built. Peter was the recognized leader of the Apostles after the death and resurrection of Christ and is called the Vicar of Christ with primacy over the entire Church. The popes, as his successors as Bishops of Rome, receive his primacy.

❀ **PRONUNCIO**   See *Legate, Papal* and *Diplomacy, Papal.*

❀ **PUBLISHING, VATICAN**   See *Libreria Editrice Vaticana; L'Osservatore Roman;* and *Polyglot Press, Vatican.*

❀ **QUID VOBIS VIDETUR?** See *Cardinal; Cardinals, Sacred College of;* and *Consistories.*

❀ **QUIRINAL PALACE**   The Palazzo del Quirinale, the palace built on the Quirinal Hill in Rome by Pope Gregory XIII (1572–1585) to serve as a summer residence for the popes. The palace was constructed by Gregory as a means of escaping the stifling atmosphere of the Vatican during the hot summer months when the air was marked by the stench of the swamps and the danger of malaria. The Quirinal offered better air and breezes, given the height of the hill. It was begun in 1574 and subsequently claimed the labors of such brilliant architects as Domenico Fontana (designer of the main facade), Carlo Maderno (the chapel), and Bernini (the wing along the Via del Quirinale). The first pope to take up summer residence was Pope Clement VIII (1592–1605). It was such a favorite place for Pope Alexander VII (1655–1667) that he considered moving the entire papal administration there, out of the Vatican. It would continue to serve as the summer residence until 1870 and the capture of Rome by the forces of King Victor Emmanuel II. The palace was the site of several conclaves, the last in 1846 with the election of Pius IX. As Victor Emmanuel's troops entered the city in 1870, Pius IX declared himself a prisoner of the Vatican, lamenting ever after the loss of his summer residence. On arriving at the palace, King Victor Emmanuel was said to have declared in his native Piedmontese, *"Finalment i sum"* ("Here I am at last!"). The Quirinal was taken over as the palace of the king of Italy, an acquisition that the popes refused to acknowledge until 1929 and the signing of the Lateran Accords between Pius XI and Benito Mussolini. Of the loss of the palace, Pius IX reportedly declared that barrels of holy water were needed to wash away the profanation. After the fall of the monarchy in 1947, the Quirinal was made the residence of the president of the Republic of Italy.

❀ **RADIO, VATICAN** The official radio station of the Holy See, the Radio Vaticana, with the call letters HVJ (merely call letters). The station was inaugurated on February 12, 1931, by Pope Pius XI, who broadcast over the transmitters built by Guglielmo Marconi, inventor of the radio. The pontiff spoke in Latin, declaring from the Bible: "Listen, heavens, while I speak; earth, hear the words that I am saying." He thus was the first pope to have his voice sent out across the world. Marconi remained in charge of the Vatican transmitters until his death in 1937; its first director was Father Giuseppe Gianfranceschi, S.J., a veteran of the Italian expedition to the North Pole in 1929. The first years were largely experimental as the directors focused on the activities of the pope, but the outbreak of World War II brought a decisive turning point as the radio earned much acclaim for its nonstop transmission of literally over one million humanitarian messages, including pleas for information about missing soldiers, separated families, and prisoners of war. After the war, the radio underwent a swift process of modernization, culminating with the inauguration in 1957 of a large transmitting center at Santa Maria di Galeria just to the north of Rome. From its tall 175-ton antenna, Vatican Radio broadcasts classical and jazz music and programs on art, science, and literature, but its primary function continues to be the one stated on the plaque unveiled by Pius XI, namely "that the voice of the Supreme Pastor may be heard over the airwaves to the ends of the earth, for the glory of Christ the King and for the good of mankind." Sending forth the words of the pontiff, uniting Catholics in Europe, Asia, the Americas, Africa, and the Middle East into the common bond of the faith, the radio airs masses, rosaries, and the speeches and exhortations of the pope. Vatican Radio is also one of the best places (obviously) for the first word on papal activities and any developments during a papal election. In all, the radio broadcasts in thirty-four languages, with different programming for each language, attuned to the cultural and religious peculiarities of the listeners in various regions; also broadcast are special messages, including secret, encoded instructions to papal ambassadors in certain hostile environments (this was most true during the days of Communist domination in Eastern Europe).

❀ **RAILWAY, VATICAN**   The official train station of the Vatican City State, located behind St. Peter's Basilica and the Mosaic Factory (where mosaics are made and repaired) and near the Palazzo of the Governatorate. The Vatican rail station was built as a gift of Benito Mussolini to Pope Pius XI after the signing of the Lateran Accords in 1929. Standing at the end of the branch line from Viterbo, it was intended to provide the pope with his own train depot, but was rarely used by the pontiff or even by the dignitaries who visited the Vatican since they found it more convenient to travel by automobile. The station saw a limited amount of activity during the Second Vatican Council (1962–1965) and was utilized by Pope John XXIII on a trip he made to Assisi and Loreto in 1962. Technically, any time the pope travels by train, the Sistine Choir is expected to sing psalms as he boards and to serenade him out of the station. The station is used today primarily as the entry point into Vatican City for the supplies used by its inhabitants and as the export site for the magnificent creations and work of the Mosaic Factory. The station is the only spot in the Vatican to be bombed during World War II. In 1943, four bombs were mysteriously dropped on the city by a plane of unknown origin, narrowly missing the basilica and exploding right next to the station. No one was hurt and no severe damage was done, but some of the station's walls were pockmarked and windows were blown out. The incident was never completely explained, as the Allied air forces were not in the habit of bombing Rome (with the exception of the two raids in July and August 1943, one of which damaged the church of San Lorenzo Fuori le Mura), and the Luftwaffe was careful about respecting its status as an open city. Historians believe that the "accidental" bombing was intended as a message from Hitler to Pius XII to express *Der Führer's* displeasure over the pope's efforts to assist refugees and especially his helping of the Jews. (See also *Vatican City, State of.*)

❀ **RAPHAEL**   One of the greatest of the Renaissance painters and architects (1483–1520), who made significant contributions to the artistic patrimony of the Holy See. Rafaello Sanzio was born in Urbino, the son of Giovanni Santi (or Sanzio), himself an accomplished artist who died when Raphael was still a boy. After studying in the Umbrian studio of Perugino Vannucci, Raphael began to assert himself artistically and in 1504 went to Florence, then the capital of the Italian

Renaissance. In 1508, he journeyed to Rome at the invitation of Donato Bramante where, at the age of twenty-five, he embarked upon a brilliant period of activity. Pope Julius II (1503–1513) commissioned him in 1508 to paint the rooms in the Vatican now called the Raphael Stanze, the chambers occupied by Pope Julius because he refused to sleep in the quarters once occupied by his enemy Alexander VI, the Borgia Pope. The rooms are the Hall of Constantine, the Room of Heliodorus, the Room of the Segnatura, and the Room of the Fire in the Borgo. The frescoes found in the rooms, the subjects chosen by Julius, are some of the greatest of the Renaissance, a superb example of Raphael's genius and the highest ideals of the era. Among the numerous frescoes is *The School of Athens,* presenting a gathering of Greek philosophers, with Aristotle and Plato in debate on the search for truth dominating the center scene. Raphael used as his models the foremost artists of the time: Leonardo da Vinci, Michelangelo, and Bramante; Raphael placed himself in the corner, peering somewhat pensively at the viewer. He supervised the completion of the loggia in the Vatican Palace begun by Bramante, decorating it himself, and in 1514, at the command of Pope Leo X (1513–1521), he succeeded his friend as chief architect of St. Peter's Basilica. In the Vatican he also built the loggetta, which was nicknamed Cardinal Bibbiena's Bathroom, although no water closet has ever rivaled it. An entire room is also dedicated to him in the Vatican Museums, including a series of magnificent tapestries created from his cartoons and his last painting, *The Transfiguration.* One of the foremost innovators and fearless experimenters, Raphael literally worked himself to death, dying in Rome on April 6, 1520, after what period writers called "a wild debauch."

✸ **RED POPE**   The nickname given to Giacomo Cardinal Antonelli (1806–1876), secretary of state to Pope Pius IX (1846–1878). The appellation was derived from the wide powers and influence he was said by some critics to wield within the papal administration, so much so that he supposedly was the near equal of the pope. The name was also used for the prefect of the Congregation for the Propagation of the Faith in recognition of the extensive authority that the cardinal wielded as head of the department overseeing the missionary effort of the Church throughout the world.

✸ **REFORMATION, CATHOLIC**   See *Adrian VI, Paul III, Julius III, Marcellus III, Paul IV, Pius IV, Pius V, Gregory XIII, Sixtus V,* and *Clement VIII.*

⚜ **REFORMATION, PROTESTANT** See *Adrian VI, Alexander VI, Clement VII, Clement VIII, Gregory XIII, Julius II, Julius III, Marcellus II, Paul III, Paul IV, Pius IV, Pius V,* and *Sixtus V.*

⚜ **RIARIO FAMILY** Relatives of Pope Sixtus IV (1471–1484) who profited handsomely from his election. The most notable was Pietro Riario, a nephew of the pope. Like the future pope Giuliano della Rovere (Julius II), Pietro was still in his twenties when made a cardinal by his uncle, receiving as well a huge series of benefices and gifts; he was the abbot of several wealthy abbeys and either bishop or archbishop at the same time of four different sees, such as Florence, Valencia, Spoleto, and Seville; to these was added the purely symbolic title of Patriarch of Constantinople. The sees gave him an income of such size that he was the envy of many of the richest nobility in Christendom. He spent over 200,000 gold florins in one of the wildest episodes of debauchery and avarice of the era; each of his acts was recorded with dedicated glee by contemporary chroniclers. Riario finally died of exhaustion and dissipation in 1474 at the age of twenty-eight. A grandnephew of Sixtus, Raffaele Riario was made a cardinal at seventeen, but barely escaped with his life when, as legate to Florence, he was accused of participating in the plot to assassinate the Medici rulers of the city while at High Mass in the cathedral. Riario was not hanged but was briefly imprisoned.

⚜ **RING OF THE FISHERMAN** Also the Fisherman's Ring, in Italian the *piscatorio,* the ring traditionally used by the pope as a signet. The Ring of the Fisherman is so called from the engraving upon it depicting St. Peter in a boat, an allusion to the declaration of Christ to the Apostle that henceforth he was to be a fisher of men (Lk. 5:10). The ring is decorated with the name of the reigning pontiff circling the node and is first mentioned during the reign of Pope Clement IV in 1265. By custom, the ring is placed upon the finger of the newly elected pontiff by the cardinal camerlengo, and is subsequently not worn on a daily basis. Its purpose henceforth is to seal all Papal Briefs, a function that dates to at least the fifteenth century. Upon the death of the pope, the camerlengo has the duty of defacing the ring and then smashing it to prevent its possible misuse. After this is done, a document is signed testifying to the deed. (See also *Alexander VI* and *Rings, Papal.*)

⚜ **RINGS, PAPAL** The rings traditionally worn or used by the pope. As Supreme Pontiff and successor to St. Peter, the newly elected pontiff receives from the hands of the cardinal camerlengo the Ring of the

Fisherman, which is subsequently not worn but kept for sealing important official documents. (See *Ring of the Fisherman* for other details.) As a bishop, the pope also wears the customary episcopal ring, a band of office used by bishops since the sixth century to mark their consecration to the highest of the sacramental offices in the Church. It is worn on the right hand and may be made of virtually any substance or stone, save for the sapphire, which is reserved exclusively for cardinals. The pope continues to wear his episcopal ring, the specifics of it in keeping with his personal tastes. Pope Paul VI, for example, wore a simple silver band, a copy of which he sent out to every bishop in the world. Pope John Paul II wears the same one he used while still a bishop in Poland, a gold, cross-shaped band.

⚘ **RISORGIMENTO**   The name meaning "revival" given to the social and political movement in Italy during the nineteenth century that culminated in the unification of Italy in 1870; the success of the Risorgimento resulted in the loss of the Papal States by the popes and the demise of the temporal power of the papacy. In 1870 Victor Emmanuel's troops marched into Rome, which became his capital. Pope Pius IX refused to acknowledge the death of his temporal power, declaring himself a prisoner of the Vatican, thereby starting some six decades of political and social strife known as the Roman Question and the *dissidio*. (See also *Italy; Papal States; Pius IX; Roman Question;* and *Vatican City, State of*.)

⚘ **ROGITO**   The official notarial act or document testifying to the death and formal burial of the pope. It includes a variety of testaments from a physician and various officials of the Holy See testifying that the pope had truly died and that his funeral and burial had followed all of the required customs and rituals. The *rogito* is then given into the keeping of the Vatican Archives where it is stored for posterity. (See also *Death of a Pope*.)

⚘ **ROMAN CURIA**   See *Curia, Roman*.

⚘ **ROMAN QUESTION**   Also called the *dissidio* ("division"), the name given to the ongoing political difficulty between the Holy See and the Italian government from 1870 until 1929. The cause of the dispute was the seizure of Rome by the troops of King Victor Emmanuel and the resulting demise of the last vestiges of the temporal power of the Holy See, which brought to a close the period of gradual Italian unification called the Risorgimento. Pope Pius IX (1846–1878) responded by declaring himself a "prisoner of the Vatican," refusing to step foot out of Vatican City, the one piece of papal property not taken over by Italian forces. Pius refused to recognize the Italian king or his regime, steadfastly rejecting the Law of Guarantees proffered by Victor Emmanuel to permit the pontiff to retain some parts of his authority. Pius maintained the Curia and its functions as always and even accepted and sent ambassadors and legates. To ensure independence in communications, Pius retained a post office. He was also supported by the so-called Black Nobility, the aristocracy of the Eternal City who refused to accept the presence of the king. Pius's policy was carried on by his successors, Leo XIII, Pius X, and Benedict XV. The Roman Question was finally resolved by Pius XI with the Lateran Accords signed with Benito Mussolini in 1929. (See also *Lateran Treaty; Pius IX; Pius XI;* and *Vatican City, State of.*)

❀ **ROMAN SEE** See *Holy See.*

❀ **ROMANUS** Pope from around August to November 897. The cardinal priest of S. Pietro in Vincoli, he was elected to succeed the murdered Pope Stephen VI (VII), probably by the party that had deposed him and desired to bring about the posthumous rehabilitation of Pope Formosus, whose rotting corpse Stephen had put on trial. Little is known about Romanus's pontificate, although he may have been deposed by the Formosan Party, based on a recension in the *Liber Pontificalis,* which seems to indicate that he later became a monk. His date of death is thus unknown. Successor: Theodore II.

❀ **ROME** The Eternal City and the ancient City of the Popes. One of the greatest cities in the history of the world, Rome today is the capital of the country of Italy, one of the fashion headquarters of Western civilization, and the seat of power for the Holy Father and the Curia, the central administration of the Catholic Church. The traditional residence of the popes in the Eternal City dates to the first century when St. Peter and St. Paul established the diocese of Rome in the year 42. While a traveling pastor to his flock—his missionary efforts took him away from the city for long stretches of time—Peter paid the ultimate sacrifice for the faith around 64: he was crucified upside down on Vatican Hill and buried near this execution site during the brutal persecutions of Nero. Peter was recognized as Prince of the Apostles and Vicar of Christ on earth, so his successors as Bishop of Rome gradually

Rome, the city of the popes; in the foreground is the Colosseum, traditional site of Christian martyrdoms. (AP/WIDE WORLD PHOTOS.)

were recognized as holding primacy first in the West and then over the entire Christian Church. The bishops' position in Rome, first city of the Roman Empire until the fourth century, certainly did not hurt, and after the demise of the Roman Empire in the West, they assumed increasing civil control in the absence of any central authority in the city. Unfortunately, the popes as rulers of the city were faced with chronic strife, political intrigue and invasions, famines, droughts, and plagues. In the ninth century the city was ravaged by Saracen raiders; in the tenth and eleventh centuries popes were routinely appointed, deposed, and even murdered by the powerful noble houses of Rome, such as the Crescenti and Tusculani; and throughout the Middle Ages pontiffs had to spend much of their time away from their own city because of squabbles (and even bloodshed) with the Roman Commune, which sought to curb their power, or with Holy Roman emperors who would seize the city in their struggles with the Holy See over such issues as the Investiture Controversy.

The relationship of the popes with the Romans has thus been one of love and hate. Romans often despised their pope for being a foreigner (such as Adrian VI); a severe religious fanatic, who might take away their lottery and gambling and imprison many Romans for heresy (such as Paul IV); or even for betraying what they saw as a commitment to Italian nationalism (Pius IX). Romans also could be quite possessive of their Holy Father, resenting any foreign interloper who might wish to drive him away, embodying the adage that we might hate him, but he is still ours. In the times when the city loves its pontiff, the relationship is a close one, as seen with John Paul I and John Paul II. The former, the Smiling Pope, captured the Romans with his transparent goodness and his innocent goodwill. John Paul II stunned and won over the hearts of the Romans with his surprising use of Italian and his immediate pastoral skills. At its ideal, the relationship has been one of mutual regard, even when the popes say things the Romans know to be true, but which they choose habitually to ignore, all the while fiercely declaring themselves devout Catholics.

ROME, BISHOP OF   The most important of all titles possessed by the pope. Technically, each election to decide a new pope is concerned only with choosing a new successor to St. Peter as Bishop of Rome. By virtue of this office, however, the pope receives the claim of primacy over the Universal Church and all of the other titles to which he is entitled. (See *Titles of the Pope.*)

ROME, DIOCESE OF   The actual diocese comprised of the parishes of the city of Rome. It is often forgotten by Catholics that the election of the pope is technically only the choosing of the next bishop of the diocese of Rome, who, by virtue of his succession to St. Peter, is Supreme Pontiff of the Church. The diocese is also surrounded by a series of other dioceses, called the Suburbicarian Dioceses from which the cardinal bishops receive their titular titles. The diocese of Rome, while under the complete authority of the pope (as Bishop of Rome), is technically administered by a vicar (or substitute), known as the Vicar General of the Pope for the Diocese of Rome. (See also *Vicar General.*)

ROME, PARISHES OF   The parishes that comprise the diocese of Rome under the care of the Bishop of Rome, the pope, the successor of St. Peter. The parishes of the Roman See number twenty-five, traditionally being first organized under Pope St. Anacletus (76–88). The parishes are some of the oldest in the entire Church and have both a practical and an important symbolic role. In a practical sense, these are the actual parishes that make up the diocese, administered by the priests of Rome and under the spiritual guidance of the pope (who is represented in administrative terms by the Vicar General of the Pope for the Diocese of Rome). Symbolically, the parishes are the sites of the churches to which the cardinal priests of the Sacred College of

Cardinals are assigned to serve as their titular sees or holdings. This gives the cardinals a direct connection to the ancient custom of having cardinals come from the parishes of the Eternal City. (See also *Cardinals, Sacred College of.*)

�֍ **ROME, SACK OF**   The Eternal City has been sacked on a number of occasions during the past centuries, often with severe consequences for the city and its inhabitants and involving the popes themselves. Arguably the most famous capture of the city came in 410 when the Visigoths under Alaric stormed into Rome and looted it with terrible loss of life. According to legend, the Visigoths took the city's treasure, gold, and its pepper, which was a rare and expensive commodity. The pope at the time, St. Innocent I (401–417) had tried to prevent the siege of the city and was away, at Ravenna trying to negotiate a truce, at the time Rome fell. While Pope Leo I the Great (440–461) was able to prevent the conquest of Rome by Attila the Hun, he could not stop the advance of the Vandals in 455 under their gifted king, Geiseric. Leo did manage to avert serious violence, but the city endured a second pillage in fifty years. More papal intervention occurred in 546 when the Goths came to the gates of Rome. Representing Pope Vigilius, his legate Pelagius (the next pope) managed to stop a massacre by King Totila; Totila even sent Pelagius to Constantinople as his ambassador to try to negotiate peace. In 846, Saracens sailed up the Tiber and not only attacked Rome but sacked St. Peter's Basilica, a calamity for the popes and the inspiration for the erection of the Leonine City under Pope Leo IV. One of the worst attacks came in 1527 when Pope Clement VII was beset by an imperial army sent into Italy by Emperor Charles V. In February 1798, French General Louis Berthier took the city, proclaimed the Roman Republic, and deposed Pius VI, who was sent into exile. The French would again occupy Rome in 1808, this time making off with the treasure of the popes, most of which was returned after the fall of Napoleon in 1814. In 1870, Rome fell before the unifying troops of King Victor Emmanuel, who made the Eternal City the capitol of a united Italy. Finally, in 1943, after the fall of Mussolini, German forces took over, placing enormous pressure on Pope Pius XII, who was aware that Adolf Hitler had been considering plans to evacuate the pope to Lichtenstein or even Germany.

❀ **SABINIAN** Pope from 604 to 606, a Tuscan by birth, he was appointed a deacon and given considerable trust by Pope St. Gregory I the Great (590–604), being sent to Constantinople in 593 as the papal representative. While there Sabinian disappointed his master in his failure to resist the Byzantine emperor Maurice (r. 582–602) in the persistent and obnoxious use by John IV, the Patriarch of Constantinople, of the title "Ecumenical Patriarch," a claim of great displeasure to the pope. Brought back to Rome in 595, he had sufficiently recovered his standing so that in March 604 he was elected to succeed Gregory. Owing to delays in receiving imperial approval (which was then needed), he was not consecrated until September 13. Aside from ongoing difficulties with the Lombards, his brief reign was memorable for several events. First, he ended the long-standing policy of his predecessor of advancing monks within the papal government, using regular clergy instead. Second, famine continued to grip the region, but he stopped Gregory's habit of giving away grain to alleviate starvation. Instead, he sold it, an act that sparked the ire of the Romans. After his death on February 22, 606, a mob blocked his funeral procession; the dead pope had to be taken around the city walls to reach Sabinian's final resting place within St. Peter's. Successor: Boniface III.

❀ **SAINT ANNE OF THE PALAFRENIERI, CHURCH OF** The small church located in the Saint Anne district of the Vatican City State, just inside the Porta Sant'Anna, which serves as the parish church for the residents of the papal city. The church was built in 1573 by command of Pope Gregory XIII for the *palafrenieri,* the papal grooms. Its architect was Giacomo da Vignola, the successor to Michelangelo as chief architect of St. Peter's Basilica. It is normally not visited by tourists. In a technical sense, the pope himself is the pastor, although the church is administered by the Augustinian Fathers. Any person who dies as a citizen of the Vatican has the right to be buried in the crypt beneath the floor of the church.

St. Peter's Basilica, the largest church in the world; the Apostolic Apartments are to the left.
(CATHOLIC NEWS SERVICE.)

✿ **SAINT PETER, BASILICA OF**   The largest, most famous, and most recognized church in the world. While not the cathedral church of Rome (that would be St. John Lateran), St. Peter's is the basilica most used by the pope for his liturgical celebrations and other important events. It is situated on the Vatican Hill, within the Vatican City State. The present basilica dates to the sixteenth century and is not the first one built; that first basilica was begun under Emperor Constantine the Great from around 320 to 350 on the Vatican Hill over the very site where St. Peter was buried following his crucifixion nearby in 64. The church was approximately 203 feet long and 184 feet wide, with five great doors. There was no fixed altar, but the focus of the building was the tomb beneath the baldacchino in the apse, which marks the grave of the Prince of the Apostles. Mosaics initially decorated the columns and arches; frescoes were added later.

The basilica survived earthquakes and pillage during the Middle Ages, but by the fifteenth century the foremost church in Christendom and one of the greatest pilgrimage shrines was in dire need of renovation. Its walls were out of plumb, its columns near collapse, and its decorations showing age. When it became apparent that more than simple repairs were required, Pope Nicholas V (1447–1455) took the decisive step of ordering an entirely new St. Peter's to be constructed. The initial architect was Bernardo Rosselino, but the initial work ceased upon Nicholas's death. It was the famed Pope Julius II (1503–1513) who began the new basilica in earnest, requesting proposed plans from the architects Donato Bramante and Giuliano de Sangallo; he chose the ideas of Bramante and, on April 18, 1506, Julius laid the cornerstone. It would require over a century to complete and, in all, there were 13 different architects, laboring over the course of 20 pontificates; the architects included some of the foremost Renaissance masters in Italy: Sangallo, Michelangelo, Pirro Ligorio, Giorgio Vasari, Giacomo Barrozzi, and Giacomo della Porta; construction was completed by Giovanni Fontana and Carlo Maderno under Paul V (1605–1621). During his reign, the last vestiges of the Constantinian basilica were demolished, although the tombs and notable monuments were carefully preserved. Paul also modified Michelangelo's long-standing design (based on Bramante's plans) of a Greek cross to form a longer Latin cross. This meant extending the nave, requiring over seven hundred workmen. Maderno also built the facade, which still stands, dominating the square and erected with two extra bays on each side to accommodate bell towers. The addition had the unfortunate effect of blotting out the view of the mighty dome from the square itself and was long the source of complaint and criticism for its pillars and the none too humble declaration carved upon it by command of Pope Paul V: IN HONOREM PRINCIPIS APOST. PAVLVS BORGHESIVS ROMANVS PONT. MAX. AN. MDCXII PONT. VII (In Honor of the Prince of the Apostles, Paul V Borghese, Roman, Supreme Pontiff, in the Year 1612, the Seventh of his Pontificate). Pope Urban VIII (1623–1644) consecrated the church at long last on November 18, 1626. Urban also commissioned the great architect Bernini to create a fitting baldacchino over the high altar and paid for the two bell towers, but work had to stop abruptly and Bernini lost much face when the roof began to sink from the weight. Bernini recovered and was later responsible for the magnificent piazza, dedicated in 1666 under Pope Alexander VII (1655–1667).

The present church is maintained by the ceaseless vigilance of the Holy See, with actual care under the authority of the Reverend Fabric of St. Peter's, with work carried out by the *Sampietrini*. Visited by millions each year and the site of the greatest celebrations of the Church calendar, the basilica boasts such unrivaled masterpieces as the *Pietà* and the *Cathedra Petri,* as well as a host of chapels, altars, statues, and decorations. But perhaps its greatest symbol of faith is the relatively small bronze of St. Peter located in the nave. Said to have

A Visit to St. Peter's

When we reached the door, and stood fairly within the church, it was impossible to comprehend that it was a *very* large building. I had to cipher a comprehension of it. I had to ransack my memory for some more similes. St. Peter's is bulky. Its height and size would represent two of the Washington capitol set one on top of the other—if the capitol were wider; or two blocks or two blocks and a half of ordinary buildings were set one on top of the other. St. Peter's was that large, but it could and would not look so. The trouble was that everything in it and about it was on such a scale of uniform vastness that there were no contrasts to judge by—none but the people, and I had not noticed them. They were insects. The statues of children holding basins of holy water were immense, according to the tables of figures, but so was every thing else around them. . . . Away down toward the far end of the church (I thought it was really clear at the far end, but discovered afterward that it was in the center, under the dome,) stood the thing they call the baldacchino—a great bronze pyramidal framework like that which upholds a mosquito bar. It only looked like a considerably magnified bedstead—nothing more. Yet I knew it was a good deal more than half as high as Niagara Falls. It was overshadowed by a dome so mighty that its own height was snubbed.

—Mark Twain,
The Innocents Abroad (1869)

St. Peter's Square, designed by Bernini, in a photograph from the early twentieth century; the central streets leading from the square to the Tiber would be demolished by Mussolini to make way for the Via della Conciliazione.

been carved by the thirteenth-century artist Arnolfo di Cambio, its right foot has been worn smooth from the devout kisses of pilgrims. (See box, *A Visit to St. Peter's,* page 311.)

❀ **SAINT PETER'S SQUARE**   The Piazza San Pietro, the large square stretching before St. Peter's Basilica, one of the most recognized landmarks in the world. St. Peter's Square in its present form was laid out by the brilliant architect Gian Lorenzo Bernini from 1656 to 1667 on behalf of Pope Alexander VII (1655–1667). The basilica had always boasted a portico or small square; the old Constantinian basilica, for example, had a forecourt called from the seventh century the Garden of Paradise. This courtyard was torn up by the construction of the new St. Peter's and, nearly a century after work had begun on the basilica, Pope Alexander commissioned a piazza worthy of the great edifice. As always, his favorite architect would not disappoint. The square is elliptical in shape, with two long colonnades, stretching like arms about to embrace; there are four rows of columns, numbering 284 in all and 63 feet high. The colonnade is topped by 140 statues of saints, along with the name and coat of arms of Pope Alexander. The square also has two beautiful fountains, and the impressive Obelisk of Caligula. When standing at the stone markers between the colonnade and the fountains the observer will notice that the columns seem perfectly aligned on that side of the square, in four perfect rows. According to Bernini's unfinished plan, the piazza was supposed to have a smaller, finishing colonnade at the entrance. This was never completed and the square retains its open front, the main route by which most tourists enter the papal city. The square is the usual site for the holding of the papal audience each week and any other special occasions. (See also *Audiences, Papal; Christmas; Conciliazione, Via della; Easter;* and *Saint Peter, Basilica of.*)

❀ **SAINTS, PAPAL**   See box, *Saints,* page 314.

❀ **SAMPIETRINI**   The collective and popular name given to the workers of St. Peter's Basilica who are responsible for its maintenance, decoration, and other repair work within the church. Their name means "the men of St. Peter's," and they have been in existence for some four hundred years, since construction of the new basilica got under way in the sixteenth century. Under the authority of the Reverend Fabric of Saint Peter's, the *Sampietrini* perform a wide variety of functions, including making repairs on the walls, floors, and areas of the church, erecting scaffolding for crowds who will attend the numerous liturgical functions of the pope, and placing decorations throughout the entire basilica complex and square during Christmas and other feasts. (See also *Tomb of Saint Peter.*)

❀ **SANCTISSIMUS DOMINIS NOSTER**   A title of address meaning "Our Most Holy Lord" in Latin that is used on formal occasions for the pope. (See also *Titles of the Pope.*)

❀ **SANCTITAS**   A form of address commonly used when speaking or writing to the pope. Meaning in Latin "Holiness," it is the Latin equivalent of the term "Your Holiness," or "His Holiness," found in English. Normally, the name Holy Father is used by members of the Vatican staff. (See also *Titles of the Pope.*)

❀ **SCHISM, GREAT**   See *Western Schism, Great.*

❀ **SECRETARIAT OF STATE**   The most important department of the Roman Curia that has extensive authority over the Curial activities and the significant work of the international relations of the Holy See. The Secretariat is under the direction of the Cardinal **Secretary of State,** ranked effectively just below the pope in the power structure of the Church, although the dean of the College of Cardinals is second in

Saints

It is hardly surprising that in the history of the papacy, many successors of St. Peter were themselves revered as saints by the Church they once governed. The early popes led the faith during eras of bloody persecution and many were martyred. Every pope, in fact, from the time of the crucifixion of Peter on the Vatican Hill until 352 has been honored as a saint. The first pontiff not ranked among the elect of heaven was the highly unlucky Liberius. The last pope—at this printing—to be canonized was St. Pius X (1903–1914) who was made a saint by Pius XII in 1954. The last pope before him to be canonized was St. Pius V (1566–1572), declared a saint by Clement XI in 1712. Among the more notable canonized saints are St. Leo I the Great (440–461), St. Gregory I the Great (590–604), St. Martin I (649–655), St. Leo III (795–816), St. Gregory VII (1073–1085), and St. Celestine V (1294). There are also some popes who are not yet saints, possessing the title of Blessed (a step on the road to canonization). They include Eugene III (1145–1153), Urban V (1362–1370), Benedict XI (1303–1304), Urban II (1088–1099), and Gregory X (1271–1276). Pope Pius IX (1846–1878) also had his cause opened in 1985 by John Paul II, thus starting him on the road to possible sainthood. (For the names of canonized pontiffs, see Appendix I.)

ecclesiastical matters. This powerful dicastery originated in the fifteenth century with the development of the offices of the Curia handling the secretarial and administrative needs of the popes. It was later joined with the department called the Congregation for Extraordinary Ecclesiastical Affairs founded in 1793 by Pope Pius VI (1775–1799) with the aim of dealing diplomatically with the states of Europe. Today, the Secretariat is divided into two sections: the Section for General Affairs and the Section for Relations with States; the former has oversight over the day-to-day operations of the Holy See and is a kind of domestic policy office, while the latter has the often difficult job of fostering diplomatic relations with states and maintaining contact with the legates of the pope posted to countries around the globe. The two sections are normally headed by a titular archbishop; the first is called the *Sostituto* to the Secretary of State and the second the Secretary for Relations with States. Both are extremely high-ranking prelates but are under the authority of the cardinal secretary and can be removed at the discretion of the pope. The secretary of state is always a cardinal and is hand-picked by the pope. The office developed in the real sense during the seventeenth century as the pope came to rely upon scrupulous and competent cardinals in place of the traditional and often greedy cardinal nephews. One of the first of the truly notable secretaries of state was Fabio Chigi, the future Pope Alexander VII (1655–1667). Over succeeding centuries, cardinal secretaries of state have included some truly brilliant statesmen, such as Ercole Consalvi (d. 1824), Giacomo Antonelli (d. 1876), Eugenio Pacelli (the future Pius XII), and Agostino Casaroli, secretary from 1979 to 1990.

❀ **SEDE VACANTE** The name given to the period during which the Holy See is vacant, between the death of a pope and the election of his successor in a conclave. Meaning "vacant see," the *sede vacante* denotes that the Church is without a Supreme Pontiff and that the affairs of state and church are being administered in a caretaker capacity by the cardinal

Rare stamps commemorating the sede vacante in 1963.

camerlengo, in conjunction with the Sacred College of Cardinals. During this time, special coins and stamps are issued; they are some of the most interesting collectors' pieces to philatelists and numismatists.

SEDIA GESTATORIA The portable throne or chair in which the pope was carried during solemn papal processions. The *sedia gestatoria* (from the Latin *sedes,* for "chair," and *gestare,* "to carry") was intended to place the pontiff in an exalted position and was one of the foremost elements in the pomp and grandeur of the papacy in the past. Surrounded by the full papal court in all of its sartorial majesty, flanked by the *flabella* (or ornate ostrich fans), and to the grand musical accompaniment of the papal choir, the pope was carried into St. Peter's Basilica; over the throne was the portable canopy, the *umbrellino,* held aloft by eight monsignori. The pope assumed a certain otherworldliness to the crowds in the basilica and even more so to the millions who would see him in newsreels or on television. By custom, dating to the sixteenth century, the newly elected pope was brought triumphantly into St. Peter's with great pomp and fanfare. Before him were burned three bundles of tow while the papal master of ceremonies proclaimed *"Sancte Pater sic transit gloria mundi"* ("Holy Father, so passes the glory of the world"). The *sedia* itself was a silk-covered armchair, attached to a *suppedaneum,* with gold rings on each side through which were passed two long rods. The rods were carried by the papal grooms, the *palafrenieri* (or *sediarii*), in red uniforms. Certainly an ostentatious means of transportation, the portable throne also had a practical purpose. When a pontiff was old or unwell, it allowed him the chance to save his limited strength for the mass or ceremonies of the day. It also gave the huge throngs in attendance the chance to see him at a great distance. Pope Paul VI (1963–1978) used the *sedia gestatoria* with less frequency than his predecessors, but found it convenient as his health declined. Pope John Paul I (1978) was quite reluctant to retain it, feeling that it was not in keeping with the pastoral image he wished to convey for the papacy, and his successor, John Paul II, dispensed with it altogether. (See also *Flabellum.*)

Pope Leo XII carried in procession on the portable throne, the sedia gestatoria; from an engraving of a painting by Vernet.

❀ **SERGIUS I** Pope from 687 to 701, a native of Palermo, Sergius was a member of a Syrian family from Antioch, although he may have been born in Syria and raised in Palermo. Ordained in Rome, he served the Roman Church throughout the reigns between Adeodatus II and Conon (672–687). When Conon died on September 21, 687, there followed the irregular elections of the two antipopes Paschal and Theodore, bringing much upheaval to the city and causing the electors to convene again and properly elect another pope. The soldiers, clergy, and government officials unanimously elected Sergius on December 15, 687. They then stormed the Lateran, which was occupied by the two other factions, and installed their new pontiff. Sergius subsequently won acceptance by the Exarch of Ravenna—the representative of the emperor in Italy—but only after paying the bribe that had been promised to him by Paschal. Once settled in as pope, Sergius was a forceful figure, standing firm in resisting the demands of Emperor Justinian II that he give his formal approbation to the decrees of the Council of Trullo (692), which had permitted clerical marriage and reemphasized the twenty-eighth canon of the Council of Chalcedon (451) giving to the Patriarch of Constantinople virtually equal status with the Bishop of Rome. Justinian decided to use force to compel the pope to his will. An imperial officer, Zacharias by name, was dispatched to Rome with orders to arrest Sergius. The Byzantine troops in Ravenna, however, chose to support the pope, storming Rome and chasing an aghast Zacharias into the Lateran, where he literally hid under Sergius's bed while the pope negotiated with the troops and the angry mobs who had come to murder the officer and save their pontiff. As it was, Zacharias returned to Constantinople to learn that Justinian had been overthrown. Sergius was devoted to restoring churches, especially St. Peter's, and was responsible for several liturgical innovations. He died on September 9, 701. Successor: John VI.

❀ **SERGIUS II** Pope from 844 to 847, whose reign was noted for the bloody sack of Rome in 846 by the Saracens. Sergius was a member of the noble class in Rome, with a distinguished career under several popes, including archpriest under Gregory IV. At Gregory's death in January 844, Sergius was already old and in poor health, but the Roman nobility chose him as a counterweight to the choice of the other Roman classes, the antipope John. The troops of the nobles then ruthlessly crushed all opposition and installed Sergius on the papal throne; John was permitted to live only at the personal appeal of the pope.

Because this election had been undertaken without seeking the approval of Emperor Lothair I, the new pope pacified the Frankish ruler by accepting a synod that investigated his legitimacy and by reaffirming imperial rights. Sergius's rule was much hindered by the odious presence of his own brother, Bishop Benedict of Albano, who came to assume a preeminent place in the papal administration, auctioning off honors and offices to raise ever more money. The papacy was thus far from efficient, its severe shortcomings glaringly exposed in August 846 when 75 ships landed at the mouth of the Tiber and disgorged 10,000 Saracen raiders upon a stricken Rome, pillaging St. Peter's of its treasures and relics. The Romans were convinced that the disaster was the result of the vices of the pope and his brother. Sergius died the next year on January 27, ending a less than successful reign. Successor: St. Leo IV.

❀ **SERGIUS III**   Pope from 904 to 911. A Roman, Sergius belonged to the nobility of the city, receiving appointment as a deacon under Pope Stephen V (VI) and then consecration as bishop by Pope Formosus. He subsequently participated in the Cadaver Synod, however, and when that body declared the acts of Formosus annulled, Sergius accepted demotion back to the rank of deacon; Pope Stephen VI (VII) ordained him a priest. In late 897, he was elected pope by the anti-Formosan Party following the death of Pope Theodore II, but he lost out in the ensuing struggle with the faction supporting Pope John IX and was exiled to Florence. In 904, he was elected once more, receiving consecration on January 29, and taking control of the papacy with the help of Alberic I of Spoleto. According to often unreliable contemporary chroniclers, he ordered the deposed Pope Leo V and the antipope Christopher to be strangled. This action, assuming it was at his behest, launched a depressing reign. He proclaimed his pontificate to have begun not in 904 but 897, thereby making John IX, Benedict IV, and Leo V illegitimate and rendering all ordinations under them annulled. When opposed in this action, he relied upon the ambitious nobleman Theophylact and his infamous wife, Theodora, to enforce his will. His pontificate thus marks the ascendancy of the house of Tusculani, which dominated the papacy in the succeeding years, plunging the Holy See into one of its darkest eras. According to legend, Sergius fathered a child, the future John XI, by Marozia, the fifteen-year-old daughter of Theodora. One of his few positive contributions was the restoration of the Lateran Basilica. He was also reportedly of an orthodox disposition in matters of theology; St. Robert Bellarmine observed that "he erred by very bad example, but never by false doctrine." Successor: Anastasius III.

🕭 **SERGIUS IV** Pope from 1009 to 1012, the son of a Roman cobbler, Sergius was originally named Peter (Pietro), receiving the nickname "Bucca Porci" (or "Pig's Snout") because of his apparently peculiar appearance. He served as Bishop of Albano from around 1004 to 1009 and was elected as successor to John XVIII on July 31, 1009. He was elected probably through the influence of the powerful patrician John II Crescentius, master of Rome and head of the Crescenti family. Little is known about his reign. He endeavored to promote sound relations with Henry II of Germany, probably in the hope of curbing the overweening authority of the Crescenti, but his plans never developed fully. He was also devoted to the poor. His death on May 12, 1012, came a mere week before the passing of John II Crescentius, a double event thought by some scholars to be more than a little suspicious. The possibility of foul play only becomes more likely, given the event that swiftly ensued: the house of Tusculani, a rival of the Crescenti, secured the election of their own candidate, Benedict VIII. Owing to his name Peter, Sergius decided to change it out of respect for the Prince of the Apostles, thereby inaugurating the custom of pontiffs adopting new names; while he was not the first to take a new name (that honor belonged to John XII), he made the practice common. Successor: Benedict VIII.

🕭 **SERVUS SERVORUM DEI** A title used by the popes, meaning "Servant of the Servants of God," that is today used on certain official documents. The name was first adopted by Pope St. Gregory I the Great (590–604) in response to the decision of the Patriarch of Constantinople to use the title Ecumenical Patriarch, implying that his authority was ecumenical (or universal), a challenge to the supremacy of the pope. Gregory hoped to stress the humility of the pope as the one who serves the very people who serve God, a calculated way of shaming the patriarch. The appellation did not come into popular usage until the ninth century, but was given formal recognition by Pope St. Gregory VII (1073–1085) and made the exclusive possession of the pope in the twelfth century.

🕭 **SEVERINUS** Pope from May 28 to August 2, 640, Severinus was from Rome, the son of Avienus, most likely a member of the city's nobility. Elected in October 638, he was faced immediately with a considerable dilemma. When petitioning for imperial ratification of his election, Severinus was informed that he would not be acknowledged until he gave acceptance to the decree of Emperor Heraclius (r. 610–641), the *Ecthesis,* which declared that Christ had only one will (as compared to the orthodox teaching that he possessed two, human and divine). Severinus declined the demand and thus spent nearly two years in negotiations, during which he suffered personal humiliations at the hands of Byzantine soldiers; the papal treasury was also ransacked and divided among the troops, the commander cunningly sending a part of it to the emperor. He was finally consecrated on May 28, 640 (the starting date of his reign), although he apparently never agreed to the *Ecthesis.* Severinus declined in health over the months of delay; his death on August 2 was hastened by the harsh treatment he received from the soldiers when they stormed the Lateran. Successor: John IV.

SFUMATA Italian for "smoke," used for the much anticipated signal that pours out of the smokestack of the Sistine Chapel announcing to the world whether a new pope has been elected; white smoke signals a new pope and gray or dark smoke denotes that the voting will continue. The sending out of smoke from the chapel is a traditional means of keeping the outside world aware of how the election is proceeding, the only communication sent by the cardinals until the election is over. In the preparations for the conclave, a special oven is brought into the chapel and attached to the chimney leading outside. Each time a session of votes is held, the ballots are brought to the oven and burned. In the past, they were burned with dry straw to make white smoke and wet straw to create a gray or black smoke. This was notoriously unreliable since the straw often did not burn properly, sending out white smoke when the cardinals meant black and black when they meant white. In 1978, a chemical

Smoke (the sfumata) billows out of the chimney on the roof of the Sistine Chapel, signaling the election of Pope John Paul I in 1978.
(CATHOLIC NEWS SERVICE.)

agent, marked appropriately *bianco* (white) or *nero* (black), was added to the ballots to ensure the right color. After the election of Albino Luciani as John Paul I in 1978, the chemical *bianco* was added to send out white smoke; the cardinal in charge, however, poured on so much that a gray smoke went up, followed at last by white smoke. The crowd's perplexity was only cleared up when the cry was given *"Habemus papam!"* ("We have a pope!"). (See also *Conclave* and *Elections, Papal.*)

❀ **SHIP OF PETER**   See *Barque of Peter.*

❀ **SHOES OF THE FISHERMAN**   The shoes worn by the pope. The traditional footwear of the pontiff was a type of velvet slipper that either had his coat of arms embroidered on the instep or was truly ornate with gold embroidery and perhaps even jewels, a cross on the instep. Customarily, a cleric entering the presence of the pope had to kneel down and kiss the crosses on the slippers, a practice found right up until the 1958 accession of Pope John XXIII, who found it absurd. The ornate slippers, however, remained in use until the accession of Pope John Paul II in 1978. Normally, the pope-elect is led away from the presence of his cardinal electors and dressed in the white robes of his new office in the nearby Chapel (or Room) of Tears. Part of the attire is the pair of slippers. Karol Cardinal Wojtyla, newly elected as pope, refused to put them on because they were too ostentatious. He reportedly greeted the cardinals as their new pontiff still wearing the battered black shoes he had worn into the conclave, a character trait not lost on many of the cardinal electors. The pope has since normally worn a kind of red or auburn leather loafer. (See also *Gammarelli's.*)

❀ **SIGNATURE, POPE'S**   The signature normally used by the pope when signing official documents. The present pope normally signs his name as *Joannes Paulus P.P. II.* The name is as it properly appears in Latin, the initials *P.P.* referring to him as *Pastor Pastorum* ("Pastor of Pastors"). For some formal documents, such as bulls, the signature reads *Joannes Paulus P.P. Servus Servorum Dei,* meaning John Paul, Pastor of Pastors, Servant of the Servants of God. He may adopt a more casual signature in personal communication with family members and longtime personal friends.

❀ **SILVERIUS, ST.**   Pope from 536 to 537, Silverius was the son of Pope Hormisdas—through a marriage prior to his entering the priesthood—and was born at Frosinone. He was serving as a subdeacon in 536 when word reached Rome that Pope Agapitus I had died in Constantinople. In the ensuing election, Silverius was chosen as his successor, receiving consecration on June 1 or 8, 536. He owed his rather unexpected elevation to the intervention of King Theodahad, the Ostrogoth ruler of Italy who was anxious to have as pope someone he could use against the Byzantines during what Theodahad anticipated was the imminent invasion of Italy. The clergy of Rome initially opposed Silverius, but they were convinced to give their acquiescence through the obvious menace of the Ostrogoths. What followed was a demonstration of Byzantine intrigue at its worst. Empress Theodora, wife of the great Byzantine Emperor Justinian I (r. 527–565) and a devoted adherent of the unorthodox movement of Monophysitism, began working for Silverius's removal since the ambitious Roman deacon Vigilius, representative of the Holy See in Constantinople, had been promised the papacy in return for the restoration of the deposed Monophysite patriarch Anthimus. Silverius thus fell under pressure to step down, especially after the capture of Rome by the Byzantine general Belisarius. After standing firm against the wishes of the empress, the pope was seized and accused of conspiring with the Goths; the evidence for this was a series of forged letters. Found guilty, he was formally deposed on March 11, 537, stripped to the rank of monk, and sent into exile to the small town of Patara on the coast of Anatolia. The local bishop, however, protested the pope's innocence, and Emperor Justinian ordered that he be permitted to return home to receive a fair trial. Anxious that this should not happen, Vigilius, now the reigning pontiff, connived to intercept Silverius, sending him to Palmaria, near Naples. Under threat of torture, Silverius was finally convinced to step down, doing so on November 11, 537. He died on December 2, 537, the victim of starvation and cruelties by his captors, who were anxious, Vigilius included, for his demise. Once dead, he was given a simple grave on the island. Successor: Vigilius.

❈ **SIMPLICIUS, ST.**   Pope from 468 to 483, his reign was overshadowed by the final demise of the Roman Empire in the West in 476. A native of Tivoli, he was elected to succeed St. Hilarus on March 3, 468. Despite its length, his pontificate is not that well known, in large measure because of the major events that were gripping the Roman Empire. He devoted much of his early years to resisting the spread of the heretical doctrine of Monophysitism. The problem of the heresy grew especially acute after the usurper Basiliscus became emperor in the Eastern Empire in 475. Basiliscus was deposed the following year, but the new emperor issued the *Henotikon,* a document intended to reconcile the Monophysites to the Christian faith but which Simplicius resisted because it lacked the essential affirmation of the belief that Christ possessed two natures, human and divine. Owing to the impasse, there began the Acacian Schism, which would divide the faith in East and West until 519, the first of many breaches over the next centuries. In 476, the pope was faced with the removal of the last emperor in the West, Romulus Augustulus by the German (Heruli) chieftain Odoacer, who established himself as the ruler of the Italian peninsula. The deposition signaled a period of Germanic domination in Italy and an influence upon the papacy, especially under Odoacer's successors, the Ostrogoths. Successor: St. Felix III.

❀ **SIRICIUS, ST.**   Pope from 384 to 399. The son of Tiburtius, he was born in Rome, serving as a lector and a deacon under Popes Liberius (352–366) and Damasus (366–384). His election as successor to Damasus in December 384 was challenged by the antipope Ursinus, but Siricius was chosen by unanimous vote and duly accepted as Bishop of Rome. Siricius would be overshadowed in history by the towering presence of such contemporaries as St. Jerome and especially St. Ambrose of Milan, but he was responsible for genuinely significant achievements in securing for the Holy See jurisdictional authority over the entire Church. He sent letters across the Church making clear his claim of primacy and universal authority of his see. His letter to Himerius, bishop of Tarragona, in February 385, is considered the first of the papal decretals. (See *Decretals.*) He also sent papal decrees to the bishops of Africa. In Rome, he convened two synods, in 386 and 392; at the former synod, he decreed that no bishop should be consecrated without the permission of the Holy See, a crucial right for the popes if they hoped to exercise their power over the future Church. Siricius also intervened in the East, settling a schism that had divided the faithful in Antioch, the so-called Melitian Schism. He dedicated the Basilica of St. Paul's Outside-the-Walls in 390; his dedication is recorded on a column dating to the fourth century outside the basilica. Successor: St. Anastasius I.

❀ **SISINNIUS**   Pope for several weeks in early 708, Sisinnius was a Syrian by birth, receiving election as successor to John VII perhaps in October 707, although he was not consecrated until January 15, 708. His consecration was delayed because of the reluctance of the exarch (the imperial representative) to give his assent, as was then customary. Sisinnius survived a mere few weeks as pope, dying on February 4; he was already so old and ill at the time of his election that he could not even raise his arms to feed himself. His only known act was to consecrate a bishop for Corsica. Successor: Constantine.

❀ **SISTINE CHAPEL** The main chapel of the papal palace of the Vatican that was first constructed under Pope Sixtus IV (1471–1484) and from whom its name is derived. Also called the Pope's Chapel (although he also has a private one in his apartments), the Sistine Chapel is one of the most famous and eagerly visited locations in all of Rome because of the presence of the world-renowned frescoes on its walls and especially its ceiling, namely the work of Michelangelo.

The chapel itself was begun in 1475 and was built by Giovanni dei Dolci, on the plans of Baccio Pontelli. Designed as a kind of fortress chapel—it was intended to serve as part of a plan of fortification for the Vatican Palace—the Capella Sistina replaced the earlier Palatine Chapel of Nicholas III, which was falling into ruin.

The great claim to fame for the chapel is the presence of the nearly incomparable art upon its walls, the result of three distinct stages of papal patronage. Sixtus IV used his considerable resources to attract some of the finest artists of the day to decorate the walls. These frescoes, painted from 1481 to 1483, are, unfortunately, often ignored by visitors,

Pope John Paul II celebrates Mass in the restored Sistine Chapel in April 1994; behind him is Michelangelo's Last Judgment. (AP/WIDE WORLD PHOTOS.)

who immediately cast their eyes heavenward to drink in the work of Michelangelo on the ceiling. The wall frescoes were painted by such masters as Perugino (said to have been in charge of the ever competing artists), Domenico and Benedetto Ghirlandaio, Cosimo Roselli, Luca Signorelli, and even Botticelli. Left undecorated by them was the ceiling,

The Last Judgment

The renowned great altar fresco of the *Last Judgment* in the Sistine Chapel is considered the crowning glory of Michelangelo's mature years. The fresco, depicting in unrelenting terms the Last Judgment, was commissioned by Pope Paul III (1534–1549) and was completed by the artist in 1541, nearly thirty years after finishing the famed ceiling in the same chapel. In order to accomplish the labor, Michelangelo found it necessary to destroy some frescoes already on the wall and to remove two inconveniently placed windows. In their place was installed a slightly sloping wall, to prevent excessive dust settling on the painting. Intended by the pope to serve as a powerful reminder to all Catholics about the faith, the fresco was devastatingly successful, since Michelangelo used stark, at times shocking imagery to present the Second Coming of Christ. The damned are especially horrifying, because Michelangelo depicted the doomed souls with unremitting intensity. Present in the fresco are Charon, the boatman of Hades; and Minos, the judge of the underworld—both from Dante's *Inferno.* As a cruel joke, Michelangelo used the visage of Cardinal Biagio da Cesena for Minos, complete with the ears of an ass, in punishment for the court official's complaint about the nudity in the fresco. The painter also placed his own face in the picture, in the skin held by the martyr St. Bartholomew. It was said that when Pope Paul III saw the completed wall, he fell to his knees and plaintively begged the rather unsympathetic Christ before him to forgive him his transgressions. The fresco stands not only as one of Michelangelo's greatest achievements but as a testament to his own deep and tormented spirituality. The fresco is clearly visible to all the members of the conclave electing a new pope in the Sistine Chapel, a silent but dynamic reminder to the new pontiff of the power of faith and the ultimate destiny of all. The fresco should not be confused— as though that were possible—with the eleventh- or twelfth-century *Last Judgment* found in the Pinacoteca, the Vatican's museum of paintings.

which was painted blue with stars. Pope Julius II (1503–1513), the ever ambitious nephew of Sixtus IV, hoped to leave his own mark on the chapel and so commissioned Michelangelo to paint the ceiling in what is now a legendary undertaking. The commission took the years 1508 to 1512 to complete and stands as one of the towering achievements of the Italian Renaissance. Michelangelo also painted the third major attraction of the chapel, the fresco of the *Last Judgment* behind the altar, which took from 1533 to 1541. (See box, *The Last Judgment,* page 325.)

The Sistine Chapel was recently the site of an extremely ambitious and significant restoration project that was funded by Japanese Nippon Television (NHK), in close cooperation with the Vatican Museums and the Vatican restoration laboratories, to remove the literally centuries of smoke, dirt, and accumulated varnish. The work of the restorers, art experts, and scientists was finally completed in 1994 and was the source of some controversy among art historians, a few of whom felt that the bright, vibrant colors of the frescoes were not at all what Michelangelo intended. Regardless, the restoration unveiled a startlingly new Sistine ceiling and *Last Judgment,* in sharp contrast to the somber work that had been known for many years. The chapel also has one other practical purpose: it is the site of the conclave where the cardinals gather to elect a new pope. (See also *Sixtus IV.*)

SISTINE CHOIR The official choir of the pope, performing at the celebrations presided over by the Supreme Pontiff. Known in full as Il Collegio dei Capellani Cantori della Capella Pontificia, the Sistine Choir is heard by audiences around the world whenever the pope says mass or attends some important gathering at which music plays a part. The Sistine Choir was started by Pope Sixtus IV (1471–1484) to serve as the source of music for his recently built Sistine Chapel. The longstanding *capella pontifica* (pontifical choir) was thus replaced by the *capella sistina.* His nephew, Julius II (1503–1513), added a new preparatory choir, the *capella Julia.* The Sistine Choir claimed as its most illustrious director, the *magister capella,* the famed composer Palestrina (d. 1594).

SIXTUS I, ST. Pope from 115 to 125, although there is some question as to the dates of his reign. Known also in earlier sources as Xystus, he was a Roman according to the *Liber Pontificalis.* Elected to succeed St. Alexander I, he is counted as the seventh pope and the sixth successor to St. Peter. According to custom, he was responsible for a number of liturgical regulations, such as allowing only the minister to touch the sacred vessels used during the mass, an innovation that established the priest as a distinctly separate class within the Church. He also is credited with establishing the movable date for Easter. Successor: St. Telesphorus.

❀ **SIXTUS II, ST.**   Pope from 257 to 258, called also Xystus II; according to the *Liber Pontificalis,* he was a Greek. Chosen to succeed St. Stephen I, he is the first pontiff to bear the same name as a predecessor (hence Sixtus II) and was called by contemporaries Sixtus Junior. Contemporaries also described him as conciliatory and peace-loving, probably because of the efforts he undertook to restore relations between Rome and the churches of Africa and Asia (Anatolia) after they had been broken by the disagreement over the rebaptism of heretics; in Rome it was decreed that heretics should not be rebaptized once they had come to their senses, because the sacrament was eternal. His reign was cut short by the sudden and extremely savage persecution launched by Emperor Valerian in 257. Sixtus avoided arrest for a while, but so conspicuous a personage as Bishop of Rome could little avoid the decree of 258, which called for the deaths of all bishops and deacons should they be caught violating a law that forbade the gathering of Christians in cemeteries. On August 6, 258, Sixtus was beheaded while still sitting in his episcopal chair delivering a sermon to his flock in the cemetery of Praetextatus on the famed Appian Way. His bloodstained chair was placed behind his tomb in the cemetery of Callistus, the traditional burial place of early popes. Sixtus is honored in a fifteenth-century fresco painted by Fra Angelico located in the Chapel of St. Nicholas in the Vatican. Successor: St. Dionysius.

❀ **SIXTUS III, ST.**   Pope from 432 to 440. Known also as Xystus III, he came from Rome and enjoyed a correspondence with St. Augustine. He was elected to succeed Celestine I by a unanimous vote, his reign beginning on July 31, 432. Much of his pontificate was taken up with the theological controversies of the time. He confirmed the doctrinal decrees of the Council of Ephesus (431) condemning Nestorianism, the heresy that had denied both a divine and human nature in Christ. Sixtus also opposed the heresy of Pelagianism, which had likewise been condemned at Ephesus. In defending papal rights, he stood firm in insisting upon the religious authority of Rome over Illyricum, which was politically dependent upon Constantinople and was eyed by the Patriarchs of Constantinople as a place of possible expansion for the Eastern Church. In Rome, Sixtus gave magnificent expression to the triumph of orthodox doctrine, in particular the decree much opposed by the Nestorians by which Mary was declared the Mother of God, by rebuilding the old Liberian Basilica and renaming it the Basilica Santa Maria Maggiore (St. Mary Major). Sixtus tweaked the Nestorians by decorating it within with scenes from the life of the Blessed Virgin Mary. Successor: St. Leo I the Great.

 SIXTUS IV Pope from 1471 to 1484, best known for building the famed Sistine Chapel. Francesco della Rovere was born near Savona, Italy, in 1414 to poor parents and entered the Franciscan order at the age of nine, later studying at the universities of Pavia and Bologna and teaching in Bologna, Pavia, Padua, and Florence. Renowned for his preaching and his theological expertise, he was appointed provincial for the order in Italy and then Minister General in 1464. Made a cardinal in 1467 by Pope Paul II, he was conspicuous over the next several years in devoting himself to a life of intense prayer and theological study. Partly on the basis of this reputation and through the influence of the Duke of Milan, he was elected to succeed Paul on August 9, 1471. Once elected as Pope Sixtus, he underwent a truly remarkable transformation from the retiring theologian and Franciscan friar to one of the fifteenth century's most worldly and political pontiffs, although he was most likely personally free of immoral conduct. A dedicated nepotist, he relied heavily upon his nephews, the most notable being Giuliano della Rovere, the future Pope Julius II (1503–1513), whom he appointed cardinals. Embarking upon a lavish and grand life of banquets and entertainments, he also declared himself a patron of the arts, bringing to his court artists, architects, and humanists. When he built the Sistine Chapel, for example, he commissioned leading Renaissance painters to decorate it; he also built churches and bridges around Rome, improved roads and widened streets, and laid the foundations for the Vatican Library. Far more troubling were his foreign ventures and involvement in Italian politics. The worst incident was the Pazzi Conspiracy in Florence where, with the connivance of the pope, a conspiracy was formed to assassinate Lorenzo de'Medici and his brother. The attempt killed only Giuliano de'Medici, and in the bloody purge that followed Sixtus was quite embarrassed by the execution of his nephew, Rafael Cardinal Riario, and the revealing of his own part in the affair. A war erupted with

Florence in which the papal troops fared badly. To make matters worse, Sixtus was led into other conflicts by his nephews, desultory but costly fights with Naples and Venice. Finally, the Italian states compelled the pope to sue for peace in 1484, a humiliating defeat for the ambitions of his family and the pontiff himself. In other matters, he tried with little result to organize a crusade against the Ottoman Turks and gave his permission for the Spanish Inquisition to be launched, appointing as Grand Inquisitor the infamous Tomas de Torquemada; the Inquisition would become a dreaded aspect of the faith in Spain over the next centuries. Sixtus also began granting plenary indulgences in return for money to pay for his building projects, an innovation that would contribute to the rise of the Protestant Reformation and the decline in papal esteem across Christendom. His relatives were so disliked because of their greed and ruthlessness that upon his death on August 12, 1484, their mansions were looted and they were ceremoniously booted out of power. It would not be forever. Successor: Innocent VIII.

SIXTUS V   Pope from 1585 to 1590, Felice Peretti was born in 1521 at Grottammare, Italy, the son of a gardener. While a lad, he supposedly labored as a swineherd before entering the Franciscans. Ordained in 1547 at Siena, he became an eminent preacher, going to Rome and earning the patronage of several powerful cardinals and two saints, Ignatius Loyola and Philip Neri. In 1557, he was appointed head of the Inquisition in Venice, where his zeal in extirpating heretics was so discomforting to the Venetians that they had him recalled in 1560. Named a consultor of the Holy Office and a professor of the University of Rome, he became procurator general of the Franciscans in 1566 and cardinal in 1570. Bishop of Fermo from 1571 to 1577, he retired from public life owing to a personal dislike for Pope Gregory XIII (1572–1585). He whiled away the time editing the works of St. Ambrose and supervising the building of a villa on the Esquiline Hill in Rome. In the conclave that followed the death of Gregory, Peretti was ranked as a candidate and was duly elected on April 24, 1585.

While pontiff for a mere five years, Sixtus was incessantly active; he was dedicated to restoring the Papal States and embarked upon a massive building program in Rome. Sixtus was committed as well to the reform of the Church and its administration. To bring peace to the States of the Church, he waged a pitiless war against the brigands infesting the cities and countryside of central Italy, earning the nickname of the "Iron Pope." In a series of blood-curdling campaigns, Sixtus put to death 7,000 brigands and confessed to the French ambassador that he regretted not being able to execute another 20,000. Once he had purged the marauders, the pope set about the task of repairing papal finances, selling government offices (not, he noted, ecclesiastical ones), and thereby raising large amounts of money. New taxes were not popular with his subjects in the Papal States, but he pointed out that they were free of pillage. He was determined to beautify Rome: streets were widened, new order was brought to the city, and Romans stared in shock at the colossal scale of his building. The dome of St. Peter's Basilica was finally finished, as was the Quirinal Palace; he also rebuilt the Lateran Palace, added a new papal palace in the Vatican, and constructed a new home for the Vatican Library. Sixtus also placed an immense obelisk in front of St. Peter's. So popular was this touch that Sixtus placed several more throughout the city.

In matters of the Church, Sixtus was bold and innovative. He commanded that there should be no more than seventy cardinals in the Sacred College at one time, administrative matters were henceforth to be taken up by a consistory of cardinals in Rome, and, most significantly, the pontiff completely reorganized the Curia into a series of fifteen permanent congregations headed by cardinals to oversee the government of the Church. His system is still in existence today. He also supported the launching of the Spanish Armada against England in 1588, although he adroitly predicted the fleet would meet with disaster. Aside from his frightful massacre of the criminals in the States, the only significant blemish on his reign was the elevation of a fifteen-year-old nephew to the cardinalate. Sixtus died in the Quirinal Palace on August 27, 1590. Successor: Urban VII.

✸ **SOTER, ST.** Pope from around 166 to around 175, he came from Campania, Italy, if the *Liber Pontificalis* can be believed, receiving election to succeed St. Anicetus. According to custom, he was especially generous to those Christians condemned to labor in the mines of Sardinia (where one eye was usually burned out and replaced by silver to serve as a perpetual identification mark) because of their deep faith. He also was said by Eusebius of Caesarea to have sent a charming letter and some gifts to the Christians of Corinth, the reply to which from the local bishop, Dionysius of Corinth, was preserved in part in Eusebius's *Ecclesiastical History.* While traditionally honored as a martyr, there is no verification of his actual martyrdom. Successor: St. Eleutherius.

✸ **SOVEREIGN OF THE STATE OF VATICAN CITY** One of the titles borne by the Holy Father. It is a statement of the absolute authority wielded by the pope over the Vatican City State as established by the Lateran Accords signed in 1929 between Benito Mussolini and Pope Pius XI, which formally established the temporal holdings of the papacy. The title also denotes the fact that the pope has control over all facets of government within the state, including executive, legislative, and judicial powers. (See also *Vatican City, State of.*)

🕸 **STAMPS, VATICAN**   The official postage stamps of the Vatican City State. While best known as collectors' items and first issued in 1852, Vatican stamps have first and foremost a practical purpose, being used on the mail departing the papal city. They are used by all elements of the papal government, but are especially prized by tourists who enjoy sending postcards to friends and family from the Vatican with the official postage of that tiny country. Vatican stamps are considered legally valid only when used within the Vatican State; the Italian government does not recognize them as valid, nor does the Vatican accept Italian postage for mailing anything from out of the papal state. The stamps are actually printed by the Italian state printing office for the Holy See, an arrangement in place since 1929 and the

An assortment of stamps issued by the Holy See.

Lateran Treaty and in Switzerland. The Vatican Post Office issues regular postage, supplemented quite often by a wide variety of commemorative items, from Holy Years to the anniversaries of saints and notable events, to the inevitable death and election of new popes. Airmail stamps were first issued in 1937. (See also *Post Office, Vatican.*)

🕸 **STATES OF THE CHURCH**   See *Papal States.*

🕸 **STEPHEN I, ST.**   Pope from 254 to 257, he is best known for his conflict with the famed St. Cyprian of Carthage and for being the first pontiff to make a formal claim for the primacy of the Holy See. A native of Rome, he was the son of Jovius and was an archdeacon of Rome at the time of the martyrdom of St. Lucius on March 5, 254. At the moment of Lucius's death, Stephen was entrusted with the care of the Church, receiving election as Bishop of Rome on May 12. While his reign fortuitously came between the persecutions of the emperors Trajanus Decius and Valerian, it was nevertheless much troubled. The cause was the controversy with St. Cyprian over several doctrinal matters, including the validity of the sacrament of baptism as administered by a heretic. The disagreements with Cyprian, especially over the baptism issue, grew more severe over time and might have led to a breach in the Church had Stephen not died on August 2, 257. While venerated as a martyr, there are no facts to support the tradition. Successor: St. Sixtus II.

❀ **STEPHEN (II)** A priest from Rome who received election as successor to Pope St. Zachary several days after his death on March 15, 752. Stephen was then properly installed in the Lateran Palace but suffered a stroke after three days and died the following day. This created an awkward situation because he had not been formally consecrated before his death and, according to the canon law of the time, only popes properly consecrated were considered legitimate, the dates of their pontificate beginning at that moment rather than at their election, as became custom in the sixteenth century. As a result, Stephen was not listed in the official lists of popes, nor was he accepted as such by writers of the Middle Ages. In the 16th century, however, as per the new custom, he suddenly became legitimate and was recognized as "Stephen II" by the Church until 1961. In that year, his name was dropped from the official list of popes as presented in the *Annuario Pontificio*. Instead, his successors named Stephen were given a dual numbering system so that the otherwise Stephen III is now Stephen II (III), the indignity of parentheses outweighing the question of legitimacy. Appropriately, the pope who followed Stephen (II) was Stephen II (III).

❀ **STEPHEN II (III)** Pope from 752 to 757 who secured the founding of the Papal States, the temporal possessions of the Holy See. A native of Rome, Stephen received appointment as a deacon under Pope Zacharias. His own unanimous election as pope on March 26, 752, came about after the extremely premature death of Stephen (II) after a mere three days. From the start, Stephen was faced with the omnipresent danger of the Lombards. His pleas, like those of his predecessors, went unanswered by the Byzantine emperors, and so the pope in desperation turned to a new potential ally, the Franks. Stephen traveled across the Alps in 754 and met with Pepin to plead with him to come to Italy and save the papacy from the barbarians. Pepin agreed—his decision assisted by the favors bestowed upon him by the pope, including the title Patrician of the Romans—marched into the peninsula and defeated the Lombards in battle. He was back two years later, but this time he seized extensive territories, including Ravenna, which had been captured from the Byzantines by the Lombards. Instead of restoring them to the Greeks, however, Pepin handed them to Stephen in a gift called the Donation of Pepin. On the basis of this gift, the papacy came into possession of temporal holdings, the Papal States. Stephen spent the rest of his reign establishing a system of government for his new properties. He was followed as Vicar of Christ by his brother. Successor: Paul I.

❀ **STEPHEN III (IV)**   Pope from 768 to 772, a Sicilian, he grew up in Rome and served in the papal government prior to his election as successor to St. Paul I. His reign, starting from August 7, 768, ended the short period of anarchy in which two antipopes, Constantine and Philip, followed each other. He owed his elevation to the powerful papal notary Christopher whose authority was shown by the wholesale cruelties inflicted by his followers upon the one-time adherents of the antipopes. Stephen was powerless to stop them, but he did convene a synod in the Lateran at which Constantine's acts were burned, his ordinations declared invalid, and the now blinded claimant sentenced to perpetual imprisonment. At the synod, the bishops also decreed that lay people should henceforth not participate in papal elections nor should a layperson be eligible for election. His reign was dominated by intrigue as the long-standing enemies of the papacy, the Lombards, were turned into allies through the cunning of their king, Desiderius. He convinced Stephen to abandon his relationship with Charlemagne and the Franks and to surrender both Christopher and his son Sergius into the hands of their enemies, the Lombards and the ambitious papal chamberlain Paul Afiarta. The pro-Frankish party of Rome was then massacred, Christopher and Sergius having their eyes gouged out before being cruelly murdered. Stephen realized too late that he had been deceived by the promises of the king and Afiarta, finding himself a prisoner who had replaced one master for another. Just how ill-advised his moves were became manifest when Charlemagne renounced his marriage to the daughter of Desiderius in 771 and thus made inevitable a war with the Lombards. Stephen did not live to see it, dying on January 24, 772. Successor: Adrian I.

❀ **STEPHEN IV (V)**   Pope from 816 to 817, a son of a noble Roman named Marinus, Stephen grew up in the Lateran and was ordained a deacon by Pope Leo III. In June 816, he was elected to succeed Leo, receiving consecration on June 22. The main achievement of his short reign was the crowning of Emperor Louis the Pious in October 816 at Reims. The coronation helped certify the tradition of papal consecration of the emperors, a rite that provided the emperors with the claim of succession to the Roman Empire of old and the popes with the right to invest the emperors and to request their military assistance when necessary. Successor: St. Paschal I.

❁ **STEPHEN V (VI)**   Pope from 885 to 891. A native of Rome and a member of a noble family, he was educated by a relative named Zachary, who also happened to be a bishop and the highly respected chief librarian for the Holy See. Appointed a cardinal by Marinus I, Stephen was so known for his personal sanctity that he won unanimous election in September 885 as successor to St. Adrian III. Despite being consecrated without the then customary imperial confirmation, Stephen did not suffer any displeasure on the part of Emperor Charles III the Fat because the ruler had far greater troubles and was, in fact, deposed in 887 by Arnulf, king of the East Franks. This political instability within the Carolingian Empire could not have come at a worse time, for Stephen was beset by a host of crises, including famine and the menace of the Saracens. Starvation was relieved through the use of his own family's money. To find a new political patron in the wake of the disintegration of the empire, Stephen turned to Guy III of Spoleto, the ambitious nobleman who would bring such pain to the Church over the next years. Stephen also made what later proved a most unfortunate decision in forbidding the use of the Slavic liturgy among the Christian converts in Moravia. His decision hastened the movement of the Slavs into the fold of the Eastern Church and the loss of the entire region by the Latins; this had considerable consequences for the conversion of Russia by the missionaries of the Eastern Church. Successor: Formosus.

❁ **STEPHEN VI (VII)**   Pope from 896 to 897, best known for his infamous summoning of the Cadaver Synod. A native of Rome and the son of a priest (or presbyter) named John, Stephen received appointment, possibly against his will, as Bishop of Anagni by Pope Formosus. He received election as successor to Boniface VI in May 896, owing his elevation to the political patronage of the House of Spoleto, a formidable party in Roman affairs. Its head, Guy of Spoleto, had been crowned Holy Roman Emperor by Stephen V (VI) in 891, and Guy's son, Lambert of Spoleto, was crowned co-emperor by Pope Formosus. The deceased Formosus, however, had earned the eternal enmity of the Spoletans by his coronation of Arnulf as Holy Roman Emperor in a challenge to the supremacy of the Spoleto family in Italy. Thus, when the pro-Spoletan Stephen was elected, he permitted Rome to undergo a brutal period of retribution against the adherents of the dead pope. Lambert and his mother Agiltrude were not merely content to besmirch the memory of the pope and to wipe out his followers. Stephen was compelled to call the Cadaver Synod in 897 in which the decaying corpse of Formosus was propped up in a chair and tried on assorted charges. (See *Cadaver Synod* for other details.) Following the mutilation of Formosus's corpse and the completion of the trial, an earthquake struck the city—as sure a sign of divine displeasure as the Romans could receive. Already sickened by the wave of murders and the sacrilege committed upon a pope, the Romans rose up in revolt and demanded that Stephen be deposed. The Spoletans removed him, threw him in a prison, and had him strangled in August 897. Successor: Romanus.

❀ **STEPHEN VII (VIII)**   Pope from 928 to 931. A native of Rome, he was the son of Teudemund and was the cardinal priest of St. Anastasia at the time of his election in December 928 to succeed Leo VI. He owed his elevation entirely to the powerful matron head of the house of Theophylact, Marozia, who was de facto ruler of Rome. Stephen's reign thus was spent under her domination and he was considered by the Romans to be a mere interregnum pope holding the see until Marozia's young son, the future John XI, was old enough for his election to be considered plausible. Stephen's death in 931 brought an end to a thoroughly nondescript reign, distinguished only by certain privileges bestowed upon monasteries in Italy and France. Successor: John XI.

❀ **STEPHEN VIII (IX)**   Pope from 939 to 942, he was born in Rome, although little of his early life is known with certainty, and tradition incorrectly declared him of German descent. At the time of his elevation to the papacy, as successor to Leo VII on July 14, 939 (after a one-day interregnum), he was serving as cardinal priest of SS. Silvestro and Martino and owed his election to Alberic II, the master of Rome from 932 to 954 who effectively controlled the papacy. Stephen was thus utterly under Alberic's shadow and exercised virtually no independent authority, although he was permitted to promote the monastic reform movement that had developed out of the famed monastery of Cluny in France. Stephen also gave his support to King Louis IV of France (r. 936–954) in a dispute with his nobles. His death in October 942 was apparently rather premature. He most likely gave offense to Alberic and found himself suddenly deposed. As was the habit of the times, he was probably imprisoned, cruelly mutilated, and either strangled or starved to death. This was not a happy time for the papacy. Successor: Marinus II.

�֍ **STEPHEN IX (X)** Pope from 1057 to 1058. While brief, the reign of Stephen was not without considerable note. He was originally known as Frederick of Lorraine, the son of the Duke of Lorraine and a cousin of Pope St. Leo IX (1049–1054). Under Leo he served as papal chancellor, librarian, and a reliable legate, although his participation in the doomed mission to Constantinople in 1054 proved less than spectacular; the Eastern and Western Churches suffered a schism that has yet to be healed. In 1055, he entered the monastery of Monte Cassino and in 1057 was chosen abbot of that famed community at the behest of Pope Victor II (who forced the reigning abbot to retire) and was then promoted to the rank of cardinal. In the election that followed Victor's death, Frederick gave his backing to Hildebrand (the future Pope St. Gregory VII) and to Cardinal Humbert of Silva Candida, but, to his own amazement, he was elected pope on August 2, 1057. He gave his wholehearted support to the reform movement in the Church, which came to be called the Gregorian Reform. He died in Florence, but not before demanding a pledge from his cardinals that they would not choose a successor without the participation of Hildebrand, who was away at the time in Germany; in this way he hoped to ensure that he would be followed by another determined reformer. Successor: Nicholas II.

✤ **SUBURBICARIAN DIOCESES** See *Cardinal* and *Cardinals, Sacred College of.*

✤ **SUCCESSORS OF ST. PETER** One of the important claims made by the Bishops of Rome to establish their supremacy over the Universal Church. The popes are considered the successors of St. Peter in that they follow him as Bishop of Rome in direct succession dating from Pope John Paul II in an unbroken line back across the centuries to the very founding of the diocese of Rome by Sts. Peter and Paul. (See *Rome, Bishop of* and *Vicar of Christ.*)

✤ **SUPREME PONTIFF** See *Pontifex Maximus* and *Titles of the Pope.*

✤ **SWISS GUARD** The Cohors Helvetica or the Guardia Svizzera Pontificia, the world-famous bodyguard of the popes, first established in 1505 by Pope Julius II (1503–1513). Of all the ceremonial trappings of the papacy, the Swiss Guard is perhaps the most well known and certainly the most colorful. The Guard was born out of the chronic strife and bloodshed in Rome at the start of the sixteenth century when Pope Julius, desiring a reliable bodyguard and largely unable to find a force willing to serve in Rome, turned to the Swiss, reaching an agreement with the Swiss cantons of Zurich and Lucerne (the Swiss had always produced outstanding troops) for several hundred soldiers "for the protecting of our palaces." He dispatched his chamberlain Peter Hertenstein to take command of the force, and he returned on January 21, 1506, marching to St. Peter's through the Porta del Popolo with the second in command, Gaspar de Silinon. Their uniform was supposedly designed by Michelangelo, but some experts feel that they probably showed up in Rome already wearing their own; their current and distinctive blue and gold outfits actually date only to 1914 and were first drawn by their commander. On their helmets can be seen the ornate tree that decorated the coat of arms of Pope Julius, from the Delle Rovere family.

New members of the Swiss Guard are given their oath of loyalty on the anniversary of the massacre of the Guard in 1527.
(CATHOLIC NEWS SERVICE.)

The corps today numbers around one hundred, including a colonel and three officers, a chaplain, twenty noncommissioned officers, and two drummers. There is also a band, which practices out at the heliport when not being used. Recruited only from the Catholic cantons of Switzerland, the potential Guardsman signs up for two years, with freedom to leave the service anytime after that on notice of three months. He must also have served in the Swiss Army, be between nineteen and thirty, and come from the ever requisite "good family." After eighteen years, each is eligible for a pension of half-pay, increasing to full pay for thirty years' service. Aside from presenting a

Vatican stamps commemorating the 450th anniversary of the Swiss Guard.

magnificent ceremonial bodyguard to the pontiff, the Guard fulfills important practical roles, such as crowd control—especially in St. Peter's Square where the audience can become quite animated—and mounting permanent guard over the three main entrances to the Vatican: Porta Santa Anna, the bronze doors just off the Court of St. Damase, and the Arch of the Bells near St. Peter's. The Guardsmen are visible during all occasions involving the pope; even when he is traveling he is accompanied by two guardsmen, in mufti. The principal weapon of the soldiers is the same as it was in 1505, a halberd, which actually proves quite useful when moving crowds or stomping on the toe of a persistently troublesome person determined to touch the pope. The Guard also receives training in the use of slightly more modern weaponry, such as rifles that can be reached quickly in the event of some serious incident. They also carry a short sword and a mace or pepper spray (for out-of-control nuns, perhaps), and have studied both judo and karate (for very out-of-control nuns). Any truly terrible event, however, falls under the purview of the Vigilanza, the Vatican security force, supported by the Italian police, but extra precautions have been taken since the assassination attempt on the pope in 1981. The Guard, however, knows that it may well be necessary to die on behalf of the pontiff, as occurred in 1527 when the Vatican and Rome were stormed by the troops of Emperor Charles V. While Pope Clement VII escaped with 42 guardsmen to Castel Sant'Angelo, 147 others stood their ground and were massacred by the imperial mercenaries, many of them Catholic. Among those killed were the commander of the Guard and his wife, who were brutally tortured to death in their quarters rather than reveal the hiding place of the pope's gold. Two important dates each year commemorate the founding of the Guard and the massacre on May 6, 1527; the latter date is used to administer the oath to all new guardsmen. Among the most notable colonels in the history of the unit are the members of the Pfyffer von Altishofen family, which has produced a large number of its commanding officers. The official chapel of the Guard is the smallest in the entire papal state; it is located in the St. Anne district, next to the barracks.

⚜ **SYLVESTER I, ST.**   Pope from 314 to 335, his reign witnessed the greatly improved legal and political position of the Church owing to the favor shown to it by Emperor Constantine the Great (d. 337). Also known as Silvester, he was probably a Roman, surviving the severe persecutions under Emperor Diocletian (r. 284–305) and serving as a presbyter at the time of his election to succeed St. Miltiades. Consecrated on January 31, 314, he was both the benefactor and the victim of the towering presence of Constantine. The emperor was immensely generous to the Church, especially that of Rome, but Sylvester played only a minor role in the formal implementation of the pro-Christian decrees that helped set the Roman Empire on the path of a Christian state. Sylvester's predicament was exacerbated by Constantine's neglect in granting any special authority to the Bishop of Rome and his own habit of involving himself directly in the affairs of the Church. Thus, Sylvester did preside over the significant Council of Nicaea in 325, although he was invited to attend as one of the Church's bishops. His legates, or representatives, to the council, however, were treated with deep respect and permitted to sign the council's decrees ahead of the assembled prelates save for the council president, the much respected Hosius, bishop of Cordoba. As a result of Constantine's munificence, Sylvester was able to construct the first of the truly great churches of Rome, most notably the first St. Peter's, St. Paul's, and the Basilica Constantiniana, the future Basilica of St. John Lateran, which Sylvester made the cathedral church of the diocese of Rome. He also received from the emperor the Lateran Palace, the residence of the popes until the end of the fourteenth century. Successor: St. Mark. (See also *Donation of Constantine.*)

⚜ **SYLVESTER II**   Pope from 999 to 1003, the first Frenchman to become Vicar of Christ. Gerbert of Aurillac was born around 940 near Aurillac, Auvergne, studying under the Benedictines at their monastery of St. Geraud, Auvergne. He later studied mathematics and science in Cordoba and Seville, Spain. In 970, he traveled to Rome and there made a favorable impression upon both Pope John XIII and Emperor Otto I. Through the emperor, he was sent to Reims where the local archbishop appointed him head of the cathedral school. Such was his reputation for learning that he was invited in 980 to debate his scientific knowledge before the emperor at Ravenna. Three years later he was named abbot of the monastery of Bobbio near Genoa. Probably the next year, he returned to Reims and, in 989, was named by Archbishop Adalbero to succeed him as archbishop. This election was contested, however, and Gerbert was deposed in 995 by John XV on the grounds that he had come to the see illegally. Gerbert traveled to the court of Otto III and there became a tutor to the ruler, accompanying him to his coronation as emperor in 996. Two years later, he was made archbishop of Ravenna. The year after that he was elected to succeed Gregory V, his reign dated from April 2, 999. Sylvester struck a careful balance between harmonious labors with the emperor to foster a kind of universal Christian empire and a careful defense of papal rights and prerogatives. He spoke out aggressively against simony and other clerical irregularities, promoted missionary work, established metropolitan sees in Poland and Hungary, and recognized King St. Stephen I as ruler of Hungary. His close relationship with Otto was not pleasing to the resentful Roman nobles, and in 1001 the pope was driven from Rome, returning only the next year after Otto's death and the collapse of their dreams of a united Christendom. Sylvester himself lived only until May 12, 1003. Aside from his pastoral work, he is honored as one of the greatest scholar popes; he is credited with introducing Arabic numbers to the West, inventing the pendulum clock, and was reputed to be a sorcerer. Successor: John XVII.

❀ **SYLVESTER III**   Pope from January 20 to March 10, 1045, his brief reign was during the anarchical period of Pope Benedict IX. John of Sabina was serving as bishop of Sabina when, on January 20, 1045, he was elected pope to succeed the unworthy Benedict who had been deservedly expelled from the papal throne in September the previous year. His elevation was owed largely to the success of the Crescenti family in the protracted negotiation that followed the departure of Benedict. Sylvester was their choice, having served as their reliable bishop in the Crescenti home territory of Sabina. His reign was terminated on March 10, when Benedict returned to Rome and tossed him out of Rome. Sylvester returned to his see at Sabina, which he had wisely retained, while Benedict went on to bring even more shame upon himself. At the Synod of Sutri, convened under the patronage of King Henry III of Germany, Sylvester was condemned as a usurper and sentenced to imprisonment in a monastery; this was apparently suspended, for he went back to his diocese and continued on as bishop until his death probably, around October 1063. While generally counted as a legitimate pontiff, there is some possibility that Sylvester can be ranked among the antipopes. Successor: Benedict IX, Gregory VI, or Clement II.

❀ **SYLVESTER IV**   Antipope from 1105 to 1111. This puppet pope was originally named Maginulfo and was created by Emperor Henry V to serve as a rival against Pope Paschal II during the bitter struggle between the emperor and the pope over the controversy of investiture. While established in Rome, Sylvester was swiftly expelled from the city, never posing much of a threat to the legitimate pontiff. He was stripped of any power in 1111, when a settlement was reached between the warring parties.

❀ **SYMMACHUS, ST.**   Pope from 498 to 514, his pontificate was much troubled by the presence and activities of the antipope Lawrence. Symmachus was probably a native of Sardinia and a convert to Christianity, receiving baptism and ordination as a deacon in Rome. On November 22, 498, he was elected to succeed Anastasius II, but the same day, a minority group in Rome chose instead to support the arch-priest Lawrence. One of the key issues in the division was Symmachus's hard position concerning the schismatic activities of a number of bishops in the Eastern Empire, part of the ongoing Acacian Schism that had begun in 484 and would not end until 519. The supporters of Lawrence desired a continuation of the generally conciliatory attitude of Anastasius II. As neither side was willing to yield in the matter, it was brought before King Theodoric of the Ostrogoths, who found in Symmachus's favor. Lawrence initially submitted, but his supporters would not give in, working to undermine Symmachus's legitimacy, including hurling charges against him ranging from simony and irregularities in the calendar to fornication. The Laurentians also seized the Lateran and assaulted the pope, during which attack several priests were murdered. Symmachus fled to St. Peter's and lodged himself within its walls. Finally, Theodoric ended the conflict by commanding the Laurentians to disperse and Lawrence to retire from Rome. In another matter, Symmachus expelled the peculiar religious adherents called the Manichaeans from Rome and burned their books. He also issued the so-called Electoral Decree of Symmachus in March 499 in Rome that sought to establish certain regulations concerning future papal elections. Successor: St. Hormisdas.

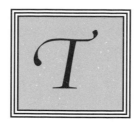

T

TELESPHORUS, ST. Bishop of Rome from around 125 to 136, the eighth pope and the seventh successor to St. Peter. Few details of his pontificate are known with certainty. He was probably a Greek, as noted by the *Liber Pontificalis,* which also claims that he had previously been an anchorite and was responsible for introducing the custom of fasting throughout the week before Easter (this was actually begun several centuries later). Perhaps most interesting, he is credited with beginning the practice of Midnight Mass, a glorious celebration that has been carried on ever since despite the hardships it imposes on the celebrants. Telesphorus most likely died a martyr. Successor: St. Hyginus.

TELEVISION A medium that has been used extensively by the popes to advance their pastoral message. The first pontiff to become well known via television was Pope Pius XII (1939–1958). Where previously the popes had used newspaper, newsreels, and radio, Pius was seen by increasingly large television audiences, especially in the years after World War II. His successor, John XXIII (1958–1963), was surprisingly adroit at attracting favorable press coverage during Vatican Council II. With improvements in technology, a worldwide audience was able to follow the events of the passing of a pope in great detail as well as the conclave that followed. Pope John Paul II is today perhaps the best known religious or political figure on the planet, thanks in large part to television. The Vatican Television Center—the Centro Televisio Vaticano (CTV)—was established by Pope John Paul II on October 23, 1983.

THEODORE I Pope from 642 to 649. A Greek and a native of Jerusalem, he was the son of a bishop also named Theodore. He came to Rome most likely after fleeing his homeland in the wake of the Arab invasions in the early seventh century. Elected to succeed John IV, he devoted much of his pontificate to resisting the spread of the heresy of Monothelitism, which proposed that Christ had only one will, a divine one, rather than the divine and human proclaimed by orthodox teaching. While he made only a little progress in challenging the heresy in the East, his work bolstered the West against it, especially in Africa and the Holy Land. Theodore was also active in building churches and aiding the poor. Successor: St. Martin I.

❀ **THEODORE** Antipope in 687. A candidate for the papacy of one of the factions in Rome following the death of Pope John V on August 2, 686, he did not succeed in securing election, losing to Conon (686–687). After his death Theodore was again advanced, but this time another party proposed the antipope Paschal (who had bribed the exarch, or Byzantine representative, to secure his own election). The two factions refused to compromise, each seizing half of the Lateran. As the Romans found this situation absurd, they voted in proper fashion and, on December 15, 687, elected St. Sergius I. Theodore accepted the will of the Romans, publicly embracing Sergius.

❀ **THEODORE II** Pope in December 897, the successor to the equally short-reigning Romanus. His election as pope came at a bleak time for the papacy since the Cadaver Synod had just been held and Pope Stephen VI (VII) strangled. He thus spent his twenty days as pontiff attempting to restore some dignity and order to the Holy See. The acts of the infamous synod were annulled, Formosus's rotting corpse, which had been fished out of the Tiber, was given a decent burial, and the numerous clergy who had been degraded by Stephen were formally reinstated. The circumstances and date of his death are unknown. Successor: John IX.

❀ **TIARA** Also the triregnum, the papal crown, a beehive-shaped ornament decorated with three diadems and a cross at the top. The tiara was not a liturgical ornament, meaning that it was not part of the pope's liturgical vestments and was not worn in such ceremonies as a mass. It was used, rather, in papal processions such as to and from the mass or at papal coronations. For liturgical celebrations like the mass, the pope wears a miter. The tiara, however, was long an important part of the symbolism of the papacy and was present in the coronation of a pope, said to represent the threefold power of the Supreme Pontiff as priest, pastor, and teacher, or the Church Militant, Penitent, and Suffering. It came as well to mark the temporal and the spiritual power that the popes had assumed as heads of the Christian Church and rulers in their own right over the Papal States. The popes would wear the triple tiara for the next six hundred years, its form remaining unchanged, so much so that when Pope Paul VI came to the

Three stamps displaying the papal tiara, as worn by Nicholas V, John XXIII, and Paul VI.

throne in 1963 he had his choice of four tiaras, including one given to Pope Pius VII (1800–1823) by Napoleon Bonaparte. Pope Paul stopped wearing the tiara after Vatican Council II (1962–1965) and upon the election of Pope John Paul I in 1978, the new pontiff refused to be crowned with the tiara; he was invested instead with the pallium, to proclaim his determination to be a purely pastoral pope. Pope John Paul II maintained the custom upon his own election such a short time later.

❁ **TITLES OF THE POPE** The formal titles possessed by the popes, handed down over the centuries and expressing his varied roles as head of the Church. The titles are: His Holiness the Pope; the Bishop of Rome; the Vicar of Jesus Christ; the successor of St. Peter; Prince of the Apostles; Supreme Pontiff (Pontifex Maximus), with primacy of jurisdiction over the Universal Church; Archbishop and Metropolitan of the Roman Province; Primate of Italy; Patriarch of the West; Sovereign of the State of Vatican City; and *Servus Servorum Dei* (Servant of the Servants of God). (See under individual titles for other details; see also *Pastor Pastorum*.)

❁ **TOMB OF PETER** The final resting place of the Prince of the Apostles, traditionally said to be located on the Vatican Hill and held now to be beneath the main altar of St. Peter's Basilica. After his crucifixion, around 62, Peter was believed to have been interred on the Vatican Hill and so, when Emperor Constantine the Great (d. 337) chose to erect a basilica in his honor, he naturally placed it upon the very spot where the bones of the first Bishop of Rome were supposedly placed. As the actual site was a cemetery, the emperor took the unusual (and cost-effective) step of leaving the honored dead where they were, simply building on top of them after filling in the tombs with earth. This had the beneficial effect of preserving the tombs completely intact. When work began on the new St. Peter's in the sixteenth century, workmen discovered the long-forgotten tombs, but the dead were left undisturbed owing to respect for the deceased, a demanding time schedule, and the oft-repeated stories of curses striking anyone who might violate the sacred ground. The cemetery was discovered again in 1939 when workers were preparing a crypt for the recently deceased Pius XI. A full investigation was undertaken, and at the deepest level, under the altar, a simple grave was uncovered; in it were the bones of an old man, with bits of fabric in gold and purple. The find caused a major stir in the Church, but the cautious Pius XII awaited further research before announcing in his Christmas message for 1950 that archaeologists had unearthed the tomb. Final declaration came only in 1968 when Pope Paul VI proclaimed that the bones were, indeed, St. Peter. There naturally remains some question as to the absolute authenticity of the bones, but the tomb is still one of the most moving sites in all of St. Peter's.

🕸 **TOWERS, VATICAN**   The medieval and Renaissance towers that still stand as part of the Vatican Palace (or Apostolic Palace) within the Vatican City State. These towers reflect the very real concern of the time that the papal residence of the Vatican should be well defended and a safe place for the popes to maintain their court and seat of government. The towers include several especially notable ones. The **Borgia Tower** (*Torre Borgia*) was constructed by the infamous Alexander VI (1492–1503) to complete the defensive plans of Nicholas V (1447–1455) for the palace by erectingh a strong tower at the northern end of the complex. It contains two very remarkable rooms, the Sala dei Santi, with paintings by Pinturicchio, and the Sala delle Sibille, both part of the Borgia Apartments. In the latter room, Pope Julius II made Cesare Borgia, Alexander's infamous son, a prisoner for a time in 1503. The **Tower of Nicholas V** is on the eastern end of the palace and is best known today as the headquarters of the Vatican Bank. Finally, the **Tower of the Winds** (*Torrei dei Venti*) stands near the Vatican Secret Archives (to which it was given in the nineteenth century). It was built during the reign of Pope Gregory XIII (1572–1585) to assist in the momentous work of the astronomers in revising the old Julian Calendar. It was also where Galileo made many of his observatoins and where he attempted—quite unsuccessfully—to demonstrate the

Copernican theories on the solar system, which were causing him such trouble with Church authorities. Interestingly, no artificial light was ever permitted into the tower, in the belief that should an invader find his way into the structure, the maze of passages and stairs would necessitate candles or torches in the night, thus alerting the guards that an interloper had penetrated the sacred confines of the Vatican. Today, the tower offers some stunning murals and breathtaking views of Rome and the papal city. **Saint John's Tower,** one of the surviving towers of the Leonine Wall, is situated to the far west of the Vatican City State, near the Heliport and past the Ethiopian College. The tower is memorable for having been converted by Pope John XXIII into a private retreat and place of meditation from the activity of the Vatican and the constant pressures of Vatican Council II. He had only a brief amount of time to enjoy it before he fell fatally ill in 1963. It has been maintained carefully ever since, his presence still felt through his coat of arms, which decorates the entrance. It is used today as a kind of guest house; one of its most distinguished occupants was Hungarian Cardinal Joseph Mindszenty in the early 1970s.

❀ **TRENT, COUNCIL OF**   See *Gregory XIII, Julius III, Marcellus III, Paul III, Paul IV, Pius IV,* and *Pius V.*

❀ **TU ES PETRUS**   A declaration of Christ, recorded in the Gospel of Matthew (16:18) in which he declared St. Peter to be the rock upon which he would build his Church. The phrase means literally "You are the rock," the Latin word being *petrus,* the source for the change of Simon's name to Peter. The Aramaic form of *petrus* is *cephas. Tu es Petrus* thus had the most significant theological implications for the successors of St. Peter as Bishop of Rome. Along the drum of the basilica of St. Peter's are carved in six-foot letters the complete Latin text from the Scriptures: *TV ES PETRVS ET SVPER HANC PETRAM OEDIFICABO ECCLESIAM MEAM ET TIBIDABO CLAVES REGNI COELORVM* ("Thou art Peter, and upon this rock I shall build my Church and I will give to thee the keys of the Kingdom of Heaven").

☙ **ULTRAMONTANISM** A movement within the Church that was known for its loyalty and devotion to the Holy See; the name was derived from the Latin phrase for "on the other side of the mountain," or "over the mountain," a reference to the fact that for those in western and northern Europe the pope was situated across the Alps in Rome. Ultramontanism began as early as the eleventh century, perdured into the seventeenth and eighteenth centuries, and flowered in the nineteenth, when the Ultramontanists found wide support from among Catholics all over who saw the revitalization of the papacy as essential to the survival of the Church. They were much aided by Pope Pius IX and played a significant role in focusing the activities of pro-papal Catholics at the approach of Vatican Council I (1869–1870) and in helping to ensure the acceptance of the doctrine of papal infallibility by that body. (See also *Infallibility, Papal.*)

☙ **UNITED NATIONS** The international organization of independent countries formed in 1945 with the general aim of promoting security, peace, and development. As an internationally recognized sovereign entity, the Holy See possesses the status of U.N. observer to the work of the U.N. and is also involved in a number of areas where the concerns of the pope or the Church might need or desire representation, including a number of international agencies. (See also *Diplomacy, Papal* and *John Paul II.*)

☙ **URBAN I, ST.** Pope from 222 to 230. Few details about Urban are known with certainty, in part because of the unreliability of details in the *Liber Pontificalis* and because of possible confusion with a contemporary bishop named Urban. He was possibly a Roman, the son of Pontianus, receiving election as successor to St. Callistus I. His pontificate is largely unknown, but it was relatively free of persecution. He also faced the continuing division of the Church in Rome through the presence of the antipope St. Hippolytus (217–235). A sarcophagus with his name inscribed in Greek was discovered by the well-known archaeologist Giovanni de Rossi (1822–1894) in the cemetery of St. Callistus. Successor: St. Telesphorus.

�֍ **URBAN II** Pope from 1088 to 1099, best known for calling for the First Crusade to capture Jerusalem from Islamic control. Odo of Lagery was born in Chatillon-sur-Marne, the son of nobles. He studied at Reims under the renowned St. Bruno, founder of the Carthusian order. Entering the reforming monastery of Cluny around 1068, he was appointed the cardinal bishop of Ostia and papal legate to Germany by Pope St. Gregory VII (1073–1085). Known for his eloquence, intelligence, piety, and commitment to continuing the reforms of Gregory, Odo was elected to succeed Victor III, his reign dating from March 12, 1088. His elevation came at a difficult time, for the papacy was still embroiled in the struggle with the Holy Roman Emperor Henry IV over the controversy of lay investiture. As part of the conflict with Gregory, Henry had orchestrated the elevation of the antipope Clement III, who was supported at the time of Urban's election by most of the bishops of Germany. Severely impoverished, Urban patiently worked to weaken Clement and was able to take final possession of Rome only in 1093, using some well-placed bribes to win control of the Lateran and Castel Sant'Angelo. Urban used a more realistic approach, which he found helpful in solidifying his position as pope. At the Council of Melfi in 1089 he issued decrees against investiture and simony, at Piacenza in 1095 he advanced more reforms, and at the famous Council of Clermont that same year he proclaimed the Truce of God (which sought to prevent bloodshed among the violent knights of the time by curbing fighting and vendettas). In response to urgent appeals for help from the Byzantine emperor Alexius I Comnenos, he called upon all Christians to march to the Holy Land and free Jerusalem. His plea launched a crusading effort that would endure for the next two centuries and have colossal consequences for Western culture. Urban cultivated good relations with the Normans of southern Italy, granting to Roger I of Sicily (d. 1101) the so-called *Monarchia Sicula,* control over the Church in Sicily, which would last until 1869. In his administration of the Church, Urban brought changes to papal finances and the papal government, first coining the term Curia Romana, still used today. Urban died on July 9, 1099. Successor: Paschal II.

✖ **URBAN III** Pope from 1185 to 1187, Umberto Crivelli belonged to a member of a noble house of Milan, receiving elevation to the cardinalate by Pope Lucius III in 1182 and appointment as archbishop of

Milan in 1185. On the same day that Lucius died, November 25, 1185, Crivelli was unanimously elected his successor. Both his election and consecration on December 1 were swiftly undertaken to avoid any interference by Emperor Frederick I Barbarossa (d. 1190) who was then embroiled in a bitter struggle with the papacy over a number of issues. The cardinals probably chose Crivelli because they knew he would be utterly devoted to resisting the emperor. This was assured by his family history. It seems that in 1162 the emperor captured and sacked Milan, and among the many Milanese massacred at the command of the brutal emperor were several relatives of Crivelli whom he saw murdered with his own eyes. Never forgetting that bloody day, Crivelli as Urban III devoted his pontificate to Frederick's defeat. He especially resisted the marriage (January 4, 1186) between Frederick's son Henry to Constance, the Norman heiress of Sicily, a union that gave Frederick's Hohenstaufen dynasty a powerful foothold in the Italian peninsula. In October 1187, Urban set out for Venice to perform the excommunication of Frederick, but near Ferrara he fell ill, dying there on October 19 or 20, 1187, his vengeance unfulfilled. Successor: Gregory VIII.

URBAN IV   Pope from 1261 to 1264. A Frenchman, Jacques Pantaleon was born at Troyes, the son of a cobbler. He earned a doctorate in canon law at the University of Paris, subsequently serving as a canon in Laon and an archdeacon in Liege. After fulfilling a papal mission to Germany, in 1253 he was named bishop of Verdun and in 1255 patriarch of Jerusalem. By chance, he was in Viterbo in 1261 at the time that the cardinals were gathered to elect a successor to Alexander IV. Since they were unable to choose a pope from among themselves, the eight cardinals (there were only eight because Alexander had failed to appoint any new ones) decided on the patriarch, formally electing him on August 29, 1261. Their choice proved a good one, for Urban IV devoted himself to the improvement of the papacy's financial position and was the architect of the eventual destruction of the Hohenstaufen dynasty of Holy Roman emperors, which had for so long troubled the Holy See. He managed to give enough support to the Guelphs in the Eternal City to secure a pro-papal local government, but he never was able to take possession there because of the endemic violence, residing instead in Viterbo and Orvieto. Recognizing that he could not liquidate the Hohenstaufen claimant Manfred, owing to his limited resources, Urban conceived of a plan to find an ambitious ally. He chose Charles of Anjou, brother of

King Louis IX of France, convincing him to accept the crown of Sicily. Within a few years, Charles would bring the Hohenstaufen dynasty to extinction. A great admirer of St. Thomas Aquinas (d. 1274), Urban gave encouragement to his truly profound theological and philosophical writings. He died at Perugia on October 2, 1264. Successor: Clement IV.

URBAN V Pope from 1362 to 1370, during the so-called Babylonian Captivity, during which the popes resided at Avignon. Guillaume de Grimoard was born in Languedoc to a noble family. Studying at Montpellier and Toulouse, he entered the Benedictine order and joined the Abbey of St. Victor in Marseilles. He received a doctorate in 1342 and appointment in 1352 as abbot of St. Germain of Auxerre; for the next years he was a reliable legate on behalf of Pope Innocent VI (1352–1362). In the conclave following Innocent's death, the brother of Pope Clement VI (1342–1352) was initially elected, but he declined; the cardinals thus turned to Grimoard, who was not a cardinal and was in Naples at the time of his elevation on a mission. Hastening to Marseilles, he arrived at Avignon and was crowned on November 6, 1362. Central to his being chosen was his reputation for saintliness, and he did not disappoint with a pontificate noted for its concern for peace in Europe and reform. A devout Benedictine, he refused to remove his black habit and insisted that he always have enough time in the day for his prayers. He took the name Urban, in fact, because those previously of that name were generally saintly pontiffs. In Avignon, Urban curtailed the often excessive extravagances of the members of the court and restored the discipline of the clergy. Two of his main concerns were improving relations with the Eastern Church and moving the papacy back to Rome. The latter ambition was actually fulfilled in 1367 when, on October 16, Urban entered Rome, despite the considerable displeasure of the French crown. While there in 1369, he greeted the Byzantine Emperor John V Palaeologus (r. 1354–1391), although Urban's hopes of a reunion were never fulfilled. Urban's sojourn in Rome lasted only three years, as the pope faced revolts in the Papal States, continuing unrest in the Eternal City, and the inconvenience of still having the papal administration in Avignon. With a heavy heart and despite the warnings of St. Bridget of Sweden that his doom would come should he leave, and ignoring the pleas of the Romans and the writer Petrarch, Urban went back to Avignon, arriving on September 27, 1370. He soon died, on December 19. He was beatified in 1870. Successor: Gregory XI.

URBAN VI Pope from 1378 to 1389, his reign brought the start of the Great Western Schism that would divide the Church until 1417. Bartolomeo Prignano was born at Naples around 1318. He received consecration in 1364 as archbishop of Acerenza and then archbishop of Bari in 1377. Prior to the latter appointment, he had enjoyed a high reputation in papal service at Avignon and, following the return of Gregory XI to Rome in 1377, had been in charge of the papal chancery. In the election that followed the death of Gregory in 1378, the cardinals were aware that the papacy faced possible schism and chaos should a new pope not be elected quickly. The popes had only recently returned to Rome and there was instability everywhere. Matters were complicated by the presence of various factions, including two different groups of French cardinals, and an Italian group anxious for the election of one of their own to make sure the papacy was not going anywhere. A Roman mob, in fact, stormed the conclave and made obvious that the cardinals would be massacred should a non-Italian be chosen. The

VRBANVS . VI . PAPA . NEAPOLITANVS .

Pope Urban VI, pontiff at the start of the Great Western Schism.

hastily arranged vote went to Prignano, who was not a cardinal (the last non-cardinal to be elected). While he was hurried to Rome, the cardinals pacified the Roman mob by falsely presenting the decrepit Cardinal Tebaldeschi as their new pontiff. When Prignano arrived, he was confirmed and consecrated on April 18, 1378, as Urban VI.

Pope Urban, whose reign began with much promise of reform, especially of the College of Cardinals, soon showed signs of uncontrollable eccentricity. The pope refused to heed St. Catherine of Siena's sage advice to be stern but to unite justice with mercy and moderation. Urban was neither merciful nor moderate. With a violently harsh nature, intemperate and imprudent attacks on the cardinals, and at times a near megalomaniacal sense of his position, Urban alienated and then outraged the College of Cardinals. Not surprisingly they departed Rome and, gathering at Anagni, a number of French cardinals proclaimed that

Urban had not been properly elected because their choice had been made under fear of death. With the backing of King Charles V of France and the patronage of Queen Joanna of Naples, the cardinals assembled at Fondi where, joined by more members of the college, they elected on September 20 Robert of Geneva as Clement VII; his coronation on October 31 launched the Great Western Schism. The Church was now torn in half as both sides gathered their allies. Urban solidified his control over Rome while Clement settled at Avignon, which was where the French cardinals had wanted the popes to return all along. To broaden his authority, Urban named twenty-nine new cardinals and established a new Curia, the old one having defected to his rival. Against a quick resolution to the crisis was Urban's highly volatile personality; he even arrested, imprisoned, and tortured six cardinals out of fear they might be conspiring against him. Embarking on a campaign to capture Naples, he was badly defeated and retired back to Rome in October 1388 since his army was melting in the absence of pay. Constant support was given by Catherine of Siena, but even the saint could not repair the pope's instability or put needed money into the treasury. By the time of his death on October 15, 1389, Urban had alienated his allies and was hated by the Romans as a despot. His passing was very likely by poison, proving the old adage that even paranoids have enemies. Successor: Boniface IX.

 URBAN VII Pope from September 15 to 27, 1590, a native of Rome, Giambattista Castagna was the son of a nobleman and a nephew of several cardinals. He studied at Padua and Bologna, earning a doctorate in law and then had a long and distinguished career in the papal government and as a diplomat, becoming a cardinal in 1583 under Pope Gregory XIII (1572–1583). During the pontificate of Sixtus V (1585–1590), Castagna was one of the most powerful figures in Rome, heading the post of Inquisitor General for the Church from 1586. His election as successor to Sixtus on September 15, 1590, was greeted with genuine joy among the members of the reform party of the Church. Contracting malaria on the night following his election, he fell rapidly ill and died before he could even be crowned. Intrigue and factionalism characterized the interregnum. Successor: Gregory XIV.

 URBAN VIII Pope from 1623 to 1644, his pontificate came during the Thirty Years' War (1618–1648) and was noted for its unrestrained opulence and nepotism. Maffeo Barberini was born in Florence to the prominent house of Barberini. Educated in his native city, he also studied in Rome and Pisa, earning a doctorate in law in 1589. Entering into the service of the popes, he had a distinguished career including the holding of the posts of nuncio to France and bishop of Spoleto; Pope Paul V made him a cardinal in 1606. Elected to succeed Gregory XV on August 23, 1623, Urban was in almost every respect a classic Baroque-era pontiff: he fought to protect Church rights and to advance the cause of the Catholic Reformation, while spending lavishly on art and architecture and ensuring his own family's political and financial aggrandizement.

On the day of his election, he canonized such important saints as Ignatius Loyola, Francis Xavier, and Philip Neri. He reformed the process of canonizations, was an avid supporter of the foreign missions, and condemned the slave trade in Brazil, Paraguay, and the West Indies. The two most important events of his reign were the trial of Galileo and the Thirty Years' War. Galileo Galilei was tried and condemned for a second time in 1633 by the reluctant pontiff, who was a friend. While Urban ordered Galileo spared any torture and gave him a comfortable incarceration, the trial of the astronomer was one of the most criticized proceedings in Church history and warranted a formal apology by Pope John Paul II in 1992. The devastatingly destructive Thirty Years' War, meanwhile, would not end in his reign, and the favor he showed to France and Cardinal Richelieu against another Catholic power, the Holy Roman Empire, actually hurt the Catholic cause in Germany, all in the hope of curbing imperial ambitions in Italy.

In Rome, the pontificate of the Barberini pope brought wild spending in the city, and Urban was a great patron of the famed architect Gian Lorenzo Bernini. On November 18, 1626, the pope consecrated the completed St. Peter's and decorated it with a baldacchino made partly from bronze torn out of the Pantheon; more bronze was stolen to make cannon, much to the outrage of the Romans. The artillery was needed because Urban was led by his rapacious nephews into a disastrous war with the duke of Parma from 1642 to 1644 that humiliated the papacy, emptied the treasury, and caused the Romans to hate their pontiff. Adding to his foul reputation in Rome was his shameless nepotism; one brother and two nephews were made cardinals, and other family and friends were given exalted positions. When Urban died on July 29, 1644, Romans celebrated in the streets. Urban was also a poet and a classical scholar. Successor: Innocent X. (See also *Barberini, House of.*)

❀ **URBI ET ORBI**   A term meaning "for the city and the world" that is traditionally used for the solemn blessing given by the pope from the balconies of the great basilicas of Rome at certain times of the year or for some major event. The name of the speech implies that the pontiff is speaking to the city of Rome and to the entire world. The blessings are customarily given from the loggia of St. Peter's Basilica at Christmas, Easter, Holy Thursday, and the feast of Sts. Peter and Paul. Other blessings are given on the feast of the Ascension at St. John Lateran and the feast of the Assumption at Santa Maria Maggiore. Perhaps the most memorable *Urbi et Orbi* blessing comes at the start of a new pontificate. It is customary for the newly elected pope to appear on the balcony of St. Peter's and address the crowd in the square below and the millions of viewers across the world. The pope gives to the throngs not merely his prayer but a glimpse of himself as Pastor of Pastors, with some clue as to what his pontificate will be like. Pope John Paul II, for example, stunned the crowd when he spoke nearly flawless Italian, proclaiming to the delighted crowd, "The reverend cardinals have called a new Bishop of Rome. They have called him from a far country, far but always so close for the communion in the Christian faith and tradition.... Even if I cannot explain myself well in your—our—Italian language, if I make a mistake you will correct me." John Paul has customarily used the blessing to give his greeting in literally dozens of languages. (See also *Christmas* and *Easter.*)

❀ **URSINUS**   Antipope from 366 to 367 during the reign of Pope St. Damasus I. A deacon at the time of Pope Liberius's death in September 366, Ursinus was elected pope by a faction of the Roman clergy opposed by a party favoring the deacon Damasus. The latter was supported by a large band of toughs who began vicious street fighting that grew so violent that the city prefect needed troops to quell it. Ursinus was exiled for a time, returning the next year on September 15. Once again ejected from the city by imperial order, Ursinus continued to scheme against the pope and was finally hustled off to Cologne where, according to the lament of a synod held at Aquileia in 381, he did not stop harassing Damasus. At the legitimate pope's death in 384, Ursinus offered himself as successor, his proposal laughed at by the electors. His followers were exceptionally loyal over the years, causing so much trouble that they were banned from Rome.

❀ **VALENTINE** Pope from August to September 827. Probably from Rome, he was the son of Leontius and was given a post in the papal government by Pope Paschal I (817–824). Known to be of especially high moral character, according to the *Liber Pontificalis,* he was unanimously elected to succeed Pope Eugene II, but survived anywhere from a month to forty days. His reign is almost entirely unknown. Successor: Gregory IV.

❀ **VATICAN** The collective name given to the residence of the pope, situated in Rome on the Vatican Hill. The use of the name Vatican is today synonymous with the Holy See, as well as the Vatican City State, of which the pontiff is sovereign. The name Vatican can also imply the Holy See, in that it is used by diplomats; one might, for example, be appointed ambassador to the Vatican when actually one is sent to the Holy See. Vatican can also denote the vast collections of art, manuscripts, palaces, and books the popes have preserved in the Vatican Museums, Library, and Archives over the centuries. (See also *Vatican Hill; Apostolic Palace;* and *Vatican City, State of.*)

❀ **VATICAN ARCHIVES** See *Archives, Vatican.*

❀ **VATICAN BANK** See *Bank, Vatican;* see also *Finances, Vatican.*

❀ **VATICAN CITY, STATE OF** The Stato della Città del Vaticano, also the Vatican City State, the independent state established in 1929 by the terms of the Lateran Treaty signed between the Holy See and the kingdom of Italy; the reigning pontiff is considered the absolute sovereign and temporal ruler of the papal city. The Vatican City State is the world's most unique sovereign nation and its smallest independent country, encompassing some 108.7 acres, its dimensions marked out by a series of walls, erected roughly between 1540 and 1640. The territorial marker of Vatican territory before St. Peter's Square is a simple white line drawn between the piazza and the square of Pius XII, which signals the beginning of Italian jurisdiction. While the city is a mere 3,428 feet at its greatest width from east to west, it should not be forgotten that this is a fully functioning state, with its own laws, population, government, currency, stamps, and even its own armed forces. Further, within the confines of the city are found gardens, churches, offices, palaces, chapels, and, above all, the immense artistic patrimony of the Holy See preserved in the Vatican Museums and the Sistine Chapel, the Basilica of St. Peter's, the largest church in the world, and the formal apartments serving as the official residence of the reigning pontiff. The Vatican State also includes a number of so-called extraterritorial possessions: office buildings around Rome, the major patriarchal basilicas (such as St. John Lateran and St. Mary Major), and the papal retreat at Castel Gandolfo. The population of the tiny state numbers around one thousand, mostly clergy and women religious (nuns and sisters), with several hundred lay people occupying apartments in the assorted palaces and buildings. There are also cardinals (whose homes and residences enjoy extraterritorial rights), bishops, priests, and nuns who serve in the

A panoramic shot of the Vatican City State; visible are the Vatican Gardens, the Vatican Museums, and the Governatorate, the headquarters of the administration of the Vatican State. (AP/WIDE WORLD PHOTOS.)

Map of Vatican City State

1 Saint Peter's Basilica
2 Bernini's Bronze Doors
3 Bernini's Colonnade
4 Saint Peter's Square (Piazza San Pietro)
5 Tower of Nicholas V
6 Apostolic Palace
7 Courtyard of San Damaso
8 Courtyard of the Marshal
9 Courtyard of the Parrot
10 Borgia Courtyard
11 Courtyard of the Sentinel
12 Sistine Chapel
13 Borgia Tower
14 Borgia Apartment/ Collection of Modern Religious Art/ Raphael Stanze (2nd floor)
15 Saint Anne Gate

16 Church of Saint Anne of the Palafrenieri
17 Vatican Printing Press
18 Vatican Post Office
19 Tapestry Workshop
20 Church of San Pellegrino
21 Offices of *L'Osservatore Romano*
22 Lapidary Gallery
23 Courtyard of the Belvedere
24 Vatican Library/ Sacred Museum/ Gallery of Maps (2nd floor)

25 Vatican Library
26 Courtyard of the Library
27 Tower of the Winds
28 Braccio Nuovo (New Arm)
29 Chiaramonti Museum
30 Courtyard of the Pine
31 Belvedere Niche
32 Vatican Library/ Profane Museum/ Gallery of the Tapestries/Gallery of the Candelabra (2nd floor)
33 Gregorian Egyptian Museum/Gregorian Etruscan Museum (2nd floor)
34 Pio-Clementine Museum
35 Octagonal Courtyard

36 Belvedere of Innocent VIII
37 Stairs of Bramante
38 Casina of Pius IV
39 Historical Museum (Underground)
40 Pinacoteca (Picture Gallery)
41 Gregorian Profane Museum/Pio Christian Museum/ Pontifical Missionary-Ethnology Museum
42 Entrance to the Vatican Museums
43 Vatican Gardens
44 Vatican Radio Station
45 Pontifical Ethiopian Museum
46 Palace of the Governorate of Vatican City
47 Floral arrangement in honor of the reigning Pontiff (displaying the Papal Coat of Arms)
48 Church of St. Stephen of the Abyssinians

49 Palace of the Tribunal
50 Mosaic Workshop
51 Railroad Station
52 Tower of Saint John
53 Papal Heliport
54 Palace of Saint Charles
55 Sacristy and Treasury of Saint Peter's
56 Piazza of the Protomartyrs
57 Arch of the Bells
58 Audience Hall (Aula)
59 Palace of the Congregation for the Doctrine of the Faith (Holy Office)
60 Holy Office Square
61 Church of San Martino degli Svizzeri (Church of the Swiss Guard)

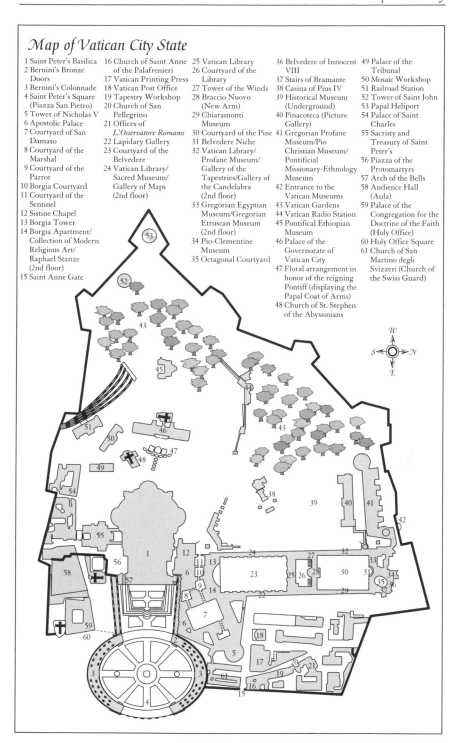

Vatican or Curia but reside outside the Vatican City in various parts of Rome; they are joined by around 3,400 lay employees, whose often small income is subsidized by the luxury of buying food and other goods in the Annona, the Vatican store, which offers shopping free of the crushing Italian taxes. The popes once had an actual army at their call, but today they are served by two main forces, the Vigilanza, which provides all police services, and the famed Swiss Guard who have been protecting the popes since 1506. (See also *Gendarmes, Pontifical; Noble Guard, Pontifical;* and *Palatine Guard of Honor.*)

The pope is absolute ruler of the Vatican State in all matters judicial, executive, and legislative, but the daily government of his tiny realm is in the hands of the Pontifical Commission of the State of Vatican City, a group of cardinals, assisted by various officials, headquartered in the Governatorate in the Vatican Gardens. The legal system is generally based on the Code of Canon Law, with the cooperation of Italian authorities in cases where canon law may not apply—such as murder, assassination attempts on the pope, burglary, or assault. After all, the dungeons of the Vatican were closed long ago and there is no jail in a formal sense, although clergy who are summoned to Rome for censure or investigation for dubious theological theories are often said to have been sent to the Vatican Prison for Bad Priests. The Vatican also has its own parish, the local church not being St. Peter's but the church of St. Anne's of the Palafrenieri; its pastor is appointed by the pope from among candidates of the Augustinian Fathers (who run it) and at the recommendation of the archpriest of the Vatican and the prior general of the Augustinian order. Citizens of the City State are permitted burial in the tiny church. The overall pastoral care for the City State is the responsibility of the archpriest of St. Peter's, who also serves as vicar general of Vatican City. The parish and the entire city are separate from the diocese of Rome, of which the pope is bishop.

Since its founding, the Vatican City State has never been invaded, although violence and war have crossed the borders of the sacred city. During World War II, Pope Pius XII housed hundreds of Jews and other desperate refugees, along with endangered manuscripts and art collections. The Vatican was also bombed during the war, one of the most mysterious events of the conflict. (See *Railway, Vatican.*) The most infamous act came in 1981 with the attempted assassination of Pope John Paul II in St. Peter's Square by Mehmet Ali Agca. The Vatican remains best known today for the presence of the pope, the mystery and mystique of the Curia, the grandeur of the palaces, churches, and basilica, and most of all for the deep faith it represents and upon which it was literally built. (*See also Canon Law; Conclave; Curia, Roman; Diplomacy, Papal; Elections, Papal; Holy See; Lateran Treaty; Library, Vatican; Museums, Vatican; Publishing, Vatican; Radio, Vatican; Vatican; Vatican Hill;* and *Vicar General.*)

❈ **VATICAN COUNCIL I**   See *Pius IX;* see also *Infallibility, Papal* and *Ultramontanism.*

❈ **VATICAN COUNCIL II**   See *John XXIII, Paul VI,* and *John Paul II.*

❈ **VATICAN HILL**   The hill just to the northwest of Rome, across the Tiber, best known today as the site of the Vatican City State and the residence of the pope. Vatican Hill occupies the territory along the right bank of the Tiber and is comprised of the Mons Vaticanus and the Campus Vaticanus. The origins of the name Vatican are quite obscure, perhaps coming from the Etruscan language. Not considered the most desirable location around Rome because of its marshes, which often teemed with the danger of malaria, Vatican Hill had a terrible reputation among Roman writers. Martial, for example, despised the wine that came from there, writing *"Vaticana bibis, bibis venenum"* ("When you drink Vatican, you drink poison"). As the city grew in size and population, any available land came into use, and the wealthy Romans acquired property there, including the infamous Emperor Gaius Caligula (d. 37), who built the Circus Gai that was completed by Emperor Nero, a stadium where games and races were held. It was here that Nero staged the first terrible persecutions of the Christians. St. Peter himself was probably put to death in the Circus around 64. Next to the circus was a cemetery, largely the resting place for the lower strata of Roman society. Christians used the cemetery as well, and, from the second century, it was revered as the burial place of St. Peter. Once Christianity was granted full recognition by the imperial government, the hill assumed increasing importance because of the presence of so many martyrs, especially the Prince of the Apostles and the first Bishop of Rome. Emperor Constantine the Great (d. 337) thus built a great basilica on the Vatican Hill, placing it directly over the cemetery of the Christians. The site soon emerged as one of the great centers of pilgrims and one of the most sacred places in the Roman Empire and later all of Christendom. (See also *Borgo, The; Rome; Vatican;* and *Apostolic Palace.*)

❈ **VATICAN LIBRARY**   See *Library, Vatican.*

❀ **VATICAN PALACE**   See *Apostolic Palace.*

❀ **VATICAN RADIO**   See *Radio, Vatican.*

❀ **VESTMENTS, PAPAL**   See box, *Papal Vestments,* pages 364–65.

❀ **VETO, RIGHT OF PAPAL**   The custom that endured until 1903 for a secular power, such as the Habsburgs, France, or Spain, to block or veto the possible election of a cardinal as pope if in their view the candidate was unacceptable or was believed to be disposed to working against their interests. The right of veto or approval dates to the sixth century when popes were required to seek confirmation from the Byzantine emperor before entering into their duties as Bishop of Rome. When this created severe delays in the installation of the new pope, the protocol was changed to the exarch of Ravenna, the leading Byzantine official in Italy. Gradually, the Byzantine influence waned, but the need for a political blessing from the dominant secular power would remain as popes later sought the approbation of the Holy Roman Emperor. From this tradition stemmed the idea that the leading nations of Europe could demand that certain candidates be vetoed or removed from consideration. By the sixteenth century, each papal election had become a kind of chess game as various kingdoms tried to defeat those cardinals favored by their enemies; for example, the French might veto a candidate favored by the imperial party, and the imperial party might oppose a cardinal known to favor the Spanish. The last attempt at using a veto was in 1903 when the Emperor Franz Josef I tried to prevent the possible election of Mariano Cardinal Rampolla, who he feared would be pro-Spanish. The cardinal was not elected—Giuseppe Sarto, St. Pius X, was chosen instead—but the new pope declared that no secular interference would ever again be permitted. Since that time, papal elections have been entirely free of secular influence. (See also *Elections, Papal.*)

❀ **VICAR GENERAL**   An ecclesiastical official who fulfills a variety of duties in the name of a residential bishop. Most dioceses around the world have their own vicar generals and the see of Rome is no exception. Termed officially the Vicar General of His Holiness, he has authority over the spiritual welfare of the Roman faithful in the name of the pope, who is bishop of the diocese of Rome. He functions with the full episcopal authority by virtue of his role as vicar (or substitute) of the Bishop of Rome. The Vicar General of Rome is an old office, dating to the early period of the papacy since the popes often appointed vicars to represent them in assorted matters. The actual office was not made permanent until 1264 when Pope Urban IV named Tommaso Lentini his vicar general. Pope Paul IV in 1558 added to the prestige of the office by declaring that the vicar was henceforth ever to be a member of the Sacred College of Cardinals. The cardinal vicar has authority over the entire diocese of Rome, but since 1929 his jurisdiction has ended at the walls of the Vatican City State, which has its own vicariate. He is assisted by his own Curia, a vice-regent, and several titular bishops who serve as auxiliaries, each with responsibility for their particular area of the diocese. The headquarters of the vicar general, called the Chancery of the Diocese of Rome, are situated in the Lateran Palace. The vicar general of Vatican City, also a cardinal, has responsibility for the pastoral care of the residents of the city and is normally the archpriest of St. Peter's Basilica; he also has authority over the papal villas at Castel Gandolfo.

❀ **VICAR OF CHRIST**   One of the titles of the pope, known in the Latin as the *Vicarius Christi,* denoting his primacy over the Universal Church. This position is derived from his place as successor to St. Peter, Prince of the Apostles, who was commissioned by Christ with the powers of a vicar, meaning he was to act in Christ's name on earth, as made clear in a number of Scriptural passages, such as his declaration in the Gospel of Matthew (16:18–19) that Peter would be the Rock upon which he would build his Church. As Vicar of Christ, the pope claims the authority to speak in Christ's name. It was first used as a title for the pope at the Synod of Rome in 495 for Pope Gelasius I.

❀ **VICAR OF PETER**   An unofficial title used by the popes until its formal rejection by Pope Innocent III (1198–1216) and replacement by the more accurate title Vicar of Christ. Vicar of Peter denotes "one who takes the place of Peter" and is considered improper for several reasons. First, it suggests that the pontiff is not necessarily a successor to St. Peter but merely a substitute and hence not in succession of authority established by Christ. It also implies that the pope holds his position not through Christ but by the will of Peter. The title Vicar of Peter, abandoned in the thirteenth century, is not used today in any document related to the Holy See.

❀ **VICTOR I, ST.**   Pope from 189 to 199, Victor was an African from a Roman family headed by a man named Felix. Little else is known about his early life, save that he is considered the first pontiff to come from a Latin rather than a Greek background. Elected to succeed St. Eleutherius, he was instrumental in strengthening the papacy, in dealing with the controversy surrounding the accepted date of Easter, and in advancing the Latin culture within the Church. Victor was quite ready to use the powers of the papacy to enforce orthodox teachings, excommunicating a number of Church leaders for resisting his authority or for teaching heretical or questionable doctrines. In the matter of the proper date for Easter, the pontiff demanded that the date used in Rome be used, replacing the custom found in the East of observing the Passover according to the Jewish calendar that did not necessarily fall on Sunday. Under Victor, the Latin language also began to serve as the official language of the Church. Victor himself wrote in Latin and from his time Greek faded as the Church took on a much greater Latin orientation. He is also known to have authored a treatise on throwing dice. Successor: St. Zephyrinus.

�֎ **VICTOR II** Pope from 1055 to 1057, Gebhard Dollnstein-Hirschberg was the son of Count Hartwig of Calw and the Countess Baliza; he was perhaps born in Germany, most likely Swabia, or perhaps Bavaria. Appointed Bishop of Eichstatt in 1042 through Emperor Henry III, he was only twenty-four years old. Despite his youth, Gebhard emerged as a leading advisor to the ruler, once convincing Henry to recall an army that was on the march into Italy to assist Pope St. Leo IX in his ongoing fight with the Normans. Not surprisingly, he thought this idea was rather ill advised once he himself became pope. Following the death of Leo on April 9, 1054, a group of legates arrived from Rome at the imperial court under the guidance of the famed reformer Hildebrand (the future Pope St. Gregory VII) to request that Henry nominate Gebhard as the next pontiff. Henry agreed, but Gebhard hesitated some months before finally accepting the papacy at Regensburg in March 1055. Receiving consecration on April 13, 1055, he established himself as a reforming pontiff very much in the mold of his predecessors. Summoned to Germany in September 1056, the pope was at the bedside of the emperor when Henry died on October 5. Before his passing Henry entrusted into Victor's care the guardianship over his son, Henry IV. Victor was faithful to his promise, securing young Henry's accession at Aachen, negotiating peace between the imperial court and the ambitious, scheming nobles of the empire, and appointing Henry's mother as regent. Unfortunately, Henry emerged as one of the most dedicated of all enemies of the Holy See. The pope returned to Italy in February 1057, dying on July 28, 1057, at Arezzo from a fever. Successor: Stephen IX (X).

❀ **VICTOR III**   Pope from 1086 to 1087 who was more than reluctant to receive election. Born at Benevento, Daufari was from Lombard stock, entering at an early age the Benedictine monastery of St. Sophia in Benevento, receiving the name Desiderius. Later moving to Monte Cassino, he was elected abbot there in April 1058. Here he earned the fully justified title of greatest of the abbots of that renowned community, his fame described by one historian as imperishable. The following year, Pope Nicholas II appointed him cardinal priest and papal vicar for southern Italy; Nicholas gave him vast authority, including the right to appoint abbots and bishops. He also negotiated an alliance between the Normans and the papacy that was to prove of considerable help to Pope St. Gregory VII (1073–1085) in his struggle with Emperor Henry IV. While he fell out of favor with the pope, Desiderius was nevertheless at Gregory's side when the pope died on May 25, 1085, at Monte Cassino. In the election that followed, the abbot was chosen by the cardinals on May 24, 1086. The electors would brook no refusal, forcibly dressing him in the papal vestments. He took the name Victor in honor of Victor II but was never pontiff with much enthusiasm. Even before his consecration he left Rome, resigned his office, and returned to Monte Cassino. Brought back to Rome despite the continuing presence of the antipope Clement III, Victor was consecrated on May 9, 1087. He survived barely over a year, returning twice to Monte Cassino out of frustration with the cardinals and the irascible Romans. During a synod at Benevento he fell ill and died on September 16, 1087. Successor: Urban II.

❀ **VICTOR IV**   The name of two different antipopes. The first was from March to May 1138 and was originally named Gregory Conti. He was proclaimed by a faction in conflict with Pope Innocent II (1130–1143). The second was from 1159 to 1164 and was known originally as Octavian of Monticelli. Known in some lists as Victor V, he was the first of a series of antipopes propped up by Emperor Frederick I Barbarossa during his bitter struggle with Alexander III (1159–1181).

❀ **VICTOR EMMANUEL II**   See *Italy, Pius IX, and Quirinal Palace.*

❀ **VIGILANCE, OFFICE OF THE**   The *Corpo di Vigilanza,* the blue-clad and formal Vatican police force with responsibility for the polic-

Papal Vestments

Vestments are the proper attire worn by a priest during liturgical celebrations and other religious events. By custom, the vestments worn by the pope are those of a bishop of the Church, but he is also adorned with the heightened spiritual authority of a Metropolitan and the Bishop of Rome, as is seen by the presence of the pallium. The pope's vestments are composed of an amice, alb, cincture, stole, and chasuble when saying mass. The amice is a white vest draped over the shoulders; an alb is a loose white gown worn over the amice and tied around the waist by the cord or belt called the cincture. Over this goes the stole, one of the most important spiritual symbols of the priesthood, basically a long, narrow strip of cloth over the neck and shoulders, hanging down past the knees and used to signify the priestly state. Next worn is the chasuble, the normally heavily decorated or brocaded garment shaped somewhat like a poncho. Its color depends on the feast day of the mass and its decoration may vary widely, depending upon the taste of the wearer. A cope, or large cape fastened at the neck, is worn on some occasions. As a bishop, the pope also wears a miter, the tall conical hat signifying his authority, and carries a crosier (or crozier), the shepherd staff. The miter (or mitre) is made of two curving, cone-shaped flaps of equal length, split at the top and joined at the bottom by a headband; when not worn, the miter can be folded into a flat shape. The crosier implies the bishop's role as pastor. Pope John Paul II has carried distinctive shepherd's staffs designed by Lello Scorzelli. The pope also wears his zucchetto, or skullcap, which he removes during the most solemn parts of the mass. (See also box *Papal Dress,* pages 120–21, and *Tiara.*)

The pope celebrates Mass in full vestments; the crosier was designed for him by the artist Lello (Scorzelli).

The pope, wearing a cope, in a ceremony.

ing and safeguarding of the Vatican City State. They work closely with the Swiss Guard (the defenders of the Holy Father) and the Italian police (who maintain watch over St. Peter's Square). The *Vigilanza* were originally the Pontifical Gendarmerie, the police force of the Papal States, but their role changed significantly after the loss of the States of the Church in 1860, their area of jurisdiction reduced to Rome. In 1870, with the loss of Rome itself, they found themselves guarding only the Vatican. Their name was changed from Pontifical Gendarmerie under Pope Paul VI (1963–1978).

❀ **VIGILIUS** Pope from 537 to 555, a native of Rome, Vigilius was the son of a Roman consul. He was made a deacon and was actually chosen by Pope Boniface II (530–532) to succeed him, although such was the uproar among the Romans that Vigilius withdrew his name from all consideration. It would appear, however, that ever after he harbored ambitions for the papacy. As representative of Pope Agapitus to the imperial court at Constantinople, he secured the full support and trust of Empress Theodora, wife of Emperor Justinian (r. 527–565). Agapitus died while visiting Constantinople in 536, and Theodora apparently connived with Vigilius to have him elected pope in return for certain promises to restore a deposed and heretical patriarch she supported. Vigilius arrived in Rome only to learn that Silverius had already been elected. Undaunted, Theodora calmly orchestrated Silverius's deposition, and Vigilius was promptly chosen as his replacement. To his lasting shame, however, the new pontiff took part in the brutal treatment of his predecessor, who died from starvation in 537. With this less than glittering beginning, Vigilius now outraged Theodora by failing to follow through on their understanding. His reign was subsequently a stormy one as the much disliked pope was faced with a series of theological controversies, most notably Justinian's condemnation of three theologians who were considered entirely orthodox in the West. Caught in a most uncomfortable position, Vigilius vacillated and was seized and carried off to Constantinople in January 547. Ill from the humiliations inflicted upon him, he agreed to the condemnation—albeit with reservations—in December 553 and was immediately assailed by the Church in the West. Finally granted his freedom, he set out for Rome in early 555, dying in Sicily on June 7 from years of abuse. Successor: Pelagius I.

❀ **VITALIAN, ST.** Pope from 657 to 672. Little is known about his early life, but according to the *Liber Pontificalis* he came from Segni, in

Campania, Italy. Chosen to succeed St. Eugene I on July 30, 657, he made as the main focus of his reign improving relations with the Byzantine Empire after years of hostility over a number of theological controversies. So improved did dealings become that Emperor Constans II even visited Rome; unfortunately he was stabbed to death in his bath while in Sicily. Constans's successor Constantine IV continued his policies toward the pope. Vitalian's work against the heresy of Monothelitism would not bear fruit during his pontificate, but it set the stage for the final defeat of the movement in 681. He also promoted the ongoing conversion of England. Successor: Adeodatus II.

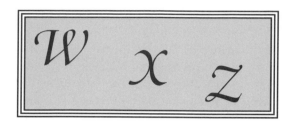

❧ **WASHING THE FEET**   See *Holy Thursday Washing of Feet.*

❧ **WESTERN SCHISM, GREAT**   See *Alexander V, Benedict XIII, Boniface IX, Clement VII, Gregory XII, Innocent VII, John XXIII, Martin V,* and *Urban VI.*

❧ **WORLD WAR I**   See *Benedict XV* and *Pius X.*

❧ **WORLD WAR II**   See *Pius XI* and *Pius XII;* see also *Railway, Vatican* and *Vatican City, State of.*

❧ **WORMS, CONCORDAT OF**   The agreement signed in 1122 between Pope Callistus II (1119–1124) and Emperor Henry V that resolved the conflict over investiture. (See *Investiture Controversy* for details.) By the agreement, abbots and bishops in the lands of the Holy Roman Empire were to be freely elected by the clergy, with the emperor deciding only contested elections. Afterward, the prelates were to receive from the ruler the proper regalia befitting the political authority that they exercised in the imperial system. This secular investing was followed by a religious one, in which the symbols of spiritual authority were bestowed upon them. The concordat is also called the *Pactum Calixtinum.* It is considered the first official concordat between the Holy See and a sovereign government.

❧ **XYSTUS**   See *Sixtus* for popes under this name.

❧ **ZACHARY, ST.**   Pope from 741 to 752. Also called Zacharias, he was a Greek born in Calabria, serving under Pope Gregory III as a deacon and succeeding him on December 3, 741. In dealing with the kingdom of the Lombards, who had been long-standing enemies of the papacy and a constant menace to Rome, Zachary negotiated a settlement with King Liutprand, also convincing the Lombards not to assail the Byzantine territory in Italy called the Exarchate of Ravenna. The pope thus won the thanks of the Byzantine Emperor Constantine V (r. 741–755). He very shrewdly gave formal recognition to the deposition of the last Merovingian king, Childeric III, and approval of the subsequent anointing of King Pepin III the Short, coining the famous phrase, "He who does the work of the king ought to be king." This move opened the door to the later dealings of the popes with the Franks, a relationship of lasting significance for the papacy. Zachary was also a generous restorer of churches. Successor: Stephen II (III).

✿ **ZELANTI** See *Gregory XVI, Leo XII,* and *Papal States.*

✿ **ZEPHYRINUS, ST.** Pope from 199 to 217, a Roman by birth according to the *Liber Pontificalis,* he was the successor to St. Victor I. His pontificate was beset by theological ferment in the Church over several heresies, and he was criticized by the antipope Hippolytus for being weak and indecisive in dealing with them. He used as his principal assistant the deacon Callistus, the future Pope St. Callistus I. The other notable event of his time was the persecution launched by Emperor Septimius Severus (202 or 203). By tradition, he died a martyr. Successor: St. Callistus I.

✿ **ZOSIMUS, ST.** Pope from 417 to 418, a Greek, he succeeded Pope St. Innocent I on March 18, 417. Nothing is known with certainty about his early life. His pontificate was characterized by a consistently unsuccessful effort to enforce the papal will over parts of the Church, often assuming broad powers where a greater amount of circumspection would have been favored. In Gaul (France), for example, he proclaimed the see of Arles a papal vicariate, thus insulting grievously the rights of the local metropolitan sees of Marseilles, Vienne, and Narbonne. He was twice forced to climb down from pronouncements made to the African churches, and died on December 26, 418, while preparing to excommunicate several clerics in Ravenna who he thought were scheming against him. Very unpopular in Rome because of his dictatorial and tactless personality, Zosimus's death brought celebrations in the streets. Successor: St. Boniface I.

✿ **ZUCCHETTO** The distinctive skullcaps worn by prelates of the Church when they are in vestments or cassock. The zucchetto derives its name from the Italian colloquial term *zucca* (pumpkin) used to denote the head. It is a sewn cap of eight triangular-shaped silk wedges, used in the past to cover the tonsure (the shaved part of the scalp of many clergy) in the cold of the winter. Over time, it came to be an accepted part of the clerical attire, with fixed colors for rank. Today the colors are black for priests, purple for bishops, and scarlet for cardinals. The pope wears a white zucchetto, which he rarely removes save for windy weather and during solemn parts of the mass. The first pope to wear the white zucchetto on a regular basis was Pius VI (1775–1799). (See also *Camauro* and box, *Papal Dress,* pages 120–21.)

Appendix 1

❀

POPES

The following list of the Supreme Pontiffs of the Church includes their places of birth, length of their reigns, their original names, and the dates of their coronations or installations. Source for dates: *Annuario Pontificio*.

Peter, St. (Simon Bar Jona): Bethsaida in Galilee; d. *c.* 64 or 67

Linus, St.: Tuscany; 67–76

Anacletus, St. (Cletus): Rome; 76–88

Clement, St.: Rome; 88–97

Evaristus, St.: Greece; 97–105

Alexander I, St.: Rome; 105–115

Sixtus I, St.: Rome 115–125

Telesphorus, St.: Greece; 125–136

Hyginus, St.: Greece; 136–140

Pius I, St.: Aquileia; 140–155

Anicetus, St.: Syria; 155–166

Soter, St.: Campania; 166–175

Eleutherius, St.: Nicopolis in Epirus; 175–189

Victor I, St.: Africa; 189–199

Zephyrinus, St.: Rome; 199–217

Callistus, St.: Rome; 217–222

Urban I, St.: Rome; 222–230

Pontian, St.: Rome; July 21, 230 to Sept. 28, 235

Anterus, St.: Greece; Nov. 21, 235 to Jan. 3, 236

Fabian, St.: Rome; Jan. 10, 236 to Jan. 20, 250

Cornelius, St.: Rome; Mar. 251 to June 253

Lucius I, St.: Rome; June 25, 253 to Mar. 5, 254

Stephen I, St.: Rome; May 12, 254 to Aug. 2, 257

Sixtus II, St.: Greece; Aug. 30, 257 to Aug. 6, 258

Dionysius, St.: July 22, 259 to Dec. 26, 268

Felix I, St.: Rome; Jan. 5, 269 to Dec. 30, 274

Eutychianus, St.: Luni; Jan. 4, 275 to Dec. 7, 283

Caius, St.: Dalmatia; Dec. 17, 283 to Apr. 22, 296

Marcellinus, St.: Rome; June 30, 296 to Oct. 25, 304

Marcellus I, St.: Rome; May 27, 308 or June 26, 308 to Jan. 26, 309

Eusebius, St.: Greece; Apr. 18, 309 to Aug. 17, 309 or 310

Miltiades, St.: Africa; July 11, 311 to Jan. 11, 314

Sylvester I, St.: Rome; Jan. 31, 314 to Dec. 31, 335

Mark, St.: Rome; Jan. 18, 336 to Oct. 7, 336

Julius I, St.: Rome; Feb. 6, 337 to Apr. 12, 352

Liberius: Rome; May 17, 352 to Sept., 24, 366

Damasus I, St.: Spain; Oct. 1, 366 to Dec. 11, 384

Siricius, St.: Rome, Dec. 15, or 22 or 29, 384 to Nov. 26, 399

Anastasius I, St.: Rome; Nov. 27, 399 to Dec. 19, 401

Innocent I, St.: Albano; Dec. 22, 401 to Mar. 12, 417

Zosimus, St.: Greece; Mar. 18, 417 to Dec. 26, 418

Boniface I St.: Rome; Dec. 28 or 29, 418 to Sept. 22, 422

Celestine, St.: Campania; Sept. 10, 422 to July 27, 432

Sixtus III, St.: Rome; July, 31, 432 to Aug. 19, 440

Leo I the Great, St.: Tuscany; Sept. 29, 440 to Nov. 10, 461

Hilarus, St.: Sardinia; Nov. 19, 461 to Feb. 29, 468

Simplicius, St.: Tivoli; Mar. 3, 468 to Mar. 10, 483

Felix III (II), St.: Rome; Mar. 13, 483 to Mar. 1, 492

Gelasius I, St.: Africa; Mar. 1, 492 to Nov. 21, 496

Anastasius II: Rome; Nov. 24, 496 to Nov. 19, 498

Symmachus, St.: Sardinia; Nov. 22, 498 to July 19, 514

Hormisdas, St.: Frosinone; July 20, 514 to Aug. 6, 523

John I, St. (Martyr): Tuscany; Aug. 13, 523 to May 18, 526

Felix IV (III), St.: Samnium; July 12, 526 to Sept. 22, 530

Boniface II: Rome; Sept. 22, 530 to Oct. 17, 532

John II: Rome; Jan. 2, 533 to May 8, 535

Agapitus I, St.: Rome; May 13, 535 to Apr. 22, 536

Silverius, St. (Martyr:) Campania; June 1 or 8, 536 to Nov. 11, 537 (d. Dec. 2, 537)

Vigilius: Rome; Mar. 29, 537 to June 7, 555

Pelagius I: Rome; Apr. 16, 556 to Mar. 4, 561

John III: Rome; July 17, 561 to July 13, 574

Benedict I: Rome; June 2, 575 to July 30, 579

Pelagius II: Rome; Nov. 26, 579 to Feb. 7, 590

Gregory I the Great, St.: Rome; Sept. 3, 590 to May 12, 604

Sabinian: Blera in Tuscany; Sept. 13, 604 to Feb. 22, 606

Boniface III: Rome; Feb. 19, 607 to Nov. 12, 607

Boniface IV, St.: Abruzzi; Aug. 25, 608 to May 8, 615

Deusdedit, St. (Adeodatus): Rome; Oct. 19, 615 to Nov. 8, 618

Boniface V: Naples; Dec. 23, 619 to Oct. 25, 625

Honorius I: Campania; Oct. 27, 625 to Oct. 12, 638

Severinus: Rome; May 28, 640 to Aug. 2, 640

John IV: Dalmatia; Dec. 24, 640 to Oct. 12, 642

Theodore I: Greece; Nov. 24, 642 to May 14, 649

Martin I, St. (Martyr): Todi; July 649 to Sept. 16, 655 (in exile from June 17, 653)

Eugene I, St.: Rome; Aug. 10, 654 to June 2, 657

Vitalian, St.: Segni; July 30, 657 to Jan. 27, 672

Adeodatus II: Rome; Apr. 11, 672 to June 17, 676

Donus: Rome; Nov. 2, 676 to Apr. 11, 678

Agatho, St.: Sicily; June 27, 678 to Jan. 10, 681

Leo II, St.: Sicily; Aug. 17, 682 to July, 683

Benedict II, St.: Rome; June 26, 684 to May, 8, 685

John V: Syria; July 23, 685 to Aug. 2, 686

Conon: birthplace unknown; Oct. 21, 686 to Sept. 21, 687

Sergius I, St.: Syria; Dec. 15, 687 to Sept. 8, 701

John VI: Greece; Oct. 30, 701 to Jan. 11, 705

John VII: Greece; Mar. 1, 705 to Oct. 18, 707

Sisinnius: Syria; Jan. 15, 708 to Feb. 4, 708

Constantine: Syria; Mar. 25, 708 to Apr. 9, 715

Gregory II, St.: Rome; May 19, 715 to Feb. 11, 731

Gregory III, St.: Syria; Mar. 18, 731 to Nov. 741

Zachary, St.: Greece; Dec. 10, 741 to Mar. 22, 752

Stephen II (III): Rome; Mar. 26, 752 to Apr. 26, 757

Paul I, St.: Rome; Apr. (May 29), 757 to June 28, 767

Stephen III (IV): Sicily; Aug. 1 (7), 768 to Jan. 24, 772

Adrian I: Rome; Feb. 1 (9), 772 to Dec. 25, 795

Leo III, St.: Rome; Dec. 26 (27), 795 to June 12, 816

Stephen IV (V): Rome; June 22, 816 to Jan. 24, 817

Paschal I, St.: Rome; Jan. 25, 817 to Feb. 11, 824

Eugene II: Rome; Feb. (May) 824 to Aug. 827

Valentine: Rome; Aug. 827 to Sept. 827

Gregory IV: Rome; 827 to Jan. 844

Sergius II: Rome; Jan. 844 to Jan. 27, 847

Leo IV, St.: Rome; Jan. (Apr. 10), 847 to July 17, 855

Benedict III: Rome; July (Sept. 29), 855 to Apr. 17, 858

Nicholas I, St. (the Great): Rome; Apr. 24, 858 to Nov. 13, 867

Adrian II: Rome; Dec. 14, 867 to Dec. 14, 872

John VIII: Rome; Dec. 14, 872 to Dec. 16, 882

Marinus I: Gallese: Dec. 16, 882 to May 15, 884

Adrian III, St.: Rome; May 17, 884 to Sept. 885

Stephen V (VI): Rome; Sept. 885 to Sept. 14, 891

Formosus: Portus; Oct. 6, 891 to Apr. 4, 896

Boniface VI: Rome; Apr. 896 to Apr. 896

Stephen VI (VII): Rome, May 896 to Aug. 897

Romanus: Gallese; Aug. 897 to Nov. 897

Theodore II: Rome; Dec. 897 to Dec. 897

John IX: Tivoli; Jan. 898 to Jan. 900

Benedict IV: Rome; Jan. (Feb.) 900 to July 903

Leo V: Ardea; July 903 to Sept. 903

Sergius III: Rome, Jan. 29, 904 to April 14, 911

Anastasius III: Rome; Apr. 911 to June 913

Landos: Sabina; July 913 to Feb. 914

John X: Tossignano (Imola); Mar. 914 to May 918

Leo VI: Rome; May 928 to Dec. 928

Stephen VII (VIII): Rome; Dec. 928 to Feb. 931

John XI: Rome; Feb. (Mar.) 931 to Dec. 935

Leo VII: Rome, Jan. 3, 936 to July 13, 939

Stephen VIII (IX): Rome; July 14, 939 to Oct. 942

Marinus II: Rome; Oct. 30, 942 to May 946

Agapitus II: Rome; May 10, 946 to Dec. 955

John XII (Octavius): Tusculum; Dec. 16, 963 to May, 14, 964

Leo VII: Rome; Dec. 4 (6), 963 to Mar. 1, 965

Benedict V: Rome; May 22, 964 to July, 4, 966

John XIII: Rome; Oct. 1, 965 to Sept. 6, 972

Benedict VI: Rome; Jan. 19, 973 to June 974

Benedict VII: Rome; Oct. 974 to July 10, 983

John XIV (John Campenora): Pavia; Dec. 983 to Aug. 20, 984

John XV: Rome; Aug. 985 to Mar. 996

Gregory V (Bruno of Carinthia): Saxony; May 996 to Feb. 18, 999

Sylvester II (Gerbert): Auvergne; Apr. 2, 999 to May 12, 1003

John XVII (Siccone): Rome; June 1003 to Dec. 1003

John XVIII (Phasianus): Rome; Jan. 1004 to July 1009

Sergius IV (Peter): Rome; July 31, 1009 to May 12, 1012

Benedict VIII (Theophylactus): Tusculum; May 18, 1012 to Apr. 9, 1024

John XIX (Romanus): Tusculum; Apr. (May) 1024 to 1032

Benedict IX (Theophylactus): Tusculum; 1032 to 1044

Sylvester III (John): Rome; Jan. 20, 1045 to Feb. 10, 1045

Benedict IX (second time): Apr. 10, 1045 to May 1, 1045

Gregory VI (John Gratian): Rome; May 5, 1045 to Dec. 20, 1046

Clement II (Suidger, Lord of Morsleben and Hornburg): Saxony; Dec. 24 (25), 1046 to Oct. 9, 1047

Benedict IX (third time): Nov. 8, 1047 to July 17, 1048 (d. *c.*1055)

Damasus II (Poppo): Bavaria; July 17, 1048 to Aug. 9, 1048

Leo IX, St. (Bruno): Alsace; Feb. 12, 1049 to Apr. 19, 1054

Victor II (Gebhard): Swabia; Apr. 16, 1055 to July 28, 1057

Stephen IX (X): (Frederick): Lorraine; Aug. 3, 1057 to Mar. 29, 1058

Nicholas II (Gerard): Burgundy; Jan. 24, 1059 to July 27, 1061

Alexander II (Anselmo da Baggio): Milan; Oct. 1, 1061 to Apr. 21, 1073

Gregory VII, St. (Hildebrand): Tuscany; Apr. 22 (June 30) to May 25, 1085

Victor III, Bl. (Dauferius, Desiderius): Benevento; May 24, 1086 to Sept. 16, 1087

Urban II, Bl. (Odo di Lagery): France; Mar. 12, 1088 to July 29, 1099

Paschal II (Raniero): Ravenna; Aug. 13 (14), 1099 to Jan. 21, 1118

Gelasius II (Giovanni Caetani): Gaeta; Jan. 24 (Mar. 10), 1118 to Jan. 28, 1119

Callistus II (Guido of Burgundy): Burgundy; Feb. 2 (9), 1119 to Dec. 13, 1124

Honorius II (Lamberto): Flagnano (Imola); Dec. 15 (21), 1124 to Feb. 13, 1130

Innocent II (Gregorio Papareschi): Feb. 14 (23), 1130 to Sept. 24, 1143

Celestine II (Guido): Citta di Castello; Sept. 26 (Oct. 3), 1143 to Mar. 8, 1144

Lucius II (Gerardo Caccianemici): Bologna; Mar. 12, 1144 to Feb. 15, 1145

Eugene III, Bl. (Bernardo Paganelli di Montemagno): Pisa; Feb. 15 (18), 1145 to July, 8, 1153

Anastasius IV (Corrado): Rome; July 12, 1153 to Dec. 3, 1154

Adrian IV (Nicholas Breakspear): England; Dec. 4 (5), 1154 to Sept. 1, 1159

Alexander III (Rolando Bandinelli): Siena; Sept. 7 (20), 1159 to Aug. 30, 1181

Lucius III (Ubaldo Allucingoli): Lucca; Sept. 1 (6), 1181 to Sept. 25, 1185

Urban III (Uberto Crivelli): Milan; Nov. 25 (Dec. 1), 1185 to Oct. 20, 1187

Gregory VIII (Alberto de Morra): Benevento; Oct. 21 (25), 1187 to Dec. 17, 1187

Clement III (Paolo Scolari): Rome; Dec. 19 (20), 1187 to Mar., 1191

Celestine III (Giacinto Bobone): Rome; Mar. 30 (Apr. 14), 1191 to Jan. 8, 1198

Innocent III (Lotario dei Conti di Segni): Anagni; Jan. 8 (Feb. 22), 1198 to July 16, 1216

Honorius III (Cencio Savelli): Rome; July 18 (24), 1216 to Mar. 18, 1227

Gregory IX (Ugolino, Count of Segni): Anagni; Mar. 19 (21), 1227 to Aug. 22, 1241

Celestine IV (Goffredo Castiglioni): Anagni; Dec. 12 (20), 1241 to Nov. 10, 1241

Innocent IV (Sinibaldo Fieschi): Genoa; June 25 (28), 1243 to Dec. 7, 1254

Alexander IV (Rinaldo, Count of Segni): Anagni; Dec. 12 (20), 1254 to May 25, 1261

Urban IV (Jacques Pantaleon): Troyes; Aug. 29 (Sept. 4), 1261 to Oct. 2, 1264

Clement IV (Guy Foulques or Guido le Gros): France; Feb. 5 (15), 1265 to Nov. 29, 1268

Gregory X, Bl. (Teobaldo Visconti): Piacenza; Sept. 1, 1271 (Mar. 2, 1272) to Jan. 10, 1276

Innocent IV, Bl. (Peter of Tarentaise): Savoy; Jan. 21 (Feb. 22), 1276 to June 22, 1276

Adrian V (Ottobono Fieschi): Genoa; July 11, 1276 to Aug. 8, 1276

John XXI (Petrus Juliani or Petrus Hispanus): Portugal; Sept. 8 (20), 1276 to May 20, 1277

Nicholas III (Giovanni Gaetano Orsini): Rome; Nov. 25 (Dec. 26, 1277) to Aug. 22, 1280

Martin IV (Simon de Brie): France; Feb. 22 (Mar. 23), 1281 to Mar. 28, 1285

Honorius IV (Giacomo Savelli): Rome; Apr. 2 (May 20), 1285 to Apr. 3, 1287

Nicholas IV (Girolamo Masci): Ascoli; Feb. 22, 1288 to Apr. 4, 1292

Celestine V, St. (Pietro del Murrone): Isernia; July 5 (Aug. 29), 1294 to Dec. 13, 1294; (d. 1296)

Boniface VIII (Benedetto Caetani): Anagni; Dec. 24, 1294 (Jan. 23, 1295) to Oct. 11, 1303

Benedict XI, Bl. (Niccolo Boccasini): Treviso; Oct. 22 (27), 1303 to July 7, 1304

Clement V (Bertrand de Got): France; June 5 (Nov. 14), 1305 to Apr. 20, 1314

John XXII (Jacques Deuse): Cahors; Aug. 7 (Sept. 5), 1316 to Dec. 4, 1334

Benedict XII (Jacques Fournier): France; Dec. 20, 1334 (Jan. 8, 1335) to Apr. 25, 1342

Clement VI (Pierre Roger): France; May 7 (19) 1342, to Dec. 6, 1352

Innocent VI (Etienne Aubert): France; Dec. 18 (30), 1352 to Sept. 12, 1362

Urban V, Bl. (Guillaume de Grimoard): France; Sept 28 (Nov. 6), 1362 to Dec. 17, 1370

Gregory XI (Pierre de Beaufort): France; Dec. 30, 1370 (Jan. 5, 1371) to Mar. 26, 1378.

Urban VI (Bartolomeo Prignano): Naples; Apr. 8 (18), 1378 to Oct. 15, 1389

Boniface IX (Pietro Tomacelli): Naples; Nov. 2 (9), 1389 to Oct. 1, 1404

Innocent VII (Cosma Migliorati): Sulmona; Oct. 17 (Nov. 11), 1404 to Nov. 6, 1406

Gregory XII (Angelo Correr): Venice; Nov. 30 (Dec. 19), 1406 to July 4, 1415 (d. 1417)

Martin V (Oddone Colonna): Rome; Nov. 11 (21), 1417 to Feb. 23, 1431

Eugene IV (Gabriele Condulmer): Venice; Mar. 3 (11), 1431 to Feb. 23, 1447

Nicholas V (Tommaso Parentucelli): Sarzana; Mar. 6 (19), 1447 to Mar. 24, 1445

Callistus III (Alfonso Borgia; Jativa (Valencia); Apr. 8 (20), 1445 to Aug. 6, 1458

Pius II (Enea Silvio Piccolomini): Siena; Aug. 19 (Sept. 3), 1458 to Aug. 14, 1464

Paul II (Pietro Barbo): Venice; Aug. 30 (Sept. 16), 1464 to July 26, 1471

Sixtus IV (Francesco della Rovere): Savona; Aug. 9 (25), 1471 to Aug. 12, 1484

Innocent VIII (Giovanni Battista Cibo): Genoa; Aug. 29 (Sept, 12), 1484 to July 25, 1492

Alexander VI (Rodrigo Borgia): Jativa (Valencia); Aug. 11 (26), 1492 to Aug. 18, 1503

Pius III (Francesco Todeschini-Piccolomini): Siena; Sept. 28 (Oct. 1, 8) 1503 to Oct. 18, 1503

Julius II (Giuliano della Rovere): Savona; Oct. 31 (Nov. 26), 1503 to Feb. 21, 1513

Leo X (Giovanni de'Medici): Florence; Mar. 9 (19), 1513 to Dec. 1, 1521

Adrian VI (Adrian Florensz): Utrecht; Jan. 9 (Aug. 31), 1522 to Sept. 14, 1523

Clement VII (Giulio de'Medici): Florence; Nov. 19 (26), 1523 to Sept. 25, 1534

Paul III (Alessandro Farnese): Rome; Oct. 13 (Nov. 3), 1534 to Nov, 10, 1549

Julius III (Giovanni Maria Ciocchi del Monte): Rome; Feb. 7 (22), 1550 to Mar. 23, 1555

Marcellus II (Marcello Servini): Montepulciano; Apr. 9 (10), 1555 to May 1, 1555

Paul IV (Gian Pietro Caraffa): Naples; May 23 (26), 1555 to Aug. 18, 1559

Pius IV (Giovan Angelo de'Medici): Milan; Dec. 25, 1559 (Jan. 6, 1560 to Dec. 9, 1565

Pius V, St. (Antonio-Michele Ghislieri): Bosco (Alexandria); Jan. 7 (17), 1566 to May 1, 1572. Canonized May 22, 1712

Gregory XIII (Ugo Buoncampagni): Bologna; May 13 (25), 1572 to Apr. 10 1585

Sixtus V (Felice Peretti): Grottamare (Ripatrasone): Apr. 24 (May 1), 1585 to Aug. 27, 1590

Urban VII (Giovanni Battista Castagna): Rome; Sept. 15, 1590 to Sept. 27, 1590

Gregory XIV (Niccolo Sfondrati): Cremona; Dec. 5 (8), 1590 to Oct. 16, 1591

Innocent IX (Giovanni Antonio Facchinetti): Bologna; Oct. 29 (Nov. 3), 1591 to Dec. 30, 1591

Clement VIII (Ippolito Aldobrandini): Florence; Jan. 30 (Feb. 9), 1592 to Mar. 3, 1605

Leo XI (Alessandro de'Medici): Florence; Apr. 1 (10), 1605 to Apr. 27, 1605

Paul V (Camillo Borghese): Rome; May 16 (29), 1605 to Jan. 28, 1621

Gregory XV (Alessandro Ludovisi): Bologna; Feb. 9 (14), 1621 to July, 8, 1623

Urban VIII (Maffeo Barberini): Florence; Aug. 6 (Sept. 29), 1623 to July 29, 1644

Innocent X (Giovanni Battista Pamfili): Rome; Sept. 15 (Oct. 4), 1644 to Jan. 7, 1655

Alexander VII (Fabio Chigi): Siena; Apr. 7 (18), 1655 to Sept. 22, 1667

Clement IX (Giulio Rospigliosi): Pistoia; June 20 (26), 1667 to Dec. 9, 1669

Clement X (Emilio Altieri) Rome; Apr. 29 (May 11), 1670 to July 22, 1676

Innocent XI, Bl. (Benedetto Odescalci): Como; Sept. 21 (Oct. 4), 1676 to Aug. 12, 1689

Alexander VIII (Pietro Ottoboni): Venice; Oct. 6 (16), 1689 to Feb. 1, 1691

Innocent XII (Antonio Pignatelli): Spinazzola; July 12 (15), 1691 to Sept. 27, 1700

Clement XI (Giovanni Francesco Albani): Nov. 23, 30 (Dec. 8), 1700 to Mar. 19, 1721

Innocent XIII (Michelangelo dei Conti): Rome; May 8 (18), 1721 to Mar. 7, 1724

Benedict XIII (Pietro Francesco Vincenzo Maria Orsini): Gravina (Bari); May 29 (June 4), 1724 to Feb. 21, 1730

Clement XII (Lorenzo Corsini): Florence; July 12 (16), 1730 to Feb. 6, 1740

Benedict XIV (Prospero Lambertini): Bologna; Aug. 17 (22), 1740 to May 3, 1758

Clement XIII (Carlo Rezzonico): Venice; July 6 (16), 1758 to Feb. 2, 1769

Clement XIV (Giovanni Vincenzo Antonio Lorenzo Ganganelli): Rimini; May 19, 28 (June 4), 1769 to Sept. 4, 1774

Pius VI (Giovanni Angelo Braschi): Cesena; Feb. 15 (22), 1775 to Aug. 29, 1799

Pius VII (Barnaba Gregorio Chiaramonti): Cesena; Mar. 14 (21), 1800 to Aug. 20, 1823

Leo XII (Annibale della Genga): Genga (Fabriano); Sept. 28 (Oct. 5), 1823 to Feb. 10, 1829

Pius VIII (Francesco Saverio Castiglioni): Cingoli; Mar. 31 (Apr. 5), 1829 to Nov. 30, 1830

Gregory XVI (Bartolomeo Alberto Mauro Cappelari): Belluno; Feb. 2 (6), 1831 to June 1, 1846

Pius IX (Giovanni M. Mastai-Ferretti): Senigallia; June 16 (21), 1846 to Feb. 7, 1878

Leo XIII (Gioacchino Pecci): Carpineto (Anagni); Feb. 20 (Mar. 3), 1878 to July 20, 1903

Pius X, St. (Giuseppe Sarto): Riese (Treviso); Aug. 4 (9), 1903 to Aug. 20, 1914

Benedict XV (Giacomo della Chiesa): Genoa; Sept. 3 (6), 1914 to Jan. 22, 1922

Pius XI (Achille Ratti): Desio (Milan); Feb. 6 (12), 1922 to Feb. 10, 1939

Pius XII (Eugenio Pacelli): Rome; Mar. 2 (12), 1939 to Oct. 9, 1958

John XXIII (Angelo Giuseppe Roncalli): Sotto il Monte (Bergamo): Oct. 28 (Nov. 4), 1958 to June 3, 1963

Paul VI (Giovanni Battista Montini): Concessio (Brescia); June 21 (30), 1963 to Aug. 6, 1978

John Paul I (Albino Luciani): Forno di Canale (Belluno); Aug. 26 (Sept. 3), 1978 to Sept. 28, 1978

John Paul II (Karol Wojtyla): Wadowice, Poland; Oct. 16 (22), 1978

Appendix 2

❀

ROMAN CURIA

The *Curia Romana* is the central governmental body of the Church, charged with assisting the pope in all administrative needs. The Curia is organized into a maze of often interconnected congregations, tribunals, councils, commissions, and agencies. For details on the history of the Curia, the reader is encouraged to consult the entry, *Curia, Roman.* See also *Cardinals, Sacred College of; Holy See;* and *Vatican.* Pope John XXIII was once asked how many people work in the Vatican. He thought for a moment and replied, "About half." While humorous, the pontiff's jest did hit upon the Roman custom of thirty-hour work weeks and the afternoon siesta, not to mention the large numbers of days off, thanks to the holidays observed by the Church. Nevertheless, the members of the Curia are normally carefully chosen officials who are well trained and supposedly conspicuously moral individuals. The present Curia is organized as per the apostolic constitution *Pastor Bonus* issued by Pope John Paul II on June 28, 1988 (effective March 1, 1989), although any pope can make changes as he sees fit, including the disbanding of the entire structure should he so choose, although this would be unthinkable. This listing has been compiled with material from the *Annuario Pontificio* and the *Catholic Almanac.*

SECRETARIAT OF STATE
The most important office of the Curia, it assists the pontiff in the care of the universal Church. It is headed by the Cardinal Secretary of State and has two main divisions:

> The Section for General Affairs, which has the responsibility of administering the day-to-day needs of the Holy See;

> The Section for Relations with States, (formerly the Council for Public Affairs of the Church), which oversees the diplomatic relations of the Holy See. It has attached to it a Council of Bishops and Cardinals.

CONGREGATIONS
These are the main departments of the Church's central government. They are powerful and influential and are always run by cardinals. Even within these offices, there are some with more clout than others.

Congregation for the Doctrine of the Faith

Congregation for Oriental Churches

Congregation for Bishops

Congregation for Divine Worship and the Discipline of the Sacraments

Congregation for the Causes of Saints

Congregation for the Clergy

Congregation for Institutes of Consecrated Life and Societies of Apostolic Life

Congregation for Catholic Education (for Seminaries and Institutes of Study)

Congregation for the Evangelization of Peoples

TRIBUNALS

Apostolic Penitentiary

Apostolic Signatura — the Supreme Court of the Church and the State of Vatican City.

Roman Rota — the court of appeal for those cases in which appeal is made to the Holy See; it is best known for its jurisdiction over marriage.

COUNCILS

Pontifical Council for the Laity

Pontifical Council for Promoting Christian Unity

Pontifical Council for the Family

Pontifical Council for Justice and Peace

Pontifical Council "Cor Unum" — Catholic aid services

Pontifical Council for Pastoral Care of Migrants and Itinerant Peoples

Pontifical Council for Pastoral Assistance to Health Care Workers

Pontifical Council for the Interpretation of Legislative Texts

Pontifical Council for Interreligious Dialogue (the Commission for Religious Relations with Muslims is attached)

Pontifical Council for Culture

Pontifical Council for Social Communications

OFFICES

Apostolic Chamber

Prefecture for the Economic Affairs of the Holy See

Administration of the Patrimony of the Apostolic See (APSA)

CURIAL OFFICES, COMMISSIONS, AND COMMITTEES

Prefecture of the Papal Household

Office for Liturgical Celebrations of the Supreme Pontiff

Commission on Latin America (attached to Congregation for Bishops)

Pontifical Committee on International Eucharistic Congresses

Central Statistics Office (attached to Secretariat of State)

Fabric of St. Peter

Office of Papal Charities

Disciplinary Commission of the Roman Curia

Council of Cardinals for Study of Organization and Economic Problems of the Holy See

Theological Commission (attached to Congregation for the Doctrine of the Faith)

Biblical Commission (attached to the Congregation for the Doctrine of the Faith)

Pontifical Commission, "Ecclesia Dei" (for the return of priests, seminarians, and others to the Church from the fraternity of Archbishop Marcel Lefebvre)

Pontifical Commission for the Revision and Emendation of the Vulgate

Pontifical Commission for the Cultural Patrimony of the Church Commission on Sacred Archaeology

Pontifical Committee for Historical Sciences

Vatican II Archives

Cardinalatial Commission for the Sanctuaries of Pompeii, Loreto, and Bari (under the Congregation for the Clergy)

Commission for Religious Relations with Muslims (attached to the Council for Inter-Religious Dialogue)

Commission for the Protection of the Historical and Artistic Monuments of the Holy See

Commission for the Preservation of the Faith, Erection of New Churches in Rome

Institutes for Works of Religion (IOR) — the Vatican Bank

Labor Office of the Apostolic See (ULSA — *Ufficio del Lavoro della Sede Apostolica*)

INTER-AGENCY COMMISSIONS

Interdepartmental Standing Commission for matters concerning appointments to local Churches and the setting and alteration of them and their constitution.

Interdepartmental Standing Commission for matters concerning members, individually or as a community, or Institutes of Consecrated Life founded or working in mission territories.

Interdepartmental Standing Commission for matters concerning the formation of candidates for Sacred Orders.

Interdepartmental Permanent Commission as part of the Congregation for Catholic Education entrusted with the task of promoting a more equitable distribution of priests throughout the world.

Permanent Interdepartmental Commission for the Church in Eastern Europe, replacing the Pontifical Commission for Russia, which was terminated.

Appendix 3

❀

THE VATICAN MUSEUMS

The Vatican Museums are a series of associated collections housing the immense artistic patrimony of the Church and the popes. In the proclamation for the exhibition of "The Vatican Collections: The Papacy and Art" in 1982, Pope John Paul II observed that the art of the popes "will have a contribution to make to the men and women of our day. They will speak of history, of the human condition in its universal challenge, and of the endeavors of the human spirit to attain the beauty to which it is attracted. And yes! These works of art will speak of God, because they speak of man created in the image and likeness of God; and in so many ways they will turn our attention to God himself." The collections are housed in former palaces and residences of the popes. Among some of the most notable buildings containing a portion of the museums' holdings are the Chapel of Nicholas V, the Borgia Apartments, the Belvedere Palace, the Sistine Chapel, and the Raphael Loggia and Stanze. The following are descriptions of the main sections of the Museums:

MUSEO PIO-CLEMENTINO
Founded by: Pius VI (1775–1799) and Clement XIV (1769–1775). The Pio-Clementino houses the world's largest assembly of ancient classical sculpture. It includes a number of important rooms: Round Room, Greek Cross Room, Room of the Muses, Room of the Animals, Statue Gallery, Bust Gallery, Octagonal Court, Gallery of Masks, Cabinet of Apoxyomenos, Room of the Biga, Gallery of the Candelabra. The Octagonal Court (Cortile Ottagono) contains the most famous sculpture pieces in the entire museum, the *Laocoön* and the *Apollo Belvedere*.

MUSEO CHIARAMONTI
Founded by: Pius VII (1800–1823). Named after the family of Pius VII, this contains a large collection of antique art, including statues of gods and emperors, and the Galleria Lapidaria, which preserves some five thousand ancient inscriptions — the pagan ones are on the east wall, the Christian ones on the west. Pius also built the Braccio Nuovo (the New Arm) for the overflow of statues and the reclaimed artistic patrimony of the Papal States that had been looted by the French. Notable pieces in the Chiaramonti are the renowned *Augustus of Prima Porta*, the *Pudicitia*, and the *Athena Giustiniani*.

MUSEO GREGORIO ETRUSCO
Founded by: Gregory XVI (1831–1846). The Gregorian Etruscan Museum is devoted to a collection of Etruscan art from pre-Roman Italy. Its basis was the art found in Lazio from 1820 to 1840; it boasts magnificent pottery of Greek, Etruscan, and South Italian origin.

MUSEO GREGORIO EGIZIO

Founded by: Gregory XVI (1831–1846). The Gregorian Egyptian Museum offers a collection of Egyptian art, including several mummies, wooden sarcophagi, and funerary papyri.

MUSEO GREGORIANO PROFANO

Founded by: Gregory XVI (1831–1846). The Gregorian Profane Museum contains the former holding of the Museo Profano Lateranense (the Lateran Museum): classical sculpture, portraits, funerary reliefs, and mosaics, as well as a remarkable assortment of sarcophagi.

MUSEO PIO-CRISTIANO

Founded by: Pius IX (1846–1878). The Christian Museum houses a valuable collection of early Christian art, including sarcophagi, inscriptions, and reliefs. The inscriptions were first assembled by the great archaeologist Giovanni Battista de Rossi (1822–1894). It also boasts the famed statue of the *Good Shepherd* from the fourth century. This museum, like the Museo Gregoriano Profano, was housed originally in the Lateran.

MUSEO MISSIONARIO ETNOLOGICO

Founded by: Pius XI (1922–1939). Originally housed in the Lateran, Missionary Ethnological Museum was moved to the Vatican in 1963. It displays a vast body of art from the lands where Christian missionaries preached the Gospels: Asia, Southeast Asia, Polynesia, India, Melanesia, Africa, South America, Central America, North America, and Christianized regions of Africa and Latin America.

PINACOTECA

Founded by: Pius XI. The Picture Gallery is the nearly unrivaled collection of paintings. Opened in 1923, the Pinacoteca offers a wide range of artistic development, from early "primitive" works predating Giotto to as late as the nineteenth century. Among the artists displayed are: Margaritone d'Arezzo, Pietro Lorenzetti, Giotto, Sassetta, Gentile da Fabriano, Fra Angelico, Leonardo da Vinci, Raphael, Guercino, Caravaggio, Michelangelo, Titian, Rubens, and Carlo Maratta.

MUSEO STORICO

Founded by: Paul VI (1963–1978). Opened in 1973, the Historical Museum houses carriages and other transports used by the pope and cardinals in earlier days; it also has an impressive array of uniforms and weapons of the old papal armed forces, such as the Noble Guard, the Palatine Guard of Honor, the Papal Artillery, and the Papal Zouaves, all of which are now long disbanded. There are also mementoes of the final tragic battles of Castelfidardo, Mentana, and Porta Pia, in which papal troops tried vainly to stem the tide of Italian unification and to prevent the fall of the Papal States in 1860 and 1870.

COLLEZIONE D'ARTE RELIGIOSA MODERNA

Founded by: Paul VI (1963–1978). The Collection of Modern Religious Art was inaugurated in 1973 and was a deep expression of Paul's commitment to continue the close relationship between the Church and the artistic life of the times, especially in keeping with the spirit of Vatican Council II. The eclectic collection boasts a wide variety of modern art, including pieces by Georges Rouault, Henri Matisse, Giorgio de Chirico, Erich Heckel, Emil Nolde, Graham Sutherland, and Pablo Serrano.

GALLERIA DELLE CARTE GEOGRAFICHE

The Gallery of Maps, located on the upper floor of the Vatican Museums along the extended length of the galleries of the Candelabra, Tapestries, and Maps. The collection is the farthest south of the three areas, running along a corridor of some 400 feet. It is one of the most remarkable areas in the entire museum complex, offering a series of 32 frescoed maps painted by the Dominican scholar and cosmographer Ignazio Danti from 1580 to 1583. The maps, of an attractive blue and gold, present the lands of the Papal States, regions of Italy (including Venice), and various sea battles, such as the vigorous painting of the Siege of Malta. Aside from the walls is the barrel-vaulted ceiling running the entire length of the gallery, which is superbly decorated with frescoes matching the regions and scenes depicted on the walls. They were done from 1573 to 1583 by painters headed by Cesare Nebbia and Girolemo Muziano.

GALLERIA DEI CANDELABRI

The Gallery of the Candelabra, one of the gallery rooms located on the second floor in the Belvedere wing. The long corridor, reached from the Greek Cross Room by the Simonetti Stairs, includes the Galleries of the Candelabra, Tapestries, and Maps. The name of the gallery is derived from the enormous candlesticks dating back nearly two millennia. It is the repository of some excellent Roman and Greek sculpture, some disfigured over the centuries at the command of a pope who did not appreciate the nakedness of some of the subjects and so ordered the strategic placement of fig leaves. Aside from the statues, the gallery is blessed by the fact that it was once an open loggia connecting the two main papal palaces. It thus still commands two excellent views. On one side is the Cortile della Pigna and on the other are Vatican Gardens, including the Casina of Pius IV, headquarters of the Pontifical Academy of Sciences.

Suggested Reading

❀

The following is a suggested reading list, including some of the books and studies used in the preparation of this work. These books have been chosen because of their accessibility for the general reader and their availability in English or English translation. This list omits those works not available in translation or too obscure or difficult to obtain for the average reader. The list of omitted works is naturally a long one, and includes the extremely useful *Annuario Pontificio, L'Attivita della Santa Sede, The Official Catholic Directory, Acta Apostolicae Sedis,* the *Liber Pontificalis,* the *Patrologia Latinae,* and the *Enchiridion Symbolorum,* as well as numerous other books in German, Latin, Italian, and French.

Ambrosini, Luisa, with Mary Willis, *The Secret Archives of the Vatican.* Boston: Little, Brown, 1969.

Andrieux, Maurice, *Daily Life in Papal Rome in the Eighteenth Century.* London: George Allen and Unwin, 1968.

Aradi, Zsolt, *The Popes: History of How They Are Chosen, Elected, and Crowned.* New York: Farrar, Straus & Cudahy, 1955.

Attwater, Donald, *Penguin Dictionary of Saints.* Baltimore, Md.: Penguin, 1965.

Baldwin, M. W., *The Medieval Papacy in Action.* New York: Macmillan, 1940.

Barraclough, Geoffrey, *The Medieval Papacy.* London: Thames & Hudson, 1968.

Barry, W. F., *The Papacy and Modern Times; A Political Sketch, 1303–1870.* London: Williams & Norgate, 1911.

———. *The Papal Monarchy from St. Gregory the Great to Boniface VIII.* New York: G. P. Putnam's Sons, 1902.

Begni, Ernesto, ed., *The Vatican: Its History — Its Treasures.* New York: Letters & Arts, 1914.

Bennett, Melba B., *Key to the Apostolic Vatican Library.* Palm Springs, Calif.: Welwood Murray Memorial Library, 1967.

Beny, Roloff, and Peter Gunn, *The Churches of Rome.* New York: Simon & Schuster, 1981.

Bergere, Thea and Richard, *The Story of St. Peter's.* New York: Dodd, Mead, 1966.

Bergin, Thomas G., ed., and Jennifer Speake, *Encyclopedia of the Renaissance.* New York: Facts on File, 1987.

Boorsch, Suzanne, *The Building of the Vatican.* New York: Metropolitan Museum of Art, 1980.

Broderick, Robert C., *The Catholic Encyclopedia.* Nashville: Thomas Nelson, 1976.

Brooke, Christopher, *The Structure of Medieval Society*. London: Thames & Hudson, 1971.

Bruscher, Joseph S., *Popes Through the Ages*. Princeton: D. Van Nostrand, 1959–1964.

Bull, George, *Inside the Vatican*. New York: St. Martin's Press, 1982.

Bunson, Matthew, *Encyclopedia of the Roman Empire*. New York: Facts on File, 1993.

———. *Our Sunday Visitor's Encyclopedia of Catholic History*. Huntington, Ind.: Our Sunday Visitor, 1995.

Burton, Margaret, *Famous Libraries of the World*. London: Grafton, 1937.

Calvesi, Maurizio, *Treasures of the Vatican*. Cleveland: World Publishing, 1962.

Cardinale, Hyginus Eugene, *Orders of Knighthood, Awards and the Holy See*. Gerrards Cross, United Kingdom: Van Duren, 1983.

———. *The Holy See and International Order*. Gerrards Cross, United Kingdom: Colin Smythe, 1976.

Carnahan, Ann, *The Vatican*. London: Odhams Press, 1950.

Chadwick, Owen, *The Popes and the European Revolution,* Clarendon Press: Oxford, 1981.

Chamberlin, Eric R., *The Bad Popes*. New York: Dial Press, 1969.

Cheetham, Nicholas, *Keepers of the Keys*. New York: Charles Scribner's Sons, 1982.

Cornwell, Rupert, *God's Banker; An Account of the Life and Death of Roberto Calvi*. London: Gollancz, 1984.

Coughlan, Joseph, *Inside the Vatican*. New York: Gallery Books, 1990.

Creighton, Mandell, *A History of the Papacy from the Great Schism to the Sack of Rome,* 5 vols. London: Longmans Greens, 1897.

Cross, F. L., and E. A. Livingstone, eds., *The Oxford Dictionary of the Christian Church*. Oxford, United Kingdom: Oxford University Press, 1983.

Dal Maso, Leonardo B., *Rome of the Popes*. Rome: Bonechi Edizioni, 1975.

Dell Arco, Maurizio F., ed., *The Vatican and Its Treasures*. London: Bodley Head, 1982.

Di Fonzo, Luigi, *St. Peter's Banker*. New York: Franklin Watts, 1983.

Empie, Paul, and Murphy T. Austin, eds., *Papal Primacy and the Universal Church*. Minneapolis: Augsburg Publishing, 1974.

Foy, Feliciano A., ed., *Catholic Almanac*. Huntington, Ind.: Our Sunday Visitor, annual.

Fremantle, Anne, *The Papal Encyclicals in their Historical Context*. Mentor-Omega, New York: New American Library of World Literature, 1956.

Gahlinger, Anton, K.S.G., *I Served the Pope*. Pittsburgh: St. Joseph's Protectory, 1953.

———. *Papal Heraldry*. Cambridge, Mass.: W. Heffer & Sons, 1930.

Galbreath, Donald Lindsay, *Papal Heraldry*. London: Heraldry Today, 1972.

Gessi, Leone, *The Vatican City.* Rome: Grafia SAI, 1930.

Gontard, Friedrich, *The Chair of Peter.* New York: Holt, Rinehart & Winston, 1964.

Graham, Robert A., S.J., *Vatican Diplomacy: A Study of Church and State on the International Plane.* Princeton, N.J.: Princeton University Press, 1959.

Granfield, Patrick, O.S.B., *The Papacy in Transition.* New York: Doubleday, 1980.

Greeley, Andrew M., *The Making of the Pope 1978.* Kansas City, Kans.: Andrews & McMeel, 1979.

Gregorovius, F., *History of the City of Rome in the Middle Ages.* London: Bell & Sons, 1894–1912.

Grisar, H., *History of Rome and the Popes in the Middle Ages.* London: Paul, 1911–1912.

Hammer, Richard, *The Vatican Connection.* New York: Holt Rinehart & Winston, 1982.

Hardon, John A., *Modern Catholic Dictionary.* Garden City, N.Y.: Doubleday, 1980.

Hasler, August, *How the Pope Became Infallible.* Garden City, N.Y.: Doubleday, 1981.

Hebblethwaite, Peter, *In the Vatican.* Bethesda, Md.: Adler & Adler, 1986.

———. *The Papal Year.* London: Geoffrey Chapman, 1981.

Heenan, Dr. John, *The Vatican State.* London: Pilot Press, 1943.

Heim, Bruno B., *Armorial.* Gerrards Cross, United Kingdom: Van Duren, 1981.

———. *Heraldry in the Catholic Church.* Gerrards Cross, United Kingdom: Van Duren, 1978.

Heston, Edward L., C.S.C., *The Holy See at Work.* Milwaukee: Bruce Publishing, 1950.

Hibbert, Christopher, *The Popes.* Chicago: Stonehenge Press, 1982.

Holisher, Desider, *The Eternal City.* New York: Frederick Ungar, 1943.

Hollis, Christopher, ed., *The Papacy.* New York: Macmillan, 1964.

Howells, T. B., *The Men of the Vatican.* London: Independent Press, 1936.

Hughes, John Jay, *Pontiffs: Popes Who Shaped History.* Huntington, Ind.: Our Sunday Visitor, 1994.

Hyde, J. K., *Society and Politics in Medieval Italy 1050–1350.* London: Macmillan, 1973.

Hynes, Rev. Harry G., *The Privileges of Cardinals.* Washington, D.C.: Catholic University of America, 1945.

John XXIII, *Journal of a Soul.* London: G. Chapman, 1980.

John Paul II, *Crossing the Threshold of Hope.* New York: Random House, 1994.

———. *Love and Responsibility.* London: Collins, 1981.

Jung-Inglessis, E. M., *St. Peter's.* Florence: Scala, 1980.

Kelly, J. N. D., *The Oxford Dictionary of Popes.* Oxford, United Kingdom: Oxford University Press, 1986.

Kinney, Edward M., ed., *The Vatican*. New York: L. H. Horne, 1964.

Kittler, Glenn D., *The Papal Princes*. New York: Dial Press, 1960.

Korn, Frank, *From Peter to John Paul II*. Canfield, Ohio: Alba House, 1980.

Lees-Milne, James, *St. Peter's*. London: Hamish Hamilton, 1967.

Letarouilly, Paul M., *The Vatican and the Basilica of St. Peter*. London: Alec Tiranti, 1963.

Levy, Alan, *Treasures of the Vatican Collections*. New York: New American Library, 1983.

LoBello, Nino, *The Vatican's Wealth*. London: David Bruce & Watson, 1968.

McDowell, Bart, *Inside the Vatican*. Washington, D.C.: National Geographic Society, 1991.

Mann, H. K., *The Lives of the Popes in the Early Middle Ages*. London: Paul, Trench Trükner & Company, 1902–1932.

Martin, Malachi, *The Decline and Fall of the Roman Church*. New York: G. P. Putnam's Sons, 1981.

————. *Three Popes and a Cardinal*. London: Hart-Davis, 1973.

Mayer, Fred, *The Vatican*. New York: Vendome Press, 1979.

Mellor, Capt. F. R., *The Papal Forces*. London: Burnes, Oates & Washbourne, 1933.

Metropolitan Museum of Art, *The Vatican: Spirit and Art of Christian Rome*. New York: Harry N. Abrams, 1982.

————. *The Vatican Collections: The Papacy and Art*. New York: Harry N. Abrams, 1982.

Miller, J. Michael, C.S.B., *The Shepherd and the Rock: Origins, Development, and Mission of the Papacy*. Huntington, Ind.: Our Sunday Visitor, 1995.

Morgan, Thomas B., *Speaking of Cardinals*. New York: G. P. Putnam's Sons, 1946.

Murphy, Francis X., C.S.S.R., *The Papacy Today*. London: Weidenfeld & Nicholson, 1981.

————. *This Church These Times*. Chicago: Association Press, 1980.

Nainfa, Rev. John, *Costumes of Prelates of the Catholic Church*. Baltimore, Md.: John Murray, 1909.

Neuvecelle, Jean, *The Vatican: Its Organization, Customs, and Way of Life*. New York: Criterion, 1955.

Neville, Robert, *The World of the Vatican*. New York: Harper & Row, 1962.

Nichols, Peter, *The Pope's Divisions*. New York: Penguin Books, 1981.

Oliveri, Mario, *The Representatives: The Real Nature and Function of Papal Legates*. Gerrards Cross, United Kingdom: Van Duren, 1981.

Packard, Jerrold M., *Peter's Kingdom,* New York: Charles Scribner's Sons, 1985.

Pallenberg, Corrado, *Inside the Vatican*. New York: Hawthorn Books, 1960.

————. *Vatican Finances*. London: Peter Owen, 1971.

Pastor, L. von, *The History of the Popes from the Close of the Middle Ages*. London: J. Hodges, 1891–1953.

Pepper, Curtis G., *The Pope's Back Yard*. New York: Farrar, Straus & Giroux, 1966.

Pirie, Valerie, *The Triple Crown*. Gaithersburg, Md.: Consortium Books, 1976.

Potter, Mary Knight, *The Art of the Vatican*. Boston: L. C. Page, 1902.

Ratzinger, Joseph, *The Ratzinger Report: An Exclusive Interview on the State of the Church with Vittorio Messori*. San Francisco: Ignatius Press, 1985.

Redig de Campos, Deoclecio, *Art Treasures of the Vatican*. Englewood Cliffs, N.J.: Prentice-Hall, 1974.

Sharkey, Don, *White Smoke over the Vatican*. Milwaukee: Bruce, 1944.

Spina, Tony, *The Making of the Pope*. New York: A. S. Barnes, 1962.

Sterling, Claire, *The Time of the Assassins*. New York: Holt, Rinehart & Winston, 1983.

Stravinskas, Peter, ed., *Our Sunday Visitor's Catholic Encyclopedia*. Huntington, Ind.: Our Sunday Visitor, 1991.

Thomas, Gordon, and Max Morgan-Witts, *Pontiff*. Garden City, N.Y.: Doubleday, 1983.

Ullmann, Walter, *A Short History of the Papacy in the Middle Ages*. London: Methuen, 1974.

Vaillancourt, Jean-Guy, *Papal Power*. Berkeley: University of California Press, 1980.

Van der Veldt, James, O.F.M., *Exploring the Vatican*. London: Hollis & Carter, 1968.

————. *The City Set on a Hill*. New York: Dodd, Mead, 1944.

Van Lierde, P. C., and A. Giraud, *What Is a Cardinal?* New York: Hawthorn Books, 1964.

Vatican Radio 1931–1971. Rome: Societa Grafica Romana, 1971.

Wall, Bernard, *The Vatican Story*. New York: Harper & Brothers, 1956.

Walsch, John Evangelist, *The Bones of St. Peter*. Garden City, N.Y.: Doubleday, 1982.

Whale, John, ed., *The Man Who Leads the Church*. San Francisco: Harper & Row, 1980.

Wynn, Wilton, *Keepers of the Keys*. New York: Random House, 1988.

Yallop, David A., *In God's Name*. New York: Bantam Books, 1984.

Young, Norwood, *The Story of Rome*. London: J. M. Dent, 1901.